New Horizons in Economic Thought

New Horizons in Economic Thought

Appraisals of Leading Economists

Edited by
Warren J. Samuels
Professor,
Department of Economics
Michigan State University

Edward Elgar

Published by
Edward Elgar Publishing Limited
Gower House
Croft Road
Aldershot
Hants GU11 3HR
England

Edward Elgar Publishing Company
Old Post Road
Brookfield
Vermont 05036
USA

HB
87
.N49
1992
15 8835
may 1993

A CIP catalogue record for this book
is available from the British Library

Library of Congress Cataloguing-in-Publication Data
New horizons in economic thought: appraisals of leading economists/
    Warren J. Samuels, editor.
      p. cm.
     1. Economics—History—20th century. I. Samuels, Warren J.,
  1933– .
  HB87.N49   1992
  330.1—dc20   91–40184
                                              CIP

ISBN 1 85278 379 6

For Michelle Jessica Nagy

Contents

Contributors

Richard P. Adelstein: Department of Economics, Wesleyan University

Elizabeth E. Bailey: Wharton School, University of Pennsylvania

Randall Bausor: Department of Economics, University of Massachusetts, Amherst

Béla Csikós-Nagy: Hungarian Economic Association, Budapest and Visiting Professor, Department of Economics, University of Vienna

Peter E. Earl: Department of Economics and Marketing, Lincoln University, New Zealand

Jon Elster: Department of Political Science, University of Chicago

Kenneth P. Jameson: Department of Economics, University of Utah

Herman B. Leonard: John F. Kennedy School of Government, Harvard University

Gary D. Libecap: Department of Economics, University of Arizona

Daniel Little: Department of Philosophy, Colgate University, and Center for International Affairs, Harvard University

Keith E. Maskus: Department of Economics, University of Colorado

Michael McPherson: Department of Economics, Williams College

Philip Mirowski: Department of Economics and Reilly Center for History and Philosophy of Science, University of Notre Dame

Mark Perlman: Department of Economics, University of Pittsburgh

Charles K. Wilber: Department of Economics, University of Notre Dame

Robert D. Willig: Department of Economics, Princeton University, and Deputy Assistant Secretary, United States Department of Justice

Introduction: Diversity and New Horizons in Economics

Warren J. Samuels

Economics in the twentieth century has had several distinctive characteristics. These include an increasing emphasis on technique, especially mathematical formalism; the growth of highly focused specialized fields, such as economic development, labour economics, public finance and so on; the predominance of neoclassical economics; the heterogeneity of neoclassical economics; and the existence of schools of thought other than neoclassical economics – such as institutional economics, Marxian or radical economics, social economics, post-Keynesian economics, neo-Ricardian economics, and so on – which are themselves each heterogeneous, so that, overall and in the aggregate, economics itself has been very diverse. The predominance of a heterogeneous neoclassical economics has therefore existed within a heterogeneous larger economics, with varying approaches within each school, all as so many sub-currents within economics.

Although there is a tendency for neoclassicists to define economics in neoclassical terms, that is, to equate economics with neoclassicism and to define being an economist with being a neoclassicist, what most accurately describes contemporary economics is the enormous diversity of work undertaken by economists. Indeed, many if not most economists are eclectic in their orientation, taking insight from where they can find it, perhaps even reinventing wheels already developed within other schools of thought, so that while much of their work is more or less narrowly derivative, some, perhaps much, is protean and more robust than if conducted within the narrow confines of one school alone. In any case, it is accurate to say that economics is a heterogeneous whole with many occasionally blending sub-currents, or that economics is a matrix formed by a diversity of schools, each of which is itself heterogeneous, each having quite different views of both itself and each other.

The predominance of neoclassicism, however, means that in the twentieth century individual economists have increasingly been defined, and generally define themselves, in relation to neoclassicism. Yet while neoclassicism is the predominant mainstream, neoclassical economics itself has been understood in quite diverse terms as the mechanics of utility, price determination or operation of the price mechanism, the working of the free enterprise system, the operation of pure markets, the mechanics of the pure theory or logic of choice, constrained maximization decision-making, the allocation of resources and so on. Not all of these are mutually exclusive; all are mutually reinforcing. Still, neoclassicism has been complex, heterogeneous, and kaleidoscopic in practice.[1]

The meaning of heterogeneity within neoclassicism and within economics as a whole means that there are ongoing deep issues which economists either sublimate, finesse, gloss over or confront directly. One of the continuing roles of criticism – in the sense of literary criticism – within economics is to compel recognition and discussion of fundamental questions. One of the sources of heterogeneity within neoclassicism is due precisely to the different positions which neoclassicists themselves take on fundamental questions: the nature and role of competition, statics versus evolutionary dynamics, uncertainty, the nature and etiology of tastes and human choices, the relations or interrelations between individual and collective action, the nature and structure of markets and of economic organizations, the relation of positive to normative economics and so on, including, as indicated above, the very meaning of neoclassicism itself in terms of the identification of its central problem. On the one hand, the power of neoclassicism means both that it has been very fecund within its own terms and that it has had impact on the work of economists of other schools. On the other hand, the variegated neoclassical solutions to conceptual problems and questions (such as those just listed) have been accompanied by limits, and therefore by attempts to both minimize and affirm the significance of those limits. At the highest levels of intellect within the discipline, in contrast to the myopic comprehensions and visions of the epigones, meaning has been a matter of the combination of strengths and weaknesses, and not simplistic rationalizations of conventional practice – though most practice is conventional and understood in largely simplistic ways. A good example is instrumentally adopted, methodologically limiting assumptions – for example, the rationality assumption – which are taken none the less to define reality.

The present volume contains essays which identify, place in perspective and appraise the work of 13 important accomplished scholars whose contributions are among the best, the most promising and the most innovative in contemporary economics. These writers have generated new substantive and interpretative horizons in economics. They present different visions of the economy and of doing economics. Some of the differences are large but some are not so large in relation to the mainstream of neoclassical economic thought. Each of these writers has influenced the work of other economists and other social scientists. Each works in diverse fields within economics, and several enter into the domains of other disciplines; all have made seminal contributions.

Several of the authors whose work is presented here consider themselves to be neoclassicists – though each has in mind an affirmation of his own version of neoclassicism. Several authors, however, are very critical of neoclassicism, or at least of what they consider fundamental aspects of its doctrine and practice. Several are fundamentally dissatisfied with the conventional treatment of the psychology of the individual economic agent, notably the assumption of rationality, including the assumption of given self-interests. Several are displeased with the approach to economic policy, especially fundamentals of the economic role of government, derivative from neoclassicism – though they disagree among themselves as to the correct approach. Several are unhappy, on diverse grounds, with the practices of mathematical and econometric technique within the neoclassical paradigm. And so on.

Because of the heterogeneity of both neoclassical economics and economics as a whole, the innovations which these writers propose to bring about underscore the operation of selective perception in at least three matters. First, it is not conclusive whether specific proposed innovations would constitute change within or of the predominant paradigm. Secondly, it is not conclusive whether their proposed changes signify (in the sense of Imre Lakatos) a progressive or a degenerating character to mainstream economics. Both are, indeed, matters of selective perception. What is clear is that no one economist is likely to applaud or agree with all the views and all the innovations proposed by the economists whose work is the subject of the essays of this book. Thirdly, the 13 economists have created new concepts and new tools of economic analysis, as well as new views of already existing tools. But they especially have presented new views of what 'economic reality' is all about. Moreover, the variation among their views of economic reality is certainly a matter of selective perception of a reality which is capable of diverse interpretation and specification, and of economic analysts having different standpoints or perspectives, so that their respective interpretations are indeed diverse.

The 13 economists whose work is examined here are but a more or less representative sample of vast new and exciting work on the horizons of economic thought by dozens of economists. Some have been included in *Contemporary Economists in Perspective*.[2] Others, including numerous other non-Americans, await future consideration.

George Akerlof starts with the conventional neoclassical views of rationality and optimality and, as Randall Bausor perceives, attempts a reformation rather than a revolutionary repudiation. Yet such a judgement depends on one's perspective. By introducing nonrational, irrational and sociological, or institutional, considerations, Akerlof may be seen as either fundamentally compromising the conventional approach or as enriching or amplifying the conventional story. Some will say that he has gone too far, others that he has not gone far enough, in reconstituting the psychology underlying economic behaviour. In so far as his analyses contemplate departures from the rational and the optimal, he is maintaining the neoclassical interpretative base but he is also saying that economic reality must be defined, willy-nilly, in substantially modified neoclassical terms.

William J. Baumol is a prolific virtuoso general theorist who has made a variety of contributions to theory and to the application, as well as to the history, of theory. Elizabeth E. Bailey and Robert D. Willig concentrate on Baumol's work in dynamic analysis, applied microeconomic theory and the welfare economics of externality theory, the latter especially in regard to the environment. By virtue of a combination of his major works, Baumol is the founder of our understanding of the service sector, especially his cost–disease model of the arts and deindustrialization; thus has Baumol responded to and interpreted a major transformation in the modern economy. Bailey and Willig also underscore certain ideas that Baumol has advanced which have even wider putative application: the subadditivity of costs, the complexity of scale economies in multiproduct firms, the sustainability of prices and contestability. Baumol has also attempted to revise and enhance standard theory in other respects: for example, a more robust set of possible specifications of the standard maximization model of the firm, the transaction demand for cash balances, and public utility pricing. In addition, Baumol has contributed important and influential insights on the welfare economics of externalities and the theory of the state, as well as on many other topics.

Jon Elster is a political scientist and in this volume both the subject of an essay by Daniel Little and the author of the essay on John Roemer. His work as a political scientist is evidence in support of the ideas that economics is both still really political economy and laden with philosophic assumptions, substance, implications and nuances. Little's essay discusses Elster's contributions to the foundations of the theory of rationality, philosophy of social science, and analytical Marxism (a field which Elster shares with Roemer). One of the conventional criticisms of standard economic theory is its research pre-empting assumption of rational behaviour. Elster refuses to take this assumption for granted and, as Little shows, explores various aspects of the theory of rationality, including the meaning of rationality, the endogenization of preference changes, and the roles of cognition and time preference. Elster's work in the philosophy of science is shown to centre on aspects of relevant practice and a very sophisticated exposition and defence of methodological individualism, especially in relation to rational-choice theory. Finally, Little examines and critiques Elster's analytical Marxism, with its striking reformulation of both the microfoundations of Marxian theory and what Marxian economics is all about. In various ways, then, Elster the political scientist uses and goes beyond the tools and theories of economists.

Nicholas Georgescu-Roegen is an economic theorist of the first rank who has made very important contributions to technical neoclassical economic theory. But he also has developed bodies of theory which both constitute and indeed are advanced by him as alternatives to traditional theory. In so doing he has become one of the most radical thinkers in economic theory, radical in the dual senses of working at the level of fundamental conceptions and of seeking fundamental change of conceptualization of economic theory. The essay on Georgescu-Roegen, by the somewhat like-minded heterodox Philip Mirowski, focuses on three themes in his work: probability theory and stochastic forms as natural laws; scientism and arithmomorphism; and value theory. In pursuing these topics, Georgescu-Roegen has critiqued conventional conceptualization and practice in such areas as the theory of rationality, econometrics, formalization, probability, 'science', determinate-solution seeking, the economy as process, and the concept of scarcity which underlies the theory of value. It is in connection with the last topic that Georgescu-Roegen has introduced the theory of thermodynamics, even as a substitute for the conventional approach to value theory.

Albert O. Hirschman is accurately presented by Charles Wilber and Kenneth Jameson as a political economist of development with an eye to the unexpected and a strategy to promote development. He is a methodologist concentrating upon the role of the participant–observer and an holistic mode of explanation. He is also a general social theorist who has introduced and made vital roles for the concepts and practices of exit, voice and loyalty, and who has contributed to our understanding of human behaviour both conceptually, or theoretically, and, with regard to the early development of economic thought, historically, by his attention to what he has called the passions and the interests.

Janos Kornai, of Hungary, has been a theorist of economic planning and therefore a theorist of socialism and a systematizer of economic theory in the light of socialism and economic planning. He has written on problems of centralization, repressed inflation and, *inter alia*, the factors which decision-makers in both planned and market economies must face. In the process, as Béla Csikós-Nagy shows, Kornai has reached (with regard to both orthodox socialist and orthodox Western economic thought) quite heterodox conclusions concerning the nature of scarcity, the role of equilibrium analysis in economic theory, the status of general equilibrium theory, and the nature of the market *qua* market. Starting from his experience under socialist economic planning of the Hungarian type, Kornai has produced quite original and unique insights and characterizations of markets, of the difference between resource- and demand-constrained systems, and of the formation and role of prices/pricing in different systems.

Edward Leamer, as Herman Leonard and Keith Maskus show, has worked successfully in two fields principally: econometrics and international trade. In the former, Leamer has developed a remarkable record and reputation both for having created important techniques and for having insisted that economists pay strict and not passing and only *pro forma* attention to the limitations of their econometric techniques, even the techniques developed by him, rather than disregard those limitations in the rush to reach empirically grounded results. In the field of international trade, Leamer has put his econometric techniques to effective use, producing a series of significant empirical papers on important topics in trade theory.

Harvey Leibenstein is concerned about interdependence between the preferences of different consumers, going beyond the conventional practice of postulating both autonomous and given preferences, and extending, for example, into the making of human fertility decisions. Leibenstein is perhaps best known for his concept of X-efficiency, which relates to the integrative and co-ordinating processes within firms. Much of what he says contributes to a richer conception of human decision-making than is permitted by the simple rationality assumption. In interpreting Leibenstein, Mark Perlman stresses the complex Marshallian, Morgenstern–Austrian and even Smithian influences on his work.

Charles Lindblom is one of a relative handful of political economists who have demonstrated that one can analyse collective behaviour, in particular the state, in substantially non-ideological terms, while incorporating and underscoring its important normative elements. His focus is on spontaneous partisan mutual adjustment in problem-solving and decision-making. Lindblom believes that decision-making is incremental in character and is so for several reasons, especially the diffusion of power and knowledge in economy and society. But he also believes in the necessity to analyse the role of co-ordinating processes and institutions, including government, in enabling and contributing to the incremental adjustments which economic actors make – including incremental adjustments in the co-ordinating processes and institutions themselves. Pervading Lindblom's analysis are, first, a concern with structure, notably the privileged position of business in general and of centres of corporate business power in particular, and, secondly, a focus on the formation of attitudes, beliefs and values or volitions. In all these matters Lindblom departs from the combinations of self-perceptions, rationalisations and technical shortcuts which characterize so much work in economics, although he himself believes that partisan mutual adjustment is both the way things are and the way they ought to be in accordance with liberal democratic values. Richard Adelstein elicits and identifies the tensions which necessarily arise within such a rich and complex view of the political economy.

Douglass North has, in a sense, tried to do for economic history what George Akerlof has endeavoured to do for microeconomics: namely, enrich the conventional neoclassical view of the world, and has done so in a manner which is both recognizably neoclassical in its larger formulations and orientation but also radical in its departures. Gary Libecap necessarily focuses on the evolution of North's view of institutional and system change. North has come to use the transaction cost mode of analysis but he has combined it with attention to power (which governs whose interests will count as costs to others) and ideology. Transaction cost analysis is very congruent with the neoclassical view of market adjustments, but power and ideology represent serious innovations in the neoclassical mode of explanation and interpretation. And like several other economists treated in other essays, North effectively stresses the methodologically collectivist role of institutions and path dependence, both serious compromises of the neoclassical emphasis on methodological individualism. As with Akerlof, North's work can be viewed as being either still too much within neoclassicism or too unsettling a set of departures.

John Roemer has developed a reputation for brilliant innovation in his combining of neoclassical analytical technique with Marxist values and general view of the world. Among other things, in Roemer's neoclassicist reformulation of Marxian economics, exploitation is divorced from considerations of class. As Jon Elster argues, this has not prevented certain normative arguments to constitute the leading thread of Roemer's work. Yet, in a manner somewhat paralleling the diverse reactions which one can take to, for example, the work of Akerlof and North, one can find in Roemer's work a reformulation of Marxism which constitutes either a serious departure from and finessing of Marx's message or a strengthening of the analytics of the Marxian approach.

Tibor Scitovsky has been an economic theorist, specializing in microeconomics and welfare economics, who has been interested in extending theory to increasingly incorporate the complexities of the real world. He has attempted to deal with the role and consequences of power in markets, the adjustment processes which operate in markets, and the psychology underlying both economic activity and economic theory. As Peter Earl indicates, Scitovsky has been interested in distribution and other aspects of power, as both cause and consequence in market processes and in the determination of welfare; in the role of information; in the differences between trading relationships predicated upon whether economic actors are price-makers or price-takers, and in the relationships between price formation and information; in the causes, consequences and cure of inflation; in the institutions which form and channel international economic relationships; in the effects of both economic growth and unemployment on human welfare; and especially the psychology of human satisfaction, with respect to which Scitovsky has also provided a critique of American culture. It is in connection with economic psychology that Scitovsky has attempted to penetrate the individual and social psychology of modern American socioeconomic life. The importance of such work, heretofore not substantively much addressed by mainstream economic theorists, is indicated by the realizations, first, that to the extent that self-interest is the driving force in a market economy, it is not a given but is formed through socialization and the appropriation of social roles and styles or philosophies of life; and secondly, that economics can contribute to serious social criticism.

Amaryta Sen, like several of our other subjects, has made striking contributions to numerous and quite varied fields in economics, not all of which could be covered in depth here. Sen has enriched the theory of rational behaviour, indeed the theory of behaviour in general, by his work on commitment. He has provided an alternative approach to utilitarian moral evaluation through his theory of capabilities. He has also enriched our understanding of the nature and role of rights and of liberty in a liberal society and its inexorable policy processes. And he has made significant contributions to the theory of social choice, to development economics, and to the study of poverty and hunger. In his own way, Sen has voiced anew many of the questions, hitherto either forgotten or given stylized formulation, raised by Adam Smith as to the meaning of the wealth of nations and the derivation and role of moral sentiments and the moral and legal rules and rights to which they give rise and which they also reflect.

One of the leading threads running through the work of the three dozen or so economists discussed in Spiegel and Samuels's *Contemporary Economists in Perspective* was uncertainty. The development of economic thought in the early post-Second World War period consisted of various approaches to uncertainty due to the radically indeterminate nature of the future. In this volume, both uncertainty and several other threads appear – which may reflect either the growth and further maturation of economic thought or the subconscious mind and predilections of the editor (after all, rational expectations, supply side and new classical economics, among other variants of economic thought, are not represented here). These threads include: elaborate attention to human psychology and decision-making, and accordingly greater sophistication with regard to the domain for which the rationality assumption has for so long precluded much substantive analysis; greater attention to the formation and operation of human institutions; the formation, role and consequences of information in the working out of economic performance; formalization not necessarily impeding greater sophistication and subtlety; the importance of both general philosophical and specifically methodological assumptions in economic theory; the importance of co-ordinating institutions and adjustment processes, even within or in conjunction with methodological individualism; the importance of power; and these and the many other respects in which conventional (and heterodox) economic theory can be enriched and made more robust than has been permitted by the relatively narrow, often ideologically and professionally myopic, and empirically uninformed and untested character of much traditional theory.

What is the process by which proposed theoretical (and other) changes are absorbed within the corpus of economic thought? How are the ideas constituting new horizons within economics filtered and reworked so as to be made compatible with received ideas? This is not the place to advance a theory of theoretical adaptation, but surely one aspect of historical practice is relevant, one which may well govern the future of the ideas surveyed in this volume. For various reasons, individual writers propose important changes in the corpus of economic theory. Often enough, these proposed changes are part of a larger definition of reality or research programme held by the individual writer. What often happens is that certain parts or facets of the proposed changes – those which are deemed by others to be consonant or congruent with the received paradigm or corpus of theory – become absorbed within the received corpus. This absorption is largely on the terms 'dictated' by the ongoing mainstream, so that both the larger definition of reality or research programme of the innovator is aborted and the innovator's own formulation of his or her innovation is finessed. Examples of this within the last half-century have been the Joan Robinson–Edward Chamberlin imperfect competition 'revolution' of the early 1930s and the price-inflexibility ideas of such writers as Gardiner C. Means and John R. Hicks. The former had a significant impact on the tools which economists use, and both have contributed some pages to treatises and texts on economic theory. But neither has effectively challenged and replaced the idealist conceptions of smoothly operating competitive markets which, indeed, seem now more strongly entrenched than ever in both microeconomics and macroeconomics – although in at least some of these cases such challenge and replacement was the intent of the innovator. Inertia has, it seems, an inexorable, erosive effect.

One further principle is exhibited by these essays. It is really a very simple principle, yet it is one which, because of ego, identification, professional specialization and (in the sense of Hirschman) loyalty, is readily neglected by all of us. The principle is that the meaning of any theory, model, tool, concept, insight, line of reasoning and so on, is a combination of its strengths and weaknesses or limitations. No theory or whatever can address every question or every facet of a problem. Accordingly, not only does the vast corpus of received economics, including all schools of economic thought, have strengths and limitations, but the innovative work of the 13 economists addressed in this collection also has respective strengths and limitations. These 13 economists are to be celebrated (though the respective authors were admonished to avoid outright celebration, an author's inclusion in the collection being presumptive of worthiness), but as they, the subjects, surely would agree individually, they have not, even on their own terms, solved all the conceptual, theoretical and practical problems which they have addressed. The remonstrations by Leamer about the limitations of econometric techniques and the pretentiousness of much econometric practice, give expression to this principle.

Finally, individual motivations both led to the creation of the innovations proposed by these 13 writers and governed the receptions given to their work. These motivations enable insights into, first, the role of intellectual and personal biography in the creation and modification of economic ideas and tools; and secondly, the sociology of the discipline. In other words, the study of the work of individual economists, and of the generation, content and reception of their innovations, is also, willy-nilly, the study of the discipline of economics.

NOTES

1. See Warren J. Samuels, 'Introduction', in Klaus Hennings and Warren J. Samuels (eds), *Neoclassical Economic Theory, 1870–1930*, Boston: Kluwer Academic Publishers, 1990, pp. 1–12.
2. Henry Spiegel and Warren J. Samuels (eds), *Contemporary Economists in Perspective*, 2 vols, Greenwich, CT: JAI Press, 1984.

1. George A. Akerlof

Randall Bausor

An economist's professional training transmits a particular and sometimes peculiar way of thinking about society. Economistic thinking embraces a penchant for disentangling the purely logical connections between propositions through the employment of mathematically formal models.

Enthusiasm for 'rationality' accompanies this strategic specialization. Most economic models adhere to mathematical optimization, presuming that economic action is motivated by, and empirically reveals, choices made in strict accordance with optimal outcomes. We imagine individuals always doing whatever leads them closest to satisfying their preferences, and impute the resulting equilibrium on to the economy.

Such an equilibrium is extraordinary. In perfect competition all markets clear, all firms receive a fair return and all households get the goods they want at the least cost. Moreover, since the labour market, like all markets, clears, an economy of rational agents achieves full employment of all resources. Here lies a conundrum, for throughout most of the twentieth century, labour in most economies has not been fully employed. Thus, the rationalistic methods invoked by neoclassical economics may be flawed.

External critiques argue that the fully optimizing image fundamentally misconstrues human nature, and thus yields a distorted sense of the economy. Attention to historical time and uncertainty, as well as to the institutional and habitual fabric of society, yields insight into problems of systemic misco-ordination, and has been woefully neglected by theories contingent upon the rational optimizing portrait of behaviour.

The work of one economist, George A. Akerlof, struggles to incorporate such concerns into the context of mainstream economic thought. In a series of elegantly argued essays he demonstrates that market signalling, habits and customs, issues of fairness and other apparently irrational behaviours, all impinge upon 'rational' optimizing. Moreover, by dealing with these complex phenomena in a way accessible to traditional economic analysis, his work greatly extends and deepens economists' thinking.

His particular genius inserts the alien phenomenon of 'irrationality' into a methodologically familiar context. As such, his prolific writing of rare clarity has fundamentally enhanced economic discourse and unarguably enriched the fund of insight with which economists tackle their task. By its very nature, however, Akerlof's work should be seen as a reformation of mainstream economics rather than as a revolutionary repudiation of it.

This chapter examines the numerous facets of George Akerlof's economics and argues that its diverse components constitute a coherent and consistent research agenda. Section 1 explores the various microeconomic elements of this programme, including writings on signalling, customs, habits, fairness and 'gifts'. Section 2 shows how these issues inform his macroeconomics of labour markets and the demand for money. With this background, Section 3 critically assesses Akerlof's economics.

'IRRATIONALITY' AND AKERLOF'S MICROECONOMICS

Akerlof's greatest talent is to locate places where the neoclassical analysis of abstract optimization might fail, to present an interesting alternative conceptualization of behaviour and motivation, and to illustrate the idea with a telling example. Rather than overwhelming the reader with technically dazzling formalization, he informs with simple and graceful arguments.

In this way he has raised issues of market signals and information, customs and habits, 'near-rationality' and tacit interpersonal relationships such as gift exchanges. In his hands, the analysis of each of these phenomena generates a potential deviation from market perfection, deviations which may be macroeconomically significant, even if the gains from rectifying them are microeconomically trivial. Thus, these tales of personal human behaviour cast a large shadow indeed.

To understand the significance of Akerlof's campaign to enrich the economist's image of human affairs, first consider the microeconomist's traditional model. Perfect competition is the microeconomist's ideal. In it all agents rationally optimize given exogenous, well-defined preferences. In this Utopia, everything works out for the best. Even casual empiricism suggests, however, that people never really have it quite so good. Actual processes of choosing are not all costless; perfect information is not freely and universally available; preferences evolve with experience; and a bevy of tacit elements interject themselves to make the icy impersonality of perfectly competitive markets personal.

Modelling such phenomena is problematic for the economist. The loss of perfect competition releases a flood of complications not easily rendered mathematically clear. The logic of irrationality is far more daunting than that of rationality. Nobody, however, has pursued it more energetically than

George Akerlof, and the obvious entrance to his microeconomics is his widely cited work on information asymmetry in markets.

His justly famous essay on 'Lemons', (1970), with its ramifications extending far beyond the market for lemons, led to work on 'Tagging' (1978a), of 'Caste' (1976) and of discrimination. Carefully recasting an assumption generates market performance far different from that envisioned for competitive equilibrium. Akerlof demonstrates how asymmetrical information among market participants can lead to failure to enact mutually beneficial trades. Using elementary modelling methods and spare mathematical formalization, he shows that when some people lack information about commodity quality, they may lose the motive to trade. This simple point, presented in a formal context allowing the reader (and the writer) to concentrate on the particular problem, brilliantly captures a fundamental problem in the theory of markets. If some people are in the know and some people are not, then the happy propositions about perfectly competitive markets dissolve in the acid of ignorance. Uncertainty and fear obstruct transacting if they prevent potential participants from marketing. Much the same point about information and market signals is further developed in (1976), (1978a) and (1985a). Trading in used automobiles is but one vivid example. Markets for labour and credit are more significant.

The earliest of these additional three essays, (1976), examines the use of indicators in labour markets to explain why 'qualified' workers may work faster to drive less-productive workers out of higher-grade employment (thus, the rat race) (p. 31), and how caste structures and the indicators attendant on adherence to caste institutions and norms may persist. Akerlof addresses issues of caste identification in a static partial equilibrium model, showing that since reliance upon caste-specific indicators may constrain the freedom to exchange, it may lead to Pareto inferior outcomes.

Similar insights inform the economics of tagging (1978a). The informational issue here involves welfare programmes in which particular groups are targeted to receive benefits under the presumption that the group qualities efficiently identify worthy recipients. In a simplified version of the Mirrlees–Fair model, Akerlof illustrates the problem, and argues that a negative income tax is not 'always superior to a welfare system that gives special aid to people with special problems or characteristics' (p. 59). Analogously, in (1985a) the problem is how a small group of discriminating customers can economically force discrimination on to the market by placing sanctions against firms which ignore the discriminatory social custom.

'A Theory of Social Custom, of which Unemployment may be One Consequence' (1980a) addresses a related issue. In this tightly argued piece, Akerlof models how reputations regarding behaviour identified with particular social customs affect adherence to those customs. Modelling this situation requires specifying codes of behaviour, identifying utility's dependence on reputation and measuring a custom's strength in society. Here we are very close indeed to an abstract model of why certain institutions – that is, social codes – maintain support, and why such codes could generate economically rational motives for further adherence to it.

> Our paper answers the question of whether economic gains must necessarily erode social customs, the violation of which results in greater utility to persons who do not care about the obedience to the custom per se. The answer, according to our model, is that such customs may, once established, continue to be followed with a stable fraction of the population believing in those customs and also following them.   (p. 95)

Within this context, moreover, Akerlof shows that multiple equilibria might exist, each with a different prevailing code.

Essential to this construction is the view that adherence to a custom is a matter of individual choice. Obedience to a tradition or adoption of an institution's behavioural norms appear not as obstructions to choice but as the venue for the exercise of 'rationality'.

Akerlof injects the complexities of social customs into optimizing models, however, in a highly simplified manner. On page 74, for example, he asserts that an agent obeys a utility function.

$$U = U(G, R, A, d^c, e)$$

where 'G is a vector representing his consumption of material goods and services; R represents his reputation in the community; A is a dummy variable representing his obedience or disobedience of the community's code of behavior; d^c is a dummy variable representing his belief or disbelief in this code of behavior, and e represents his personal tastes' (pp. 74–5). Although this presentation permits the application of the static-optimization apparatus to the problem, it trivializes the richness with which those customs can be symbolized, that is, by a real-valued variable. Thus, Akerlof adapts static optimization to a problem in which personal preference may be socially contingent, but the sophisticated reader might question whether the neoclassical depiction of static choice adequately describes the human psychology of social bonding.

Fortunately, 'Loyalty Filters' (1983a) and 'The Economic Consequences of Cognitive Dissonance' (1982c) pursue these concerns further. These papers profoundly enrich the economic understanding of loyalty and the psychology linking beliefs and experience. 'Loyalty Filters' proposes that experience may filter values. Certain behaviours may be inculcated through deliberately sanctioned experiences, and may indirectly lead to rewards. Thus, you can be honest without being the 'systematic sucker' (p. 55). With a simple model he shows why people may not be undeviatingly selfish, but honest or loyal. Since the model is static, however, only comparative static results and neither the dynamics nor the morphogenesis of values can be addressed.

'The Economic Consequences of Cognitive Dissonance' takes the argument further, since psychological insights regarding cognitive dissonance connect experience and belief. What people believe is modelled as the outcome of choice, as an optimal psychological adaptation to the stresses generated by one's experiences and position in the world. Someone employed in a nuclear power plant, for example, may choose to believe that such work is safe. Although this essay is a particularly good example of Akerlof's immense talents to motivate ideas with apt illustrations (here with convincing discussions of job safety and the deterrence of crime), one should hesitate at the spectre of agents rationally selecting beliefs in order to minimize the distress of cognitive dissonance. That they so adapt is not the issue, that they deliberately and intentionally *choose* to do so is.

Consider the positing of preferences over a space of beliefs. If agents merely choose to believe what they believe, what generates the preferences at this level? Why not argue that these preferences are themselves the outcome of choice over some other space? Either the construction essentially begs the question, or it launches analysis on an infinite regress of choice over schemes of choice. What reason have we, other than familiarity with the mechanics of optimization, to agree that psychological adaptation should be construed as choice? Do people choose beliefs any more than they choose to be in pain when they fall down the stairs? Is the socially embedded construction of personality truly the outcome of rational choice?

Despite such doubts, we should recognize that Akerlof's microeconomics is not so much the extension of rationality *per se* as the recognition that lapses from it are ubiquitous, and that even when they are microeconomically trivial, they can be collectively significant. In a series of articles (1985c, 1985a and 1987), he and Janet L. Yellen present a remarkably cunning argument linking inconsequential lapses from strict economic rationality for the individual to displacement of equilibrium from optimality.

Their argument is vitally important to economics, and is also easily grasped by anyone familiar with microeconomic modelling. They introduce the concept of near-rationality:

Near-rational behavior is nonmaximizing behavior in which the gains from maximizing rather than nonmaximizing are small ... (1985b, pp. 823–4)

If an individual's gains from optimizing are insignificant, he or she may not bother to do so, yet if enough people replace optimization with some alternative practice, for example, habits or rules of thumb, then these acts may be collectively significant. According to the envelope theorem, marginal deviations from the optimum value of the objective function are independent of whether or not an agent responds to an infinitesimal change in a parameter. Thus, the comparative static rewards to optimizing compared to 'inertia' are trivial, and the agent may not do it. If enough of the population adopts 'inertial' behaviour, however, then the aggregate consequences may not be infinitesimal. Near-rational behaviour, that is, may lead to aggregate irrationality.

This simple argument has truly profound implications for economics. We are reminded that the marginal reward to recomputing an optimum following a marginal change in a parameter is zero. Thus, agents have no motive to do so if optimization is not costless. On the contrary, they may inertially persist in their current acts. Hence, with no reference to information asymmetries or varying preferences or incompatible contracting, we see why individuals may not always occupy an optimizing outcome. This social inertia opens the door to considering particular behavioural rules and institutional arrangements without relying upon *ad hoc* tales of irrationality. Akerlof and Yellen beautifully show why strict optimizing might be abandoned, even in the most elementary of textbook cases. Furthermore, near-rational individuals may not compose collectively optimal systems.

These essays penetrate deep into the microeconomic foundations of macroeconomics. They reveal that the happy results of Classical and New Classical economics are less generally applicable than frequently alleged. When people have little or no motive to maximize, near-rational behaviour emerges and if a sufficiently high proportion of the population adopts it, then systemic performance suffers, and the macroeconomic presumptions of New Classical economics need not apply.

Akerlof's microeconomics explores a variety of ways in which behaviour might deviate from the perfectly competitive norm. Information asymmetries, filtering of preferences and beliefs, tagging of groups and near-rationality may all lead people to stray from the simple maximizing ideal. We now examine how the possibility of such wanderings informs a micro-founded macroeconomics.

AKERLOF'S MACROECONOMICS: LABOUR MARKETS AND THE DEMAND FOR MONEY

Although Akerlof is justly famous for the microeconomic analysis of customs, beliefs, market signalling and near-rationality, the full force of his contribution can be recognized only when that microeconomics is perceived as the foundation for his macroeconomics. Building in the Keynesian tradition (if not in that of Keynes), he first constructs the microfoundations for a theory of persistent involuntary unemployment, and secondly, examines the demand for money in terms of rule-of-thumb, rather than strictly optimizing management of bank accounts. This yields new insights into the quantity theory of money.

His work does not challenge the orthodox image of aggregate demand and aggregate supply vaulted over ISLM curves. Rather, it rejuvenates that analysis with microfoundations informed by asymmetric information, customs, fairness and habits. His contribution is not politically conservative (by American standards), but since it acquiesces in the traditional conceptualization of macroeconomic modelling, it cannot be truly considered methodologically, and at least at the explicitly macro level, conceptually radical.

'The Case against Conservative Macroeconomics: an Inaugural Lecture' (1979b) presents Akerlof's most cogent statement of his macroeconomics. Here he ties together many of the disparate strands of his research, and reveals himself to be a Keynesian in the Cambridge, Massachusetts, sense. His terminology and arguments are cast in terms of ISLM and of aggregate demand and aggregate supply, allowing him to engage the New Classical economics within orthodox conceptualizations.

His difference from 'conservative' economics rests primarily with their dependence upon strictly rational microfoundations. As he and Yellen (1987) put it:

> Keynesian analysis violates the commonly regarded sine qua non of good economic theory – a microeconomic foundation based on perfectly rational, maximizing behavior. In our reading, economists have accorded the assumption of rational, self-interested behavior unwarranted ritual purity ...   (1987, p. 137)

The problem of unemployment, that is, arises not from a systemic failure of a market-clearing positive price vector logically to exist, but from the failure of the system to achieve the rationally optimal outcome. Quoting again from (1987),

> most Keynesians accept the verdict of Patinkin and Pigou that, in the presence of a real balance effect, the aggregate demand curve is *not* vertical and thus a full-employment equilibrium exists. What to Keynes was a minor assumption in a theory rationalizing business cycles is now interpreted as the key assumption. ... During the past two decades Keynesian theorists have struggled to formulate a 'sensible' microeconomic foundation for Keynesian economics based on individualistic optimizing behavior, by relaxing the assumptions of the perfectly competitive Walrasian model and introducing instead a dizzying array of market imperfections: asymmetric information, incomplete contingent claims markets,

staggered contracts, transactions costs, imperfect competition, specific human capital, efficiency wages, etc. ... While each of these innovations has enriched economics by modeling important aspects of reality, the introduction of these imperfections has still not provided a *total* rationalization of Keynesian economics when judged according to the rule that the proposed theory be *fully* consistent with rational optimizing behavior and the absence of any unexploited gains from trade. In the end, it invariably turns out either that there is an unrealistic assumption or that some clever, complicated neoclassical contract will eliminate involuntary unemployment. ... This paper begins with the premise that theory which fits the real world will be based on assumptions that individuals are not fully rational. (pp. 137–8)

The issue is not that ideally aggregate demand and aggregate supply could be co-ordinated, but that any descriptively valid theory must recognize the prevalence of individuals who are not fully rational, and that their behaviour may displace the macroeconomy from the Classical Utopia. Thus, macroeconomic problems are ultimately microeconomic concerns.

We see this strategy explicitly in his three main thrusts against conservative macroeconomics contained in (1979b). The first regards the LM curve, and involves the elasticity of demand for money with respect to income:

The fault of the quantity theorists, I will argue in this lecture, is to dismiss the very reasonable possibility that fiscal policy works because the short-run income elasticity as well as the short-run interest elasticity is low. (1979b, p. 219)

A second complaint against New Classical thinking can be articulated in terms of aggregate supply. Exponents of the 'rational expectations' school argue that if actual output prices exceed market-clearing prices, then aggregate supply will be greater under the mistaken belief of firms that equilibrium prices have grown more favourable. The deception lasts, however, only so long as it takes agents to reformulate their price expectations. Thus, unemployment should be comparatively brief, and no expansionary fiscal policy permanently increases output. Akerlof contends that this argument is empirically specious since 'most unemployment belongs to spells of sufficient length that it cannot plausibly be accounted for by misinformation regarding prices' (1979b, pp. 219–20).

His third basis for disagreement with conservative macroeconomics regards the theoretical characterization of aggregate supply as contingent upon market clearing for both goods and labour. Only then is full employment manifested. Akerlof rightly contends that for several institutional reasons, including workplace norms, social customs and perceptions of fairness, firms may rationally offer and workers accept a wage above that which clears the labour market. Thus, long-term involuntary unemployment can be traced to institutional features of labour markets.

Akerlof's macroeconomics is Keynesian in its reliance on aggregate demand and aggregate supply microfounded through ISLM. His disagreement with Classical assertions focuses on their presumption that agents are fully rational. Since each of his chosen battlefields involves near-rational or irrational microfoundations, we now examine each in more detail.

Labour-Market Customs and Institutions

Akerlof theoretically attacks the enigma of labour markets persistently failing to clear with two partial-equilibrium arguments. The lesser of these imagines the job itself as a scarce resource to be rationed. The greater examines the nexus of social customs, habits and psychological responses to the employment relation which might induce employers to offer a wage higher than that which clears the market to their employees.

The former argument, that the employment opportunities given by the stock of capital may not profitably match all available labour, sees jobs as scarce resources to be rationed among job seekers. Akerlof's presentation of this view appears in (1967, 1969a, 1969b, and 1981a). The first three of these invoke a neoclassical aggregate production function of the sort fashionable in the 1960s to model structural unemployment as misco-ordination between incompatible types of capital and labour. Here, kinds of capital generate productively efficient employment niches. Just as some vintages of capital may be unemployed if one exhausts labour first, all of the available capital may be employed before every potential worker gets a job. 'Jobs as Dam Sites' (1981a) provides a partial-equilibrium, optimizing presentation of much the same idea. Here Akerlof argues that jobs are scarce resources, just as dam sites are, and that efficiency requires that they be rationed among the labourers who yield the best use of the job. Just as, even at zero cost, a dam which underutilizes a dam site may be wasteful, an unskilled worker matched with a scarce job, for which the elasticity of substitution is low, may be wasteful, even at a zero wage. Thus, not only may involuntary unemployment result, but it would tend to be concentrated among the unskilled. He writes:

> This image of the job gives reason for pessimism about the wage elasticity of demand for labour of a given skill, since it says that unskilled workers, no matter how low they bid their wages, may still be unable to bid jobs away from skilled workers.   (1981a, p. 101 in 1984 edn)

Inflexibility either in job descriptions or in skills is central to this case. Correctly emphasizing that people have distinct skills that cannot be quickly and costlessly altered, Akerlof writes:

> much specific technology consists of fixed job descriptions that relate how dis-
> crete persons (as opposed to abstract labour units, as in most economic models)
> relate to each other to accomplish the economic goals of the firm. (1981a, p.
> 109 in 1984 edn)

How mismatches might arise leads to models of the workplace as governed
by 'efficiency wages'. Of that approach, he and Yellen write:

> All these models have in common that in equilibrium an individual firm's pro-
> duction costs are reduced if it pays a wage in excess of market-clearing, and,
> thus, there is equilibrium involuntary unemployment.
>
> Without equivocation or qualification, we view efficiency wage models as
> providing the framework for a sensible macroeconomic model, capable of ex-
> plaining the stylized facts characterizing business cycles. Such a macroeconomic
> model must have at least five features: It must have involuntary unemployment;
> shifts in aggregate demand must change equilibrium output and employment, at
> least in the short run; over the course of the business cycle, productivity must
> behave procyclically; more skilled workers must have lower unemployment
> rates; and the quit rates should decrease with higher unemployment. (1986, pp.
> 1–2)

Efficiency-wage microfoundations focus attention on events in labour markets, and assert that in equilibrium it is to the advantage of firms to pay more
than the market-clearing wage. Moreover, the problem cannot be dismissed
as the consequence of implicit contracting between employers and their risk-
averse employees fearful of termination. For, as Akerlof and Miyazaki argue,

> Because both firms and workers prefer full-employment to layoffs in any given
> state, it follows that unemployment cannot occur in an equilibrium with rationally
> negotiated contracts. (1980f, p. 321)

Thus, lapses from full and strict rationality *per se* are required, and the
enigma such models must explain is why employers gain from higher wages.

The efficiency-wage argument contends that firms get something for paying a wage higher than that necessary to clear the labour market. What it gets
is work. If worker productivity rises when they are treated well, and high
wages treats them well, then managers of the firm may validly offer a wage
too high to clear the market in order to cajole work from workers. Sophisticated employers understand that merely hiring workers does not in itself get
the work done. People get the work done, and static production functions
employing abstract units of labour cannot explain what the firm must do to
extract labour from workers.

In a powerful series of essays, Akerlof argues that by treating their workers fairly and adhering to accepted codes of behaviour, firms can cultivate
the bond with their employees and facilitate the extraction of work from

them. Those who feel fairly treated and who are loyal to the firm are more likely to work. They will work 'harder' and more co-operatively, will be more appreciative of the job, will be more productive and thus more valuable to the firm. One obvious way to cultivate their goodwill, of course, is to pay them more than they could get in the 'market'.

Additional insights into the tacit human component of employer–employee relations appear in several more papers by Akerlof. In 'Workers' Trust Funds and the Logic of Wage Profiles' (1989), Akerlof and Katz show that a rising wage profile is not equivalent to a 'trust fund' of deferred wages, and generates an additional motive not to shirk among veteran employees. 'A Theory of Social Custom, of which Unemployment may be One Consequence' (1980a) presents a static optimization model of competing social customs and reputations regarding those customs. Such customs may persist, even in the presence of ostensible economic costs. If such a custom involves the employment and use of labour, especially regarding the reputable wage, which may be required to maintain the goodwill and productivity of one's employees, it may also become associated with 'involuntary' unemployment. Similarly, 'Fairness and Unemployment', with Janet L. Yellen (1988), contains a simple efficiency-wage model with a clever *ad hoc* assumption about the effort function, and reveals otherwise obscure concerns about equity. If people think they are being paid fairly, especially in relation to others in the enterprise, then they are more likely to participate enthusiastically. If they feel they are being treated meanly, and consider themselves underpaid, then they may effectively sabotage the firm's work. Succinctly, 'if people do not get what they think they deserve they get mad. This is the basic simple proposition underlying the fair wage/effort hypothesis' (p. 48). Thus, a firm may benefit from paying a wage higher than market clearing for some types of labour in order to convince its workers that they are being treated fairly, and thus get more work from them.

Akerlof generalizes many of these concerns for the tacit human dimension of labour relations in terms of 'gifts' between employer and employee. 'Labor Contracts as Partial Gift Exchange' (1982a), one of the most innovative and insightful essays recently appearing in the economics literature, and 'Gift Exchange and Efficiency-Wage Theory' (1984) understand labour contracts and work-place decisions in terms of 'gifts'. Here a gift is a noncontractually obligatory benefit extended to someone else in tacit expectation of a *quid pro quo*. This context consolidates analysis of the many tacit, perhaps even unconscious, elements of a worker's bond to work and employer. Accommodation by the worker (working hard and being productive) may be construed as a gift to the employer with the implicit expectation of something (job security or a 'high' wage) in return. According to efficiency-wage arguments, it may be in the best interests of the firm to maintain a psychologically positive environment evincing a gift from employees of better-than-required performance. In order to reap such gains, the firm may wisely eschew the market-clearing wage. Both the gift and the expectation, however, are matters of social custom.

These psychological and institutional insights carry static optimization far beyond the conservative 'orthodoxy' of fully rationally optimized labour-market decisions. Akerlof immensely stretches the usual methods but does not fracture them. Although the manifestation of rationality takes an odd turn, agents are still maximizing something. As Akerlof writes:

> An explanation for either the firm's behavior or the workers' behavior must depend either on maximization of something other than profits by the firm or on interaction of the workers with each other and with the firm that alters their utility functions.   (1982a, p. 150 in 1984 edn)

Macroeconomically, pervasive microeconomic decisions of this kind yield labour markets that do not explicitly clear, and involuntary unemployment persists.

The Duration of Unemployment and of Jobs

Uneasiness about long-term involuntary unemployment would be misplaced without empirical justification for it. Consequently, Akerlof also investigates the duration and seriousness of unemployment experienced in America. Unless there is an empirical reason to agree that involuntary unemployment is persistent and frequently lengthy, the New Classical claim that deviations from full employment are merely temporary displacements arising from exogenous shocks remains unchallenged.

During the 1970s the 'new view' of Feldstein (1973), Hall (1972) and Perry (1972) argued that unemployment spells tend to be brief, so that unemployment can be construed as a period during which one quickly searches for the best wage. Further, if the duration of employment empirically tends to be brief, then the New Classical presumption of 'rational expectations' (in which all displacements from full employment are temporary and provoked only by current random shocks) is also supported.

In a series of articles with Brian Main (1980b, 1980c, 1981b, 1981c, 1983b) and with Janet Yellen (1985d), Akerlof argued that some measures of both job duration and unemployment spells can mislead. Differences analogous with those between the average age of a population with the average age of death of a population underlie alternative estimates of unemployment duration. Since the average length of a spell of unemployment in progress underestimates the true experience of unemployment, an experience-weighted measure of unemployment was constructed. According to this technique American unemployment spells and job tenures both appear to be much longer. Regarding unemployment spells, Akerlof and Main write:

> Every group, persons with single spells, double spells, and three or more spells, experienced more unemployment than indicated by the average length of a completed spell. Persons with single spells have more unemployment because multiple spells are on the average shorter than single spells; persons with more than one spell have more unemployment because of the multiplicity of their spells. (1980c, p. 888)

And regarding job duration they write:

> While the average job may be quite short because there are many short jobs, most employment experience is spent in jobs that are quite long. This is somewhat contrary to the popularized view of the U.S. labor market as one where everyone is on the brink of changing jobs. ... This popular view that jobs are quite short is, however, a statistical artifact based on an erroneous interpretation of turnover statistics. (1980b, 1008–9)

Their evidence supports the contention that unemployment is typically sufficiently long that it cannot be explained in terms of 'job search'. Similarly, tenure also tends to be of long duration. The first of these contentions undermines the empirical power of the new classical description of labour markets, and the second bolsters the institutional orientation of efficiency-wages models.

The Demand for Money

Macroeconomics remains incomplete without a theory of money. The New Classical macroeconomics focuses on monetary aggregates, and regards interventionist policies as simultaneously temporarily disruptive and permanently inefficacious. 'Keynesian' economics, on the other hand, casts monetary theory within the context of ISLM, and focuses on the elasticities of the demand for money with respect to the interest rate and income. Given the IS curve, if the interest elasticity of the demand for money is small, then an increase in the supply of money will leak into speculative demand only slowly, thus forcing much of its impact on to the income-expenditure flow. If the income elasticity of the demand for money is also low, then expansionary monetary policy produces a relatively large outward shift in the LM curve. Thus, if, at least in the short term, the IS curve is not vertical, then monetary policy can affect the level of income. Monetary policy's power to affect income levels depends on low income and interest-rate elasticities of the demand for money.

With these macroeconomic concerns in mind, Akerlof examines the microfoundations of the demand for money. Six essays (1978b, 1978c, 1979a, 1980e, 1980f, 1982b) explore the microeconomics of bank-account monitoring in terms of near-rational behaviour. Whereas the rewards to strict optimization in managing one's bank account can be 'quite trivial' (1982b, p. 35), many people may meet their transactions demand by target-threshold monitoring of accounts. A person adjusts his or her account if the balance hits either a maximum or minimum allowable. At the maximum, funds are shifted to other assets, and at the minimum, nonmonetary assets are sold to obtain liquid funds. Compared with Irving Fisher's periodic monitoring scheme and with full optimization, this leads to a low income-elasticity of the transactions demand for money. Under such a regime, Akerlof and Milbourne argue that 'velocity, rather than being constant, will be almost proportional to income' (1980e, p. 898). Similarly, Akerlof wrote in 1979:

> Economic theorists have usually assumed that the short-run income elasticity of the transactions demand for money is quite large, being approximately unity. ... this paper shows that if habits are defined differently, in terms of threshold-target monitoring, velocity is not constant in the short run, but instead if proportional to income. (1979a, p. 182)

Hence, the Quantity Theory is undermined and interventionist policies gain power. In (1980d) a very low income elasticity of the demand for money recurs. There, however, the source is the postponing of disbursements when money is not at hand. People who have bills to pay but no money, may delay, pay with near-money or obtain credit:

> they delay their payments by the use of credit cards for example, or by the temporary nonpayment of their bills (the taking of trade credit). Payment is completed at times when the cash balance is more liquid. This is equivalent to a payments rationing procedure at times of illiquidity. (1980d, p. 146)

With such a rationing scheme, velocity again varies with income, and the basic premiss of quantity theorists, both old and new, degenerates. To complete the story, Akerlof and Milbourne estimate aggregate income and interest-rate elasticities of the demand for money in (1978c). They find them to be very low indeed.

This approach to monetary theory is tightly tethered to Akerlof's other work. He introduces an alternative to strict rationality, justifies near-rational depictions of behaviour, and demonstrates that in the aggregate such behaviour surprises the received doctrines. This combination of rule-of-thumb bank account monitoring and credit-rationing perfectly illustrates his more general work on 'near-rationality'. Central to all of this is the characterization of behaviour inconsistent with classic 'rationality'.

People routinely rely upon customs, habits, rules of thumb, social conventions and institutional structures to navigate their way through their economic lives. They do so for good reasons, even if those reasons are not easily ameliorable to classical and neoclassical economics. Although such near-rational acts are individually justified, they aggregately pull the system from optimality. Involuntary unemployment is but one important consequence.

George Akerlof's extraordinary talent is for identifying precisely where habitual behaviour can be found, and in developing its consequences for both the individual and the macroeconomy. Among living economists he is unsurpassed at lucidly analysing the motivations for, manifestations of and consequences to the truly human failure to be perfectly, fully rational. These institutional and near-rational microeconomic insights then generate the microfoundations for 'Keynesian' macroeconomics.

Section 3 questions this aggregative approach to macroeconomics. Especially when perfectly rational agents absent themselves, we need to understand what macro institutions and cultures form the social matrix within which individual customs and habits emerge. The authentic macroeconomic issue is not simply how to accumulate macro results from micro behaviour, but how to constitute micro behaviour from a social nexus of macroeconomic institutions understood as socially organic entities, not just collections of people.

INSTITUTIONS, AND THE MACROFOUNDATIONS OF MICROECONOMICS

In telling microeconomic tales without fully rational optimization, Akerlof dramatically veers from neoclassical orthodoxy. In one vital methodological respect, however, he remains staunchly neoclassical. He first analyses micro phenomena and only then aggregates to a derived macroeconomics. Macroeconomics arises from microfoundations, and microeconomics is told with no macroeconomic contingency. Compositionally, he is fully reductionist. The institutions and patterns that arch across the macroeconomy do not impinge upon individuals.

Here lies a mystery. To an amazing extent, his microeconomics is the analysis of economic acts guided by near-rational inertia, habits, customs and social norms. Gift exchange and efficiency wages rely upon implicit, tacit social norms, upon institutions. Yet his microeconomics neglects the critical embedding of those institutions within a culturally and historically contingent macroeconomic story of its own. The microeconomic manifestation of institutions cannot be adequately grasped without embedding them in an organically constituted macroeconomic social matrix. That social matrix, of course, is itself an institution. Thus, one ultimately needs a macrofoundation of microeconomics.

Regrettably, however, Akerlof's methodology conforms to the neoclassical norm so that, like them, he cannot transcend the craving for microfoundations to recognize the need for the organic study of macro institutions *per se*. This methodological choice reverberates through both his microeconomics and his macroeconomics.

A microeconomics richly endowed with sensitivity for the impacts of social norms through 'gift exchange' and 'loyalty' begs for an integrated sense of the institutional fabric governing the environment of the agent. The efficiency-wage story, for example, is written in terms of the firm's ability to get workers to work. Without an understanding of the firm's position in society, however, and of how it functions as but one institution in the lives of its employees, the efficiency-wage parable cannot truly emerge as a coherently integrated tale. Without macrofoundational bearings, that is, the story retains *ad hoc* elements, and its true complexity cannot be told.

The need for an organically construed institutional framework can also be seen in both components of Akerlof's macroeconomics. He models the transactions demand for money, for example, in terms of target-threshold monitoring, but the story is told given autonomous flows of expenditures and receipts. Consequently, one cannot employ his model to integrate credit and finance into the determination of the autonomous income-expenditure flow. At the micro level, a false dichotomy between autonomous expenditures and monetary phenomena appears and cannot be expunged from a microfounded macro.

The reductionist craving for microfoundations taints the theory of employment as well. Attention is diverted from the macroinstitutional basis of misco-ordination (through financial intermediation, for example) and thrust entirely upon partial equilibrium images of the labour market. That the macroeconomy may systemically suffer loses ground to a view that chronic unemployment reflects peculiarities in only one market. Lacking a rich depiction of the complete institutional network within which both firms and employees live, for example, the story of worker motivation and loyalty cannot be integrated with the story of consumer motivation and loyalty. Consequently, one of Keynes's great insights, that in the aggregate, fear and uncertainty can constrain expenditure so that microdecisions not to spend, that is, to save, are not equivalent to other microdecisions to spend, that is, to invest, is lost. Thus, when viewed as an authentic problem of macroeconomic co-ordination, one recognizes that there may be no price vector at which planned spending warrants the full employment of all resources, including labour, and despite the microinstitutional details of the labour market. One sees how persistent unemployment may not be a matter of just the markets for labour but of the entire system whereby expenditures for outputs generate the income from which expenditures can be planned.

Fixating the problem of unemployment solely within the labour market necessarily ignores other stories in which other institutions, including those affecting the financing of consumer expenditure, the debt-carrying capacity of firms, the expected return to investment and the confidence of wealth holders all influence macroeconomic outcomes, including the level of employment.

Regardless of these methodological worries, George A. Akerlof is unarguably one of his generation's greatest economists. Through a series of authentically original, innovative and insightful essays, he has personally resuscitated an approach to economics that otherwise would have been institutionally barren. More than any other, he has demonstrated that economists can productively incorporate issues of loyalty, customs, caste and 'gift-giving' into their models. Further, he has persuasively argued that microeconomic near-rationality blossoms into macroeconomic malaise. And all of this he crafted with a skilful pen of rare clarity. Economists of all persuasions should listen to his tales.

REFERENCES

Akerlof, George A. (1967), 'Stability, Marginal Products, Putty, and Clay', in *Essays on the Theory of Optimal Economic Growth*, ed. Karl Shell, Cambridge, Mass.: MIT Press.

—— and Stiglitz, Joseph E. (1969a), 'Capital, Wages and Structural Unemployment', *Economic Journal*, **79**, (314), 269–81.

—— (1969b), 'Structural Unemployment in a Neoclassical Framework', *Journal of Political Economy*, **77**, 339–407.

—— (1970), 'The Market for "Lemons": Quality, Uncertainty, and the Market Mechanism', *Quarterly Journal of Economics*, **84**, 488–500; reprinted in *An Economic Theorist's Book of Tales*, New York: Cambridge University Press, 1984.

—— (1976), 'The Economics of Caste and of the Rat Race, and Other Woeful Tales', *Quarterly Journal of Economics*, **90**, 599–617; reprinted in *An Economic Theorist's Book of Tales*, New York: Cambridge University Press, 1984.

—— (1978a), 'The Economics of "Tagging" as Applied to the Optimal Income Tax, Welfare Programs, and Manpower Planning', *American Economic Review*, **68**, 8–19; reprinted in *An Economic Theorist's Book of Tales*, New York: Cambridge University Press, 1984.

—— (1978b), 'The Microeconomic Foundations of a Flow of Funds Theory of the Demand for Money', *Journal of Economic Theory*, **18**, 190–215.

—— and Milbourne, Ross D. (1978c), 'New Calculations of Income and Interest Elasticities in Tobin's Model of Transactions Demand for Money', *Review of Economics and Statistics*, **60**, (4), 541–6.

—— (1979a), 'Irving Fisher on his Head: the Consequences of Constant Threshold-Target Monitoring of Money Holdings', *Quarterly Journal of Economics*, **93**, (2), 169–87.

—— (1979b), 'The Case against Conservative Macroeconomics: an Inaugural Lecture', *Economica*, **46**, 219–37.

—— (1980a), 'A Theory of Social Custom, of which Unemployment may be One Consequence', *Quarterly Journal of Economics*, **94**, 749–75; reprinted in *An Economic Theorist's Book of Tales*, New York: Cambridge University Press, 1984.

—— and Main, Brian (1980b), 'Maximum Likelihood Estimation with Pooled Observations: an Example from Labor Economics', *International Economic Review*, **21**, (3), 507–15.

—— and Main, Brian (1980c), 'Unemployment Spells and Unemployment Experience', *American Economic Review*, **70**, (5), 885–93.

—— and Milbourne, Ross D. (1980d), 'Irving Fisher on his Head, II: The Consequences of the Timing of Payments for the Demand for Money', *Quarterly Journal of Economics*, **95**, 145–57.

—— and Milbourne, Ross D. (1980e), 'The Short-Run Demand for Money', *Economic Journal*, **90**, 885–900.

—— and Miyazaki, Hajime (1980f), 'The Implicit Contract, Theory of Unemployment Meets the Wage Bill Argument', *Review of Economic Studies*, **47**, 321–38.

—— (1981a), 'Jobs as Dam Sites', *Review of Economic Studies*, **48**, 37–49; reprinted in *An Economic Theorist's Book of Tales*, New York: Cambridge University Press, 1984.

—— and Main, Brian (1981b), 'An Experience-Weighted Measure of Employment and Unemployment Durations', *American Economic Review*, **71**, (5), 1003–11.

—— and Main, Brian (1981c), 'Pitfalls in Markov Modeling of Labor Market Stocks and Flows', *Journal of Human Resources*, **16**, 141–51.

—— (1982a), 'Labor Contracts as Partial Gift Exchange', *Quarterly Journal of Economics*, **97**, 543–69; reprinted in *An Economic Theorist's Book of Tales*, New York: Cambridge University Press, 1984.

—— (1982b), 'The Short-Run Demand for Money: a New Look at an Old Problem', *American Economic Review*, **72**, (2), 35–9.

—— and Dickens, William T. (1982c), 'The Economic Consequences of Cognitive Dissonance', *American Economic Review*, **72**, (3), 307–19.

—— (1983a), 'Loyalty Filters', *American Economic Review*, **73**, (1), 54–63.

—— and Main, Brian (1983b), 'Measures of Unemployment Duration as Guides to Research and Policy: Reply', *American Economic Review*, **73**, (5), 1151–2.

—— (1984), 'Gift Exchange and Efficiency-Wage Theory: Four Views', *American Economic Review*, **74**, (2), 79–83.

—— (1985a), 'Discriminatory, Status-based Wages among Tradition-oriented, Stochastically Trading Coconut Producers', *Journal of Political Economy*, **93**, (2), 265–76.

—— and Yellen, Janet L. (1985b), 'A Near-rational Model of the Business Cycle, with Wage and Price Inertia', *Quarterly Journal of Economics*, **100**, 823–38.

—— and Yellen, Janet L. (1985c), Can Small Deviations from Rationality Make Significant Differences to Economic Equilibria?', *American Economic Review*, **75**, (4), 708–20.

—— and Yellen, Janet L. (1985d), 'Unemployment through the Filter of Memory', *Quarterly Journal of Economics*, **100**, 747–73.

—— and Yellen, Janet L. (1986), 'Introduction', in *Efficiency Wage Models of the*

Labor Market, ed. George A. Akerlof and Janet L. Yellen, New York: Cambridge University Press.

—— and Yellen, Janet L. (1987), 'Rational Models of Irrational Behavior', *American Economic Review*, **77**, (2), 137–42.

—— and Yellen, Janet L. (1988), 'Fairness and Unemployment', *American Economic Review*, **78**, (2), 45–9.

—— and Katz, L.F. (1989), 'Workers' Trust Funds and the Logic of Wage Profiles', *Quarterly Journal of Economics*, **104**, 525–36.

Feldstein, M.S. (1972), *Lowering the Permanent Rate of Unemployment*, United State Congress, Joint Economic Committee, Washington, D.C.: US Government Printing Office.

Hall, R.E. (1972), 'Turnover in the Labor Force', *Brookings Papers*, **3**, 709–56.

Perry, G. (1972), 'Unemployment Flows in the U.S. Labor Market', *Brookings Papers*, **2**, 245–92.

2. William J. Baumol

Elizabeth E. Bailey and Robert D. Willig

INTRODUCTION

At a time when political and economic freedoms are issues of immense moment, it is fitting indeed to undertake a retrospective on the contributions of William J. Baumol. Baumol has been spending his career addressing fundamental matters that economists have pondered since before Adam Smith framed them in the capitalist mould two centuries ago. He has influenced both basic viewpoints on the economic problem – the framework of static allocation and the dynamic focus on evolution and growth. Baumol has been among the very few who have been able to glide repeatedly and productively between microeconomic theory and practice, often creating new and insightful theory to illuminate pressing practical problems, and equally often generating from theoretical foundations practical solutions ripe for implementation. On the family tree of the economics profession, he is a great-grandfather of many important ideas and researchers, who is himself still productively creating.

Baumol's work is in essence pragmatic even while approached through theory. He has changed the landscape of economics by providing bridges among theory, policy and practice. He has been the seminal researcher on the imbalance in growth between the manufacturing and service sectors, and he has taken the lead in studying productivity convergence among industrial countries. He has been a pioneer in research on microtheory, contributing significantly to our understanding of business behaviour. His work on contestability theory and 'Baumol–Bradford' pricing principles offers influential insights into the nature of regulatory and deregulatory mechanisms that best serve the public interest. From the very outset of his career, he has been a research leader in welfare theory across a wide spectrum of concerns, commencing with a theory of the State built up from the foundations of the influence of externalities on the beneficial organization of government operations. His concerns about the environment drove him to generate and disseminate leading ideas on harnessing market incentives for environmental protection. His bold study of fairness is responsive to on-going issues facing government.

Our review of Baumol's research will focus on work that is representative of his contributions to each of three areas: dynamic analysis; applied microtheory; and welfare theory. We attempt to highlight research we find particularly influential and compelling, rather than attempting to review all the areas touched upon by this extremely prolific scholar.

DYNAMIC ANALYSIS

Baumol's fascination with dynamic models stemmed from his first teaching experience. His lectures on economic dynamics, delivered while he was a PhD student at the London School of Economics, are encapsulated in his first book, *Economic Dynamics* (1951). His working definition of economic dynamics is that it is the study of economic phenomena in relation to preceding and succeeding events. He views the models of Harrod, Marx and Schumpeter as having these features, and his treatment of their work is sensitive and intuitive. In contrast, he portrays the work of Hicks as statics incorporating time rather than as true dynamics. Here, the process of change is not of primary concern. Rather, Hicksian analysis aims to study a photograph, a 'still' of a system in motion. The 'still' must be dated, but the economic analysis of it can be static.

Baumol in his own work sometimes uses one and sometimes the other perspective on the economic problem. His most influential contribution to dynamics exposes the relationships over time between more- and less-productive sectors of the economy. His cost–disease model (sometimes called Baumol's disease) describes the inexorable relative increase in costs facing the service sector. Paradoxically, he shows that this sector with relatively stagnant productivity will experience relatively fast growth as labour resources are freed by rising productivity in technologically progressive sectors.

Baumol has also developed a theory of productivity convergence among countries that leads eventually through technology transfer to similar levels of productivity. This focus on productivity in broad aggregates – industry and country-wide performance – has provided a much-needed balance of perspective to the recent preoccupation with industrial competitiveness cast in terms of operating differences among firms in different countries, especially between those in the US and Japan.

The Cost-Disease Model: The Arts

A quarter of a century ago, Baumol published 'Macroeconomics of Unbalanced Growth: the Anatomy of Urban Crisis' (1967a). This theoretical study divides economic activity into two types. There are technologically progressive activities in which innovation, capital accumulation, scale and organizational learning all lead to continuing and cumulative increases in output per worker-hour. Then there are technologically nonprogressive activities which, by their very nature, permit only occasional increases in productivity.

The basic source of difference resides in the role played by labour in the activity. In the former case, labour is primarily an instrument. The consumer cares little how much labour is used in manufacturing, and is concerned only with the price and quality of the final product. By contrast, for the latter sector, labour for all practical purposes is itself the final product. For example, a string quartet takes as much time for training and delivery of an excellent performance today as it did a hundred years ago. There is little opportunity for improved productivity.

For such a dichotomization of economic activity, a very simple model yields startling dynamic consequences. Productivity per worker-hour grows cumulatively in one sector relative to that in the other, while wages rise commensurately in all areas. In the progressive sector, productivity increases will serve as an offset to rising wages. However, for the nonprogressive sector, every rise in wages will yield a corresponding addition to costs. As a result, relative costs in the nonprogressive sector must inevitably rise, and do so cumulatively.

These propositions provided illumination and explanation to Baumol of the data he and William F. Bowen had collected on the performing arts. In their book *Performing Arts: The Economic Dilemma* (1966), they argue that the continual financial strain in the provision of those services is due not to extravagance or mismanagement, but instead follows as an inevitable consequence of the constant nature of productivity in the delivery of artistic performances. The effective dissemination of this powerful insight contributed substantially to the significant success of the campaign for public support of the arts.

Due to the reception accorded his work on the performing arts, Baumol found himself with the opportunity to influence the conduct of business by the legitimate theatres of New York City. He had long been appalled by the misallocation of resources apparent from the considerable number of seats that remained empty during many theatrical performances, while so many potential theatre-goers were discouraged by the ticket prices. Yet, the typical theatre manager was convinced that a general lowering of ticket prices would decrease total revenues, and add to the theatre's financial distress. Baumol's unique ability to apply microeconomic analysis to puzzles posed by reality yielded a practical solution that was implemented. A direct result of Baumol's efforts is the long-standing and highly successful organization called 'TKTS' that offers previously unsold tickets for seats at Broadway shows at substantial discounts on the day of performance.

Baumol is a painter and sculptor in his own right, and he has exercised his artistic talents since his earliest days of study at the Art Student's League in New York City. He teaches sculpture at Princeton, and his works have been exhibited in New York and New Jersey. The genesis of the significant intellectual contribution Baumol has made to understanding the evolution and problems of the service sector is clearly closely linked to his passion for the arts.

Cost–Disease Model: Deindustrialization

Baumol vastly extended beyond the arts the domain over which his cost–disease theory provides important illumination. Early on, Baumol (1967a) applied this theory to explain 'the crisis of the larger cities'. He found that a large proportion of the services provided by cities are activities falling in the relatively nonprogressive sector of the economy, because there is little scope for labour-saving substitution of other inputs in their provision. Consequently, Baumol articulated the following implication of the cost–disease model (p. 423):

> Since there is no reason to anticipate a cessation of capital accumulation or innovation in the progressive sectors of the economy, the upward trend in the real costs of municipal services cannot be expected to halt; inexorably and cumulatively, whether or not there is inflation, administrative mismanagement or malfeasance, municipal budgets will almost certainly continue to mount in the future, just as they have been doing in the past. This is a trend for which no man and no group should be blamed, for there is nothing that can be done to stop it.

While Baumol clearly understood from the outset the broad economy-wide implications of his cost–disease theory, the recent concerns and policy debates about the direction of the US economy have motivated him to return to the subject. His latest insights on the state of the US economy in the context of its modern history and that of other national economies are presented in *Productivity and American Leadership: The Long View* (1989, with Sue Anne Batey Blackman and Edward N. Wolff). Here, Baumol's cost–disease theory is applied to explain long-term trends and cross-national regularities in divisions of production and labour among sectors of the economy.

According to the theory, secularly rising productivity in agriculture and manufacturing, together with low to moderate levels of the income elasticity of demand for such goods, leads to concomitant declines in the shares of the labour force working in these sectors. This is so despite the fact that the productivity-driven decline in relative cost of these goods induces greater demand for the volume of these sectors' outputs. The labour resources freed in this fashion by rising productivity in the technologically progressive agriculture and manufacturing sectors move to newly emerging sectors and to the technologically stagnant service sector.

While the services produced with relatively stagnant productivity rise in relative prices, their demand does not fall off dramatically due to the rise in the level of real income that results from the productivity gains in the other sectors. As a result, Baumol's theory predicts that the share of nominal GNP

Figure 2.1   Sector shares, US labour force, 1800–1980

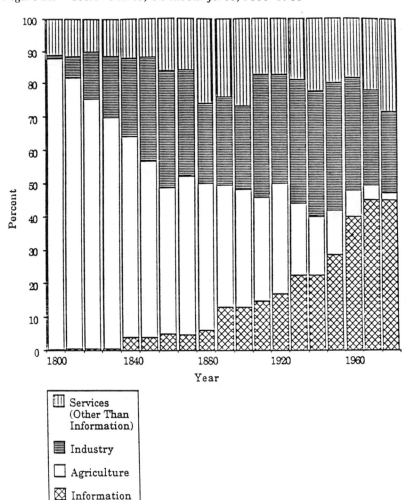

SOURCE: Baumol *et al.* (1989, p. 146).

accounted for by stagnant services evaluated at their nominal prices will rise over time, that the share of real GNP accounted for by stagnant services evaluated at their real prices may remain relatively stable over time, and that the share of the labour force producing stagnant services will grow over time.

It is remarkable how these seemingly paradoxical predictions of Baumol's theory are borne out by empirical evidence. As displayed in Figure 2.1, the US employment shares of agriculture and manufacturing have declined over time, with the most dramatic decreases occurring in agriculture as a result of its intense productivity growth. The corresponding increases in employment shares have occurred in the emergent information sector and in the sector of other services with stagnant productivity.

The relative prices of services with stagnant productivity have clearly increased over time. This fact is consistent with the predictions of Baumol's cost–disease theory. Most important, this fact helps in the choice between Baumol's theory and the deindustrialization model that provides the alternative and more conventional explanation of why the US service sector has expanded its employment share. According to the deindustrialization theory, the employment share of US services has expanded as a result of the decreasing ability of US manufacturing to compete successfully in its world markets. It is an implication of the deindustrialization model that the relative prices of services would fall, glutted by the push of labour from the slack manufacturing sector into the services sector. Thus, the deindustrialization theory is belied by the fact that the relative prices of services have risen, while this fact is precisely what Baumol's theory predicts.

Finally, in the post-war era in the US, the nominal value of the output of the service sector has grown about twice as fast as has the nominal GNP, while in real terms the two have grown at similar rates. Internationally, Figure 2.2 displays the nominal and real shares of services versus per capita income, ranging from very poor countries like India to highly industrialized countries like the United States. Across the full range of economic development, when expressed in constant prices, the service sector share of gross domestic product (GDP) is roughly constant, while in nominal terms that share markedly increases with real GDP per capita.

Thus, Baumol's theory finds striking empirical support (yet more can be found in the book) both in US and international data. Well beyond its importance for the progress of economic modelling and for aiding in the organization of economic history, Baumol's theory provides fundamental perspective on current trends in the US economy that drive consideration of pivotal policies. From this perspective, increases in labour employed in the service sector and decreases in labour employed in manufacturing are not indicators of a deindustrialization that calls for remedial measures. Instead,

Figure 2.2A   Nominal (unadjusted for inflation) share of services vs per-
capita income, 39 countries, 1975

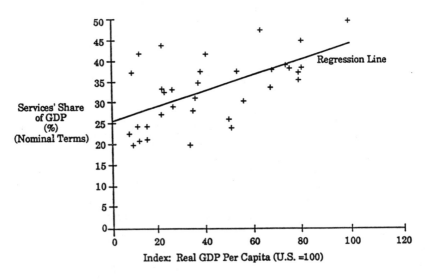

Figure 2.2B   Real (inflation-adjusted) share of services vs per-capita
income, 39 countries, 1975

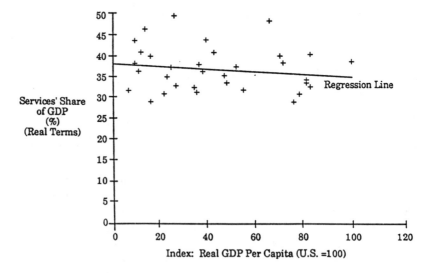

SOURCE: Baumol *et al.* (1989, p. 123).

these trends emerge from Baumol's research as inevitable consequences of technological progress in manufacturing, coupled with the intrinsic human component of the provision of services.

The profound significance of Baumol's theory for our viewpoint on the US economy is summarized well in a recent review of his book (Williamson, 1991, p. 57):

> While the deindustrialization model implies that the service sector's relative employment expansion is due to the 'push' of labor from industry where productivity is failing in the face of foreign competition, the cost disease model, in contrast, implies that it is due to the 'pull' of labor into services where productivity growth is failing ...
> The moral of the cost disease model is that America would deindustrialize faster if she were a technological leader in manufacturing, rather than a relative laggard struggling to retain her share of world markets. Indeed, our more successful competitors should exhibit a more rapid rise in the relative price of services and a more rapid rise in the share of workers employed in services. The evidence seems to be consistent with this indirect inference from the cost disease model and it turns the popular deindustrialization story on its head.

Productivity Convergence

Another theme of Baumol's research on dynamics is that, over long term eras, there is convergence in the levels of productivity experienced by industrial nations. He has studied this matter both from the standpoint of the mechanisms of technology transfer that historically have brought about such convergence, and the standpoint of what the data show. Figure 2.3 is sufficient to bring home the point, by displaying the labour productivity (GDP/work-hour) for seven leading industrial countries over the past century. Indeed, statistical treatment of the data supports the hypothesis that the bigger the productivity gap in 1950 between the US and another industrial country, the faster has been the catch-up by that country in the subsequent period, 1950–79. Baumol and his co-authors view that erosion of the American lead in many segments of technology as a natural consequence of convergence or closure of productivity differentials across industrialized countries. Thus here too, as in the analysis of employment in the service and manufacturing sectors, Baumol's theoretical and empirical work provide invaluable perspectives on trends that many have myopically construed as symptoms of a crisis requiring emergency policy responses.

Nevertheless, as Baumol is quick to point out, there is no determinism to productivity that obviates attention to considered measures by firms and by government aimed at keeping productivity high and growing as fast as is cost-effective. He emphasizes the critical role of incentives in motivating individuals and firms to expend efforts and investments to produce with

*Figure 2.3   Labour productivity (GDP/work-hour), 7 leading industrial
countries, 1870–1979*

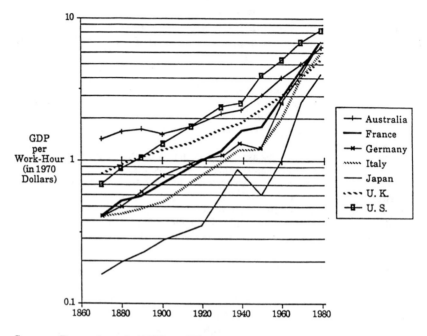

SOURCE: Baumol *et al.* (1989, p. 92).

efficiency, high quality, and innovation, and he raises alarms about institutions that dampen and misdirect such incentives.

APPLIED MICROTHEORY

Baumol's lifelong interest in microtheory and its applications began during his undergraduate years at CCNY (City College of New York) from 1939 to 1942. He was concerned that the modern theories of market imperfections, as being developed by Edward Chamberlain and Joan Robinson, were not being taught. So he became part of a pro-active group of students who organized self-teaching seminars. He accepted the assignment to learn about microeconomics and to lecture to his fellow students about the topic.

   The link to government was made in his first job, at the Department of Agriculture in 1942, where he began to learn how microtheory could be applied to concrete issues. Upon completion of military service, he returned to Agriculture and was part of a group charged with the responsibility of allocating US grain resources among countries. Here, he learned about the complexities of fairness and about the importance of transactions costs, and was confronted by the difficulties faced by even the best intentioned and most skilled officials with the mandate of performing the allocation of resources that markets otherwise might automatically effect.

In the field of applied microtheory, Baumol's research has provided a balanced counterweight to the unqualified faith in markets espoused by the Chicago School. His new, often paradoxical, propositions in economic theory offer concrete examples of when economic freedoms are appropriate and when they are likely to lead to outcomes that can be improved with intelligent interventions. His signature is exploration of the extent to which there can be robust performance and efficiency in the absence of the usual simplifying assumptions, such as no transactions costs, no externalities, no large or multiproduct firms, and no motivations other than profit maximization. In each instance, Baumol's contributions have been those of an economist entrepreneur. He has spawned research enterprises, with others inspired by his lead to supply a steady flow of papers incorporating his ideas as major building blocks of their own research.

The style Baumol has adopted as a scholar relies stimulatingly on posing problems through paradox. This style began when Baumol was a young assistant professor at Princeton engaged in avid and energetic dialogue with his older colleague, Jacob Viner. Viner set himself the task of presenting a fresh paradoxical proposition before his young friend each week. And Baumol would become locked in intellectual ferment as he unravelled the mystery. This delight at solving economic puzzles has remained with Baumol throughout his career, and has made it a true pleasure for his many co-authors, such as ourselves, to engage in research quests with him.

Baumol's early research in microeconomic theory identified and gave shape to concepts now intrinsic to modern business decision-making and education. He was one of the first to construct reductionist mathematical models of business phenomena for the purpose of deriving propositions with significance to economic theory. At the same time, he was able to represent fundamental microeconomic ideas in terms that were linked to tools employed by business analysts and practitioners. These penchants of Baumol came together in his textbook *Economic Theory and Operations Analysis* (first published in 1961, revised three times, and translated into many languages) which exposed large numbers of students in many fields to the insights of microeconomics in terms they could integrate into their own analytic frameworks. Of course, Baumol's talents in textbook authorship are well-known even to our youngest readers, as a result of the currently best-selling Econ 1 text that he coauthored with Alan Blinder, *Economics: Principles and Policy* (1979a).

In the following sections, we review a few of Baumol's most memorable contributions to microtheory from the 1950s and 1960s. Then we turn to the later portion of his work that deals with pricing, regulation, market structure, entry, and the formulation of public policy in these areas. Perhaps most dramatically, the theory of contestable markets that he co-authored (in part, with ourselves) has provided one of the pillars of the intellectual framework for the deregulatory movement. Contestability theory provides guidance in ascertaining where regulatory and antitrust intervention are and are not warranted, apart from the degree of concentration in the market structure. This work also yields innovative principles for the design of governmental policies towards businesses whose appropriate regulation would promote economic welfare.

Budget Management

Two of Baumol's papers from the 1950s and 1960s dealing with budget management are noteworthy examples of his trademark mathematical modelling of business phenomena, with important conclusions for both economic theory and business practice. The first that we review, 'The Transactions Demand for Cash: An Inventory Theoretic Approach' (1952a), is one of Baumol's first papers and one of the most cited. This research is based on the insight that a stock of cash provides its holder with an inventory of the medium of exchange. Cash is held so that it can be surrendered conveniently at the moment required for an exchange. Cash is costly to hold due to the loss of interest that could have been earned had the funds remained invested. On the other hand, holding more cash means that fewer withdrawals from invested funds need be made to finance expenses, thereby saving on the transactions cost or broker fee incurred for each withdrawal. By applying a result from inventory theory, Baumol shows that the minimum cost method of paying for transactions in this model is to demand cash in proportion to the square root of the value of transactions.

While the model is thus simple, the implications were profound. One prevalent view of economists at the time was that in a stationary state there would be no demand for cash balances. This view could not withstand Baumol's insight that it will generally pay to maintain an inventory of cash in order to economize on transactions costs. Another prevalent view at the time was that the transactions demand for cash was proportionate to the money value of transactions. This view was proven by Baumol to be logically inconsistent with the economies of scale in the use of cash which follow from the square root formula. In general, the demand for cash as an optimal inventory rises less than in proportion to the volume of transactions. A third consequence of the perspective generated by Baumol's modelling is that the demand for money moves inversely with interest rates even though it is held only to facilitate transactions.

The second paper we review here, 'Investment and Discount Rates under Capital Rationing – A Programming Approach' (1965, with Richard Quandt), explores situations in which the investment decisions of government agencies and/or company divisions are constrained by budgets whose magnitudes are largely beyond their control. The paper brings together the mathematical analysis of capital budgeting with the indifference curve approach common in the neoclassical theory of capital. The model studies the maximization of the utility generated by the net cash flow over time from undertaking various investment project combinations, subject to exogenous constraints on each period's cash flow. Even while making use of a subjective utility index, the Baumol–Quandt model for capital rationing for the first time provided an objective measure of the applicable discount rate. This is the ratio of the dual prices corresponding to the budget constraints for the two periods, or the objective rate of exchange across the periods permitted by the available investment opportunities. The analysis is widely applicable to practical problems of how to choose the discount rate for investment project selection under capital rationing, and, at the same time, provides a demystification of discount rates for economic theory.

Several other papers by Baumol during the same decades are also worthy of mention for the role they played in disseminating and interpreting mathematical programming methods to the economics profession. 'Integer Programming and Pricing' (1960, with Ralph Gomory) links Gomory's method of solution of integer linear programming problems to a discussion of the dual prices and their relationship to the marginal yields of scarce indivisible resources and their efficient allocation. 'The Dual in Nonlinear Programming and its Economic Interpretation' (1968, with Martin Balinsky) discusses the circumstances under which duals can be paired with primal nonlinear programming problems. The paper shows that for primal problems which are characterized by diminishing returns throughout, many of the powerful duality properties of linear programming retain their validity, including the economic interpretation of Lagrange multipliers as shadow prices. A third paper in this vein, 'Decomposition, Pricing for Decentralization and External Economies' (1964, with Tibor Fabian) will be discussed later.

Business Behaviour

In his contributions to the theory of the firm, Baumol displays a fascination with changing the assumptions inherent in standard economic models in order to better correspond with real behaviour. 'On The Theory of Oligopoly' (1958) presents Baumol's view that a large corporation may seek to maximize not its profits but its total sales revenues. Once profits exceed some satisfactory level in a period of time, such a firm will sacrifice further increases in profits in the same period if larger revenues can thereby be attained. The satisfactory stream of profits (which may lie below the short-run profit maximizing levels) will be determined by long-run considerations such as the firm's ability to finance the maximization of long-run sales. Sales maximization may be a managerial goal, regardless of the impact on shareholders, or it may be an effective rule-of-thumb for short-run behaviour that in fact promotes long-run profits.

This model continues to be highly relevant today, as it has been advanced as an apt description of the behaviour of Japanese firms, with their very long run perspective. To clarify the point, consider Figure 2.4. The standard profit maximizing model would have the firm producing output Q_p, the short-run profit maximizing level. Under the Baumol model, an American firm might view its long-run satisfactory level of profit to be at P^*, permitting the firm to operate at Q^*, which is larger than Q_p but less than the revenue maximizing level, Q_s. If a Japanese firm is willing to settle for the lower profit level of P_s because of differing expectations of acceptable short-run return in

Figure 2.4   Revenue maximization model

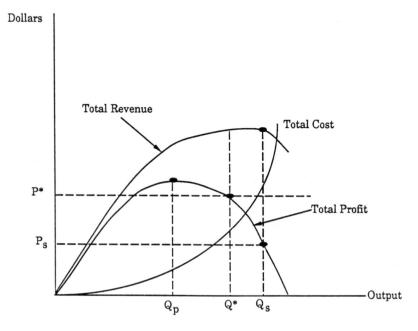

SOURCE: Baumol (1958, p. 189).

Japan, the Japanese firm could attain the larger output level, Q_s, and this may yield increased long-run profitability.

Baumol extends the model to the multiproduct case, showing that even in the sales maximizing firm, relatively unprofitable inputs and outputs are to be avoided, whatever the level of outlay and total revenue. He also uses it to explain a number of otherwise puzzling features of oligopolistic behaviour, including non-price competition, advertising policy and reactions by firms to changes in the level of overhead costs.

Baumol's research on the theory of oligopoly was enlarged from a static to an explicitly dynamic analysis in 'The Theory of Expansion of the Firm' (1962) and *Business Behavior Value and Growth* (1959). In these works he

Figure 2.5 Growth–equilibrium model

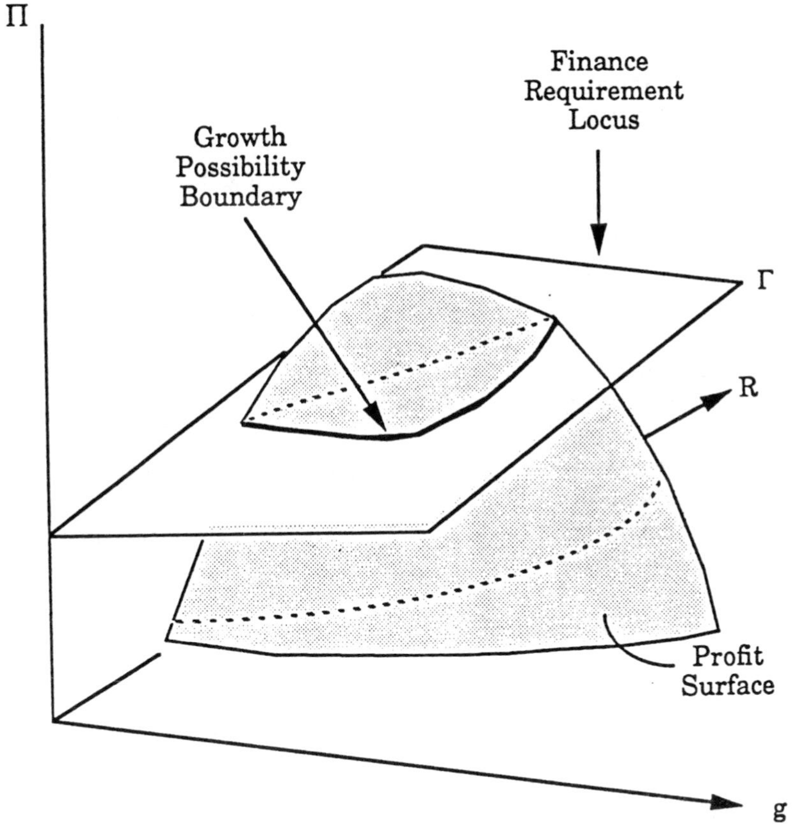

SOURCE: Baumol (1959, p. 99).

argues that the extraordinary long-run growth record of the Western capitalist economies can to a considerable extent be ascribed to the motivation for growth in the business firm. Thus, he generalizes his earlier static model employing a sales-level objective to a growth-equilibrium model. From the longer-run point of view, profit no longer acts as a period-by-period constraint on the maximization of each period's sales. Instead, profits are the means for obtaining capital needed to finance expansion plans. The optimal profit stream will be that consistent with the largest flow of output (or rate of growth of output) over the firm's lifetime. Figure 2.5 shows the dome-like profit surface over the plane where revenues, R, and the rate of growth of company output, g, are represented. The finance requirement locus depicts the levels of investment needed by the company to attain various values of g and R. The growth possibility boundary shows the values of g and R that are consistent with these financial requirements being met with the firm's earnings. Thus, the analysis indicates that the firm can effect tradeoffs between growth and revenues according to its objectives, which may be the maximization of growth, or of revenues, or of some balance between the two.

In addressing competitive strategies of businesses, Baumol also generalized other aspects of the then standard models of the firm. In particular, he felt that the received models failed to shed light on how firms deal with the diversity of consumer tastes that characterize most real markets. Firms' choices of competitive strategies that encompass the characteristics of their products and their marketing activities are at the heart of product differentiation. Baumol's contributions (with Richard E. Quandt) in 'The Demand for Abstract Transport Modes: Theory and Measurement' (1966) and in 'Calculation of Optimal Product and Retailer Characteristics: The Abstract Product Approach' (1967b) developed the abstract products approach in which goods and retail establishments are represented as bundles of attributes. The seminal theoretical perspectives presented by Baumol and Quandt were developed simultaneously with the similar ones of Kelvin Lancaster (1966). Baumol and Quandt were the first to conduct an empirical study of demand in which products are represented by their characteristics.

Regulation of Natural Monopolies

Baumol has made major and extremely influential contributions to the theory and practice of the regulation of natural monopolies. While much of our description of his accomplishments in this area must await our explanation in the next section of the development of contestable market theory, here we focus on his earlier work. The most prominent is presented in his paper (with David Bradford) 'Optimal Departures from Marginal Cost Pricing' (1970a). This classic poses and answers the question of how to characterize the prices that are welfare optimal for a firm to charge, subject to the constraint that the prices must generate revenues sufficient to cover the firm's costs of production. This is a key question for an unsubsidized multiproduct natural monopoly firm, whose increasing returns to scale imply that its costs cannot be covered by first-best prices set equal to marginal costs. 'Baumol–Bradford' prices or 'Ramsey' prices are now the common short-hand terms to denote second-best optimality (or 'quasi-optimality) for natural monopolies that are not subsidized. (The quasi-optimality conditions were recognized to be equivalent to those first derived by Frank Ramsey (1927) in a taxation context. In addition, Baumol and Bradford were careful in their article to give credit to A.S. Manne, M. Flemming, M. Boiteux, P. Samuelson, and others for their independent derivations of similar results during the 1950s.)

Baumol and Bradford show that the quasi-optimal prices that maximize consumer welfare subject to a binding profit constraint deviate in a systematic manner from marginal costs. In the simplest case, where the cross-elasticities of demand among the firm's products are all zero, the percentage deviations from marginal costs of the firm's quasi-optimal prices are inversely proportional to the price elasticities of demand for the firm's goods. This inverse elasticity rule says that to minimize welfare loss, the most inelastic demanders bear the brunt of making up the loss that would result from pricing at marginal costs. The clearest intuitive explanation is still found in an earlier Baumol piece (1968) on the topic:

> For if we consider as a distortion in demand any departure in demand patterns from those that result from prices set at marginal costs then, if it is necessary in order to meet a revenue requirement to vary prices from marginal costs, the least distortion will be caused if the largest price changes fall on those items whose demand is inelastic, i.e., those items whose demand will not change markedly in response to a departure from marginal cost pricing.

Baumol was well aware of the enormous significance of these results for the conduct of rate regulation. It had been, and in many venues still is, traditional for regulators to require that rates be set equal to costs, product by product, even where there are substantial common or joint costs that are incurred for the production of no one product alone. Baumol has long railed against the regulatory practice of creating systems of 'fully allocated costs' that divide up the joint and common costs among the firm's products, for the purpose of pricing. He points out (see Baumol, Koehn, and Willig, 1987, for a recent articulation) that allocation of the logically unallocable joint and common costs is inherently arbitrary and sensitive to the accounting methodology. But most important, Baumol emphasizes the Baumol–Bradford conclusion that the public interest requires that regulated prices be sensitive to conditions of demand as well as to conditions of cost. Since no system of fully allocated costs can reflect the various elasticities of demand of the firm's products, different and more flexible methods of rate regulation are needed to serve the interests of consumer welfare.

In the example of the regulation of railroad freight rates, the Baumol–Bradford results imply that movements with no effective transportation or other substitute alternatives, such as some coal shipments to electric utilities, should bear proportionately more of the railroad's overhead costs than movements, for example by boxcar, for which there are effective alternatives such as delivery by truck. Although the Interstate Commerce Commission (ICC) has been somewhat resistant to abandoning fully allocated costs, and following the principles adduced from the theory by Baumol and Bradford, remarkable progress has been made towards acceptance of their lessons in this domain.

In related work, Baumol (1971) studied the welfare optimal pricing of products requiring durable irreversible investments for their efficient manufacture. He showed that optimal prices in any specific time period reflect that period's assignment of capital depreciation costs, but that errors costly to the public interest might often result from application of rigid depreciation formulae. Instead, optimal prices reflect 'economic depreciation', which is the marginal opportunity cost of the use of the capital stock. Some specific practically useful lessons that emerge are that depreciation should be confined to wear and tear expenses when there is excess capacity in the capital stock, that depreciation charges should be permitted to grow as the time for replacements by innovations approaches, and that the straight-line depreciation formulae generally employed by regulators are almost always distinctly suboptimal. This work was substantially generalized in Baumol, Panzar, and Willig (1982).

Baumol has also contributed more broadly to the analysis of the impacts of different types of regulation on the incentives of firms to behave in a manner that is compatible with social goals. His clarification and extension of the analysis by Averch and Johnson (1962) is a fine example. In 'Input Choices and Rate of Return Regulation: An Overview of the Discussion' (1970b), Baumol and Alvin K. Klevorick confirm that the profit-maximizing response to rate-of-return regulation is overcapitalization, that is, the adoption of a capital/labour ratio that is greater than that which minimizes cost for the level of output. However, they show that other alleged versions of the overcapitalization effect are not accurate. It is not the case that the capital/labour ratio of the regulated firm must be larger than that of the unconstrained profit-maximizing monopolist, and the regulated firm need not produce an output larger than that which maximizes profit.

Since he completed that paper, Baumol has studied a number of regulatory solutions designed to mitigate the incentives for inefficiency. These include the deliberate introduction of lags into the process of rate-of-return regulation, and price caps which share with consumers those extra profits earned by the firm as a result of cost-saving measures. The most significant ideas for new regulatory solutions are an outgrowth of the development of contestability theory, to which we now turn.

Contestability Theory

A major research achievement has been the development, by Baumol, John Panzar and Robert Willig, of the theory of contestable markets, as described most fully in their book *Contestable Markets and the Theory of Industry Structure* (1982). Contestability theory is built up from several independent modules, each providing its own fundamental insights.

The first module provides new analyses of the nature and properties of the cost structures of multiproduct firms. A firm will produce more than one product as a consequence of 'economies of scope'. The concept of economies of scope, developed by Panzar and Willig (1981), provides a powerful new language appropriate for describing efficiencies in multiproduct firms, where as a consequence of shared inputs, the cost of producing products in combination is less than the total of the 'stand-alone costs' – the costs of producing each product or subsets of products separately. Baumol invented the concept of trans-ray convexity, a strong form of economies of scope, where there is continuous complementarity in the production of different goods as output proportions change.

For a multiproduct firm, another key cost concept is 'incremental costs' – the costs of adding a product or a subset of products to the others that the firm is producing. The returns to scale properties of both incremental costs and total costs are critical for predicting the cost efficient configuration of the industry. For example, decreasing returns in the incremental costs of a product indicate that it will be produced by more than one firm in an efficient configuration. Natural monopoly results from cost subadditivity, whereby single-firm production minimizes industry costs. This occurs from the combination of overall economies of scale and trans-ray convexity, or from the combination of economies of scope with increasing returns to scale in incremental costs.

The contribution to economic science of these new cost structure concepts is highlighted in the review of the book by Michael Spence. Spence (1983, p. 981) asserts:

> Cost structures constitute one of the foundations of competitive strategy, and strongly influence industry structure. Notwithstanding this fact, the amount of microeconomic theory directed toward competitively relevant attributes of costs

has been, if not minimal, then certainly more limited than the subject deserves. In fact, prior to the work of our authors, economists and business strategists did not have a language or a set of concepts with which to talk precisely about scale economies in a multiproduct setting. We now have the beginning of such a language, and a body of theory that provides a grammar for using it.

The second module of contestability theory is the conceptualization and analysis of a sustainable industry configuration. This is a set of prices for the industry's products and a set of market-clearing output levels for each of the industry's firms that together satisfy two conditions: (i) each incumbent earns revenues that cover its costs; and (ii) no entrant can earn positive profits at or below the industry prices with any set of outputs within total market demand. Sustainable industry configurations have striking positive and normative properties. They must minimize industry-wide costs, and earn incumbents no rents. Where more than one firm produces a given product, the marginal costs of the producers must equal the market price. Prices for each product and for each subset of products lie between average incremental costs and average stand-alone costs. Under plausible conditions, Ramsey optimal industry configurations are sustainable. This holds where the technology drives the industry to be unconcentrated, as under perfect competition. And it also holds where natural monopoly cost conditions drive the industry to be monopolized.

The third building block is contestability itself, which is the vehicle for using the work on subadditivity and sustainability to construct a systematic theory of industry structure. The concept of contestable markets offers a generalization of the model of perfect competition, a generalization in which fewer assumptions need to be made to obtain the applicable efficiency results. What drives contestability theory is the possibility of costlessly reversible entry. Where such 'hit and run' entry is feasible, market equilibrium must be a sustainable configuration, or else an entrant could profit from disturbing it. Thus, in contestable markets, equilibrium is characterized by all the efficiency properties discussed above, regardless of whether the industry is monopolized, is concentrated, or is so unconcentrated that it also fits the mould of perfect competition.

Because of the observability of its properties, Bailey (1981) pointed out that the theory of contestable markets has been extraordinarily helpful in the design of deregulatory and antitrust policy. The key element is the conclusion of contestability theory that sunk costs, not economies of scale, constitute the entry barrier that confers monopoly power. The prescription is policies that enhance the contestability of markets. Increased freedom of entry and exit are clearly important. Benefits may also be forthcoming from other policies that assure that entrants are not denied access to leased or shared use of a monopolist's essential sunk-cost facilities on fully compensatory terms.

The theory also has much to offer for the diagnosis of market power, where it turns attention away from exclusive reliance upon traditional market share measures and towards assessment of the degree of structural contestability in the industry. Thus, contestability theory is not synonymous with a libertarian philosophy. It does not conclude that unrestrained market freedom automatically solves all economic problems. It does not imply that antitrust and regulatory policies are pointless. Instead, it points the way towards careful delineation of when small numbers of large firms, and vertical or even horizontal mergers may be rendered harmless by the presence of contestability. It guides policy-makers to a process of analysis, layer-by-layer, market-by-market, to locate sources of market power and to identify targeted policies crafted to solve competition problems with minimized appropriate intervention.

Baumol's partnership role in creating this theory has deep roots from his earlier work. The link from contestability theory to his work on 'Baumol–Bradford' or 'Ramsey' pricing is delightfully described by Baumol (1986a, p. xxiv) himself:

> As we know, where average costs are declining (and in a variety of related multiproduct cases), a firm which prices its products at their marginal costs must suffer losses. The question to which Ramsey addressed himself is if marginal cost prices are therefore precluded, what deviations of prices from marginal costs are required for the second-best allocation of resources, that is, for Pareto optimality under the constraint that supplying firms just cover their total costs? Ramsey was able to derive a formula for these second-best prices which was ignored by much of the economic literature for several decades but had by the 1970s received a great deal of attention. I was then able to prove (though the result took me completely by surprise) that a monopolist who decided to adopt Pareto optimal Ramsey prices would (under a set of rather reasonable assumptions) find those prices to be sustainable. In other words, such a commendable pricing decision would reward the monopolist by granting him immunity from entry.
>
> I arrived at this result in rather curious circumstances. My wife and I were attending a fundraising performance at one of New York's experimental theaters, and we were waiting in line to get in surrounded by persons in bizarre dress and make-up when, according to my wife, my face took on a rather distracted look. I told her that a theorem which hardly seemed plausible to me had come to me from nowhere, along with what seemed to me to be its entire proof.
>
> Indeed, it transpired that the rigorous proof that emerged eventually did follow the outline that came to me suddenly in that theater lobby, but it took weeks of hard labor by (a skeptical) Willig, Bailey (and myself) before it could be put into satisfactory form. [See Figure 2.6 for the graphical depiction of Baumol's insight.]

As is the case with the cost disease model, contestability runs counter to the trend of what others have been studying. Most microeconomic theory since the mid 1970s has focused on strategic interactions arising from com-

Figure 2.6   Ramsey-optimal sustainable solution

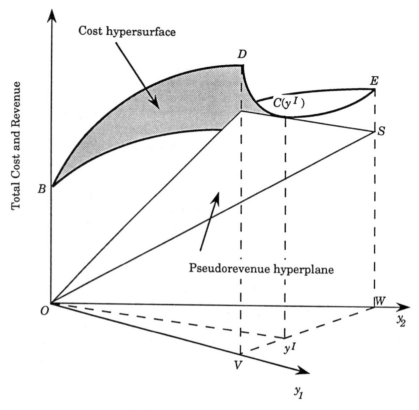

SOURCE: Baumol *et al.* (1977, p. 358).

mitments to irreversible investment and from asymmetry of information. Again, Spence (1983, p. 998) provides perspective:

> I also have a strong feeling, for which I cannot give a rigorous defense, that in the long run, costs and technology ultimately dominate the fine structure of demand, while sunk costs give rise to the vagaries of history and the play of competitive strategy in determining industry structure. This feeling is based partly upon (or is perhaps equivalent to) another intuition or conjecture, and that is that entry barriers lack permanence or durability. If this is correct, it follows for certain analytical purposes relating to the long-run evolution of industries, [contestability] theory's range of descriptive applicability may be greater than many of us whose eyes are trained mainly upon competitive strategy and entry barriers might imagine.

Apart from its possible descriptive applicability, and its diagnostic power, contestability theory has provided a new model for regulation. Bailey and Baumol (1984) discussed the possibility that concepts such as stand-alone costs and quasi-optimal pricing could be employed to replace rate-of-return regulation with methods better suited to an environment that mixed elements of natural monopoly and competition. In fact, as documented in Willig and Baumol (1987), the ICC adopted just such a new regime of railroad regulation in 1985, termed Constrained Market Pricing. The ICC rejected fully allocated costs as a method of pricing, endorsed the principles of Ramsey pricing as a general guide, and accorded railroads the freedom to choose their rates, even where there is found to be market dominance, at levels between incremental costs and stand-alone costs. As stated by the ICC:

> A rate level calculated by the stand-alone cost methodology represents the theoretical maximum rate that a railroad could levy on shippers without substantial diversion of traffic to a hypothetical competing service. It is, in other words, a simulated competitive price.

Thus, the new Constrained Market Pricing regulatory system attempts to impose on railroads the same constraints on pricing that the railroads would experience were they actually everywhere (which they are not) operating in a contestable market. So far, as reported in Willig and Baumol (1987), this regulatory mechanism seems to be working far better than its antecedents.

WELFARE ECONOMICS AND THE ROLE OF EXTERNALITIES

Another major strand of Baumol's research originated in his PhD dissertation, written under Lionel Robbins at the London School of Economics, and later published as *Welfare Economics and the Theory of the State* (1952b). Baumol developed from the logic of the Marshall–Pigou theory of externalities the rationale for government intervention in the workings of the economy. The work delineates conditions under which economic agents are or are not led by their self interest to act in a manner that is consistent with the maximization of the welfare of the group taken as a whole. In cases where activities of members of a community depend or impinge upon one another, it is shown that governmental action in the form of pricing and taxation policies may well benefit the individual agents by helping them attain their own ends. Many of these ideas, echoed in the latter works of James M. Buchanan, Gordon Tullock and M. Olson, established the philosophical foundation for the subsequent work on applied welfare economics by Baumol and the rest of the profession. It is not an exaggeration to report that Baumol's first book developed a fundamental theory of the State that is not only thoroughly consistent with the lessons of welfare economics, but that also shows the proper role to be played by economists in applying welfare economics to advise on the policy of the State.

Decentralized Decision Making

A more detailed and less fully optimistic picture was presented in Baumol's work with Tibor Fabian, 'Decomposition, Pricing for Decentralization and External Economies' (1964). This article interprets the decomposition method of mathematical programming as an instrument of economic analysis rather than as a method for numerical calculation.

The paper indicates how the decomposition method can take advantage of the economies associated with decentralized decision-making by divisions within a firm or by larger units in an economy. The method contains within it a coordinating mechanism which prevents the decentralized decisions from working at cross purposes. The mechanism maintains control over the external economy or diseconomy problems that arise because a division of the firm or of the economy may not take into account the benefits or the costs created by its activities that fall on other divisions.

Specifically, the method reaffirms that the way to deal with externalities is to modify the pricing system, offering bonuses in the case of external economies and imposing penalties on the producers of external diseconomies. Moreover, the provisional dual price system of the decomposition method embodies these penalties and bonuses, and the decomposition algorithm offers a method for determining when the divisional programs have been properly coordinated to yield a solution that is optimal for the economic unit as a whole. It is demonstrated that in some cases there exist no prices which will lead divisions to make independent decisions that are optimal from the point of view of the company or the economy as a whole. Thus, the mathematics of the decomposition method reveal the unfortunate fact that externality problems will not always admit a decentralized solution.

Externalities and the Environment

Baumol returned to the topic of externalities with 'On Taxation and the Control of Externalities' (1972). He directs attention to those externalities of the public goods variety, such as pollution, where Coasian negotiation between the polluters and those who are harmed by the pollutants is not feasible. As a matter of theory, he shows that taxation of polluters to provide full compensation to those affected by pollution may be incompatible with optimal resource allocation. For such compensation to victims provides an incentive for them to devote inadequate attention to protecting themselves against the deleterious effects of the externalities. Baumol also shows that a subsidy tends to be more effective than a tax in inducing the firm to reduce its emissions. However, paradoxically, a tax on emissions will tend to reduce emissions by the industry while a subsidy actually tends to increase total emissions by attracting more polluting firms into the industry.

His books with Wallace Oates, *The Theory of Environmental Policy* (1975) and *Economics, Environmental Policy and the Quality of Life* (1979b) further explore these issues. They point out (with considerable prescience, we now recognize) that the basic pollution problem is not unique to either free market economies or centrally planned economies, but arises in both systems from incentives to treat clean air and pure water as common property, made available for the taking at virtually zero cost. Placing a price on clean air and water induces individuals to economize on their use. While many economists focus only on financial incentives for environmental protection, however, it has been found that systems of effluent fees can encounter difficult problems of implementation. A wide range of policy instruments thus should be considered and tailored to specific situations. The books abound with both theoretical and pragmatic suggestions for the design of effective environmental policies.

Fairness versus Allocative Efficiency

In light of his contributions to both regulatory and environmental policy, and true to his early roots in government, Baumol has recently focused on generating from coherent theory guidance for policy makers having natural concerns about 'fairness'. The book *Superfairness* (1986b) stems from Baumol's recognition that issues of fairness are often more to the point than the literature of welfare economics seems to suggest, even with respect to matters with strong efficiency implications, such as the pricing of goods to consumers or to competing firms. He makes accessible recent advances in the formalization of games of fair division, and rigorously develops the novel concept of superfairness. He proceeds to apply his superfairness theory to such concrete issues as the intertemporal redistribution achieved by the employment of pricing devices to conserve scarce resources (for example, taxes on gasoline consumption), the fairness of different rationing devices considered for use in periods of scarcity, and the fairness of peak-load pricing.

CONCLUSION

There are several distinct talents that an economist can have: originality and creativity in conceptualization and model building; the ability incisively to exposit and explain complex issues on an intuitive but accurate level; policy analysis that is true to economic theory, while still accommodating of the complexities of reality and capable of practical implementation. Few economists develop even one of these talents to the extent necessary to make a major contribution to economic science. William J. Baumol has mastered all these talents, and has enthusiastically exercised them continuously from the start of his career to the time of this writing, with no slackening in sight.

The style of Baumol's work has clearly been shaped by the values that he has shared with his mentor, Jacob Viner. Viner (1958, pp. 112–13) wrote:

> No matter how refined and how elaborate the analysis, if it rests solely on the short view, it will still be ... a structure built on shifting sands.

It should then come as no surprise that so many of Baumol's major contributions have unravelled paradoxes that deal with change and with the long run. His lead issues are those of the evolution of capitalist economies; how more and less progressive and productive sectors of an economy coexist and interrelate; how microeconomic theory can be developed and enriched to illuminate complex reality; how government policy can promote efficiency where externalities or monopoly power warrant intervention; and why the government should refrain from intervening in overreaction to concentration in contestable markets or to shifts in sectoral labour employment that are driven by inevitable long-term trends. In grappling with these issues, Baumol has created elegant and enduringly influential benchmark theories for the public and private sector that have helped to shape economic theory and to guide policy. Whether conducted in 1991 or 1950, his research is applicable to an amazing degree to the economic phenomena and problems of today.

APPENDIX

Biographical Statement – Submitted by William J. Baumol

William J. Baumol is Professor of Economics by joint appointment at Princeton University and New York University. A graduate of the City College of New York (BSS, 1942) and the University of London (PhD, 1949), he is the author of some 15 books (which have been translated into about as many languages), as well as some 500 professional articles. His books include: *Economic Dynamics* (1951, 1959, 1970); *Welfare Economics and the Theory of the State* (1952); *Economic Processes and Policies* (1954, with L. V. Chandler); *Economic Theory and Operations Analysis* (1961, 1966, 1972, 1976); *The Stock Market and Economic Efficiency* (1965); *Performing Arts: The Economic Dilemma* (1966, with W.G. Bowen); *Precursors in Mathematical Economics: An Anthology* (1968, with S.M. Goldfeld); *Portfolio Theory: The Selection of Asset Combinations* (1970); *Economics of Academic Libraries* (1973, with M. Marcus); *The Theory of Environmental Policy* (1975, 1988, with W.E. Oates); *Economics, Environmental Policy and the Quality of Life* (1979, with W.E. Oates and S.A. Batey Blackman); *Economics: Principles and Policy* (1979, 1982, 1985, 1987, 1990, with A.S. Blinder); *Contestable Markets and the Theory of Industry Structure* (1982, 1987, with J.C. Panzar and R.D. Willig); *Inflation and the Performing Arts* (1984, editor with Hilda Baumol); *Productivity Growth and US Competitiveness* (1985, editor with K. McLennan); *Superfairness: Applications and Theory* (1986); *Microtheory: Applications and Origins* (1986); *Productivity and American Leadership: The Long View* (1989, with Sue Anne Batey Blackman and Edward N. Wolff).

Among his professional positions, he is a member of the Board of Trustees of the Joint Council on Economic Education, a founding member of the Advisory Committee of the World Resources Institute, and a member of the Joint Advisory Committee on Behavioural Economics of the Russell Sage Foundation and the Alfred P. Sloan Foundation. He is the Director of the C.V. Starr Centre for Applied Economic Research, at New York University. He is past president and Distinguished Fellow of the American Economic Association; past president of the Atlantic Economic Society, the Eastern Economic Association and the Association of Environmental and Resource Economists; and past member and chairman of the New Jersey Economic Policy Council. He is a fellow of the Econometric Society, honorary fellow of the London School of Economics, and holds honorary degrees from Rider College, Stockholm School of Economics, Knox College and the University of Basel. He has received the John R. Commons Award from Omicron Delta Epsilon, the Townsend Harris Medal from the Alumni Association of the City College of New York, and the Frank E. Seidman Distinguished Award in Political Economy. He is an elected member of the American Academy of Arts and Sciences, the American Philosophical Society, and the National Academy of Sciences. He is a director of Consultants in Industry Economics, Inc., and has acted as a frequent consultant for government and private industry, in the US and in many other countries.

REFERENCES

Averch, Harvey A. and Leland L. Johnson (1962), 'Behavior of the Firm under Regulatory Constraint', *American Economic Review*, **52**, 1053–69.

Bailey, Elizabeth E. (1981), 'Contestability and the Design of Regulatory and Antitrust Policy', *American Economic Review*, **71**, 178–83.

Bailey, Elizabeth E. and William J. Baumol (1984), 'Deregulation and the Theory of Contestable Markets', *Yale Journal of Regulation*, **1**, 111–32.

Balinski, Martin L. and William J. Baumol (1968), The Dual in Nonlinear Programming and its Economic Interpretation, *Review of Economic Studies*, **35**, 237–56.

Baumol, William J. (1951), *Economic Dynamics*, London: Macmillan; 2nd edn., 1959; 3rd edn., 1970.

—— (1952a), 'The Transactions Demand for Cash: an Inventory Theoretic Approach', *Quarterly Journal of Economics*, **66**, 545–56.

—— (1952b), *Welfare Economics and the Theory of the State*, London: Longmans, Green.

—— and Lester V. Chandler (1954), *Economic Processes and Policies*, New York: Harper.

—— (1956), 'Acceleration without Magnification', *American Economic Review*, **46**, 409–12.

—— (1958), 'On the Theory of Oligopoly', *Economica*, **25**, 187–98.

—— (1959), *Business Behavior, Value and Growth*, New York: Harcourt, Brace & World; rev. edn., 1967.

—— and Ralph E. Gomory (1960), 'Integer Programming and Pricing', *Econometrica*, **28**, 521–50.

—— (1961), *Economic Theory and Operations Analysis*, Englewood Cliffs, N.J.: Prentice-Hall; 2nd edn, 1966; 3rd edn, 1972; 4th edn, 1976.

—— (1962), 'The Theory of Expansion of the Firm', *American Economic Review*, **11**, 1078–82.

—— and Tibor Fabian (1964), 'Decomposition, Pricing for Decentralization and External Economies', *Management Science*, **11**, 1–32.

—— and Richard E. Quandt (1965a), 'Investment and Discount Rates under Capital Rationing – a Programming Approach', *Economic Journal*, **75**, 317–29.

—— (1965b), *The Stock Market and Economic Efficiency*, New York: Fordham University Press.

—— and William Bowen (1966), *Performing Arts: The Economic Dilemma*, New York, 1966.

—— (1967a), 'Macroeconomics of Unbalanced Growth: The Anatomy of Urban Crisis', *American Economic Review*, **57**, 415–26.

—— (1967b), 'Calculation of Optimal Product and Retailer Characteristics: the Abstract Product Approach', *Journal of Political Economy*, **75**, 674–85.

—— and Stephen M. Goldfeld (eds) (1968), *Precursers in Mathematical Economics: an Anthology*, London: London School of Economics and Political Science.

—— and David F. Bradford (1970a), 'Optimal Departures from Marginal Cost Pricing', *American Economic Review*, **60**, 265–83.

—— and Alvin K. Klevorick (1970b), 'Input Choices and Rate-of-Return Regulation: An Overview of the Discussion', *Bell Journal of Economics and Management Science*, **1**, 162–90.

—— (1971), 'Optimal Depreciation Policy: Pricing the Products of Durable Assets', *Bell Journal of Economics and Management Science*, **2**, Autumn, 365–76.

—— (1972), 'On Taxation and the Control of Externalities', *American Economic Review*, **62**, 307–22.

—— and Wallace E. Oates (1975), *The Theory of Environmental Policy*, Englewood Cliffs, N.J.: Prentice Hall (2nd edn., 1988).

——, Elizabeth E. Bailey and Robert D. Willig (1977), 'Weak Invisible Hand Theorems on the Sustainability of Prices in a Multiproduct Monopoly', *American Economic Review*, **67**, 350–65.

—— and Alan S. Blinder (1979a), *Economics: Principles and Policy*, New York: Harcourt Brace Jovanovich (2nd edn 1982, 3rd edn 1985, 4th edn 1987, 5th edn 1990).

——, Wallace E. Oates and S.A. Batey Blackman (1979b), *Economics, Environmental Policy and the Quality of Life*, Englewood Cliffs, N.J.: Prentice Hall.

——, John C. Panzar and Robert D. Willig (1982), *Contestable Markets and the Theory of Industry Structure*, New York and London: Harcourt Brace Jovanovich (2nd edn 1987).

—— and Hilda Baumol (eds) (1984), *Inflation and the Performing Arts*, New York: New York University Press.

—— (1986a), *Microtheory: Applications and Origins*, Brighton, Sussex: Wheatsheaf Books.

—— (1986b), *Superfairness: Applications and Theory*, Cambridge, MA: MIT Press.

——, M.F. Koehn and Robert D. Willig (1987), 'How Arbitrary is Arbitrary – or Toward the Deserved Demise of Full Cost Allocation', *Public Utilities Fortnightly*, **20**, 16–21.

——, Sue Anne Batey Blackman and Edward N. Wolff (1989), *Productivity and American Leadership: The Long View*, Cambridge, MA: MIT Press.

Lancaster, Kelvin J. (1966), 'A New Approach to Consumer Theory', *Journal of Political Economy*, **74**, 132–57.

Panzar, John C. and Robert D. Willig (1981), 'Economies of Scope', *American Economic Review*, **71**, 268–72.

Quandt, Richard E. and William J. Baumol (1966), 'The Demand for Abstract Transport Modes: Theory and Measurement', *Journal of Regional Science*, **6**, 13–26.

Ramsey, Frank (1927), 'A Contribution to the Theory of Taxation', *Economic Journal*, **37**, 47–61.

Spence, Michail (1983), 'Contestable Markets and the Theory of Industry Structure: a Review Article', *Journal of Economic Literature*, September.

Viner, Jacob (1958), *The Long View and the Short*, New York: Free Press.

Williamson, Jeffrey G. (1991), 'Productivity and American Leadership: Review Article', *Journal of Economic Literature*, **29**, March.

Willig, Robert D. and William J. Baumol (1987), 'Using Competition as a Guide', *Regulation*, **1**, 28–35.

3. Jon Elster

Daniel Little

Jon Elster has made important contributions to several fields, including rational choice theory, political science and philosophy. The breadth and depth of his writings are striking in a time of high specialization; he is read and discussed by political scientists, economists and philosophers. His work is difficult to summarize in a slogan, but virtually all of it has to do with problems of rational choice explanation in social science, much of it has a methodological dimension, and it is generally informed by a broad and deep acquaintance with relevant literatures in economics, political science, history, philosophy and psychology. In what follows I shall discuss Elster's contributions to a series of problem areas: the foundations of the theory of rationality; social welfare theory; philosophy of social science; and analytical Marxism. It is impossible to touch on every point of interest, or even a representative sampling; instead I shall single out several important areas of controversy for closer inspection. And since I shall dwell at times on points of criticism, it must be emphasized at the outset that I regard Elster's work with enormous respect. He has made possible a deeper understanding of a variety of important issues in a handful of disciplines. And he has drawn attention to important conceptual issues in the foundations of economic theorizing. The fertility of his mind combined with his prolificacy have combined to make a singularly important contribution to the human sciences.

FOUNDATIONS OF RATIONAL CHOICE THEORY

Much of Elster's work involves explication of the central assumptions of rational choice theory. Economists and decision theorists tend to adopt a thin and unnuanced conception of rationality, in which rational choice is strictly characterized by fixed preferences, cardinal utilities, subjectively construed probabilities and conformity to appropriate axioms of choice. Call this the 'thin' theory of rationality. This theory makes it possible to represent problems of choice in a highly compact and formal manner, and to arrive at provable results in decision theory, game theory and microeconomics. Many observers would now agree that the thin theory is a poor description of actual human decision-making behaviour.[1] Elster shows, however, that there are also unresolved conceptual problems contained within this theory. And he demonstrates that it is desirable to provide a more elaborated account of rational decision-making if rational choice theory is to be of much use in understanding social behaviour in all but the most narrowly defined market contexts.

What is Rationality?

Before we can consider non-standard cases of rational choice we need a more detailed account of what we understand by rational behaviour in the clear cases. Elster's work contains a number of discussions of this central topic. In *Ulysses and the Sirens* he analyses rational choice as the outcome of a two-step process:

> To explain why a person in a given situation behaves in one way rather than in another, we can see his action as the result of two successive filtering processes. The first has the effect of limiting the set of abstractly possible actions to the *feasible* set, i.e. the set of actions that satisfy simultaneously a number of physical, technical, economic and politico-legal constraints. The second has the effect of singling out one member of the feasible set as the action which is to be carried out. (1979/1984, p. 76; see also 1989c, pp. 13–14).

This is a useful preliminary statement of the concept of rationality. It serves well as a framework within which to understand the fields of microeconomics, game theory and the like; for these fields concentrate on the techniques of optimization through which an agent can select the optimal choice among the feasible set (the second filter). But the definition also sheds light on the importance of social and natural constraints on action (the first filter). This feature of rational action implies that there may be patterns of choice that can be explained, not as the result of optimizing deliberation, but as the result of a particular set of institutional constraints. Economists are inclined to emphasize the importance of optimization within stylized environments (markets); whereas political scientists often focus on variations in the environment of choice as the critical variable underlying patterns of social behaviour. Elster's characterization of rationality leaves room for both forms of social explanation.[2]

Turn now to problems deriving from foundational assumptions of rational choice theory. Perhaps the cornerstone of rational choice theory is the theory of preference. Individuals are assumed to have complete, consistent preference orderings which can in turn be represented by cardinal utility functions through von Neumann lotteries on pairs of alternatives. In the thin theory preferences are taken as exogenous and fixed; the theory is designed to answer the question: How should I act *given* this set of preferences? But Elster shows that a number of problems arise in interpreting the theory of preference. I shall consider several of these topics briefly and then look in greater detail at Elster's treatment of the problem of time preference.

Endogenous Change of Preference

The thin theory of rationality takes the agent's preferences as given or exogenous; microeconomics and decision theory have to do with optimization *given* a particular preference ranking of alternatives. But what if my actions today can lead to a shift in my preferences tomorrow? This expands the problem of choice dramatically; for now I must deliberate, not only over how best to achieve my current preferences, but what preferences to cultivate for tomorrow. Are there rational grounds for making such choices?[3]

Suppose my preference structure today is this: I place very high value on becoming one of the world's ten best chefs. All other careers pale in comparison. If this is a fixed preference (or at least a circumstance out of my control) then the options available to me are limited to the means I might choose to pursue this goal (chef school, a sou-chef position in a Paris restaurant and so on). Now suppose that my options are extended by allowing the possibility that I might voluntarily change my preferences. I can now choose between pursuing my old preferences or undertaking a course of psychotherapy that will rid me of this demanding ambition and establish a new and more attainable goal. The conceptual problem is this: on what basis should I deliberate about this choice? It cannot be on the basis of my existing preference structure, since that is what is up for grabs. We might attempt to deal with this problem through recourse to the idea of a second-order preference ranking: a preference ranking of preference rankings (Sen 1982a; Harsanyi 1982). In this case we might reason that it is preferable to adopt a lifeplan (first-order preference structure) in which the chief goals are reasonably attainable, over one in which the prospects of success are vanishingly small. The central point, however, is clear: the thin theory of rationality lacks resources for resolving this problem of choice. The problem of choosing to change one's preferences or utility function cannot be reduced to a problem of utility maximization; other rational considerations must be brought into play.

Self-Imposed Constraint

Turn now to problems of imperfect rationality. Elster has written a great deal on the issue of the role of self-imposed constraint within rational choice.

Here the problem derives from the fact that real decision-makers are less than completely regulated by rationality. Thus we suffer from weakness of the will (an inability to execute a decision we have determined to be for the best, all things considered), emotion, impulsiveness, habit and self-deception. These failures of rationality raise two sorts of problems. First, we need to have a more adequate conceptual analysis of the features of human practical cognition that interfere with reason. How is self-deception possible, since it seems to involve believing what I know to be false? Does weakness of the will derive from factors outside of rationality, or is it a feature of the process of rational deliberation itself?[4] Secondly, we need to consider another second-order problem of rational choice: how the rational agent can choose to act in the present so as to minimize the consequences of these features of imperfect rational capacity in the future. Elster contributes to both topics, but particularly useful is his discussion of the latter under the general topic of the problem of Ulysses and the Sirens. It is possible for rational agents to anticipate failures of rationality in the future and arrange constraints on their future choices that will guarantee the behaviour selected today as optimal. Suppose I undertake a plan for tomorrow that I judge today to be best, all things considered: I shall arise, breakfast and spend the day completing an important professional task. Suppose I also anticipate, however, that the day will be fine, the sand and sun will beckon, and I shall be irresistibly drawn to the beach – with the result that the task will remain unfinished. Finally, suppose I prefer that the task be finished to the pleasures of a day on the beach. Under these circumstances, what actions are available to me today to see that my will is accomplished tomorrow? Elster argues that the central resource available is that of precommitment – creating a constraint on my future actions that will compel me to act in the future as I decide today (1979/1984). In this example I might break the legs of my beach chair, knowing that the prospect of a day on the beach without a chair will be entirely less attractive to me tomorrow than it would in the presence of the chair. If I were perfectly rational such stratagems would not be necessary; if I were entirely immune to the call of reason they would be unavailable.

Hysteresis

Turn now to a problem of methodology in the theory of preference. The Bayesian treatment of subjective probabilities and the von Neumann approach to cardinal utilities both depend on working out the agent's probability and utility space through a series of questions about alternatives: do you prefer x with certainty or a lottery with probability p of winning y and probability $1 - p$ of winning z? The probability p is then altered until we arrive at a probability $p*$ for which the agent is indifferent between the two options;

this information can then be used to assign a cardinal utility to x. The problem that Elster raises is this: do we have any reason to think that the resulting value $p*$ is path-independent; or is it likely, on the contrary, that the agent will arrive at different values depending on whether the starting value is high or low (1979/1984, p. 129)? (This argument converges to some extent with Kahneman and Tversky's analysis of the sensitivity of choice to the decision frame; Kahneman, Slovic, and Tversky, 1982.) The path-dependence of the outcome of a causal process is sometimes referred to as *hysteresis*; and this sensitivity of the outcome to the particular order of questions raises a serious problem for the interpretation of subjective probabilities and cardinal utilities. For if we are not confident that the agent would have arrived at $p*$ no matter what order the choices were presented to him, then it is no longer justifiable to regard $p*$ as a unique measure of the agent's relative valuation of x, y, and z.[5]

Time Preferences

Each of these is a topic where Elster has focused our attention on an underlying conceptual or methodological problem in the foundations of the theory of rational choice. I now consider a final topic in somewhat greater detail with a more critical eye. Elster broadens the usual framework of rational choice by raising the problem of intertemporal planning: how should rational agents take future utilities into account in current choices? When they consider it at all, economists generally treat this problem along the lines of an annuity: future utilities are discounted by a uniform rate, compounded by the number of periods into the future the utility occurs.[6] This account may be represented formally as:

$$PVU(u) = \frac{u}{(1 + r)^n}$$

Where PVU is the present value of utility, u is the future utility, r is the discount rate, and n is the number of time periods. We may refer to this as 'uniform exponential discounting'. If we adopt this approach, then the problem of the rationality of time preferences reduces to this: is it rational to adopt a positive discount rate, or does rationality require that $r = 0$? And secondly, if a positive discount rate is rational, are there any rational grounds for selecting one value of r rather than another; or is this simply a matter of individual preference?[7]

Elster formulates the problem more generally. He considers a general intertemporal utility function governing n periods of the following form:

$$U = d_1{}^*u(x_1) + d_2{}^*u(x_2) + \ldots + d_n{}^*u(x_n) \tag{3.1}$$

where d_i are the discount coefficients for each period; $d_{i+1} < d_i$ for each i; and u is the agent's intratemporal utility function (which is assumed to be unchanging over time, reflecting the assumption that preferences do not change over time). The problem of time preference then concerns the allocation of a quantity of resources over n periods. If u is a diminishing function of resources and if the agent has no pure time preferences, then U is maximized by distributing resources equally over n periods.

Elster poses two questions about this construction. First, is there any rational basis for discounting the future at all? And secondly, are there any consistency requirements governing the discount coefficients? He accepts the point argued by others that pure time preference for the present over the future is irrational.[8] If faced with the choice of one unit of utility today or next year, Elster contends (assuming that next year is certain), that the agent should be indifferent between the two options; it is irrational for the agent to prefer today's consumption over next year's consumption merely because it is the present. The only justification for time preference, therefore, is the element of risk and uncertainty posed by the future. (I will refer to this as 'actuarial discounting'.) Elster further shows that it is possible to define a precise sense of intertemporal consistency using this formulation (1979/1984, pp. 68–72). Some settings of the discount coefficients give rise to inconsistent time preferences: the allocation that maximizes U in period 1 gives rise to a different value for consumption in period 2 than will be chosen in period 2. The agent is thus led repeatedly to change his plan from one year to the next. And Elster maintains that only uniform exponential discounting satisfies this condition (1979/1984, p. 71; 1983e, p. 7; 1989a, pp. 20–21).

Elster concludes, then, that rationality requires, first, that agents ought not discount the future over and above what risk requires; and secondly, that if they do discount the future it should be done on the basis of uniform exponential discounting. I shall argue here that Elster's formulation of these issues is infelicitous, however, and that his central conclusions are unconvincing. To the extent that discounting is based on actuarial risk, it will not be exponential; non-exponential discounts are not always inconsistent; and, more tentatively, I shall hold that rationality *requires* time discounting if we are to make sense of savings, investment and interest.

The clearest rationale for discounting the future is the element of risk and uncertainty. There is a finite probability – increasing over time – that the agent will not live to enjoy the fruits of his savings. However, it emerges that the riskiness of the future does not give rise to uniform exponential discounting. Actuarial tables provide a statistical estimate of the probability of an individual's surviving any particular year (for example, age 40 to age 41). Let p_i represent the probability of surviving the ith year once having attained the (i–1)th year. From these data it is easy to compute the probability today (in my fortieth year) of my surviving to enjoy the fruits of my fifty-second year; it is simply the product of the probabilities of my surviving each intervening year. Let the series cp_i represent the cumulative probability of surviving the ith year. This will be a decreasing series. We may now represent the problem of intertemporal planning along the lines of a problem of decision-making under risk, which can be solved by maximizing expected utility. Suppose that utility is a diminishing function of income $u(m)$. Then in allocating resources today I should choose an allocation m_i of funds M over n time periods that maximizes the expected utility of the intertemporal allocation. This construction reduces time preference to risk; on this approach, there is no pure time preference, but only an expected utility maximization. Here again we have an expression that represents intertemporal planning in terms of discount coefficients and a fixed utility function:

$$U_r = cp_1{}^*u(x_1) + cp_2{}^*u(x_2) + \ldots + cp_n{}^*u(x_n) \qquad (3.2)$$

Here the coefficients cp_i are the cumulative probabilities of surviving to the ith year. In this case, however, the coefficients are not uniform or exponential. The coefficients are diminishing since they are cumulative products of probabilities; but each coefficient is specific to the period to which it corresponds (since that year is characterized by a specific actuarial probability of survival). So if time discounting reflects actuarial risk, we can conclude that it should *not* take the form of uniform exponential discounting. Figure 3.1 illustrates the marked difference between actuarial and exponential discounting.[9]

Turn now to the problem of consistent time preference. Elster proposes that consistency of time preferences requires that we make use of an intertemporal utility function that produces allocations in the first period over n periods that will not be overturned when applied in the second period. He contends that the only consistent scheme of time preferences is one based on exponential discounting (1979/1984, p. 71; 1983e, p. 7). However, this conclusion follows from an artefact of his construction. Elster assumes that the coefficients in expression 3.1 are indexed on the current year; so when the agent deliberates next year he or she will once again be faced with coefficient d_1. However, the actuarial-discount construction requires that the coefficients be fixed by a particular starting point (for example, the agent's birth year), because the coefficient reflects the probability of surviving that particular year. So as the agent moves through life his utility function loses terms on the left; whereas Elster's construction loses terms on the right. It is

Figure 3.1 Exponential discount versus actuarial discount

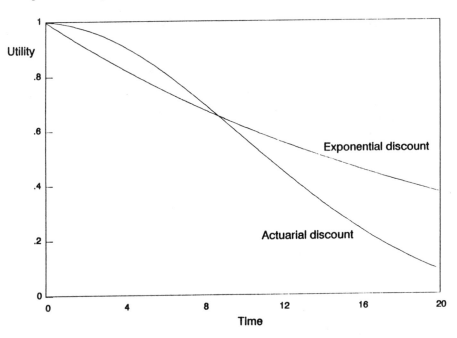

this aspect of Elster's construction that gives rise to inconsistent preferences over time. If we accept Elster's formulation, then only exponential discounting is consistent over time. However, the more general expected utility formulation with fixed indexing (expression 3.2) produces consistent preferences as well, in Elster's sense; when the agent reconsiders the allocation problem for the remaining years in the following period, he will arrive at the same distribution over the remaining years. But it requires that each year remain dated within the utility expression. And with fixed coefficients indexed to birth year the problem of inconsistency disappears.

Finally, let us consider Elster's contention that pure time discounting is irrational. (Pure time discounting disappears on the actuarial approach: here the agent prefers the present not merely because it is the present, but because the future is increasingly uncertain.) Is it irrational to prefer today's utility over tomorrow's? I do not have a general answer to this question, but we get some further grip on the question by considering how time preference relates to the existence of a positive interest rate on resources. Upon reflection it can be seen that a zero rate of utility discounting implies that the rate of interest on money should be zero as well. This is plainly not the case; therefore it follows that agents do discount future utilities. Time discounting of utilities is thus interwoven with the fact of a positive interest rate on resources, which in turn corresponds to a positive real growth rate.

Suppose that utility is produced only by income and that income shows diminishing marginal utility. And suppose that money is compounded and discounted by the interest rate i. The question is whether there is a utility discount function that follows from this set of facts. Let $PVU(u)$ be the hypothetical utility discount function. If we assume that the interest rate is an equilibrium rate reflecting agents' savings choices, then the following condition must be satisfied:

$$U(m) = PVU((1 + i)^n * m)$$

That is, it must be the case that the utility of the cost of an annuity is equal to the present discounted utility of the future value of the annuity. If the utility of current money is greater than the discounted future utility of the annuity, then individuals will choose not to save at the prevailing interest rate, which will lead to an increase in i to the point where the condition is satisfied; whereas if the current utility of the annuity is greater than the utility of its cost, then there will be excess demand for annuities, leading to a drop in the interest rate. For any utility function there is a utility discount function that corresponds to this equilibrium condition, in this respect: it discounts future utilities so that the present utility of the future value of an annuity equals the price of the annuity. If the utility function is assumed to be a Cobb–Douglas function, then we get a particularly simple outcome; the equilibrium discount rate for utility is an exponential function as well:

$$PVU(u) = \frac{1}{(1+i)^{\alpha * n}} * u$$

Thus in the Cobb–Douglas case the utility discount rate is exponentially related to the interest rate.[10] These considerations give rise to an indirect argument for the rationality of time-discount of utilities: only if there is such a discount can we make sense of the existence of a positive interest rate.

THEORY OF SOCIAL WELFARE

Turn now to Elster's contributions to the theory of social welfare. Elster has written frequently on topics falling broadly within the theory of social choice broadly construed; here I shall briefly describe several topics of interest. A good example of Elster's contributions in this area may be found in his introduction (with Aanund Hylland) to *Foundations of Social Choice Theory*

(Elster and Hylland, eds. 1986). In just a few pages Elster clarifies the original motivations of the theory of social choice (the practical problems of designing voting schemes and aggregating social welfare; pp.2–3); he illustrates some of the connections between the theory of social choice and other topics – for example, distributive justice and game theory; and he focuses attention on several conceptual problems lying at the heart of the theory – for example, the assumption that preferences are exogenous to processes of public decision-making or the problem of defining the boundaries of a given electorate (pp. 6–8).

Social Decision Processes and Individual Preferences

As we saw in the first section, Elster is interested in the problem of endogenous preference change. He believes that this problem recurs in the case of social decision-making, giving rise to a serious foundational problem in social choice theory. The central problem of social choice theory is usually formulated along these lines: given a set of individuals and fixed preference rankings, what decision rule or voting scheme can be put forward to arrive at a consistent social preference ranking? And what social preference ranking emerges from these individual preferences? In 'The Market and the Forum' Elster argues that this formulation misses a crucial element of the political process within a democracy: the fact that individual preferences are formed through the process of political decision-making itself (1986e, pp. 106–12). So individual preferences are not prior or exogenous; instead, they take form through the process of political discussion and debate.[11] And Elster takes this fact to cast some doubt on the adequacy of social choice theory: the theory abstracts from a feature of social deliberation that is essential to understanding the process of social decision-making.

Is this a telling objection? I think not. Elster is right to draw attention to the ways in which preferences are shaped through debate. But once we acknowledge this fact and admit of an extended process of discussion and persuasion, we are once again confronted with the same problems that first engaged Arrow and others. At some point it is necessary to aggregate individual preferences into a single social preference ranking; and at this point the original problem of social choice arises once again. This point emerges most clearly if we consider a comparison that Elster does not consider: the contrast between a formal social choice function and Rawls's conception of wide reflective equilibrium.[12] In each case we are attempting to characterize a rational process of collective decision-making. In the former case, however, individual beliefs and preferences are fixed, and the sole problem is how to generate a consistent social choice. In the latter case, we are to suppose that individuals retain an open mind concerning their beliefs and preferences as they consider arguments, moral reasons and alternative factual beliefs advanced by other citizens. The group reaches individual-level equilibrium when all relevant considerations (moral, theoretical, factual) have been voiced and each individual has settled on a coherent set of preferences and beliefs. We may imagine that each individual has altered his or her beliefs and preferences in various ways. Now, however, we are faced anew with the problem of *social* choice: how can these beliefs and preferences be aggregated to a consistent collective preference ranking? There is nothing in this process that allows us to conclude that unanimity will emerge through debate; instead, it is perfectly consistent, even probable, to suppose that individuals will still disagree in their rankings of social alternatives. So the point that beliefs and preferences are themselves affected by the process of social deliberation does not alter the fact that some rule or other of aggregation must be chosen to move from individual preferences to social choice.

It may be noted that this discussion raises once again the problem of hysteresis, at two levels. To the extent that citizens' preferences are affected by the character and order of arguments to which they are exposed during an extended period of debate, there is no reason to expect a unique equilibrium set of individual preference rankings; rather, different equilibria result from different discussion pathways. And secondly, different schemes of preference aggregation (social choice rules) may lead to different social preference rankings. On this view, then, problems of social choice have large stretches of indeterminacy (a conclusion that is distressingly familiar from our ordinary experience of political and group decision-making).

Alternatives to Capitalism

Are there alternatives to capitalism? This question has acquired new significance following the collapse of the bureaucratic socialist economies of Eastern Europe. It is now fairly clear that state-owned and managed enterprises have serious economic defects – incentive problems, inefficient patterns of investment, misallocations of resources across industries, and insufficient production of consumer goods. Do these defects entail that capitalism is the only economically viable form of economic organization for modern industrialized societies, or are there alternative institutions that are more democratic and less exploitative than those of contemporary industrialized capitalism, and that achieve comparable levels of productivity and efficiency?

Elster has written a good deal on several alternative possibilities. He discusses the viability of worker-owned co-operatives in 'From Here to There; or, If Cooperative Ownership is so Desirable, Why are there so few Cooperatives?' (1989b). Here his central conclusion is that the usual complaints about the inefficiency of worker-owned co-operatives are *not* compelling, and that the demands of justice give a strong reason for an economic democracy to experiment with this form of economic organization (p. 111).

Elster also considers a major institutional reform within capitalism: the creation of a state-backed right to work. 'A legally enforceable right to work would be part of the broader spectrum of rights that make up the modern welfare state' (1988c, p. 55). Elster discusses the concept of a right to work within the context of current discussions of rights more generally, and he outlines a Marxian rationale for emphasizing the positive value of work, based on the ideal of self-realization through work. Meaningful work is a prerequisite for self-respect, on this account.[13] This latter point, however, yields a normative argument *against* institutionalizing a right to work: the fact that the state must heavily subsidize one's work undermines the satisfaction and self-respect that one can derive from it (1988c, p. 74). And Elster further concludes that the economic constraints any economy is likely to face make a guaranteed right to work impossible. For both economic and moral reasons, then, Elster argues that it is better on balance *not* to institutionalize a legal right to a job.[14]

PHILOSOPHY OF SOCIAL SCIENCE

Turn now to another large area in which Elster has made an important contribution: the philosophy of social science. The philosophy of social science has changed a great deal in the past 15 years, and Elster's writings have contributed a good deal to the progress in this area. This field is concerned with problems in the logic and methodology of the social sciences: What is a good social explanation? How should social explanations relate to facts about individuals? Is there a distinctive social science method, or should the social sciences emulate the natural sciences? How do empirical methods constrain social hypotheses? Through the early 1970s this field was dominated by writings that were largely aprioristic and uninformed by much current social science research. Since that time, however, philosophers have increasingly recognized the need for a close acquaintance with extensive examples of social science inquiry so that the philosophy of social science will bear a recognizable relationship to the empirical work currently being done on social phenomena. Elster has written extensively in the philosophy of social science in the past ten years, and his writings have had a substantial effect.

The Importance of Social Science Practice

In his book *Explaining Technical Change* (1983a) Elster offered a novel approach to the study of the philosophy of social science. Instead of posing a series of *a priori* questions about the social sciences in general, Elster organized his discussion around an important instance of social inquiry – the explanation of the incidence and diffusion of technical change – and undertook to extract methodological lessons from several empirical research traditions. This approach involved a 'case-study' method for the philosophy of social science, and Elster was among the first to employ this method for this purpose. As Elster puts the point, 'empirical work conducted in isolation from the philosophy of science may be no worse for that, whereas the philosophy of science atrophies if it is not in close and constant touch with the development of current thinking on empirical matters' (1983a, p. 11). (Historians and philosophers of natural science had adopted this perspective in the 1960s, but philosophers of social science were slow to follow.) The resulting book is successful on several levels. It provides a very useful exposition of some of the central ideas in the philosophy of social science – in particular, the relation between causal, functional and intentional explanation. It offers an extensive development of Elster's important criticisms of functional explanation in social science (discussed below). And, substantively, it presents and discusses the main theories of technical change clearly and with insight, effectively clarifying and enriching future debate on this issue.

Linked with this view of the importance of the actual practice of social scientists is Elster's insistence on what may be called 'methodological pluralism' in the social sciences. Against the idea that there should be one comprehensive social theory, or one coherent set of theoretical ideas that are used to ground all social explanations, Elster offers the metaphor of a tool-box. A good tool-box consists of a number of different implements, no small number of which will do to replace all the rest. Rather, it is the diversity of the tools that constitutes the real utility of the collection. Likewise, Elster suggests that the social sciences need to resort to a large collection of theoretical tools – models, modes of analysis, quantitative techniques, and the like – in order to explain diverse social phenomena. There is a tendency within philosophy to try to reduce complexity to simplicity; Elster refreshingly affirms complexity and casts doubt on the goal of unification of the social sciences. His book *Nuts and Bolts for the Social Sciences* (1989c) puts the case clearly and well: in order to explain social phenomena it is necessary for the investigator to have recourse to a variety of theoretical tools. These tools may then be used to construct accounts of the mechanisms that underlie various social processes. Rational choice theory and game theory represent one section of the box; but sociologists' analysis of the workings of normative systems, cognitive psychologists' accounts of inference and illusion, even psychoanalysts' treatment of self-deception constitute other – and non-reducible – sections of the box as well.

Methodological Individualism

Elster's most important substantive contribution to the philosophy of social science is his renewed defence of the doctrine of methodological individualism.[15] He describes this doctrine in these terms: 'By [methodological individualism] I mean the doctrine that all social phenomena – their structure and their change – are in principle explicable in ways that only involve individuals – their properties, their goals, their beliefs and their actions' (1985b, p. 5). Methodological individualism is really two doctrines: a claim about social entities and a claim about social explanations. The ontological thesis denies that there are social entities independent from individuals; the thesis about explanation holds that assertions of explanatory relations among social facts need to be reduced to explanatory relations among individual-level facts. To explain a social phenomenon it is not sufficient to assert causal or functional regularities among social entities. Rather, it is necessary to provide a detailed account of the mechanisms at the individual level by which the causal properties or functional needs of the social system are imposed on other social institutions and practices. (That is, it is necessary to provide an account of the *microfoundations* of a given social process.[16]) Thus macroexplanations are insufficient unless accompanied by an analysis at the level of individual activity that reveals the mechanisms giving rise to the pattern to be explained. This line of argument represents a sophisticated form of methodological individualism, and unlike earlier arguments for methodological individualism it has the merit of being informed by knowledge of a variety of examples of social explanation.

Elster's commitment to methodological individualism aligns closely with his emphasis on the utility of the tools of rational choice theory in social explanation. Methodological individualism forces the social scientist to turn to the individual-level processes that produce social outcomes; and rational choice theory offers a general account of what those individual-level processes are. Rational choice theory thus functions as a research programme for social science: to explain social outcomes as the aggregate result of individuals' calculating efforts to pursue their interests given their beliefs about the environment of choice. This programme is plausible because human beings are purposive beings capable of forming beliefs and choosing actions on the basis of their goals and beliefs. This is not to say that human beings are perfectly or always rational; and in fact, much of Elster's effort is spent analysing failures of rationality. But it does imply that rational choice theory provides a common starting-point for analysis of social phenomena.

The rational choice approach generally gives short shrift to the workings of norms and values in human action. However, much of Elster's more recent work gives more attention to the role of norms and values in motivating or constraining individual choice. Whereas some social scientists within a rational choice framework have sought to minimize the role of norms and values (for example, Samuel Popkin in *The Rational Peasant*, 1979), Elster has come to recognize that reference to normative systems has a place within an individualistic theory of social action.[17] This is a step forward in the direction of a more empirically adequate theory of individual motivation, and one that can eventually be deployed to produce more complex models of social processes that reflect both prudential and normative motivations. But Elster rightly emphasizes that it is perfectly consistent for an individualist theory to introduce social norms into its explanations (1989a, p. 105); contrary to Durkheim's familiar view that norms have a supra-individual status, it is plain enough that norms can only be embodied in the actions, sanctions, gestures of approval and disapproval and so on, of particular individuals.

A particularly successful application of the doctrines of methodological individualism may be found in Elster's critique of functional explanation in social science (1983a, pp. 49–68; 1979/1984, pp. 28–35; 1982c). Social scientists have often been inclined to offer functional explanations of social phenomena – explanations of social features that explain the presence and persistence of the feature in terms of the beneficial consequences the feature has for the ongoing working of the social system as a whole. It might be held, for example, that sports clubs in working-class Britain exist because they give working-class men and women a way of expending energy that would otherwise go into struggles against an exploitative system, thus undermining social stability. Sports clubs are explained, then, in terms of their contribution to social stability. This type of explanation is based on an analogy between biology and sociology. Biologists explain traits in terms of their contribution to reproductive fitness, and sociologists sometimes explain social traits in terms of their contribution to 'social' fitness. However, Elster shows that the analogy is a misleading one, because there is a general mechanism to establish functionality in the biological realm that is not present in the social realm. This is the mechanism of natural selection, through which a species arrives at a set of traits that are locally optimal. There is no analogous process at work in the social realm, however; so it is groundless to suppose that social traits exist *because* of their beneficial consequences for the good of society as a whole (or important sub-systems within society).

This discussion shows that Elster's defence of methodological individualism has been an important corrective to some tendencies within the social sciences. However, Elster has sometimes been accused of having an *excessively* individualist approach to social explanation (for example, by Andrew Levine in his review (1986) of *Making Sense of Marx*). Elster holds that good social science explanations need to have microfoundations, and putative explanations that lack such foundations must be revised or rejected. On the whole this is a salutary recommendation for the social sciences; in too many instances it is possible to find sociologists or historians explaining outcomes as the result of group interests, latent functions or other ungrounded social processes. Here I suggest, however, that Elster's formulation of the doctrine of methodological individualism is in the end overly restrictive; there is a class of satisfactory social explanations that do not *require* microfoundations as a condition of adequacy (though it is certainly a reasonable research goal to attempt to provide such foundations). If this criticism is convincing, then Elster is guilty of the sort of over-generalization about social science method that his tool-box metaphor would reject: he is extending a perfectly legitimate but partial methodological strategy to a comprehensive requirement on all social explanation.

The macro-explanations whose adequacy I will defend fall generally within the category of causal-structural explanations. The claim that the alliance structures within which the European powers were located between 1912 and 1914 was a proximate cause of the outbreak of war is an instance of such an explanation (Williamson, 1989). In such explanations the social scientist asserts a causal relation between two or more elements of social structure, and offers empirical support for this causal hypothesis that depends on historical evidence pertaining to the patterns or regularities of these structures across a number of cases.[18]

How are such hypotheses to be empirically evaluated? First, comparative study of a set of cases permits a direct empirical test of causal hypotheses of this sort. A comparative study identifies a small class of relevant cases; it specifies the social variables under scrutiny (state structure, land tenure relations, existence of élite parties and so on); and it determines whether there are credible causal sequences among these variables in the several cases. And secondly, it is possible to provide qualitative analysis of the social mechanisms that lead to changes of state in the social variables. For example, it is perfectly credible that an overextended state will have more difficulty suppressing banditry on the periphery than one in the fulness of its powers; we can easily sketch in the institution-level causal mechanisms that lead to this outcome. Causal-structural explanations, then, represent examples of causal analysis that depend only on the relations between various elements of social structure – without identifying the individual-level processes that give rise to these structural relations.

In defending the adequacy of this sort of structural explanations I do not mean to suggest that such explanations cannot be provided with microfoundations; in fact I believe that they can.[19] Rather the methodological point is that the social scientist is not *obliged* to provide such foundations as a minimal condition of adequacy; it is possible to have the right sort of empirical support for a causal hypothesis about the connection between two or more elements of social structure, so that it is not necessary to derive this connection from underlying individual-level processes.[20]

ANALYTICAL MARXISM

Turn now to a final area of Elster's work: critical analysis of Marx's theories of society and politics. Marxism underwent a renaissance in the English-speaking world in the 1970s through the contributions of a generation of analytically gifted political scientists, economists and philosophers. Now referred to as 'analytical Marxism',[21] this body of work shed new light on central topics within classical Marxism: historical materialism, the theory of exploitation, the class-conflict model of social change, the theory of ideology, and much else. Elster was one of the central contributors to these developments, emphasizing particularly the rational choice foundations of many of Marx's central arguments. Elster argues that Marxist explanations require microfoundations, and that the tools of rational choice theory, including particularly game theory, are well-suited to provide such foundations. His book *Making Sense of Marx* (1985b) represents a largescale development of his interpretation of Marx's position on all the central issues; in addition he has published a large number of articles on these topics as well as a brief introduction to Marxism (1986d).

Rational Choice Marxism

G.A. Cohen's book *Karl Marx's Theory of History* (1978) was one of the most influential of the flurry of publications within analytical Marxism. Cohen argued that Marx's theory of historical materialism was coherent and plausible, and that it depended essentially on a pattern of functional explanation. He conceded that it is also possible to attempt to identify the causal processes that underlie functional relations (what Elster calls microfoundations and Cohen calls 'elaborations' of a functional explanation), but he maintained that it is not mandatory to do so in order to assert a functional explanation. As shown above, Elster has formulated a powerful critique of the use of functional explanations in social science, so it is unsurprising that Elster challenged Cohen's formulation. In a series of publications Elster deployed these arguments against Cohen and appears to have the stronger case. Elster's arguments show that Cohen's reconstruction of functional relations among social phenomena requires supplementation with an account of the microfoundations of these functional relations. General claims like 'the capitalist state functions to stabilize capitalist property relations' must be supplemented with accounts of the processes within capitalist society through which the needs of stability are impressed on the structure and behaviour of the capitalist state.

The call for microfoundations for Marxism is all well and good; but what sorts of underlying mechanisms are available for grounding Marxist explanations? Elster argues that Marx's chief arguments are generally compatible with a rational choice model of explanation, and that the relevant microfoundations may be constructed on the basis of rational choice analysis of the choices made by participants within the context of the institutions of capitalism. Along with several other theorists (particularly John Roemer, 1981, 1982b; and Adam Przeworski, 1985a, 1985b), Elster made a strong case for joining classical Marxism with some of the tools of rational choice theory and game theory.[22]

Elster puts this perspective to particularly useful work in his treatment of the problem of class politics: under what circumstances are classes capable of achieving collective action in pursuit of shared interests (1985b, pp. 359ff.)? Classical Marxism holds that classes tend to become class-conscious (that is, aware of shared interests) and class-active (that is, motivated to act as a group in pursuit of shared interests). But once we adopt a rational choice perspective this assumption is suspect, since it takes no account of public goods problems (free-rider problems and collective action problems). If we are to put forward a theory of class politics at all, it must include an account of the processes through which classes are capable of constituting themselves as political agents; and this means we need an account of the micromechanisms of collective action within a class society. In 'Three Challenges to Class' (1986i) and 'Marx, Revolution, and Rational Choice' (1988d) Elster turns his attention to this set of problems. He emphasizes the importance of providing an account of the microfoundations of collective action, since most instances of political collective action involve the pursuit of public goods. It is not sufficient, therefore, to refer to the shared interests that members of a class have in the attainment of a political end; it is necessary to identify as well the individual-level circumstances that given potential participants an incentive to involve themselves in the collective action. Otherwise we should expect free-riding and prisoners' dilemmas to make collective action unattainable. Others have treated this problem as well;[23] but Elster's discussions carry the issue a step forward. Here again is an instance of Elster's ability to bring some of the results of one area of social research fruitfully to bear on a topic in a non-standard area.

Marx's Economics

Much of Elster's discussion of Marx and Marxism is admirable and useful. He avoids sterile debates over the meaning of various passages in Marx's work, reflecting a concern to make sense of the doctrines rather than the texts. And he provides a provocative and extended treatment of virtually all the major ideas in Marx's writings – exploitation, freedom, alienation, socialism, materialism, and the labour theory of value. Whether the reader agrees or disagrees with a particular claim of Elster's, there is enough extensive discussion of the topic to permit a high level of specific and focused argument. In the remainder of this section, however, I shall take issue with one of Elster's central claims about Marx: that his economics are hopelessly dated and that we have little to learn from his economic analysis of capitalism. He writes in his short introduction to Marx, 'Today Marxian economics is, with a few exceptions, intellectually dead' (1986d, p. 60). This is an excessively negative and sweeping judgement, however; Marxist economic theory has more analytical scope and power than Elster credits it with. This bears out the impression that occasionally arises in Elster's book that he sometimes makes rather less sense of Marx than he might.

Elster's critique of Marx's economics (1985b, pp. 119–65) focuses on the labour theory of value (LTV). The labour theory of value can be summarized in these terms: the value of a good is equal to the total quantity of socially necessary labour time involved in its production. If we make several debatable assumptions (fixed coefficients of production, constant returns to scale, homogeneous labour and no joint products), it is possible to give a coherent economic statement of the LTV. For *n* sectors we have:

$$x_j = a_{oj} + a_{1j}{}^*x_1 + \ldots + a_{nj}{}^*x_n$$

where x_i are the labour values for each good, a_{ij} are the production coefficients and a_{oj} is the direct labour involved in producing x_j (1985b, pp. 128–30). This gives us a system of *n* linear equations from which it is possible to solve for the vector $\{x_i\}$ of labour values for *n* goods. This in turn permits us to define the basic concepts of Marxist economics: surplus value, the rate of surplus value, the organic composition of capital, and the rate of profit (p. 132). The labour theory of value can thus be formulated consistently and precisely. Elster argues, however, that the theory has absolutely no economic significance: it cannot be used as a theory of price, profits, accumulation, crisis, or to derive predictions about the systemic tendencies of the capitalist mode of production.

Elster's criticisms of the labour theory of value as a theory of price are compelling but familiar. The fact of a uniform rate of profit across sectors with differing capital–labour ratios guarantees that values and prices will systematically diverge. This is the familiar 'transformation problem' that has been treated convincingly by Morishima, Roemer and other mathematical Marxist economists. Elster concludes that labour values have no explanatory role; labour values are determined by the production function which also determines profits and prices, so we can bypass labour values without difficulty (1985b, pp. 137–8). He goes on to argue that the Marxian framework fails to explain the imperative toward technical change within capitalism (pp. 143ff.) and that Marx's theories of economic crisis are defective as well. These negative conclusions are taken to justify the sweeping judgement quoted above: Marxian economics is a dead-end.

I believe that Elster's summary treatment of the Marxian economic framework is precipitous. There is no doubt that Marx's own mathematical formulations of the labour theory of value and the economic tendencies of the capitalist system are weak by contemporary standards. The more important questions are these: Is there a core of economic insight contained in Marx's economics? Can these insights be given rigorous mathematical formulation? And do the resulting models have some utility in analysing the dynamics of contemporary capitalism? I hold that a more sympathetic reading of Marx's economics suggests an affirmative answer to each of these questions.

The central economic insights in *Capital* are these: first, Marx, like other classical economists, placed priority on the process of production. The labour theory of value is Marx's attempt to capture the idea that the social value of a commodity (and eventually its price) is ultimately related to its social cost of production; and the embodied labour time in a commodity is a measure of its social cost of production. It emerges from the work of Sraffa, Leontief, Roemer and others that this insight can be better captured in terms of the linear algebra of an input–output system (a Leontief production system). Using such a system it is possible to define the equilibrium conditions of prices, quantities, wages and profits that serve to satisfy a given level of final demand, given the assumption of fixed coefficients of production. (This construction also permits us to derive labour values for commodities.) In the end, then, the labour theory of value has been superseded by a superior system for representing the structure of a capitalist economy. But it is reasonable to regard this as a technical refinement to a substantive economic insight – not a profound reversal or repudiation of Marxian economics. Marxian economics without the labour theory of value is still recognizably Marxian.

The second major insight in Marxian economics is the emphasis on the process of surplus extraction and distribution of wealth across wages and profits. Again, Marx's own formulation of this point occurs within the context of the labour theory of value; Marx analyses profits in terms of his concept of surplus value. But we can admit the technical inadequacies of the LTV without abandoning the substantive point that economic surpluses are created and distributed by a market economy, and that distribution matters.

Here Stephen Marglin's work is a strong example of fruitful contemporary research within a broadly Marxian framework. Marglin shows that a neo-Marxian economic model sheds a good deal of light on the growth and distribution features of modern capitalist economies (Marglin, 1984). Likewise, current research within structuralist economics has absorbed this basic Marxian insight. Thus Lance Taylor summarizes the programme of structuralist economics in terms of the centrality of the 'extended functional distribution' of income (the differential distributive effects of alternative economic policies), the economic power of various institutions and groups (landlords, rentiers, organized labour) in determining economic outcomes, and the importance of changes in income and wealth distributions in macroeconomic dynamics (1990, pp. 2–4). The models that structuralist economists construct are generally couched in terms of linear Leontief production systems, not the labour theory of value; but their attention to distribution, class and the economic significance of social and political institutions owes much to Marxian economic theory.

Finally, Marx's economics must be credited for its emphasis on discerning the long-term dynamic properties of a capitalist economy. Elster directs severe criticism against Marx's theory of economic crisis (1985b, pp. 154–65), but this appears to reflect excessively high expectations of predictive success from a first-generation economic theory. (The successes of neoclassical theories of recession, unemployment or inflation are not staggeringly impressive either.) What Marx's economics encourages us to do is to attempt to arrive at models of capitalist economies that begin in the production process, that focus analysis on the distributive processes through which real wages and profits are determined, and that permit us to derive some predictions about the medium-term and long-term behaviour of a system of labour-hiring, profit-maximizing firms in a global economic system. And the achievements of neo-Marxian economists along these lines are not insignificant.[24]

Elster's dismissal of Marxian economics, then, is unjustified. Neoclassical economics, Keynesian economics, structuralist economics and Marxian economics each represent more or less coherent constellations of analytical techniques, substantive assumptions about economic causality, and assumptions about the social context of economic activity. In order to compare these theories we need a view of the criteria that ought to be used to evaluate alternative economic programmes of research. Mathematical rigour is one virtue of a research framework in economics, but there are others as well: fruitfulness in stimulating further research, realism of assumptions, ability to handle new economic problems, predictive success, and conformity to accepted theories in other areas of social science.[25] The problem of choice among research frameworks in economics is no simpler than the problem of theory or paradigm choice in other areas of science, and it is certainly not the case that the neoclassical framework wins hands down. This means, in turn, that it is justifiable to continue to pursue the programme of Marxian economics, and my own judgement is that this framework is able to explain some features of the capitalist economy that other approaches are unable to do.

CONCLUSIONS

I have only touched on a few main themes drawn out of Elster's work. I hope, though, that I have made it plain that there is much to be learned from careful reading of this body of work. In his treatment of the foundations of rationality, in his extensive discussions of the logic of the social sciences, and in his sustained critical perspectives on Marxist theory, Elster has made important contributions to several areas of the social sciences. And even in those instances where other scholars will disagree with his analysis of a particular issue, his clarity and detailed grasp of the issues lead to a higher level of debate.

Can we draw any general conclusions about Elster's contributions? It may be said that Elster's particular significance is not to have put forward profoundly original solutions to longstanding technical problems in economics; instead, his work serves two other important functions. First, he aims to establish linkages between the technical economic literature and other areas of social and political thought. Elster's work often serves as a power belt, conveying some of the results of a technical area of economic theory to applications in various areas of social science and philosophy. Unlike A.K. Sen or Kenneth Arrow whose writings have changed the ways in which we think about various topics in economic theory, Elster's work is primarily of value for his ability in bringing technical insights and models to bear on problems outside the traditional economic domain.

A second virtue of Elster's work is equally important: Elster is more inclined than most economists to consider the philosophical foundations of various domains of economic theory. There is a tendency within economic theory for fascination with the mathematical apparatus to crowd out reflective analysis of the underlying assumptions that the apparatus depends on – for example, the significance of utility functions. Elster, however, is prepared to step back and consider the background assumptions more fully, and to attempt to say how well or poorly a given formalisation succeeds in capturing the original intuition. There is a need for both kinds of work within economic theory, but Elster's contributions to the philosophical analysis of economic presuppositions are particularly valuable.

NOTES

1. See work by Kahneman, Slovic, and Tversky (1982), Herbert Simon (1979, 1983) and Cherniak (1986) for arguments to this effect.
2. A more comprehensive statement of Elster's conception of rationality occurs in Chapter I of *Sour Grapes* (1983e). This chapter serves both as an extensive introduction to the central ideas of rational choice theory and a thoughtful posing of a number of current problems in the theory of rational choice. See also his introduction to *Rational Choice* (ed., 1986a).
3. Elster discusses this problem in 'Imperfect Rationality: Ulysses and the Sirens' (1979/ 1984, pp. 76–85).
4. Elster discusses self-deception in *Ulysses and the Sirens* (1979/1984, pp. 157–79), and in *Sour Grapes* (1983e, pp. 141–66). He treats weakness of the will in a number of places: in *Ulysses and the Sirens* (1979/1984, pp. 37–47), in *Solomonic Judgements* (1989d, pp.17–19), and in 'Weakness of Will and the Free-Rider Problem' (1985e).
5. Elster raises a number of other interesting problems in the foundations of subjective probability theory in *Solomonic Judgements* (1989d, pp. 36–62).
6. See, for example, Shubik, 1982, pp. 287–9; and Axelrod, 1984, p. 13.
7. It is not self-evident that utilities should be treated along these lines; the rationale for discounting utilities, if any, must be different from that for discounting resources or money. It is rational to discount future sums of resources because current use of those resources would lead to increase over time (through the rate of real growth or the interest rate). Utility is produced by the expenditure of resources; but utility itself cannot be 'invested' productively.
8. Examples of philosophers who make this assumption include Norman Daniels (1988, pp. 158, 164–9) and Derek Parfit (1984, pp. 158ff.). Parfit discusses another way in which time preferences might come to be inconsistent: I might have different discount rates for near and distant future utilities (1984, p. 161).
9. If the probability of survival were constant over time, then actuarial discounting *would* be exponential, with p^n as coefficient for the nth term. It might be possible to argue that agents have sufficient concern for future generations that their savings behaviour is not driven by the risk of death (which is the factor that leads to steadily rising estimates of risk); in this case it would be plausible to postulate a constant risk factor – thereby producing an exponential rate of discount.
10. However, exponential discounting of utilities arises only if the utility function itself is exponential. If we go through the same line of reasoning on the assumption of a logarithmic utility function ($u = k \cdot \log(m)$), then the corresponding discount function will be linear: $PVU(u) = u - n \cdot k \cdot \log(1 + i)$.
11. Here Elster draws on Jurgen Habermas's theory of the ethics of discourse.
12. John Rawls, *A Theory of Justice* (1971).
13. Elster returns to this theme in 'Self-Realization in Work and Politics', in Elster and Moene (eds), 1989, pp. 127–58.
14. Elster raises related issues in his discussion of Krouse and McPherson's (1986) conception of a 'property-owning democracy' in 'Comments on Krouse and McPherson's "A 'mixed'-property regime"' (1986a).
15. Earlier exponents of methodological individualism include J.W.N. Watkins and Karl Popper.
16. See Roemer (1982b) and van Parijs (1983) for arguments that Marxist explanations require microfoundations.
17. Other rational choice attempts to incorporate norms into the model include Margolis (1982); Sen (1982a, 1987); and Levi (1986).
18. Theda Skocpol's comparativist study of the causes of successful revolution is a well-known example of such explanations. Skocpol asks what explains the success of revolutions in a small number of cases and the failure of revolutionary movements in many more cases; her explanation is couched at the level of such structural variables as administrative competence, land tenure systems and form of military organization.

19. For consideration of this point in application to Skocpol's argument consider Michael Taylor's valuable essay, 'Rationality and Revolutionary Collective Action' (1988).
20. For further discussion of the shortcomings of strong reductionism or individualism in social science, see my *Varieties of Social Explanation* (1991).
21. Some of the chief writings within analytical Marxism include: John McMurtry, *The Structure of Marx's World-view* (1977); G.A. Cohen, *Karl Marx's Theory of History: A Defence* (1978); John Roemer, *Analytical Foundations of Marxism* (1981); and Adam Przeworski, *Capitalism and Social Democracy* (1985a). Two collections of articles have appeared as well: Terence Ball and James Farr (eds), *After Marx* (1984) and John Roemer (ed.), *Analytical Marxism* (1986).
22. The rational choice foundations of Marx's economics are explored in my *Scientific Marx* (1986).
23. See, for example, Buchanan (1982); Michael Taylor (1988; and Shaw (1984).
24. Work by Ernest Mandel (1978), John Roemer (1981, 1982a), and Wolff and Resnick (1987) illustrates the continuing utility of this framework.
25. Recent work in the philosophy of science bears out the point that theories are evaluated on the basis of multiple desiderata. See Newton-Smith (1981); Laudan (1977); and Brown (1987), as well as a number of the essays in *Scientific Revolutions* (Hacking (ed.), 1981).

REFERENCES

Elster's Publications

Elster, Jon (1976a), 'Some Conceptual Problems in Political Theory', in Barry (1976).
—— (1976b), 'A Note on Hysteresis in the Social Sciences', *Synthese*, 33, 371–91.
—— (1978a), 'Exploring Exploitation', *Journal of Peace Research*, 15, 3–18.
—— (1978b), 'The Labor Theory of Value', *Marxist Perspectives*, 3, 70–101.
—— (1978c), *Logic and Society*, Chichester: John Wiley.
—— (1979/1984), *Ulysses and the Sirens: Studies in Rationality and Irrationality*, Cambridge: Cambridge University Press.
—— (1980a), 'Cohen on Marx's Theory of History: Review of G.A. Cohen, *Karl Marx's Theory of History*', *Political Studies*, 28, 121–28.
—— (1980b), 'Negation active et negation passive', *Archive Européennes de Sociologie*, 21, 329–49.
—— (1980c), 'Reply to Brian Barry', *Political Studies*, 28, 1.
—— (1980d), 'Reply to Comments on *Logic and Society*', *Inquiry*, 23, 213–32.
—— (1980e), 'Un historien devant l'irrationel: lecture de Paul Veyne', *Social Science Information*, 19, 773–804.
—— (1981a), ' "Introduction" to Kolm (1981) and van der Veen (1981)', *Social Science Information*, 20, 287–92.
—— (1981b), 'Un Marxisme anglais', *Annales: Economies, Sociétés, Civilisations*, 36, 745–57.
—— (1982a), 'Belief, Bias and Ideology', in Hollis and Lukes (1982).
—— (1982b), 'A Paradigm for the Social Sciences?', *Inquiry*, 25, 3.
—— (1982c), 'Marxism, Functionalism, and Game Theory', *Theory and Society*, 11, 453–82.
—— (1982d), 'Roemer versus Roemer: a Comment on "New Directions in the Marxian Theory of Exploitation" ', *Politics and Society*, 11, 3.

—— (1982e), 'Sour Grapes – Utilitarianism and the Genesis of Wants', in Sen and Williams (1982).

—— (1983a), *Explaining Technical Change*, Cambridge: Cambridge University Press.

—— (1983b), 'Exploitation, Freedom and Justice', *Nomos*, **26**, 277–304.

—— (1983c), 'Marx et Leibniz', *Revue philosophique*, **173**, 167–77.

—— (1983d), 'Reply to Comments', *Theory and Society*, **12**, 111–20.

—— (1983e), *Sour Grapes: Studies in the Subversion of Rationality*, Cambridge: Cambridge University Press.

—— (1984), 'Historical Materialism and Economic Backwardness', in Ball and Farr (1984).

—— (1985a), 'The Nature and Scope of Rational-Choice Explanation', in Le Pore and McLaughlin (1985).

—— (1985b), *Making Sense of Marx*, Cambridge: Cambridge University Press.

—— (1985c), 'Rationality, Morality, and Collective Action', *Ethics*, **96**, 136–55.

—— (1985d), 'Sadder but Wiser? Rationality and the Emotions', *Social Science Information*, **24**, 375–406.

—— (1985e), 'Weakness of Will and the Free-Rider Problem', *Economics and Philosophy*, **1**, 231–65.

—— (1986a), 'Comments on Krouse and McPherson's "A 'Mixed'-Property Regime" ', *Ethics*, **97**, 146–53.

—— (1986b), 'Comments on van Parijs and van der Veen', *Theory and Society*, **15**, 709–22.

—— (1986c), 'Further Thoughts on Marxism, Functionalism, and Game Theory', in Roemer (1986).

—— (1986d), *An Introduction to Karl Marx*, Cambridge: Cambridge University Press.

—— (1986e), 'The Market and the Forum: Three Varieties of Political Theory', in Elster and Hylland (eds) (1986).

—— (1986f), 'The Possibility of Rational Politics', *Critica*, **18**, 17–62.

—— (1986g), 'Reply to Symposium on *Making Sense of Marx*', *Inquiry*, **29**, 65–77.

—— (1986h), 'Self-realization in Work and Politics: the Marxist Conception of the Good Life', *Social Philosophy and Policy*, **3**, 97–126.

—— (1986i), 'Three Challenges to Class', in Roemer (1986).

—— (1988a), 'Consequences of Constitutional Choice: Reflections on Tocqueville', in *Constitutionalism and Democracy*, in Elster and Slagstad (eds) (1988).

—— (1988b), 'Economic Order and Social Norms', *Journal of Institutional and Theoretical Economics*, **144**, 357–66.

—— (1988c), 'Is There (or Should There Be) a Right to Work?', in Gutmann (1988).

—— (1988d), 'Marx, Revolution and Rational Choice', in M. Taylor (1988).

—— (1989a), *The Cement of Society: A Study of Social Order*, Cambridge: Cambridge University Press.

—— (1989b), 'From Here to There; or, If Cooperative Ownership is so Desirable, Why are there so Few Cooperatives?', *Social Philosophy and Policy*, **6**, 93–111.

—— (1989c), *Nuts and Bolts for the Social Sciences*, Cambridge: Cambridge University Press.

—— (1989d), *Solomonic Judgements: Studies in the Limitations of Rationality*, Cambridge: Cambridge University Press.

—— (1990), 'Local Justice and Interpersonal Comparisons', in Elster and Roemer (eds) (1990).

—— (ed.) (1986a), *Rational Choice*, New York: New York University Press.

—— (ed.) (1986b), *The Multiple Self*, Cambridge: Cambridge University Press.

—— and Aanund Hylland (eds) (1986), *Foundations of Social Choice Theory*, Cambridge: Cambridge University Press.

—— and Karl Ove Moene (eds) (1989), *Alternatives to Capitalism*, Cambridge: Cambridge University Press.

—— and John Roemer (eds) (1990), *Interpersonal Comparisons of Welfare*, Cambridge: Cambridge University Press.

—— and R. Slagstad (eds) (1988), *Constitutionalism and Democracy*, Cambridge: Cambridge University Press.

Other References

Axelrod, Robert (1984), *The Evolution of Cooperation*, New York: Basic Books.

Ball, Terence and James Farr (eds) (1984), *After Marx*, Cambridge: Cambridge University Press.

Barry, Brian (ed.) (1976), *Power and Political Theory*, Chichester: John Wiley.

Brown, Harold I. (1987), *Observation and Objectivity*, Oxford: Oxford University Press.

Buchanan, Allen (1982), *Marx and Justice*, Totowa, N.J.: Littlefield, Adams.

Cherniak, Christopher (1986), *Minimal Rationality*, Cambridge, Mass.: MIT Press.

Cohen, G.A. (1978), *Karl Marx's Theory of History: A Defence*, Princeton, N.J.: Princeton University Press.

Daniels, Norman (1988), *Am I My Parents' Keeper? An Essay on Justice Between the Young and the Old*, Oxford: Oxford University Press.

Gutmann, Amy (1988), *Democracy and the Welfare State*, Princeton, N.J.: Princeton University Press.

Hacking, Ian (ed.) (1981), *Scientific Revolutions*, Oxford: Oxford University Press.

Hahn, Frank and Martin Hollis (eds) (1979), *Philosophy and Economic Theory*, Oxford: Oxford University Press.

Harsanyi, John C. (1982), 'Morality and the Theory of Rational Behavior', in Sen and Williams (1982).

Hollis, Martin and Steven Lukes (eds) (1982), *Rationality and Relativism*, Cambridge, Mass.: MIT Press.

Kahneman, D., P. Slovic and A. Tversky (1982), *Judgement under Uncertainty: Heuristics and Biases*, Cambridge: Cambridge University Press.

Krouse, Richard and Michael McPherson (1986), 'A "Mixed" Property Regime: Liberty and Equality in a Market Economy', *Ethics*, **97**, 119–38.

Laudan, Larry (1977), *Progress and its Problems*, Berkeley, Cal.: University of California Press.

Le Pore, Ernest and Brian P. McLaughlin (eds) (1985), *Actions and Events: Perspectives on the Philosophy of Donald Davidson*, Oxford: Basil Blackwell.

Levi, Isaac (1986), *Hard Choices*, Cambridge: Cambridge University Press.

Levine, Andrew (1986), 'Review of *Making Sense of Marx*', *Journal of Philosophy*, **83**, 721–8.

Little, Daniel (1986), *The Scientific Marx*, Minneapolis: University of Minnesota Press.

Little, Daniel (1991), *Varieties of Social Explanation: An Introduction to the Philosophy of Social Science*, Boulder, Col.: Westview Press.

Mandel, Ernest (1978), *Late Capitalism*, London: Verso.

Marglin, Steven (1984), *Growth, Distribution, and Prices*, Cambridge, Mass.: Harvard University Press.

Margolis, Howard (1982), *Selfishness, Rationality, and Altruism: A Theory of Social Choice*, Chicago: University of Chicago Press.

McMurtry, John (1977), *The Structure of Marx's World-view*, Princeton, N.J.: Princeton University Press.

Morishima, Michio (1973), *Marx's Economics*, Cambridge: Cambridge University Press.

Newton-Smith, W.H. (1981), *The Rationality of Science*, Boston, Mass.: Routledge & Kegan Paul.

Parfit, Derek (1984), *Reasons and Persons*, Oxford: Oxford University Press.

Popkin, Samuel L. (1979), *The Rational Peasant*, Berkeley, Cal.: University of California Press.

Przeworski, Adam (1985a), *Capitalism and Social Democracy*, Cambridge: Cambridge University Press.

Przeworski, Adam (1985b), 'Marxism and Rational Choice', *Politics and Society*, **14**, 379–409.

Rawls, John (1971), *A Theory of Justice*, Cambridge, Mass.: Harvard University Press.

Roemer, John (1981), *Analytical Foundations of Marxism*, New York: Cambridge University Press.

Roemer, John (1982a), *A General Theory of Exploitation and Class*, Cambridge, Mass.: Harvard University Press.

Roemer, John (1982b), 'Methodological Individualism and Deductive Marxism', *Theory and Society*, **11**, 513–20.

Roemer, John (ed.) (1986), *Analytical Marxism*, Cambridge: Cambridge University Press.

Rotberg, Robert I. and Theodore K. Rabb (eds) (1989), *The Origin and Prevention of Major Wars*, Cambridge: Cambridge University Press.

Sen, Amartya K. (1982a), 'Rational Fools', in Sen (1982b).

Sen, Amartya K. (1982b), *Choice, Welfare and Measurement*, Cambridge, Mass.: MIT Press.

Sen, Amartya K. (1987), *On Ethics and Economics*, New York: Basil Blackwell.

Sen, Amartya K. and Bernard Williams (eds) (1982), *Utilitarianism and Beyond*, Cambridge: Cambridge University Press.

Shaw, William (1984), 'Marxism, Revolution, and Rationality', in Ball and Farr (1984).

Shubik, Martin (1982), *Game Theory in the Social Sciences: Concepts and Solutions*, Cambridge, Mass.: MIT Press.

Simon, Herbert (1979), 'From Substantive to Procedural Rationality', in Hahn and Hollis (1979).

Simon, Herbert (1983), *Reason in Human Affairs*, Stanford, Cal.: Stanford University Press.

Skocpol, Theda (1979), *States and Social Revolutions*, Cambridge: Cambridge University Press.

Sraffa, Piero (1960), *The Production of Commodities by Means of Commodities*, Cambridge: Cambridge University Press.

Taylor, Lance (ed.) (1990), *Socially Relevant Policy Analysis: Structuralist Computable General Equilibrium Models for the Developing World*, Cambridge, Mass.: MIT Press.

Taylor, Michael (1986), 'Elster's Marx', *Inquiry*, **29**, 3–10.

Taylor, Michael (1988), 'Rationality and Revolutionary Collective Action', in M. Taylor (ed.) (1988).

Taylor, Michael (ed.) (1988), *Rationality and Revolution*, Cambridge: Cambridge University Press.

Van Parijs, Philippe (1983), 'Why Marxist Economics Needs Microfoundations', *Review of Radical Political Economics*, **15**, 11–24.

Williamson, Samuel R., Jr (1989), 'The Origins of World War I', in Rotberg and Rabb (1989).

Wolff, Richard D. and Stephen A. Resnick (1987), *Economics: Marxian versus Neoclassical*, Baltimore, Md.: Johns Hopkins University Press.

4. Nicholas Georgescu-Roegen

Philip Mirowski*

'One and one make two' assumes that the changes in the shift of circumstance are unimportant. But it is impossible for us to analyze the notion of unimportant change.

Alfred North Whitehead

Nicholas Georgescu-Roegen, born in Constanta, Romania in 1906, now Emeritus Professor at Vanderbilt University, has seen more changes in circumstances of a geographical, cultural and intellectual variety than any three other economists. The biographical particulars of his peripatetic quest are related with great verve in his (1988), where one learns how he was diverted from his original intention to become a mathematics teacher into statistics in the Paris of Borel, Fréchet, Aftalion and Divisia; thence to study with Karl Pearson at the Galton Laboratory; and then once more diverted in 1934 to Harvard and economics by Joseph Schumpeter. In 1936 he voluntarily returned to Romania (a choice he rues to this very day), only to be forced to flee for his life back to the USA in 1948, accepting a professorship at Vanderbilt in 1949. But that safe harbour did not portend an end to his intellectual travels; in many ways, the most profound changes began to accelerate only after he settled in Nashville. This cosmopolitan background left its mark upon his writings, whose purview and scope are unrivalled by any living economist with whom I am familiar. His command of the literatures of economics and philosophy of the various European languages have been matched in history only by Marx and Edgeworth and perhaps Schumpeter; but he dominates those three in his seemingly effortless command of the literature of mathematics and physics, as well as his pellucid English. (Apparently it takes an émigré to teach the locals how to use their own language.) In an era when minor tinkering with the neoclassical status quo qualifies one as a candidate for a Nobel Prize, he brooks no peer. And yet, I should like to argue that he has been misunderstood by both his admirers and detractors.

I am aware of the dangers of trying to reconfigure the significance of the works of a living author. Indeed, recently Professor Georgescu-Roegen has given us an enumeration of what he regards as his most significant contributions.[1] His list, slightly condensed and summarized, goes as follows:

1. Clarification of the problem of integrability in neoclassical choice theory (*AE*, ch. 1; *EEM*, ch. 13);
2. Innovation of the concept of a stochastic choice theory (*AE*, chs 1,3,6);
3. Demonstration of the inapplicability of the neoclassical theory of marginal cost pricing in underdeveloped countries (*AE*, ch. 11; *EEM*, chs 5,6,8);
4. The neoclassical nonsubstitution theorem for Leontief technologies (*AE*, ch. 9);
5. The analytical representation of business cycles by nonsymmetrical waves and relaxation phenomena (*AE*, ch. 8);
6. The relative significance of dialectical vs arithmomorphic reasoning in economics (*AE*, Introduction; *ELEP*);
7. Clarification of the difficulties involved in modelling production as a process (*ELEP*; *EEM*, chs 4,11); and
8. Thermodynamics as the ultimate taproot of economic scarcity (*ELEP*).

My hesitation concerning simple acquiescence in this list is two-fold. First, most economists are unaware that these ideas originated with Georgescu or of his interpretations of them. For instance, 1 and 4 are often mistakenly attributed to Paul Samuelson; while 5 is ignored by the huge modern literature busily reinventing the wheel whose cam is the asymmetrical business cycle. As an historian, I fear that if your contribution is highjacked in the name of others, no matter how unjustly, then you have effectively not made a contribution. Secondly, I cannot shake the impression that this list is much too skewed towards the vantage point of an orthodox neoclassical economist. It is as if Georgescu wanted to lull the orthodoxy into complacency with entries 1 to 5, so as not to become too perturbed upon encountering entries 6 to 8.

Without in any way denigrating the early mathematical results, I would instead suggest that the profound importance of Georgescu-Roegen for the future of economics rests upon his writings as an economic philosopher. He alone has tackled the most pressing analytical questions of the twentieth-century economics profession: What image of science should the profession hold as its inspiration? What is the role and significance of mathematical formalism in twentieth-century developments? Why do so many economists and engineers persistently misunderstand the physical character of the economic process? How should we regard the rise of indeterminist strands in twentieth-century science? Can economists hope to discover 'laws of motion' of an economy? What are the invariants in economic analysis? It should be signalled from the outset that his lucid explorations of these issues does not enjoin the reader (and thus the present author) to agree with each and every answer he gives to these questions; one doubts that this would be what Georgescu would want, in any event. Thus, in what follows we shall freely criticize some of his work as we attempt to summarize it, in the same spirit as much of his own writing.

One possible reading of the spirit of this interpretation is to juxtapose his work with that of another towering rebel of the twentieth century, Thorstein Veblen, and to see the two as the strongest bulwark against the dominant conception of economics as a social physics, which has dictated both form and content of explanation in the West (Mirowski, 1989a). Another, perhaps more idiosyncratic, interpretation is to see Georgescu as the Michel Foucault of economics. Before the reader rejects this latter analogy out of hand, let him/her read the following quote from *The Order of Things*, and ask, were it not for the awkward writing, whether it might come from the pen of our subject:

> like any other domain of knowledge, these sciences may, in certain conditions, make use of mathematics as a tool ... But despite the specificity of the problems posed, it is unlikely that the relation to mathematics (the possibilities of mathematicization, or the resistance to all efforts at formalization) is constitutive of the human sciences in their particular positivity. And for two reasons: because, essentially, they share these problems with many other disciplines (such as biology and genetics) even if these problems are not always identical; and above all because archaeological evidence analysis has not revealed, in the historical *a priori* of the human sciences, any new form of mathematics, or any sudden advance by mathematics into the domain of the human, but rather a sort of retreat of mathesis, a dissociation of its unitary field, and the emancipation, in relation to the linear order of the smallest possible differences, of empirical organizations such as life, language, and labour.[2]

In either of these readings it will become apparent that the primary narrative line in the life of Georgescu-Roegen is a growing conviction that 'changes in the shift of circumstances' are what is most important in the economy, and that the rise to dominance of the Walrasian organon, or what he has called the 'mechanistic dogma', has exiled consideration of the flux of social life to the very margins of the discourse. As he has put it (Georgescu-Roegen, 1978, p. 3):

> practically all modern economists ... have become infatuated with the mechanistic dogma. By itself, this is not an undesirable development. At the beginning, you could actually do a lot of economics with just a little mechanics. But nowadays, exaggeration has turned things bad: we use a lot of mechanics to do only a little bit of economics, sometimes none.

In reaction to these distressing trends, Georgescu has taken of late to providing a third reading of his work, claiming he is 'the only true Schumpeterian'. While one can readily understand how Schumpeter's stress upon nonperiodic waves of creative destruction and entrepreneurial imagination would indeed appeal to those who feel disaffected from the subsequent evolution of the neoclassical school, I think this comparison also reveals one of the weaknesses of his own position, namely, why Georgescu has not had the impact upon the economics profession that the power of his ideas would warrant. However much Schumpeter consciously wanted to privilege substantive change in economic theory, he remained a staunch partisan of the neoclassical organon, and as such, maintained in his *History of Economic Analysis* that all philosophy was a 'garb' that could be harmlessly removed from the real 'scientific' economics underneath. To a certain extent Georgescu also sometimes seems to adopt something resembling this stance, asserting, 'My philosophy is in spirit Machian: it is a particular kind of epistemology which is little concerned with the science of knowledge, nor with the cognitive process itself, but mainly with the problem of valid analytical representations of the relations between facts.'[3]

It would seem that most readers of *AE*, and more particularly of *ELEP* and *EEM*, experience great cognitive difficulty in situating Georgescu on their mental map of economics precisely for this reason. It is one thing to denounce neoclassical theory as a shoddy bowdlerization of mechanics; but it is a more profound question to ask how it was that things have come to this impasse. It is enlightening to suggest how mathematics might hamper our attempts to discuss real change; but it will take us further down the road to ask what our limitations have been in conceptualizing change in Western thought in general. It may be instructive to point to lessons neoclassical economics has not learned from physics; but it restores our sense of balance to ask also what lessons physics may not have taken from economics, and to ask at what point all the borrowing to and fro simply obscures the fundamental problems. And to maintain that ultimately value is individualist and psychologistic, in the absence of any curiosity over the 'cognitive process itself', effectively leaves us back where we started, that is, as dutiful and credulous partisans of the neoclassical theory of value. Hence we find readers of Georgescu skimming over the parts of the text most clearly critiquing their own positions: Paul Samuelson ignores the devastating critique of revealed preference and integrability of preferences; proponents of an energy theory of value are silent about the critique of energetics; econometricians are oblivious to the critique of estimators and information theory; risk theorists are ignorant of the critique of their presumptions about the theory of probability; energy economists are unaware of the deep critique of the production function. I cannot think of any other instance of an economist so persistently cited favourably (and thus uncomprehendingly) by those on the receiving end of his scorn.[4]

In this paper, we shall strive to provide a bit more context in order that the economist can more easily situate the work of Georgescu-Roegen on his or her mental map. Much of this will be based on the present author's history of neoclassical economics and econometrics (Mirowski, 1989a; 1989b). To this end, we shall identify three broad themes in his work (not necessarily in their chronological order) and show their relations to larger movements in science and to parallel movements in economics. They are:

1. Probability theory ⇔ the crisis in the physics of the 1920/30s;
2. Anti-scientism ⇔ issues of how economists should not emulate physics; and
3. Value theory ⇔ what modern physics could potentially teach social theorists.

STOCHASTIC FORMS AS NATURAL LAWS

Georgescu-Roegen still holds his teacher Karl Pearson in very high esteem, and often quotes his dictum (found in *The Grammar of Science*) that 'the stochastic form is not a peripheral representation of natural laws, but the only one possible for us'. In this respect he resembles many other tyros of the 1920s and 1930s, such as Frederick Mills, Charles Roos and Gerhard Tintner,[5] who saw the rise of probability theory in quantum mechanics and statistical mechanics as heralding an entirely novel approach to the idea of lawlike behaviour in social theory (Mirowski, 1989b). Unlike that other economist-student of Karl Pearson, the much-maligned Henry Ludwell Moore (Mirowski, 1990c), it seems Georgescu embibed an enthusiasm for the Pearsonian method of moments, and this point of embarkation led him ultimately to a position diametrically opposite to Moore, to the extent of disdaining the nascent 'econometrics'. Since most of those drawn to probabalism in the 1930s became foot soldiers of the 'econometrics revolution', this case stands out and warrants our extended attention.

The issue of the meaning of the statistical regression line, often phrased as the question of what could legitimately be regressed upon what else, was the first topic to engage the talents of Georgescu. In his PhD thesis, summarized in (GR, 1947; *EEM*, pp. 263–6), he confronted this question. This inquiry was a common theme in the 1920s (Morgan, 1990, chs 5 and 6), and was only subsequently banished to oblivion by the Cowles Commission's definition of the whole problem of 'identification'. Georgescu's approach was somewhat different, essentially pronouncing a negative verdict upon the likelihood of choice of the 'true' regression line, due to the fact that any given scatter of observations could have been generated by many different stochastic structures. The way this objection was avoided in the Cowles approach was baldly to assume that the right-hand-side regressors were non-stochastic, a bit of hand-waving that Georgescu could not accept, due to his belief in the intrinsic stochastic nature of all laws. As he later wrote, 'There is no good purpose in overrunning logic by a makeshift and presenting the makeshift as a product of the highest form of scientific procedure' (*EEM*, p. 266).

The divergence between the partisans of 'Econometrics' and Georgescu was due to the fact that he always kept his sights focused upon the stochastic aspects of the question, whereas they would look for ways to 'get around' the randomness to uncover the (neoclassical) determinism beneath the phe-nomenon. For instance, he would warn his American students to check both their economic variables and their regression residuals for Gaussian distri-butions, and to eschew standard econometrics when they did not pass that test. Or, in a later attack upon the Neyman–Pearson orthodoxy in econometrics, he insisted that the pretence of a realization of economic data masquerading as a sample from some larger 'population' was a sham for two reasons: one, he rejected the 'frequentist' definition of probability which underlay most orthodox justifications of regression analysis; and two, since economists relinquished any means of gauging the biased character of their 'sample' from the ghostly population of all possible realizations of an eco-nomic variate, the only legitimate set of techniques are those branded as descriptive statistics. 'To use a statistical test to test the randomness of a sample is, therefore, a patent vicious circle' (GR, 1967, p. 83).

Thus although a member of the Econometrics Society and for a time associate editor of *Econometrica*, he was profoundly out of step with the bulk of the membership. This in turn led to a sharp exchange with Guy Orcutt (*EEM*, pp. 297–304), and fostered some of his increasing isolation within the profession in the 1950s. This disaffection had not been openly evident earlier, due to the fact that Georgescu's earliest work was concerned with the introduction of stochastic considerations into the heart of the neo-classical theory of choice. As early as his 1936 work in the *Quarterly Jour-nal of Economics* (*AE*, pp. 151–62), he asked what it would mean for us to doubt our own preference orderings, in the sense that we attach probabilities to the prospect of various commodity bundles actually being preferred in a given situation. The consequences of this amendment of the orthodox theory were then treated as fairly drastic: one lost all guarantee of transitivity of choice, and all hope of recovery of the underlying demand function was deemed forlorn.

Such pyrrhic statements did not immediately thrust one beyond the pale in the 1930s – after all, sweeping the Augean stables clean was one option then – but it certainly is the case that Georgescu's pioneering work was subsequently thoroughly ignored.[6] Partly this was due to the appearance in the 1940s of versions of the 'theory of risk and uncertainty' in the guise of the von Neumann–Morgenstern axioms and the Friedman–Savage geometry which were much more amenable to preserving the underlying neoclassical orthodoxy; but again partly it was due to the fact that Georgescu was inclined to bring the philosophical issues to the forefront, whereas the bulk of the orthodox neoclassicals (Morgenstern *et al.* included) were not.

A good example of this aversion for anything philosophical was the neglect suffered by the paper written by Georgescu for an 1955 National Bureau of Economic Research conference on expectations and uncertainty, and published in *AE* (ch. 6). Tjalling Koopmans was the assigned discussant of the paper, and in private correspondence with Mary Jean Bowman counselled that the paper should either be stripped of its philosophical discussion or else be rejected for the conference proceedings. In public he was a bit more politic:

> We must be grateful to Professor Georgescu-Roegen for his scholarly review of alternative concepts of probability. The grand debate on the meanings of probability, in which philosophers, mathematicians and physical as well as social scientists have taken active parts over several centuries, has certainly not yet run its full course. At the same time, one cannot help feeling that some of the fine points in this debate have little relevant to the preoccupations of the social scientist. For instance, the distinction between quasi-certainty and certainty ... becomes relevant only in a world where either observation is infinitely exact or experiment is infinitely often repeatable. We should of course not blame the sharpness of mathematical reasoning for producing a distinction that could only be regarded as irrelevant to the world of experience.[7]

It was precisely responses such as these, where a primary defender of abstract formalization in economics could swat away any mathematical results which did not resonate with the bland self-satisfaction of neoclassicism in the 1950s, that prompted Georgescu to reconsider the effect of mathematical formalization on economic theory. (This subset is discussed in the next section.) In the paper on expectations we observe the first hints that numbers cannot adequately express the full range and shape of human thought.

The theme of the paper on expectations is that 'the real number system does not suffice to represent all expectations and that those expectations which can meaningfully be connected with a real number form a special class' (*AE*, p. 242). Georgescu saw the root of the problem, as did Keynes before him, in the distinction between the specification of personal knowledge and the credibility of evidence, on the one hand, and some inductive relation between observed frequencies and the theoretical probability coefficient on the other. He prosecuted this inquiry by writing perhaps the best summary of the implications of the predominant schools of probability for the concept of economic expectations in that era. Curiously enough, he comes down very hard on the Subjectivist school, devoting much criticism to Shackle and Savage. As for the idea that betting forces people to commit themselves to some personal numerical estimate, he noted that

> the substitutability of consumers' goods rests upon the tacit assumption that all the commodities contain something called utility – in a greater or lesser degree ... The crucial question in expectation theory is whether credibility and the betting quotient have a common essence so that compensation of this common essence would make sense. (*AE*, p. 267)

As we have noted, all this subtlety was for naught, since in the 1970s the ideas of non-calculable probabilities, information as lacking the properties of a commodity, distinctions between certainty and quasi-certainty, and so forth were bulldozed by the juggernaut of 'rational expectations' in the interest of saving the conventional neoclassical model of deterministic constrained optimization.

By the time of *ELEP* it seems that Georgescu had innovated his own distinctive solution to the impasse of the schools found in the 1955 expectations paper. There he began to insist that probability was a dialectical and not a numerical concept:

> the conditions associated with a random mechanism – statistical regularity and irreducible irregularity – are analytically contradictory. In this lies the reason why every attempt at defining either random or probability analytically is perforce abortive ... [The Borel–Cantelli definition] is a complete thought in the Hegelian sense because it defines probability by probability. (GR, 1967, p. 78)

At this juncture, Georgescu became the sworn enemy of all attempts to reconcile probability to an analytical analogue of determinism, in neoclassical price theory or wherever else it might be found. This included fields outside the normal purview of the economist, such as 'information theory' (GR, 1975), and even in statistical mechanics (*ELEP*, ch. 6). It seems that the concern to uphold his vision of probability in the large led him to look more closely at thermodynamics: and this brings us to his most famous later themes: entropy and the problem of scientism.

SCIENTISM AND ARITHMOMORPHISM

There have been many economists who have forsworn the siren song of 'science' in the twentieth century; one thinks of the American Institutionalists, the German Historicists and Gunnar Myrdal. And yet few have had much of an impact upon neoclassical thought in any shape or form. The only viable candidates for these particular laurels are Friedrich von Hayek and Nicholas Georgescu-Roegen, and it is instructive to contrast their positions. While both have been congenitally suspicious of statism in all its forms, it appears that Hayek actually associated scientism with socialistic thought, regarding both as greasing the skids down the road to serfdom. Since for Hayek scientism was more or less identical to the engineering mentality (Hayek, 1979), he was convinced that mechanistic models embodied the hubris of the engineer in his desire to control and adjust. It seems that Hayek's understanding of the history of science and of neoclassical theory was deficient in this respect, since he did not notice that 'energetics' had been the inspiration of the orthodox neoclassical theory which he had championed up until that time, nor did he see that scientism had been used just as efficaciously to argue for the natural character of the market as against statist intervention (Mirowski, 1989a, ch. 7). Thus, the deficiency of familiarity with science and its history resulted in Hayek's case in a rather jumbled and unfocused attack upon scientism in economics.

The case of Georgescu-Roegen was rather different in this regard. Georgescu's hesitations about the scientific character of orthodox economics grew out of a sure control of the technical aspects of the model and a familiarity with scientific theories, particularly those of physics. Because of this competence, he understood rather early on that conventional neoclassical theory was simply a poor simulacrum of rational mechanics – 'Indeed, any system that involves a conservation principle (given means) and a maximization rule (optimal satisfaction) is a mechanical analogue' (*ELEP*, p. 318) – and dedicated his earliest work to exploring the options for loosening up this conception. One observes this in the 1936 *Quarterly Journal of Economics* paper, where a threshold in the comparison of satisfaction leads to an indeterminacy in equilibrium; and here we find the first use of the term 'penumbra', which later grows in significance in the work on 'dialectics' (*AE*, p. 164). One can also see it in the 1950 *QJE* paper (*AE*, ch. 2) where concern over the irreversibility of trade led to a questioning of the very idea of historically invariant laws of exchange, long before the present muddle over 'hysteresis' and the like in orthodox discourse.

What is notable about the progress of Georgescu's anti-scientism is the way in which it began in contemplation of the formal analytics of neoclassical choice theory, and only later blossomed out into such areas as production theory, econometrics, the role of mathematics and the direct relationship to physics. Yet in the early period, the similarities with Hayek again come to the forefront, since it is clear that Georgescu has adopted a quasi-Austrian approach to the whole issue of the psychology of wants and needs. As he has written in his 'Life Philosophy', 'the principle of marginal utility is just a shorthand for the law that any human satisfies his wants in their hierarchical order'.[8] This insistence upon an Aristotelian conception of psychology is out of step with the mainstream development of neoclassicism, because it violates the very concept of a physical 'field' which provided the inspiration for neoclassical value theory (Mirowski, 1989a, ch. 5), and introduces a temporal element into a phenomenon which is virtual and therefore irredeemably static. This quasi-Aristotelian rejection of a pure continuum undoubtedly inspired Georgescu's early claim that preference does not pass insensibly through indifference on the way to nonpreference; it also explains his rather incongruous campaign to resuscitate Heinrich Gossen as a serious economic theorist (GR, 1983).[9]

In any event, what was at first a scepticism with respect to the meaning of indifference later became a scepticism with regard to the use of number in describing choice, and then change. He came to define 'arithmomorphism' as: 'the fundamental principle upon which Logic rests is that the property of discrete distribution should cover not only symbols but concepts as well ... every real number retains a distinct individuality ... Arithmomorphic concepts do not overlap' (*ELEP*, pp. 44–5). These were differentiated from 'dialectical' concepts, which do overlap and interpenetrate. Examples of dialectical concepts are democracies (a nation can be a democracy and a non-democracy at one and the same time) and life (think of the problematic status of the virus). The geneaology of his concern is expressed in the following quote:

A penumbra separates a dialectical concept from its opposite. In the case of an arithmomorphic concept the separation consists of a void ... The procedure is most familiar to the student of consumers' choice where we take it for granted that between preference and non-preference there must be indifference. (*ELEP*, p. 47)

But once this distinction was applied to choice, Georgescu also began to see it as the key to his various other concerns. For example, he subsequently became convinced that 'random' was itself a dialectical concept, incapable of being sharply distinguished from the non-random in formal definition (*ELEP*, pp. 53–9; GR, 1967). He also became an advocate of the Hegelian position that number, being concerned with identity, cannot adequately express the phenomenon of change.[10] There is even a hint that the conviction that number was inadequate to capture the multiform complexity of social relations nudged him in the direction of a much more evolutionary conception of science, one which later made him an advocate of a future 'bioeconomics': 'If want had been a rigid arithmomorphic element, the human species would not have been able to survive under the radically different environments of the past.'[11]

In my opinion, this fundamental critique of the role of mathematical formalism in constraining the bounds of discourse has been responsible for many of Georgescu's most profound and potentially pregnant observations regarding economic theory. These contributions range far and wide, but we shall only briefly identify four: the stress on the importance of qualitative difference and invariance; the vain attempt to measure preferences; the great difficulties with measuring production relationships; and the suggestion of the future importance of abstract algebra.

His invocation of qualitative difference began with a very provocative thesis concerning fundamental physical laws, such as $F = ma$, or $E = mc^2$, namely that they expressed simple proportional relationships (*ELEP*, p. 102):

> this simple pattern is not a mere accident: on the contrary, in all these cases the proportional variation of the variables is the inevitable consequence of the fact that every one of these variables is free from any qualitative variation. In other words, they are all cardinal variables. The reason is simple: if two such variables are connected by a law, the connection being immediate in the sense that the law is not a relation obtained by telescoping a chain of other laws, then what is true for one pair of values must be true for all succeeding pairs. Otherwise, there would be some difference between the first and say, the hundreth pair which could only mean a qualitative difference.

An economist might think this merely an artefact of the arbitrarily chosen reference scale, but Georgescu denied this and insisted, rather, that it was an index of the success of the particular science in abstracting away all irrelevant qualitative variation. To my knowledge, he did not delve into the issue of the extent to which this abstraction might itself be due to cultural convictions of identity and difference, and the extent to which they might be a simple reflection of the inherent diversity of the phenomenon itself.[12] Nevertheless, on these grounds alone he postulated that non-linear relationships must be the norm in economics; and this well in advance of the present craze for such non-linear models taken over wholesale from physics and biology as chaotic models, Volterra predator–prey models, and models of 'increasing returns'.[13] Yet he did not counsel the eschewal of mathematical models altogether, because the construct of a world entirely free of qualitative variation was required for a benchmark of inquiry, or as he put it, 'Since cardinality is associated with the complete absence of qualitative variation, it represents a sort of natural origin for quality. To remove it from our box of descriptive tools is tantamount to destroying any point of reference for quality' (*ELEP*, p. 112).

In 1954 Georgescu had tried to deploy this argument for the intrinsic character of non-linearity to provide a novel justification for the convexity of preferences, asserting that it was *qualitative* differences which mattered to the individual, so it was necessarily the case that indifference curves must be convex. Upon some criticism by Carl Kaysen, however, he came to realize that non-linearity of preferences did not imply convexity (in the sense that some combinations would not be complements but might actually reduce the attractiveness of any combination); from that point onwards he became a harsh critic of all neoclassical models of preferences and expectations, primarily because of his conviction that arithmomorphic models misrepresent and obscure the importance of quality in human life. Unlike the common run of neoclassical theorists, who felt that by invoking ordinal utility they somehow evaded any need to measure preferences or treat them seriously, Georgescu kept insisting that the impossibility of measurement of preferences was the clearest symptom of the failure of the orthodox neoclassical model. 'Time and again, we can see the drawback of importing a gospel from physics into economics and interpreting it in a more catholic way than the consistory of physicists' (*ELEP*, p. 335).

Turning away from neoclassical utility, he trained the spotlight of arithmomorphism upon neoclassical production theory, with equally devastating consequences. Earlier, he had been absorbed with the Leontief input/output model, and had taken issue with the common practice of inscribing non-zero entries on the diagonal of the matrix, primarily because the Leontief matrix was a pure flow model, and flows within analytical boundaries should not be observable anywhere in the model (*ELEP*, pp. 260–1). Such carelessness engendered all sorts of stock/flow confusions, of which the most notable was the fallacious model of underconsumptionist tendencies in Paul Sweezy's *Theory of Capitalist Development* (*AE*, ch. 12). Yet wherever he looked, be it Marxist macromodels or the neoclassical production function, it seemed that the cavalier treatment of the measurement of inputs and outputs had resulted in all manner of outlandish statements in economics. For instance, when economists indifferently pass between production functions relating stocks and those relating flows per unit time, he showed that they implicitly assume that all production processes must be homogeneous of the first degree (*EEM*, p. 38).[14] The transgressions seemed all the more grievous when compounded by the claim that the economists were merely reproducing the physical or technical specifications of engineers, when in fact they knew absolutely nothing about the physical and design laws of any production process in any industry.

To begin to sort out the confusions, Georgescu posited a distinction between 'funds' – the requisites of production which must be present in their entirety during the process – and 'flows' – amounts of goods and services which cross the analytical boundary as inputs and outputs. He then specified what he considered to be a generic production 'functional', where an output function was related to a set of flow and fund functions, such as raw materials, intermediate goods, maintainance flows, waste flows, and funds of land, capital equipment and labour power. As he observed, 'This is a far cry from the notion inherited from Wicksteed, according to which a process is represented by a point in ordinary (Euclidean) space' (*EEM*, p. 65). The explicit consideration of land, natural resources and waste flows again pointed in the direction of the importance of the laws of thermodynamics, a theme we shall take up in the following section.

Even though the analysis was carried out at a high level of generality, Georgescu saw that it would have important implications for many controversies in economics. One such endemic dispute was over the inevitability of constant returns to scale versus the very idea of an optimum scale of production. In an article which asserted that the notion of scale had been misunderstood (*EEM*, ch. 11), Georgescu discussed how the axioms of cardinally measurable items might impinge upon the formalization of the production process (*EEM*, pp. 274–7). Although he did not mention it there, his axioms essentially described the axioms of an algebraic group. This exercise, as well as the discussion in (GR, 1986a), has prompted the introduction of abstract algebra and measurement theory as an alternative foundation for a mathematical formalization of value theory (Mirowski, 1991). In a sense, Georgescu has cleared the path for an economics that could learn some important lessons from physics without feeling it had to be physics.

THERMODYNAMICS AND THE THEORY OF VALUE

As Georgescu denounced the twin vices of arithmomorphism and scientism, his position on the question of the theory of value increasingly isolated him from the rest of the economics profession. He had rejected constrained optimization of utility as a flawed imitation of mechanics, but still insisted upon the central place of scarcity in any analysis. He insisted upon the indeterministic and irreversible nature of economic activity, but this raised the question of whether there was any object or purpose of the economy that one could readily identify. Sometimes in response he would suggest that the purpose of the economy was the pursuit of an 'immaterial flux of pleasure' (*ELEP*, p. 284), while on other occasions he would cite the survival of the human species as the teleological objective (*ELEP*, p. 277). Yet neither of these would provide the basis for any sort of analytical endeavour, and therefore I believe they left both the author and his audience unsatisfied.

For this reason, as well as those cited in previous sections, the laws of thermodynamics progressively tended to occupy the place of a theory of value in the writings of Georgescu-Roegen, generally under the rubric of a prospective promised 'bioeconomics'. It is necessary to quote at length to see how this happened:

> of all physical concepts only those of Thermodynamics have their roots in economic value ... the concept of order-entropy cannot be divorced from the intuitive grasping of human purposes ... It is again thermodynamics which explains why the things that are useful have also an economic value – not to be confused with price. For example, land, although it cannot be consumed, derives its economic value from two facts: first, land is the only net with which we can catch the most vital form of low entropy for us, and second, the size of the net is immutable. Other things are *scarce* in a sense which does not apply to land, because first, the amount of low entropy within our environment (at least) decreases continuously and irrevocably, and second, a given amount of low entropy can be used by us only once. (*ELEP*, pp. 277–8)

Now, while he was careful to warn that he was not equating energy with economic value in a literal sense (*ELEP*, p. 284), one could find numerous passages where such an interpretation seemed warranted, such as: 'All the so-called "limited wars" of our time, in Vietnam, in Korea, in the Middle East, in Africa, have occurred precisely because natural resources are so important for our existence ... Natural resources are the central element of mankind's evolution' (GR, 1978, p. 9). The fact that he had cut himself loose from the orthodox neoclassical value theory also encouraged the tendency to read Georgescu as the advocate of some species of an energetics theory of value.

The OPEC oil embargo in 1973 gave a great boost to *ELEP*, but at the cost of lumping Georgescu together with a whole host of energeticists who came out of the woodwork. These energeticists attempted to enlist Georgescu in their cause (Costanza, 1980); in reaction, Georgescu set out to publish in-depth critiques of the energy theory of value (GR, 1979; 1986b), which surely must have disorientated many of his readers who had very little background in history or physics. For this reason, as well as the fact that he has written the only sophisticated discussion of this perennial phenomenon, it is worthwhile to examine his most recent position in some detail.

> My position has been (and still is) that the Entropy Law is the taproot of economic scarcity. In a world in which that law did not operate, the same energy could be used over and over again at any velocity of circulation one pleased and material objects would never wear out. But life would certainly not exist either ... It is for these reasons that the economic process is entropic in all its material fibres. But I have also maintained (without being read correctly) that although entropy is a necessary condition for usefulness, it is not also a sufficient one (just as usefulness is a necessary but not sufficient condition for economic value ...) It is now perfectly clear that in *absolutely* no situation is it possible for the energy equivalents to represent economic valuations. (GR, 1979, pp. 1041, 1042, 1048).

Georgescu prosecuted four separate indictments against the neo-energeticists and the burgeoning neoclassical speciality known as 'energy economics'. The first, retailed under the slogan that 'matter matters too', was a warning about the misuse of the theory of relativity by economists and some natural resource specialists. Although Einstein's ubiquitous $E = mc^2$ has become a totem for those who know nothing else about physics, the conventional interpretation which asserts the physical interchangeability of matter and energy is a mistake. Georgescu pointed out that, with the exception of some extremely transient events at the sub-atomic level, matter has never actually been precipitated solely from energy. All the common transformations have proceeded in the opposite direction. The dearth of reversible transformations illustrates that no Philosopher's Stone is available, and most conversions of matter from one form to another are effectively prohibited. Here Georgescu opted to go beyond the normal boundaries of disciplinary discourse and state this prohibition as a parallel to the entropy law in the domain of matter: like energy, matter also continuously undergoes degradation and is dispersed in more and more unusable or inaccessible forms. However, there is one profound distinction between matter and energy that should block such a parallel formulation of this proto-entropy law in a manner similar to Gibbs' free energy:

> the rub is that unlike mass and energy, matter is a highly heterogeneous category. Every chemical element has at least one property that characterizes it completely and hence renders it indispensable in some technical recipes. We must therefore expect that, in contrast with the general theory of energy (thermodynamics), the study of transformations of matter in the bulk should be hard going.   (GR, 1979, p. 1035)

The energy concept was invented ultimately for the purpose of expressing certain symmetries and invariants in physical phenomena, abstracting away all other 'secondary' heterogeneous properties (Mirowski, 1989a, ch. 2). For various cultural and historical reasons, energy itself became reified in the popular mind as a homogeneous substance. When Einstein derived certain mathematical implications of a world consisting solely of symmetries and invariants, the temptation was to regard his work as a final vindication of the tenacious image of a single homogeneous substrate that suffused all physical phenomena. What had become lost was the realization that the energy concept had consciously abstracted away the heterogeneous nature of physical phenomena, dumping it into the portmanteau concept of matter. Hence it was a category fallacy to assert that matter and energy were identical.

This blind spot with regard to the importance of matter was but one manifestation of what Georgescu called the 'energetics bias', namely, the predilection to downplay the change and diversity of phenomena in favour of simple homogeneous relations. (One observes here the echoes of his position on arithmomorphism and his critique of neoclassicism as a species of energetics.) In neo-energetics, matter/energy is treated as a conserved entity, denuded of the multiform ideosyncracies of matter so crucial for the understanding of production processes. It is just these properties which continually experience degradation, and this fact constrains production processes just as surely as the second law of thermodynamics. Further, it is these properties of matter which are crucial for harnessing various energy sources. In this context, Georgescu has noted that fossil fuels have been especially cheap in the past because they required little in the way of extensive matter configurations for their utilization. The prospect is not nearly so rosy in the future.

Georgescu's second indictment of neo-energetics is that there can be no rigorous definition of 'net energy'. In their empirical work, the neo-energeticists predominantly opted to express energy content in calorific values of fuels – most commonly British Thermal Units: the quantity of heat required to raise the temperature of one pound of water by one degree Fahrenheit. Yet the neo-energeticists elided the fact that there exist no accepted calorific values for nuclear fuels, and that calorific estimates for solar energy were only indirect estimates, dependent upon ideal conversions (GR, 1986a, p. 266). These and other considerations suggested that physics alone did not provide operational algorithms for the reduction of all fuels to energy equivalents.

His third indictment was that a theory of value that asserts the proportionality of prices to embodied energy has already abstracted away the effects of the dissipation and degradation of energy, and therefore violated the second law of thermodynamics (GR, 1986a, p. 272). This fundamental mistake then exfoliates throughout the structure of neo-energetics, ranging from an inability to confront the fundamental irreversibility of economic processes to the absence of an energy content index independent of context. In Georgescu's view, all that really happens when coal is mined and burned to generate electricity is that humanity has drawn upon a fixed a limited store of low entropy and degraded much of it into dissipated heat.

His fourth and final complaint about neo-energetics is that it frequently does not practise what it preaches. Neo-energetics aims to usurp orthodox economics by reducing all phenomena to their energetic essences; but when it comes down to the nitty-gritty, they persistently and stubbornly confute energetic and monetary categories. For example, the input–output matrices so beloved of the neo-energeticists are generated from purchases and sales data which are not derived from technical specifications. Since the so-called energy coefficients are calculated from these tables, what masquerades as a reduction is in fact a circular argument (GR, 1986a, p. 272). The ensuing close correlation of economic variables and 'energy values' results from a hat trick, and has no bearing upon any issues of causality.

Georgescu's bill of indictments against neo-energetics betokens a familiarity with the physical issues which no 'energy economist' has yet shown; and yet it was not a sympathetic critique. His most recent pronouncements, especially after *ELEP*, have been uncompromising on that score. In the following quote, M_0 represents the matter requirements of a technology, while e_1 represents the energy requirements of the same technology (GR, 1986a, pp. 269, 272):

> The upshot is that since there is no potential $\psi(M_0,e_1)$ = constant on which to base a technological grid (similar to that of utility preference), the choice between two technologies such that $e_1^1 > e_1^2$ and $M_0^1 > M_0^2$ cannot be decided by physico-chemical relations alone. The upshot is that the nature of the choice between any two technologies is essentially bioeconomic ... Economic phenomena certainly are not independent of the chemico-physical laws that govern our external and internal environment, but they are not determined by those laws. It is because the economy has its proper laws that one dollar spent on caviar does not buy the same free energy as when spent on potatoes.

However correct these indictments of the various energetics movements, the great weakness of the later work has been the tantalizingly vague character of those 'proper laws' of the economy and that delectable-sounding alternative 'bioeconomics', especially when one takes into account the devastating critiques of utility, expectations and production outlined above. Although he has promised a work sketching the outlines of bioeconomics, no such tome has issued from his pen; and the prognosis is that it is unlikely to appear in the future. I believe it is not due to lack of ability or imagination (for there has been no one else so able or imaginative in the twentieth century); but rather Georgescu's conception of his own place in the economics profession. While willing to discredit the neo-energetics movement with their puerile scientism, he has never been willing to go the full nine yards and turn his wrath upon the orthodox neoclassical profession, even though, as we have seen, the sum total of his work leaves few stones standing. Although autobiography may account for some of this hesitation (the escape from Romania, the refused positions at Harvard and Chicago, the Harvard ethos), I believe that another complex of causes may be at work here. If I am right about this, then the next step in the Georgescu-Roegen research programme should diverge at this point from the path of the master.

The problem seems to lie in a residual attachment to older value-theoretic and scientific notions. As already mentioned, Georgescu has seemed unwilling to venture beyond the vague idea that value is a psychological flux, and seems to prefer to take his inspiration largely from physics. The former makes him retain some sympathy for the neoclassical project (and in this he resembles his teacher Schumpeter), while the latter encourages the appropriation of metaphors from physics and biology to anchor his conceptions of economic laws. His work, however, can be read in a different manner: namely, that value should not be based in tendentious scientific metaphors, and that, rather, the arithmomorphic character of trade should be confronted directly and explained as a social phenomenon. One version of this project, begun in Mirowski (1991), hews to the spirit of the master by trying to learn from physics without feeling impelled to copy physics. Given the rather patchy record of recognition of Georgescu's own accomplishments, this is clearly not an optimal path to a Nobel Prize in economics; rather, it is a manifesto for a future economics willing to stand up for its own specific integrity.

NOTES

* I wish to thank Nicholas Georgescu-Roegen for providing me with some of his harder-to-locate publications, as well as for that dialectical imponderable, inspiration.

1. This is an as-yet-unpublished manuscript entitled 'My Life Philosophy', for publication in a volume tentatively entitled *The Life Philosophies of Eminent Economists*, to be published by Cambridge University Press. The following abbreviations for the books of Georgescu-Roegen will be used in this Chapter: *AE*: *Analytical Economics* (1966); *ELEP*: *The Entropy Law and the Economic Process* (1971); *EEM*: *Energy and Economic Myths* (1976). Other publications will be referred to by the convention '(GR, date)'.
2. Foucault (1973, p. 349), translation of *Les Mots et les choses* (1966). Foucault aptly captures the tension which inheres in the work of Georgescu-Roegen, namely, 'the endless controversy between philosophy, which objects to the naiveté with which the human sciences try to provide their own foundation, and those same human sciences which claim as their rightful object what would have formerly constituted the domain of philosophy' (p. 346).
3. Georgescu-Roegen, 'My Life Philosophy', p. 2.
4. His citation record remains strong, considering that he has not published much if anything new in over a decade. The *Social Sciences Citation Index* lists 60 citations in 1987; 58 in 1988 and 51 in 1989.
5. The history of the impact of the perceived breakdown of determinism in the 1930s and the way it made various aspects of stochastic theory acceptable in economics remains yet to be written. My *Who's Afraid of Random Trade* (Princeton, N.J.: Princeton University Press, forthcoming) will be a first instalment in such a history.
6. For examples of this oblivion towards his work, which clearly predates any of the other cited texts, see McCall (1978); Diamond and Rothschild (1978).
7. Tjalling Koopmans Collection, Sterling Library, Yale University, box 5, folder 81. Koopmans the technician missed the significance of Georgescu's distinction between 'certainty', defined as logical implication, and 'quasi-certainty', defined as convergence in the limit to frequency ratios other than the predicted constituting a set of measure zero. The distinction has nothing in particular to do with infinite repetition, but rather simply points out in the latter case that anomalies cannot be entirely ruled out, so the certainty must be of a lower grade.

8. Georgescu-Roegen, 'My Life Philosophy', p. 14; see also *ELEP*, p. 41. The connection between his latent Aristotelianism and the overall narrative theme of concern with change is illustrated by the following quote: 'For quite a while change by generation and annihilation lingered in Scholastic speculation. But after the various principles of conservation discovered by physics in the last hundred years, we became convinced that this type of change was buried for good... It is thus quite possible that we shall return to Aristotle's views and reconsider the modern axiom that "the energy concept without conservation is meaningless" ' (*AE*, p. 30). Those familiar with *More Heat than Light* will recognize it as one meditation upon the implications of this statement.

9. We say 'incongruous' because Gossen was precisely one of those people who attempted an imitation of rational mechanics without any sure grasp of the subject matter; but also because Georgescu explains in his lengthy 'Introduction' the numerous mathematical infelicities which add up to the verdict that Gossen's model is entirely incompatible with neoclassical theory. See, especially, GR, 1983, fn.101; pp. cxv, lxxxi, xcii.

10. He has repeatedly quoted the dictum in *The Phenomenology of Mind* that 'Number is just that entirely inactive, inert and indifferent characteristic in which every movement and relational process is extinguished' (*ELEP*, p. 72).

11. Georgescu-Roegen, 'My Life Philosophy', p. 14.

12. The person most involved with discussing how different cultures use projections of the natural upon the social to reify their notions of identity and difference has been the anthropologist Mary Douglas, particularly in Douglas (1986). An introduction to the possible uses of her thesis in economics can be found in Mirowski (1990a). The present author thinks that Georgescu has not taken the issue of identity and difference so far as to question its character in the physical sciences, but that extension would be a necessary prerequisite for a thoroughgoing anti-scientism.

13. A critique of the modern chaos literature in economics from precisely the vantage point of the central importance of invariance and difference is Mirowski (1990b).

14. This constitutes a retrogression to a substance theory of value, as explained in Mirowski (1989a, ch. 6).

REFERENCES

Berndt, Ernst (1985), 'From Technocracy to Net Energy Analysis', in A. Scott (ed.), *Progress in Natural Resource Economics*, Oxford: Clarendon Press.

Colvin, Phyllis (1977), 'Ontological and Epistemological Commitments in the Social Sciences', in E. Mendelsohn, P. Weingart and R. Whitley (eds), *The Social Production of Scientific Knowledge*, Boston, Mass.: Reidel.

Costanza, Robert (1980), 'Embodied Energy and Economic Valuation', *Science*, **225**.

Currie, M. and I. Steedman (1990), *Wrestling With Time*, Ann Arbor, Mich.: University of Michigan Press.

Demetrescu, M. and J. Dragan (1986), *Entropy and Bioeconomics*, Milan: Nagard.

Diamond, Peter and Michael Rothschild (eds) (1978), *Uncertainty in Economics*, New York: Academic Press.

Douglas, Mary (1986), *How Institutions Think*, Syracuse, N.Y.: Syracuse University Press.

Foucault, Michel (1973), *The Order of Things*, New York: Vintage Books.

Georgescu-Roegen, Nicholas (1947), 'Further Contributions to the Scatter Analysis', in *Proceedings of the International Statistical Conference, 1947*, vol. v, pp. 39–43.

—— (1966), *Analytical Economics*, Cambridge, Mass.: Harvard University Press.

—— (1967), 'An Epistemological Analysis of Statistics as the Science of Rational Guessing', *Acta Logica*, **10**, 61–91.

—— (1969), 'A Critique of Statistical Principles in Relation to Social Phenomena', *Revue international de sociologie*, **5**, 347–70.

—— (1971), *The Entropy Law and the Economic Process*, Cambridge, Mass.: Harvard University Press.

—— (1975), 'The Measure of Information: a Critique', in *Proceedings of the Third International Congress of Cybernetics and Systems*, ed. J. Rose and C. Bilciu, New York: Springer Verlag.

—— (1976), *Energy and Economic Myths*, Oxford: Pergamon Press.

—— (1978), 'Mechanistic Dogma and Economics', *British Review of Economic Issues*, **5**, 1–10.

—— (1979), 'Energy Analysis and Economic Valuation', *Southern Economic Journal*, **44**, 1023–58.

—— (1983), 'Introduction', in Heinrich Gossen, *The Laws of Human Relations*, Cambridge, Mass.: MIT Press.

—— (1986a), 'Man and Production', in M. Baranzini and R. Scazzieri (eds), *Foundations of Economics*, Oxford: Basil Blackwell.

—— (1986b), 'The Entropy Law and the Economic Process in Retrospect', *Eastern Economic Journal*, **12**.

—— (1988), 'My Life Philosophy, unpublished manuscript.

Hayek, Friedrich (1979), *The Counter-Revolution of Science*, Indianapolis: Liberty Press.

Katzner, Donald (1986), 'The Role of Formalism in Economic Thought', in P. Mirowski (ed.), *The Reconstruction of Economic Theory*, Boston, Mass.: Kluwer.

McCall, J. (1978), 'Probabalistic Microeconomics', *Bell Journal of Economics*, **2**, 403–32.

Mirowski, Philip (1986), 'Mathematical Formalism and Economic Explanation', in Mirowski (ed.), *The Reconstruction of Economic Theory*, Boston, Mass.: Kluwer.

—— (1988), 'Energy and Energetics in Economic Theory', *Journal of Economic Issues*, **22**, 811–32.

—— (1989a), *More Heat Than Light*, New York: Cambridge University Press.

—— (1989b), 'The Probabalistic Counter-Revolution', *Oxford Economic Papers*, **41**, 217–35.

—— (1990a), 'The Rhetoric of Modern Economics', *History of the Human Sciences*, **3**, 243–57.

—— (1990b), 'From Mandelbrot to Chaos in Economic Theory', *Southern Economic Journal*, **57**, 289–307.

—— (1990c), 'Problems in the Paternity of Econometrics', *History of Political Economy*, **22**, 587–610.

—— (1991), 'Postmodernism and the Social Theory of Value', *Journal of Post Keynesian Economics*, **13**, 565–82.

Morgan, Mary (1990), *The History of Econometric Ideas*, Cambridge: Cambridge University Press.

Rifkin, Jeremy (1980), *Entropy: A New World View*, New York: Viking Press.

Schumpeter, Joseph (1954), *History of Economic Analysis*, New York: Oxford University Press.

van Gool, W. and J. Bruggink (eds) (1985), *Energy and Time in the Economic and Physical Sciences*, Amsterdam: North-Holland.

5. Albert O. Hirschman

Charles K. Wilber and Kenneth P. Jameson*

A BIOGRAPHICAL PORTRAIT

Albert O. Hirschman's prolific publication record began in 1938, the year in which he received his doctorate in economics from the University of Trieste. By 1943 he was publishing in major US journals, for example, 'The Commodity Structure of World Trade' in the *Quarterly Journal of Economics*, and 'On Measures of Dispersion for a Finite Distribution' in the *Journal of the American Statistical Association*. The two most recent publications, listed on the *curriculum vitae* which he kindly provided for us, are the Tanner lectures published by the University of Utah entitled 'Two Hundred Years of Reactionary Rhetoric: the Case of the Perverse Effect' and 'The Case Against "One Thing at a Time" ' in *World Development*.

The contrast of the early and recent publications, combined with a more detailed overview of his life's work, suggests the low-level generalization that Hirschman's analytical concerns have moved from narrowly technical matters of economics to issues of a broad social science nature. His evolution has countered the direction of the mainstream in the economics profession which has moved toward ever more mathematical precision and narrowness of scope.

Many economists might feel uneasy at being so out of step with the trends in their discipline; however, Hirschman's self-described stance as a dissenter or a maverick explains the direction and persistence of his efforts. Economics and the social sciences in general have been the beneficiaries. In some sense his self-appointed role has been to point out that the emperor (social science) and the queen (economics) are not clothed quite as we would like to believe. He goes beyond mere innocence, however, and has been able to teach us that working from a different and richer perspective, while being careful about the meaning of 'clothed', we can indeed see 'clothing' of an interesting and intriguing sort.

An overview of Hirschman's work finds a notable characteristic which distinguishes him from many other economists – the clear link between his involvements as an economist and his own work and writing. He lived and studied in Europe during the rise of Hitler, an experience that spawned his first book *National Power and the Structure of Foreign Trade* (1945) which showed how a more powerful nation can use that position to extract greater gains from its trade with a smaller nation. He worked in Washington at the Federal Reserve Board from 1946 to 1952, during the Marshall Plan period, leading to his less-known work on the dollar shortage and on the European Payments Union. More importantly, this period exposed him to the governmental decision-making processes which became a theme in much of his later work.

His writing on economic development was stimulated by four years as an economic adviser to the Colombian government, under the initial sponsorship of the World Bank. He took a very different stance from the 'balanced growth' development perspective dominant at that time. Hirschman has often ascribed his dissent to his unfamiliarity with existing research on development at the time he went to Colombia, implying that his thinking was mainly inductive and a response to his observations there. More recently, in 'A Dissenter's Confession: the Strategy of Economic Development Revisited' (1986, pp. 3–34) he has admitted that his earlier work and its themes had already given him a series of preconceptions before he arrived in Colombia.

From Colombia his path took him to the academy, first at Yale (1956–8), next to Columbia (1958–64), then a decade at Harvard (1964–74), and finally to the Institute for Advanced Study at Princeton where emeritus status in 1985 did not signify any slowing of activity. The university connection allowed him to turn to broader issues of social theory and the history of economic thought, though he always built on and elaborated concepts and constructs that originated in his earlier work as an applied economist.

Albert O. Hirschman was 75 in 1990 and remains productive and involved. In recent years he has spent time in such activities as membership of the Executive Panel of the Ford Foundation Project on Social Welfare Policy and on the Advisory Board of the World Institute of Development Economic Research (WIDER). In addition he has been reaping the fruits of his productive life and his contributions to the social sciences by his election to the National Academy of Sciences and the reception of honorary doctorates from universities in the United States, Italy, Germany, France, Argentina and Brazil. That the honorary degrees are in such varied disciplines as Political Science, Law and Humanities may be less a result of universities' bureaucratic decisions than a recognition of the breadth of Hirschman's scholarship.

HIRSCHMAN AS A POLITICAL ECONOMIST OF DEVELOPMENT

The Strategy of Economic Development (1958) was Hirschman's central contribution to development economics. He staked out a position which was in opposition to the reigning view and set out a series of themes that Hirschman and other development economists would use extensively.

Of the four Hirschman entries in the *New Palgrave: A Dictionary of Economics*, his concept of 'linkages' stimulated the greatest amount of Kuhnian normal science activity among economists. The idea was deceptively simple: that development can be stimulated by products with forward linkages, for their producers will naturally search out other activities which could use the product as an input. Similarly, a product with backward linkages would stimulate domestic production of inputs. Of greatest importance at the time was that linkage analysis suggested very different investment criteria from the other two competing schools of thought. The 'big push' strategy implied that broad-scale investment across all industries was required. Neoclassical maximization suggested that those investments be undertaken which had the highest discounted present value. Linkage analysis provided criteria for choosing among competing investments, rather than attempting to undertake them all; however, the criteria were dynamic and took into account a much broader range of effects than any simple present-value test could incorporate.

Policy analysis was facilitated when linkages were cast in terms of input–output analysis. As a descriptive device, the underdeveloped countries' input–output tables, with their many empty cells, were easily differentiated from the developed. As a prescriptive device it was clear that some industries, such as steel, had a wealth of both forward and backward linkages, and the effort of countries such as Brazil to develop a domestic steel industry might not be so irrational as neoclassical analysis would suggest. An entire field of analysis by economists was encouraged, based on input–output tables compiled for a remarkable number of countries: measures of linkages, direct and indirect, forward and backward, were developed and refined, and in many cases development policy was guided by the implications of the linkage construct.

Time has not been kind to this use of input–output analysis. One survey of the field and its techniques notes:

> The problems of using linkage analysis as an industrialization strategy are now familiar. The rankings of sectors in terms of output, incomes, and employment creation is not consistent ... , while confusion arises over interpretation of linkages as *potential* or *actual*. ... Linkage analysis pays no attention to comparative advantage and, indeed, implies policies contradicted by international trade theory ... (Sohn, 1986, p. 117)

The list of problems indicates a misunderstanding of Hirschman's use of linkages, for he would never reduce the construct to such narrow technical matters. Its dismissal symbolizes the failure of the 'disciples' rather than of the master. Hirschman, in his characteristic fashion, continued to use the constructs fruitfully and to investigate their implications. For example, he extended linkages to consumption and fiscal linkages in 'A Generalized Linkage Approach to Development' (1977a).

His second major contribution to development economics was the more general concept of 'unbalanced growth'. With another simple insight he dissented from the popular balanced-growth strategy of development, the 'big push', without returning to the alternative market-guided strategy of *laissez-faire*. His was a dissent from a dissent, but not a return to the status quo; and this has been a consistent characteristic of his analytical stance. In its simplest form, unbalanced growth suggested that economies would develop best by concentrating on a subset of activities that were more appropriate for them, rather than by trying to do everything at once. But the approach was not simply an argument for specialization according to comparative advantage, for development is a dynamic process which defies our efforts at reductionism. The reality he encountered in his observations of developing countries was too complex for any simple formula.

For example, his development field work uncovered many 'hidden rationalities', choices that seemed at first blush to be incorrect or irrational; but closer observation disclosed the reasons for the choices and showed they were likely to be more successful than the 'rational' alternative. It may seem absurd to install a high-technology plant in an economy without the slightest concept of the importance of maintenance; however, such a step may serve to focus so much attention on this essential element that maintenance may be carried out better than in a more forgiving atmosphere.

'Inverted sequences' also abounded in his observations of development processes. For example, logic and planning suggest that physical infrastructure such as roads and ports should be built before certain types of directly productive activities are undertaken; Hirschman found that the reverse sequence, the production of goods which had to be transported to market, could induce the construction of the infrastructure necessary (1985b, pp. 83–97). Development could be stimulated through a *shortage* of social overhead capital. Similarly, rather than discouraging domestic production, imports of particular goods could actually foster domestic production by providing both market creation and an assessment of the size of the domestic market to be satisfied when foreign exchange became scarce and limited import capacity – another example of imbalance in development.

It took only two years from the publication of *The Strategy* for Hirschman to move to the political economy of development, embarking on case studies of public decision-making in Brazil, Chile and Colombia. As he put it in the acknowledgements of *Journeys Toward Progress* (1963, p. 11):

> In planning the present study, it became clear to me that I would be setting out on a hazardous expedition into the vast no man's land stretching between economics and other social sciences such as political science, sociology, and history.

The subject matter – government decision-making – was new; however, Hirschman's conclusions had a familiar ring. Non-market responses to change are not necessarily less automatic than private responses. Public decision-making is not necessarily of poorer quality than private, though public decision-makers do not always carry out their tasks with an acceptable level of efficiency. So the questions could be better viewed from a different vantage point: the examination of policy-making sequences. Some would be inherently flawed, but most would have a hidden rationality to them which should be respected and would on occasion serve and nurture progress. Policy-making sequences would often incorporate resources to overcome obstacles to change.

From the case studies of land use and land reform in Colombia, inflation in Chile, and the regional disparity of Brazil's north-east, Hirschman drew a wealth of insights to the political economy of change. He found much that was positive in the efforts of Latin American decision-makers and gently encouraged them to dwell less on their failures, their 'fracasomania' (from the Spanish word *'fracaso'* or failure). And he was able to suggest sequences and processes that seemed to have a high promise of success and could support the contriving of reform, 'reform-mongering'.

Hirschman's work on economic development and the political economy of development was complemented by two later forays into applied development work. The first was an analysis of eleven World Bank development projects which resulted in *Development Projects Observed* (1967), the second, a six-month study of grassroots development projects sponsored by the Inter-American Foundation chronicled in *Getting Ahead Collectively: Grassroots Experiences in Latin America* (1984b).

Both show the same concern with and ability to isolate the unexpected, the unpredictable and the uncontrollable, to find the pattern of unbalanced growth in observations of change processes. In *Projects* it is described as the 'principle of the hiding hand': that the true outcomes of projects cannot be estimated *ex ante* and there is a desirable tendency to overestimate project benefits as a device to overcome the inertia that is likely to prevent initiating any difficult project. The actual outcomes are often affected more by the uncertainties of the project, by the latitudes and disciplines it incorporates. The final outcome will depend fundamentally on how decision-makers react to the unexpected. So development projects cannot simply be reduced to a benefit–cost calculation, though the opposite flaw of treating them as an art must also be avoided. In *Getting Ahead* inverted sequences and hidden rationalities are found in the ability of groups to organize themselves to better their existence collectively, a theme alluded to in *Strategy* when the ego-focused image of change is contrasted with the co-operative reality of entrepreneurial ventures (pp. 16–17). The most notable element of this effort is captured in the 'principle of conservation and mutation of social energy', which documents how leaders in collective enterprises were very often leaders in earlier and different enterprises that either failed or were repressed. So imbalance in development efforts is incorporated into the behaviour pattern of participants and will recur at unexpected places!

The writings mentioned above are the basis of Hirschman's place in contemporary development studies. Of the 228 citations to Hirschman's work in the 1988 *Social Science Citation Index*, 32 were to *Strategy* and nine were to *Projects*. There were no citations to *Getting Ahead*, indicating that much of Hirschman's current impact is outside his initial area of development economics, and that his early work continues to be the most important within the development subdiscipline. In part this reflects his tendency to 'trespass', to move outside economics to broader issues of social theory. As noted above, this is exactly the opposite of the direction of movement within economics, including development economics. For those who seek comfortable certainty in the capacity to reduce issues and analyses to mathematical precision, Hirschman's work is quite unsatisfactory.

There may be another reason as well, captured in the title of a book of his collected essays, *A Bias for Hope* (1971). Hirschman accepts and is excited about the process of social change, and has a bias toward the hope that it will result in positive changes in the human condition. He is no Dr Pangloss, though where others might find failure and an argument to resist change, Hirschman finds social energy conserved or the intriguing hidden hand. The only instance in which one detects doubts was in the turn to authoritarianism in Latin America in the 1960s and 1970s.

Hirschman's reaction to these events was to turn to the history of ideas in his book, *The Passions and the Interests* (1977b), to cast light upon the connections between economic development and political upheaval. He found a body of thought that claimed the expansion of a modern market economy would result in economic *interests* taming political *passions*. The workings of a market economy are so interrelated and delicate that it would force governments to restrain their arbitrary interference with both individual rights and economic institutions. This implicit assumption led development economists to ignore the continued existence of the 'passions'. As Hirschman pointed out (1977b, p. 124):

If it is true *that the economy must be deferred to*, then there is a case not only for constraining the imprudent actions of the prince but for repressing those of the people, for limiting participation, in short, for crushing anything that could be interpreted by some economist-king as a threat to the proper functioning of the 'delicate watch'.

Thus is was not development that caused the turn to authoritarianism; rather, the 'passions' of the policy-makers led them to impose their will on the development process.

Hirschman was correct in noting that it was impossible to draw any simple correlation between the economic changes of development and the turn to authoritarian governments; more recent events and the return of democracy have certainly borne out his scepticism. Those who equate economic liberalization and the return to democracy would do well to heed the cautions he raised.

His bias toward hope may be one reason he distanced himself from development economics and announced the decline of the discipline in 'The Rise and Decline of Development Economics' (1982a). For him the subdiscipline had been characterized by its rejection of 'monoeconomics', the belief that economic laws hold in all circumstances, and by its assertion that development could be a process of mutual benefit. The claim for a separate development economics was attacked by both orthodox and Marxist economists, and it was now charged with intellectual responsibility for all the failures of political and economic development. The attack was partially successful because development economics had based its theories upon a construct of a 'typical underdeveloped country' which was becoming ever less credible as differentiation within the Third World dramatically increased. Also the political (and now economic) disasters that struck many developing countries were laid at the door of development economics.

However, for Hirschman the decline of development economics is a result of the reaction of development economists to these problems. Some retreated from the early view that 'all good things go together' to claim that 'good economics is good for people'; some sought refuge in the belief that development can be 'downgraded to a technical task exclusively involved with efficiency improvements' (1982a, p. 21). Others took a more critical view of development performance and concentrated on income distribution or on basic human needs, partial objectives requiring specialized experts on 'nutrition, public health, housing, and education' (p. 23). This avoided the challenge posed by dismal politics and economics, at the cost of abandoning the excitement generated by the belief that the subdiscipline of development economics could make a central contribution to 'slaying backwardness'.

Hirschman accounts for this loss of hope by finding a subtle contemptuousness for less-developed countries among development economists, based on their attitude that the 'underdeveloped countries were expected to perform like wind-up toys and to "lumber through" the various stages of development single-mindedly' (1982a, p. 24).

He has always seen development as a complicated process and in *Strategy* (1958b) he noted that unbalanced growth could result in retrogression. None the less his 'bias for hope' sets him apart from many contemporary development economists. Development economics is much like Phaethon, child of the Sun, who tried to drive his father's chariot across the sky and failed dismally, endangering the entire world. Most development economists have fled to technical specificities to avoid any guilt by association. Hirschman has not but acts like one of the naiads who carved on Phaethon's tomb:

> Here Phaethon lies who drove the Sun-god's car.
> Greatly he failed, but he had greatly dared.

There is a sweet irony in Hirschman's selection as one of the 'pioneers of development' in a series of lectures sponsored by the World Bank. He began his development field-work in Colombia in 1954 under World Bank sponsorship, and quickly rejected their pressure to impress the natives with a set of magical planning and modelling tools. He was not to play the role of the gypsies and Melquiades in Garcia Marquez' *100 Years of Solitude*. The irony is that the Bank, the centre of technification of development economics, honoured the person who was implicitly pointing his finger at the same Bank for causing the decline of development economics. The Bank's *World Development Report, 1990* proves Hirschman's point by rediscovering poverty and reducing it to a set of technical issues for experts.

Once again, Albert Hirschman shows himself a dissenter. An examination of his methodology can crystallize the dimensions of the difference between his approach and that of mainstream development economics.

HIRSCHMAN VERSUS MAINSTREAM METHODOLOGY: VIVE LA DIFFÉRANCE!

Specific consideration of Hirschman's methodology serves two purposes: it isolates features of his method of inquiry which differ significantly from those of mainstream economics and it provides examples of insights which, in some cases, better explain social phenomena.

The formal methods utilized by mainstream economists produce models that are capable of yielding law-like statements. These formal laws are not empirical generalizations but are logical deductions that make *a priori* statements about necessary connections between abstract entities. Hirschman recognizes that formal methods often fail to explain the nature of social reality. Thus he has engaged in the task of developing his own explanation of social phenomena, the nature of which has ruled out other than incidental use of formal methods.

His approach looks behind such abstract variables of mainstream economics as savings, investment, competition, utility/profit maximization and efficiency to the attitudes and behaviours of real economic actors and to the institutional environment in which they must operate. He focuses on what in their circumstances leads people or firms to save or invest. For example, traditional growth theory talks about the effect on output of changes in capital/output ratios or saving rates. Hirschman wants to know what causes the mobilization of savings, capital and labour. Thus he is necessarily drawn to look at social, political and cultural factors as well as purely economic variables.

Hirschman's work has stimulated debate and research across a wide range of disciplines – sociology, political science and economics. How he has gone about researching questions, developing ideas and extracting conclusions from a lifetime of observation and reflection can tell a great deal about why he has had such a broad influence. We are interested not so much in what Hirschman wrote, although that certainly is important, as in how he constructed his particular explanations of social issues.

Hirschman as Participant-Observer

His exploratory method used in constructing explanations can best be described as participant-observer analysis. In the preface to *The Strategy of Economic Development* (1958b, p. v), he describes his role as a participant-observer:

> I was engaged primarily in an attempt to elucidate my own immediate experience in one of the so-called underdeveloped countries. In the course of this attempt, the various observations and reflections I gathered began to look more and more like a common theme. So I undertook to discover this theme and then used it in reinterpreting a variety of development problems.

The book distills the observations Hirschman made while working as a consultant to the Colombian government in 1952–6. He went to Colombia as a relative newcomer to the field of Third World economic development, though he had six years' (1946–52) experience working on the reconstruction of Europe for the Federal Reserve Board. As he says in the World Bank retrospective (1986, p. 5):

When I returned to the U.S. after four and a half years' intensive experience as
an official adviser and private consultant, I began to read up on the literature and
discovered I had acquired a point of view of my own that was considerably at
odds with current doctrines.

In describing his approach to observing Colombian development patterns
Hirschman relates (p. 8) that:

my instinct was to try to understand better *their* patterns of action, rather than
assume from the outset that they could be 'developed' only by importing a set of
techniques that they knew nothing about.

In addition to Hirschman's obvious reluctance to impose on to Colombia
ideas and norms from outside, he claimed that his purpose as an observer of
Colombian development experience was to 'look for elements and processes
of the Colombian reality that *did* work, perhaps in a roundabout and unappreciated fashion' (p. 9). In research for *Development Projects Observed*
(1967) Hirschman steeped himself in the experiences of 11 projects in Asia,
Africa and Latin America, and first allowed the projects to impress upon him
the themes or lessons of each particular success and failure.

To the participant-observer, the importance of a theme depends on the
number of connections it has with other themes, because the ultimate end is
the construction of a model which emphasizes the interconnectedness or
unity of the system. Thus, loyalty becomes an important theme because the
presence of loyalty makes exit less likely and gives scope to voice. It is the
connection between loyalty, voice and exit that makes the theme more important and relevant to the observer's analysis.

Hirschman constructs tentative hypotheses about the system out of the
recurrent themes that become obvious to him in the course of his participa-
tion-observation. The themes are then woven into a complex, multidimensional story which includes some generalizations from observed experience.
For example, in *Development Projects Observed*, he constructs hypotheses
about the importance of latitudes or 'the characteristic that permits project
planners and operators to mold a project' (1967, p. 86).

Instead of looking at these decisions from the point of view of the 'objective'
analyst and his optimizing techniques, our inquiry shall deal with the propensities
and pressures to which decision-makers themselves are subject. (1967, p. 87)

In his detailed examination of why Nigerian railroads failed to respond to
competition from highways, he attributed the problem, at least partially, to the
latitude for poor performance permitted by the existence of an alternative
method of transport, a theme which had been found in his observations. This

particular theme is picked up later in *Exit, Voice, and Loyalty* (1970) to provide an explanation for the special difficulties in combining exit and voice.

Hirschman evaluates an hypothesis or interpretation by means of a process of cross-checking different kinds and sources of evidence for their consistency with the themes. One form of this contextual validation occurs
when his earlier themes are elaborated on and expanded in later works. In
fact, *Essays in Trespassing* (1981) is organized in thematic categories based
on previous work, and as one reads the studies chronologically a remarkable
thread of consistency runs throughout. Exit and voice are applied in different
contexts, the elements of unbalanced growth are extended, and backward
and forward linkage are expanded to include consumption and fiscal linkages.[1]

Hirschman identifies 'technological alienness' and other compelling technical characteristics as additional key variables in the linkage 'hypothesis'.
This example is important in showing how Hirschman altered his original
linkage idea and expanded it to a more generalized approach. Contextual
validation serves as a means of cross-checking different kinds and sources of
evidence, and serves as an indirect means of evaluating the plausibility of
one's initial interpretations. The technique can never produce the rigorous
'certainty' espoused by formalists; it can only indicate varying degrees of
plausibility. In addition, a test of a particular theme at the initial stages can
never be conclusive, since later tests are likely to catch errors that were
missed earlier. Consequently, Hirschman's later reflections on exit and voice
reminded him that the costs of voice (that is, in time and effort) can quickly
turn into a benefit and become a 'sought-after, fulfilling activity' (1981, p.
215).

Certainly a weakness in Hirschman's work is the failure to specify in
detail the process of contextual validation. Often a reader is left with the
feeling that his 'themes and patterns' were not subjected to extensive cross-
checking of different types and sources of evidence.

The Structure of Hirschman's Explanations

His work is further distinguished by the structure of its explanations. To use
Abraham Kaplan's terminology, the structure of explanation is concatenated
(linked together) rather than hierarchical, as in formal theories. Several
relatively independent parts are linked together in composing his explanations, rather than being logically deduced as hypotheses from a formal
theory. A concatenated explanation with its relatively independent subsections
provides a many-sided, complex picture of the subject matter, and much of
Hirschman's earlier work appears to be composed this way. The theory of
unbalanced growth, for example, links together clearly identified themes
such as the scarce resource of 'genuine decision-making', imbalances on the

supply side, bottlenecks, balance of payments disequilibria and demand imbalances, and combines these themes to form a theory of development characterized by unbalanced growth.

Hirschman steps further outside the discipline of economics and links market forces to nonmarket forces in the unbalanced growth process, contrasting his view to that of classical economics (1958b, p. 63):

> Tradition seems to require that economists argue forever about the question whether, in any disequilibrium situation, market forces acting alone are likely to restore equilibrium ... As social scientists we surely must address ourselves to the broader question, is the disequilibrium situation likely to be corrected at all? It is our contention that nonmarket forces are not necessarily less 'automatic' than market forces.

Here, Hirschman has not only linked together economic phenomena but has also connected those economic forces to broader societal concerns and has created a coherent, multidimensional view of the development process.

Hirschman's Holistic Approach

For Hirschman there is an interconnectedness of the elements that make up an economic system with the political and social context in which they function. This vision of the social world is essentially 'holistic' – in place of abstracting a part from the whole for individual study, the relation of the parts to each other and to the whole is the focus of study. When he investigates the development of Brazil's north-east, land reform in Colombia and inflation in Chile he does so, not with the tools of traditional micro and macro economics but through a detailed discussion of each country's historical, political and economic situation. Within that context, Hirschman analyses the particular role of public policy in order 'to learn something about the problem solving capabilities of public authorities in Latin America' (1963, p. 1).

Hirschman has criticized the application of 'economic laws' which were discovered in a developed-country context to problems in the developing world. Traces of this rejection of universally applied laws can be found in his earliest works, in which he questions the applicability of the then new macro growth models of Harrod–Domar to the less-developed world: 'theories which, because of their high level of abstraction, [may] look perfectly "neutral" as between one kind of economic system and another, often are primarily relevant to the conditions under which they are conceived' (1958b, p. 29). As a result he suggests that 'the economics of development dare not borrow too extensively from the economics of growth ... it must work out its own abstractions' (1958b, p. 33).

In the remaining chapters of *Strategy* Hirschman does just that: he works out his own abstractions about the development process which are not based on general laws but centre more on the interrelations of the many aspects of development in an entire social system. Thus, backward and forward linkages are identified as important elements of dynamic development processes that proceed in sequences or spurts of growth activity. The focus of his schema is not on macroeconomic variables but on imbalances that exist in the society and the way in which they operate to energize human action in a certain direction. The forces of development are not those that have been identified by 'monoeconomic theory' (that is, savings rates, capital/output ratios and the like) but are powerful stimuli, such as mechanisms to induce investment, 'pacing devices', imbalances in supply and demand, and important social side effects of the creative role of imports in the development process.

The insights in this work are only possible through a method that rejects a rigid, disciplinary approach to development, based on universal laws, and proceeds by identifying the dynamics of development in a pattern that characterizes the ongoing processes of change in the whole society. A crucial element is the concept of interrelationship or unity. In *Exit, Voice, and Loyalty* (1970), Hirschman observes the economist's neglect of the role of voice, typically associated only with politics, in response to the decline in quality of a firm's product, and he notes a similar neglect of exit (that is, ability to leave) in the realm of politics. Analysis of the role of voice and exit in relation to the economy as well as to the body politic is undertaken, and Hirschman argues that the incorporation of both into a unified treatment of the political–economic system is vital to improving our understanding.

Some of the policy conclusions which are reached based on this unified analysis are quite striking, and run contrary to traditional economic prescriptions derived from general laws. Breaking up monopolies may not result in greater efficiency because such action could tend to reduce the role of voice in improving the firm's performance (1970, ch. 5). The consumers who exit are likely to be the ones who would ordinarily exercise the loudest voice and prompt improvement of the firm's product. In this example we see a result that runs counter to traditional economic wisdom. Analyses that run counter to 'traditional economic wisdom', we might add, are Hirschman's speciality!

Hirschman argues that it is inappropriate to take parts of an interdependent system out of context, and indeed, that such an approach leads to erroneous conclusions. For example, Milton Friedman's voucher plan for education, whereby private schools compete with public education, disregards the role of voice in the performance of public education. Hirschman maintains that the first to leave public education under such a system, at the first sign of quality decline, may be those who have the strongest voice in improving the schools' quality. Thus, the plight of public education and the good of the general public may not be served by greater competition. The neglect of the role of voice in this case is the culprit. The whole has been broken up into its parts, and as a result the policy conclusions are questionable.

HIRSCHMAN AS A GENERAL SOCIAL THEORIST

We now turn our attention to how Hirschman builds a more general theoretical model from particular observations and hypotheses which have been tested contextually. This type of model is constructed by linking validated themes into a network or pattern and the theorist's account of a particular part refers to the multiplicity of connections between that part and the whole system. In this way the investigator attempts to capture the interactive relationship between the part and the whole system.

As the model is constructed, earlier descriptions of the parts are continually tested by how well they fit together in a pattern and how new evidence can be explained within the pattern (Wilber and Harrison, 1978).

For example, the pattern developed by Hirschman in *Strategy of Economic Development* (1958b) was the basis for an analysis of import substitution undertaken more than ten years after initial publication. In the process he obtained a finer and finer degree of coherence between his account of the system as a pattern of interconnected parts and the real system. However, since new data and observations are constantly evolving, the model must be continually revised and can neither be completed nor rigorously confirmed.

Looking at the historical evolution of Hirschman's writing one can see this process at work. The themes elaborated in *Strategy of Economic Development* show up continually in later works, sometimes in slightly revised form. An observation and its accompanying theme in early works can be the takeoff point for an entire book, as the Nigerian railway experience was the basis of *Exit, Voice and Loyalty* (1970). Indeed, this is one of two 'social theories' which Hirschman has developed and which have provided the framework for many others' work on social theory.

Exit, Voice and Loyalty: A New Social Theory

In *Development Projects Observed* (1967) Hirschman tried to explain why the Nigerian railways had performed so poorly in competition with road transport even for low-value, bulky cargo on long hauls, in which the railways have a comparative advantage. He was specifically interested in the apparent inability of railway management to correct its most glaring inefficiencies, despite the fact that they were losing customers to the haulage industry. He proposed the following explanation (1967, pp. 146–7):

The presence of a ready alternative to rail transport makes it less, rather than more, likely that the weaknesses of the railways will be fought rather than indulged. With truck and bus transportation available, a deterioration in rail service is not nearly so serious a matter as if the railways held a monopoly for long-distance transport – it can be lived with for a long time without arousing strong public pressures for the basic and politically difficult or even explosive reforms in administration and management that would be required. This may be the reason public enterprise, not only in Nigeria but in many other countries, has strangely been at its weakest in sectors such as transportation and education where it is subjected to competition: instead of stimulating improved or top performance, the presence of a ready and satisfactory substitute for the services public enterprise offers merely deprives it of a precious feedback mechanism that operates at its best when the customers are securely locked in. For the management of public enterprise, always fairly confident that it will not be let down by the national treasury, may be less sensitive to the loss of revenue due to the switch of customers to a competing mode than to the protests of an aroused public that has a vital stake in the service, has no alternative, and therefore will 'raise hell'.

A reviewer objected to the paragraph claiming that hidden assumptions were necessary for Hirschman to arrive at that conclusion. Hirschman decided to 'pursue these assumptions into their hiding places' (1970, p. vii). He found that the explanation for the Nigerian experience could be generalized and he developed that generalization into 'a manner of analyzing certain economic processes which promised to illuminate a wide range of social, political, and indeed moral phenomena' (1970), p. vii).

Hirschman has used the resulting exit–voice–loyalty model to analyse both political and economic phenomena. Exit has traditionally been associated with economics and voice with politics. Exit means to withdraw from a relationship with a person or organization – to quit working for a particular employer, to stop buying a particular product, to stop buying an input such as steel from a particular supplier. Withdrawal from a relationship is facilitated by the existence of alternatives and economists usually see these alternatives as provided by competitive markets. Exit provides signals to the other party in the relationship that something is wrong. However, exit by itself gives little information about what is wrong.

Voice is traditionally associated with politics and has been ignored by economists. An alternative to quitting a relationship when there is dissatisfaction is to voice the complaint to the other party, which provides more information as to what is wrong. Voice becomes more important as exit becomes more difficult. This is the case for families, ethnic and religious communities and the nation. Also it is the case of those long-term relationships that one enters – husband/wife, student, member of a political party, employee of a firm.

While exit is cheap when markets provide alternatives, voice is always expensive. Exit means to withdraw from a situation, person or organization, and depends on the availability of choice, competition and well-functioning markets. It is usually inexpensive and easy to buy or not, sell or not, and hire or fire on your own. Voice means to communicate explicitly your concern to another individual or organization. The cost to an individual in terms of time and effort to persuade, argue and negotiate will often exceed any prospective individual benefit.[2]

In addition, the potential success of individual voices frequently depends on the possibility of all members joining together for collective action. This presents the 'free-rider' problem; if people cannot be excluded from the benefits of collective action, they have no incentive to join the group.

The problem is further complicated by the possibility that what started as a simply self-interested or even benevolent relationship will become malevolent. Face-to-face strategic bargaining may irritate the parties involved if others are perceived as violating the spirit of fair play. This can result in a response of hatred rather than mere selfishness. Collective action is unlikely if the members of the group are hateful and distrustful of one another.

Despite these problems, voice plays an important role in the economy as well as the political system, and voice has grown along with the rights of dissent and due process. Trade unions, consumer protection groups, consumer unions have all increased the importance of voice.

In addition, the presence of loyalty – to employer, to a product, to a supplier – strengthens the role of voice. When the economic view of people as calculating self-interested maximizers is broadened to include 'the pursuit of truth, beauty, justice, liberty, community, friendship, love, salvation, and so on' (1986, p. 149), loyalty and voice can no longer be ignored. Thus consumers out of loyalty will continue to patronize a store in the face of falling quality, and will voice their concerns in the hope of improvement, before giving up and exiting. Firms understand this and cultivate loyalty to their products. Also they seek to hear voice through market surveys of consumer attitudes toward their products.

Hirschman and many others have applied the exit–voice model to a number of different situations.[3] A fruitful application is in Freeman and Medoff's book *What Do Unions Do?* (1984). Traditional economics views unions as monopsonies that raise wages of unionized workers above the competitive level at the expense of the unemployment of non-unionized workers. However, in the exit–voice model, the collective voice provided by the union channels information to employers about workers' grievances and desires. This voice is more efficient than exit by individual workers because it provides the employer with more information. This reduces labour turnover – exit – which reduces search and training costs and thus increases labour productivity. Also if the employer responds to the workers' complaints and accepts union-negotiated fringe benefits, grievance procedures, seniority and working conditions, it is likely that employee shirking with its attendant supervision costs can be reduced.

The second more general social theory which Hirschman developed grew out of his attempts to understand human behaviour, especially when it seemed irrational and self-destructive.

The Passions and the Interests: An Enhanced Theory of Human Behaviour

Hirschman again captured the interaction between the parts and the whole in *The Passions and the Interests* (1977b) and in *Shifting Involvements* (1982b). In the former work he synthesized the thought of previous writers such as Adam Smith, John Calvin, James Steuart, Thomas Hobbes and Bernard Mandeville. Upon this foundation he built a theory of human behaviour that enriches the dominant self-interest view of human action by providing a role for the passions. The passions and the interests were seen as two counteracting forces, one of which may predominate over the other at different times. In *Shifting Involvements* he analysed the role that disappointment plays in shifting collective behaviour between 'concern with public affairs and the pursuit of a better life for oneself and one's family' (p. 7). This theme was also part of his *Essays in Trespassing* (1981) where in Chapter 5 he examined the 'turn to authoritarianism in Latin America'. The hope of Latin Americans was much like that of the seventeenth- and eighteenth-century philosophers and political economists, a hope that 'an expanding and industrialized economy would discipline the excesses of power-seeking and passionate politics in general' (1981, p. 100). But in reality the privileged position that the 'modern economy' was given led to a justification of despotism, exactly what was to be avoided. As mentioned earlier, that the economy *must be deferred to* meant that there was a case for constraining the actions of the ruler *or* for repressing those of the people. In Latin America in the 1970s the smooth functioning of the economy took precedence over the demands of individual citizens or social classes.

Hirschman used the concept of disappointment to analyse the experience of the many popular movements in Latin America. As promised economic improvements failed to bring the expected increases in welfare, the people's focus turned from private gain to social action. The turn to social action may be further reinforced by the 'rebound effect' (1982b). As the confidence in the present government's ability to deliver improved welfare dissipated into disappointment, the promises of an alternative government become more appealing. The social action that results can often be expressed, as in Latin America, in the form of popular movements, revolutions or *coup d'états*, depending on the extent of the collective disappointment. In Hirschmanian terminology, disappointment results in exit from the private sphere into the public sphere. In this case not only is there exit, but exit is reinforced by voice as the population engages in action to make its disappointment known. In the process an ideology is formed that encourages social action to promote the common good.

Hirschman's thought in *The Passions and the Interests, Shifting Involvements,* 'Against Parsimony' in *Rival Visions* (1986) and scattered throughout his writings provides an enhanced picture of human behaviour in the social sphere. He questions the scientific pretensions of orthodox models: 'Could it be that the behavioral assumptions built into them proceed from an excessively simplistic image of both human nature and the social system?' (1981, pp. 287–8). His response to this question was to introduce a richer view of human behaviour. His analysis posits a person motivated not only by self-interest but also by passions. For example, in *Shifting Involvements* he demonstrated how disappointment is a key element in human behaviour and citizen activities. Disappointment stimulates us to change our focus from the public to the private sphere and vice versa.

Hirschman used this change in focus or shift in preference caused by disappointment to discuss the volatility of consumer preferences. He built on the work of Harry G. Frankfurt who proposed that it is a 'peculiar characteristic of humans ... to form second-order desires, wants, and volitions' (1982b, p. 69). That humans have this ability means that, in addition to first order desires for food, leisure, status and the like, they can reflectively self-evaluate their preferences and modify them. He extended Frankfurt's work by showing how disappointment may be a catalyst in changing our preferences about preferences.

He also introduced 'social facts' into the analysis. These affect the way that people, and society in general, behave. They are 'facts about human social institutions, like families or businesses, and facts about large aggregations of people, like social classes, religious groups, or even whole societies which have implications for behavioral patterns' (Rosenberg, 1988, p. 113). For example:

> [Each] time economic progress has enlarged the availability of consumer goods for some strata of society, strong feelings of disappointment in, or of hostility toward, the new material wealth have come to the fore. Along with appreciation, infatuation, and even addiction, affluence seems to produce its own backlash, almost regardless of what kinds of goods are newly and more abundantly marketed. (1982b, p. 46)

This passage captures many of the elements that make Hirschman a social scientist. Not only does he set the stage for a shift in preferences and allow for passions such as infatuation and for unchosen behaviour such as addiction, but he also places the subject within a 'social fact' such as society, thereby presenting us with a richer picture of the individual economic actor.

But the challenge to the prevailing model of economic behaviour goes further. He argues that individual behaviour is also shaped by values that transcend the narrow self-interest of the economic model. We must rethink our view of people as simply self-interested maximizers. Economists have made a major mistake in treating love, benevolence and particularly public spirit as scarce resources that must be economized lest they be depleted. The analogy is faulty because, unlike material factors of production, the supply of love, benevolence and public spirit is not fixed or limited. As Hirschman says (1986, p. 155): 'first of all, these are resources whose supply may well increase rather than decrease through use; second, these resources do not remain intact if they stay unused'. Of course, these moral resources are not inexhaustible, can be overused, and are not substitutes for self-interest, but complements. Up to a point they respond positively to practice, in a learning-by-doing manner, and negatively to non-practice.

Hirschman's portrayal of economic actors as more than self-interested maximizers places him within the broad intellectual movement in the social sciences that rejects that paradigm. His attempt to generalize from the facts of experience about the working of the economy as a whole and the role of human behaviour within it has resulted in a fruitful theory – exit, voice and loyalty. Traditional economists do not generalize from the facts of experience; rather, they attempt to construct models based on assumptions about how economic agents would behave if they acted rationally in their self-interest; this rationality is bounded by the competitive equilibrium model of economic theory. If one is interested primarily in how economic actors behave, in fact, Hirschman's approach may prove to be more fruitful.

HIRSCHMAN'S STRENGTHS AND WEAKNESSES

Of the 228 citations to Hirschman in 1988, only one was in the *American Economic Review*, one in the *Journal of Economic Literature* and only 30 others were in recognizably 'economics' journals, most of those in the development area. These data illustrate the strengths and weaknesses of his work.

As an economist his greatest weakness is the limited impact he has had on the field. His earlier technical work on the structure of world trade and on measures of dispersion has been forgotten, the use of linkages in input–output analysis and in choice of investments has been dismissed. His central development construct, unbalanced growth, won the battle against the balanced growth–big push theories; however, the war seems to have been won by their common enemy, orthodox *laissez-faire* economics. Perhaps there is a Gresham's Law of Economic Theory operating here; none the less, the end result is that economists do not learn and follow Hirschman, there is little 'normal science' ongoing in his tradition of economics.

There are two reasons that account for this marginal role. The first is methodological. Hirschman's approach is highly inductive and relies heavily upon his observation of social phenomena. It lends itself much less readily to replication, although one can fancifully conceive of training courses on Hirschmanian observation skills, financed by AID or the World Bank. This might ensure the creation of whole generations of Hirschman disciples and change the approach to economic policy.

Such an event is unlikely, given the second problem. At a fundamental level, Hirschman stands in opposition to one of the main dynamics of economics: the effort to discover regularities and mechanisms which can be used to exert control over the economy. From linear programming to monetary theory, the goal has been to control the direction of the economy. Hirschman's analysis implies that this can be done only imperfectly and with many surprises along the way, since social reality and human behaviour are far too complex. Nor is it clear that such control is desirable since it can easily distort and stifle the human energies and creativities that are essential for any real development. So his followers are relegated to the role of observers, attempting to understand processes that must unfold without their intervention. The best they can do is to stand on the side and to support and encourage the process of change, while maintaining their bias toward hope about its outcome.

And where should that bias for hope come from, why should it exist, and is change necessarily progress? Answers to these questions are fundamental, and a failure to address them has been a weakness in Hirschman's work. He has turned to them recently. His Tanner lectures critique the reactionary view that social change will lead to a worsening of the human condition. And an article in the *American Economic Review*, 'Having Opinions – One Element of Well-being?' (1989b) is one of his ventures into defining the elements of the good life, toward which social change should presumably move us.

This is little and late. Once it was realized that the dragon of backwardness could not be slain, and that the processes of social change could have very detrimental effects as well as the beneficial ones, certainly there was a necessity to re-examine the whole concept of development. And that process has occurred, though without Hirschman's participation (see Wilber and Jameson, 1991; Griffin, 1988). Hirschman has argued in *Shifting Involvements* (1982b, p. 8) that there are 'swings from private concerns to public action and back'. This holds out hope that a clearer understanding of the development process in all its dimensions may combine with the shift toward public action to restore development to the forefront of economic concerns. Along with that may come the courage to undertake those steps that may lead to the progress of human beings.

While Hirschman's influence within the economics profession has not been great, the same is not true in the broader area of social science and social theory. Perhaps a greater sense of humility opens the other social science disciplines to Hirschman's ideas. The remaining 198 citations were in journals from law, business ethics, political science, social science, sociology, economic history, social philosophy; and the list could go on. There is a fecundity to Hirschman's ideas that is rare in economics; and while he admits to trespassing into other disciplines, he seems to encourage reciprocal behaviour from others. Certainly *Exit, Voice, and Loyalty, Shifting Involvements*, and *The Passions and the Interests* are alive and well in history, political science and philosophy.

So in the last analysis, Hirschman has greater strength as a social scientist than as an economist, at least as the discipline defines itself. When looked at from the perspective of the methodology of social science and of the philosophy of social science, he may indeed be successful as an economist and seeker of truth; the problem is with those who would not follow him.

In any case he has been, and no doubt will continue to be, the eternal heretic, casting doubt upon our discovered 'truths' and presenting his unique interpretation of society, exciting some, inciting others, but always 'trespassing' on other disciplines, and in the process stimulating many of us to carry on with what he calls the 'passion for the possible'.

NOTES

* We would like to thank Solomon Namala of the University of Utah for his assistance in the early stages of the project and Ginger Head of the University of Utah and Steven Brinks of the University of Notre Dame for their help on the final manuscript.

1. See Hirschman, 'Further Reflections on Exit, Voice, and Loyalty' in (1981) and Exit and Voice: An Expanding Sphere of Influence' in (1986, pp. 64–6); 'A Generalized Linkage Approach to Development, with Special Reference to Staples' in (1981).
2. Exit is more difficult in Japan where the Confucian tradition is more binding. As a result, with much greater emphasis on harmony and consensus at all levels, voice is more appreciated and cultivated.
3. See Pierre Bourdieu, 'An Antinomy in the Notion of Collective Protest'; Carol Gilligan, 'Exit–Voice Dilemmas in Adolescent Development'; Guillermo O'Donnell, 'On the Fruitful Convergences of Hirschman's *Exit, Voice, and Loyalty* and *Shifting Involvements*: Reflections from the Recent Argentine Experience'; Rebecca J. Scott, 'Dismantling Repressive Systems; the Abolition of Slavery in Cuba as a Case Study', all in *Development, Democracy, and the Art of Trespassing: Essays in Honor of Albert O. Hirschman*, ed. Alejandro Foxley, Michael S. McPherson and Guillermo O'Donnell, Notre Dame, Ind.: University of Notre Dame Press, 1986. See also the following, cited in Hirschman

(1986), pp. 99–101: Freek Bruinsma, 'The (Non-) Assertion of Welfare Rights: Hirschman's Theory Applied', *Acta Politica*, no. 3 (1980); Lena Kolarska and Howard Aldrich, 'Exit, Voice, and Silence: Consumers' and Managers' Responses to Organizational Decline', *Organizational Studies*, no. 1 (1980); Jean Laponce, 'Hirschman's Voice and Exit Model as a Spatial Archetype', *Social Science Information*, no. 3 (1974); Carl M. Stevens, 'Voice in Medical Markets: "Consumer"', *Social Science Information*, no. 3 (1974).

REFERENCES

Albert O. Hirschman Bibliography

Albert O. Hirschman (1943), 'On Measures of Dispersion for a Finite Distribution', *Journal of the American Statistical Association*, **38**, (223), 346–57.

—— (1945), *National Power and the Structure of Foreign Trade*, Berkeley, Cal.: University of California Press.

—— (1957), 'Investment Policies and "Dualism" in Underdeveloped Countries', *American Economic Review*, **47**, (5), 550–70.

—— (1958a), 'Investment Criteria and Capital Intensity Once Again', *Quarterly Journal of Economics*, **72**, (3), 469–71 (with Gerald Sirkin).

—— (1958b), *The Strategy of Economic Development*, New Haven, Conn.: Yale University Press.

—— (1963), *Journeys Toward Progress: Studies of Economic Policy Making in Latin America*, Twentieth Century Fund.

—— (1967), *Development Projects Observed*, Washington, D.C.: Brookings Institution.

—— (1970), *Exit, Voice, and Loyalty: Responses to Decline in Firms, Organizations, and States*, Cambridge, Mass.: Harvard University Press.

—— (1971), *A Bias for Hope: Essays on Development and Latin America*, New Haven, Conn.: Yale University Press.

—— (1977a), 'A Generalized Linkage Approach to Development, with Special Reference to Staples', *Economic Development and Cultural Change*, **25**, Supplement; reprinted in *Essays* (1981).

—— (1977b), *The Passions and the Interests: Political Arguments for Capitalism before its Triumph*, Princeton, N.J.: Princeton University Press.

—— (1979), 'The Turn to Authoritarianism in Latin America and the Search for its Economic Determinants', in David Collier (ed.), *The New Authoritarianism in Latin America*, Princeton, N.J.: Princeton University Press; reprinted in *Essays* (1981).

—— (1981), *Essays in Trespassing: Economics to Politics and Beyond*, Cambridge: Cambridge University Press.

—— (1982a), 'The Rise and Decline of Development Economics', in Mark Gersovitz *et al.* (eds), *The Theory and Experience of Economic Development: Essays in Honor of Sir W. Arthur Lewis*, London: Allen & Unwin; reprinted in *Essays* (1981).

—— (1982b), *Shifting Involvements: Private Interest and Public Action*, Princeton, N.J.: Princeton University Press.

—— (1983), 'The Principle of Conservation and Mutation of Social Energy', *Grassroots Development* (Journal of the Inter-American Foundation), **7**, 42–4.

—— (1984a), 'A Dissenters Confession: Revisiting the Strategy of Economic Development', in Gerald M. Meier and Dudley Seers (eds), *Pioneers in Development*, Oxford: Oxford University Press, 1984; reprinted in *Rival Visions* (1986).

—— (1984b), *Getting Ahead Collectively: Grassroots Experiences in Latin America*, New York: Pergamon Press.

—— (1986), *Rival Visions of Market Society and Other Recent Essays*, New York: Viking Penguin.

——(1987), *The New Palgrave: A Dictionary of Economics*, London: Macmillan, entries for: 'Exit and Voice'; 'Interests'; 'Linkages'; 'Jean-Gustave Courcelle-Seneuil (1813–92)'; reprinted in *Rival Visions* (1986).

—— (1989a), 'Two Hundred Years of Reactionary Rhetoric: the Case of the Perverse Effect', *Tanner Lectures in Human Values*, vol. 10, Salt Lake City: University of Utah Press, pp. 3–31.

—— (1989b), 'Having Opinions – One of the Elements of Well-Being?' *American Economic Review*, **79**, (2), 75–9.

—— (1990), 'The Case Against "One Thing at a Time" ', *World Development*, **18**, (8), 1119–22.

Other References

Freeman, Richard and James L. Medoff (1984), *What Do Unions Do?*, New York: Basic Books.

Griffin, David Ray (ed.) (1988), *Spirituality and Society: Postmodern Visions*, Albany, N.Y.: State University of New York Press.

Rosenberg, Alexander (1988), *Philosophy of Social Science*, Boulder, Cal.: Westview Press.

Sohn, Ira (ed.) (1986), *Readings in Input–Output Analysis*, Oxford and New York: Oxford University Press.

Wilber, Charles K. and Robert Harrison (1978), 'The Methodological Basis of Institutional Economics: Pattern Model, Storytelling and Holism', *Journal of Economic Issues*, **12**, (1), 61–89.

Wilber, Charles K. and Kenneth P. Jameson (1991), *The Political Economy of Development and Underdevelopment*, 5th ed, New York: McGraw-Hill.

6.   Janos Kornai

Béla Csikós-Nagy

KORNAI'S SCHOLARLY ACTIVITIES AND BACKGROUND

At the end of the Second World War, during Janos Kornai's youth, the Soviet occupation and the communist takeover of Hungary was completed. Kornai was not yet 20 years old when he was appointed to the *Szabad Nep*, the official daily news organ of the Communist Party. He was assigned to organizational duties and public relations tasks. From such a vantage point he quickly discovered the built-in contradictions and paradoxical features endemic to the Soviet type of centrally planned economic systems. By 1955 he had had his fill of journalism and opted out.

He resolved to devote his life to scientific research and was curious to investigate why centrally planned systems malfunction and how improvements in the plan could correct their sub-par operations. Under communist rule such an inquiry requires the shield of a protective institutional umbrella. He joined the Institute of Economics, the economics research division of the Hungarian Academy of Sciences.

In 1959 Oxford University Press published his first critical book on the Soviet type of planning in the West, *Over-Centralization in Economic Administration*. This work launched Kornai overnight into the limelight of international acclaim. His celebrity status was further enhanced by the havoc and angry denunciation the Hungarian publication evoked among the communist officialdom. Western experts generally believed that such an unfavourable Hungarian backlash was mainly indicative of Kornai exposing the soft underbelly of the Soviet type of central planning system. In a normative sense in the West there was a certain understanding of how such a planning system should work; Kornai explained retrospectively why the system did not.

The rage fuelled by its publication in his home country had a bizarre undertone. As early as 1956 a specially commissioned economic committee was created by the authorities and charged with making recommendations to restore the rate of economic growth and to move the economy out of stale-mate. The report of this committee almost paralleled Kornai's later publica-tion. It has to be mentioned that Kornai wrote the manuscript of *Over-Cen-tralization in Economic Administration*, which was his 'candidate thesis' (the East European equivalent of a PhD thesis) in 1955–6. The manuscript was widely circulated in Hungary in the summer of 1956, that is, before the revolution. The late Istvan Varga, who in 1957 became the chairman of the blue ribbon committee was much impressed and learned many aspects about the operation of a command economy from this work. The substantive dif-ference between these two reports was the publicity generated. In the com-mittee report, their recommendations were shelved; whereas Kornai's work by letting the cat out of the bag brought the problem into international focus.

In 1956 the popular Hungarian uprising toppled the orthodox communist Rakosi regime, and then the Russian armed intervention installed another communist regime under Janos Kadar. Initially, the Kadar government had a weak foothold and lacked practically all but minimal support. But by 1958–9 the leadership felt it had turned the tide and started to flex its muscles. The time had come for the communists to settle old scores and discipline their adversaries. Kornai, in the process of this house-cleaning, was dismissed from his job at the Academy of Sciences. He was kept out of circulation till 1963. Then, badly in need of his expertise, the Institute of Economics reap-pointed him. From then on his success was witnessed by the books, articles and hundreds of pamphlets published and by the worldwide acclaim his work received. His personal résumé is attached in Appendix I, and his most distinguished works are listed in Appendix II.

To place Kornai's work in proper historic perspective, one has to be familiar with the state of economic theory which prevailed at the time when Kornai initially entered into his scholarly investigation. The history of the early socialist economic efforts in the USSR, from the October revolution on, was well documented. The economy and some of its shortcomings were subject to heated debates among contemporary Russian economists. The great industrialization debates of the pre-quintennial plans of the 1920s have since moved into the classics of economic annals. Even today Western students of comparative systems are exposed to their deliberations. Eco-nomic policy in the USSR was subject to constant critical review by those licensed to criticize. It was a tricky license with shifting parameters, as witnessed decades later by Kornai's personal experience.

Novozhilov explored profoundly the situation which prevailed in the Soviet Union's economy in the period of transition from war communism to the new economic policy. The policy pursued had been one of low prices adapted to the level of wages paid for the production of the goods con-cerned. These prices had a very slight effect on the realization of any net social income. Those responsible for price policy in that period strove to open up the market for workers in the lower income brackets. In his analysis of the situation Novozhilov found that the policy of low prices has a similar effect to that of inflation, replacing price rises by an increasingly acute scarcity of goods. He termed this situation 'credit inflation'.

When studying the restrictive economy during the Second World War, Western economists revived the discussion which had taken place in the Soviet Union in the 1920s. The difference lies only in the terminology: 'inflationary gap' was substituted for 'commodity shortage' and 'credit inflation' was replaced by the term 'repressed inflation'. Repressed inflation is manifested in disguised price rises, forced purchases and forced savings. These manifestations exist even today in the economies of socialist societies, as a consequence of the fact that excess demand has been institutionally integrated into the economies of most of them. Economists in socialist countries refer time and again to the presence of inflationary pressure, though they generally avoid using the term 'inflation'. We meet with the following designations: sellers' market, disguised price rise, delayed demand, unsatisfied demand, non-voluntary savings, and so on.[1]

Kornai, entering into his investigation, had access to comprehensive data and literature on the nature and operation of the socialist economy. He was intrigued by the causative aspects of shortages and the multi-spectral nature of their manifestation. But sheer diagnosis did not suffice for his analytical mind. He felt compelled to penetrate beyond the diagnostic stage of observation into the causes which germinate into such malfunctions. He became fascinated by the mounting criticism of the General Equilibrium Theory of market economies, and wholeheartedly joined the foray by analysing two different interpretations: the 'reformist' and the 'revolutionary' approaches. The 'reformist' approach he believed is characterized by modifying one, two or three basic assumptions of the General Equilibrium Theory, while leaving other assumptions intact. The 'revolutionary' approach discards or neglects the traditional theory in its entirety, as shown in Kornai's original work (1971, pp. 363–4):

> These activities are directed toward improving equilibrium theory, without discarding its bases. This work is being performed by the initiators, pioneers of the modern general equilibrium theory and their disciples. Their intention is to retain as many of the results of the equilibrium school as is possible, thus maintaining its traditions and authority; on the other hand, in order to render it more efficient ... they try to relax the strong assumptions and exchange the unrealistic assumptions for more realistic ones. The other main current is 'revolutionary'; it either discards the equilibrium theory, sharply criticizing some of its features, or simply neglects equilibrium theory without argument, simply pushing it aside and starting novel investigations quite independent of the equilibrium theory.

In his celebrated study *Anti-Equilibrium* he moves into a more detailed analysis of the 'revolutionary' approach. His basic assumption radiates a firm belief that the theories and approaches he analysed pertaining to the General Equilibrium Theory only represent a partial equilibrium. None of the solutions (referred to by Kornai as fragmented) incorporated into the General Theory qualify for the consideration of an all-embracing comprehensive theory of economic systems. This even applies to some part of his earlier work on *Anti-Equilibrium* which he felt necessary to amend in his successive treatise in the *Economics of Shortage* (1980). This he considers part of the routine shake-out process, which is why he believes one discovers hardly any supporting or opposing arguments in the General Theory which have no precedent in some other earlier work. His intention was to move the theory one step ahead collating fragmented arguments of various treatises into one single all-embracing body and correlating them into a 'super'-system. It should be stressed that in his work *Anti-Equilibrium* he moved far beyond the initial framework he set out for himself. It is not merely the socialist economy which is scrutinized under its analysis but the economic discipline as a whole. It is viewed as an embracing heuristic super-model built to sort out those conditions which are pertinent in developing the acme of a perceptual instrument, whose theoretical framework is easily adaptable to everyday life.

Kornai is frequently short-changed by his peers, who limit his major contribution to his *Economics of Shortage* as an inherent characteristic of socialist economies, together with his reasoning developed on 'soft budget constraints'. These indeed are powerful ideas but also merely elements in a complex system which identify and point towards additional unmonitored observations behind the shortages in a socialist economy.

The preceding comments may carry an element of surprise that in addition to his acclaimed contributions, his close associates and readers have discovered and fine-tuned into some of his remote reverberations allusions to further dimensions of analysis.

I don't think it is hyperbolic when we acknowledge that the sophistication of Kornai's ideas generated in his seminal work *Anti-Equilibrium* placed him among the truly distinguished theorists of our time.

CRITICISM OF THE GENERAL EQUILIBRIUM THEORY

On an international level it was Malinvaud who recognized Kornai's outstanding contributions in the development of economic thought. He believed that Kornai was bold enough to demolish the entire structure of accepted theory and to search for new grounds on which a 'real' theory of economics, compatible with practical life, could be established.[2] This is a cardinal point in Kornai's reasoning. He became frustrated by the lag he complains exists between economics and the natural sciences, which was particularly depressing when the comparison was narrowed down to economics and physics. But let him voice his views (1971, p. 360):

> Physics has acted in a pressing way to the concept of economic thought not only with the example of its maturity but also directly, with the formulation of its questions, and its mathematical apparatus. At the time when Cournot, Walras and Pareto were active, classical mechanics was the brilliant star of natural sciences: it was from classical mechanics that economics took over a whole series of notions and formulation, as the equilibrium of opposing forces, stability, static and dynamic equilibrium and so on. Economics also borrowed from the same place the whole mathematical formalism of differential and integral calculus.
>
> Since then other formalized branches of physics have adopted classical mechanics (partly amalgamating classical Newtonian mechanics); also other formalized natural sciences have appeared. But the general equilibrium school has not been able as yet to free itself from the spell of classical mechanics.
>
> The narrow mathematical apparatus used in economics is also related to the above. It is true that economics applies not only calculus but also linear algebra, theory of sets, and probability theory. Last but not least, it was precisely at the urging of economists that mathematical programming, and the theory of games and decision theory have developed into more or less autonomous branches of mathematics. But even if taken together these are but a few fields from the much broader science of mathematics. Application of other mathematical disciplines is entirely sporadic. ... Economics must break away from the narrow framework of its present mathematical apparatus. It seems according to Kornai this will be achieved only with the cooperation of professional mathematicians who are well versed in many branches of mathematics.

To clarify Kornai's views let's juxtapose them with those who believe that economics is now in a state similar to that of physics at the turn of the century. We already have a 'classical physics': the general equilibrium theory. Now we must create the 'modern physics' of economics, which would have more general validity but would comprise – as a special case – our classical physics, the general equilibrium theory. He believes that the simile does not hold. The laws of classical Newtonian physics are a very good approximation of an extremely wide field of phenomena in the material world – for bodies moving considerably slower than light and consisting of many atoms. True, the new physics, the beginnings of which are present in the elaboration of Einstein's special theory of relativity, covers a much more general field; but – within its own scope – Newtonian physics is still valid. One can read in *Anti-Equilibrium* (p. 363):

> We could be quite satisfied if we had attained the situation in our discipline that had been attained in physics before 1905. But the situation is different. ... The

general equilibrium school cannot be accepted as verified real-science theory, or if it has any real science content, it covers but a small field. Each of its assumptions is very special, and combined they can explain a class of phenomena comprising an even smaller, narrower field.

Analysing Kornai's treatise in detail, we start our summation by a Walrasian equilibrium, in Pareto optimum and by price theory as presented by Böhm-Bawerk, where:

1. The Walrasian equilibrium means a perfect market clearing function of prices. There is no shortage nor slack; supply is fully equated with demand.
2. Pareto optimum prevails when there is no necessity (reason) for change, because you can no longer make everyone better off. 'You can help Joe only by hurting Tom.'
3. Böhm-Bawerk's interpretation of price theory correlates the market with economic policy. The state is free to influence the supply and demand but should not constrain the automatic price mechanism, as prices give signals for rational economic behaviour.

Kornai uniformly rejects the Walrasian equilibrium, Pareto optimum and Böhm-Bawerk's price theory.

If we leave the world of models to enter into reality, we can recognize, according to Kornai, that there does not exist an economic system with a Walrasian equilibrium as its normal state. Every system – not only in its instantaneous fluctuations but in its intertemporal average as well – departs from the strict Walrasian equilibrium. It is, however, highly characteristic of any existing system how, in which direction and how far its normal state deviates from the Walrasian equilibrium. To the narrow concept (Walrasian equilibrium) the world 'equilibrium' is connected with a value judgement. If a system is not in equilibrium it is 'bad'. This is, of course, related to the problem already mentioned. It is considered obvious that equilibrium means Walrasian equilibrium, and any state in which supply does not satisfy demand is disapproved of.

Equilibrium in the broad sense (that is to say, a normal state) in Kornai's interpretations, is a *descriptive* category in social science. We neither praise nor condemn a system by saying that it is in equilibrium, that is 'normal'. In addition, this statement does not imply that the members of the system in question, or even the majority of them, are satisfied with the system. A social system may be in equilibrium even if a large number of its citizens are dissatisfied – but they are dissatisfied for different reasons, and so their actions have opposing effects. An equilibrium establishes itself if these opposing forces counteract each other; even though some internal tension persists, an enduring compromise develops in actual conduct (see 1980, pp. 144, 145).

And what about the price law? According to his view, the role of physical (non-price) indices are rather important in the mechanism of decision-making. The explanation of consumer demand is restricted too much to the examination of price and income effects. This corresponds to the view of the general equilibrium school – but, in general, reality is more complicated. The effect of prices and income is great indeed, but there are also other, important explanatory variables; information of a non-price character has its influence too. Some examples are:

- Imitation, fashion, following the lead of reference groups;
- Continuous restratification of the pattern of consumption in favour of *new* products at the expense of the old ones;
- Consumer behaviour as a function of social position, e.g., the effect of urbanization or the development of suburbs.

In the same way, according to his judgement, there are very few empirical observations available regarding the demand functions of firms. The explanation of changes in the input pattern of production which relies exclusively on prices is a poor one. Changes in factor combinations are explained, in the final analysis, by changes in the volume of available resources, and in this relation by processes of technical progress. To a certain extent, technical progress has a life of its own. Information of a price character reflects more or less these real changes, and also the lags in adaptation to those real changes (the temporary disproportions). Necessity for technical changes is partly conveyed by information of a non-price character.

There are few reliable empirical works on supply functions of firms. Real observation is mostly replaced by an *a priori* assumption: the supply function should coincide with the marginal cost function. If it is true that price is set independently of the firm, that the firm maximizes profits and the cost function is convex, the volume of production will always be at the point where price equals marginal cost, provided average variable costs are covered. In fact, according to his view, all these assumptions are rather weak. Both the volume of production and the intention to sell develop under the influence of many kinds of impulses: stock reports, direct information from buyers, expectations regarding the future, instructions or recommendations obtained from central organs, and so on.

With his radical rejection of the General Equilibrium Theory he is usually considered an adherent of the disequilibrium school. This was his own view, also, when in 1971 he gave his work the title *Anti-Equilibrium*. But one can read in the *Economics of Shortage* (1980, p. 147):

I must acknowledge that my book, *Anti-Equilibrium*, was itself insufficiently precise in its interpretation of the word 'equilibrium'. On the one hand, what I said at the beginning of the present discussion, namely that there exists an equilibrium in the wide sense, was not clearly stated. The reader could have formed the impression that I was denying it. And yet to deny it would be almost equivalent to rejecting the idea that there exist in each system deeply rooted intrinsic regularities which constantly reproduce the essential properties of the system.

The *broad* interpretation of equilibrium – in general use in the natural sciences – is the following: it is that state of a system to which it always returns on account of its own regularities. The system is in equilibrium if the forces operating in it mutually counteract and compensate each other. Here equilibrium is a descriptive category. It leaves entirely open the question of whether this equilibrium – meant in the broad sense – of the system in question is to be considered 'good' or 'bad' by anybody (either an external observer or a participant in the system). The forest as a system of living things is in equilibrium if the wolf devours the hare; if it did not do so, the predatory animal would perish and so the customary proportions between the various species of animal would be disturbed. This event is part of the equilibrium even though the hare obviously finds it 'bad'. Counterforces operate to offset the actions of the predator and ensure the normal proportion of hares in the animal population. Such forces include the defensive and self-preservative activities of the hares (they try to escape from the wolf), and their appropriate rate of multiplication. A synonym for equilibrium in its broad sense – and an exact and equivalent synonym – is the expression 'normal state'.

The category of equilibrium is applicable to social systems in a similarly wide sense. Its precise conditions are always system-specific. They depend on the state which is permanently reproduced by the general economic laws and by the system-specific intrinsic regularities. Therefore, if we try to clarify in regard to some social system whether it is capable of being in equilibrium, we always have to analyse whether there are internal control mechanisms or social regularities which – as trends or long-term tendencies of deviations and fluctuations – bring about and permanently reproduce the normal state. It is not by relying upon criteria brought into the analysis from outside by an observer but the specific internal regularities and norms of the system that allow us to characterize the normal state of a particular system.

NORMAL STATE OF THE MARKET

It was the disequilibrium theory which started to investigate the notion of demand in the presence of a shortage economy. The disequilibrium theorists have recognized the possible separation between intention and realization when demand and supply are not in equilibrium. Kornai made use of this knowledge by establishing the non-Walrasian equilibrium theory.

Kornai's starting point is the following: the adjustment of the supply to the demand can never be instantaneous and perfect. Everybody knows what the phenomenon is like: inconsiderate planning, disorganization, bad co-operation, lack of foresight, failure to fulfil contractual obligations, lack of discipline, and so on. All these are frictions of adjustment. Kornai determines the general contents of friction indicators as follows:

1. The actors/individuals and groups, for example, firms, households, non-profit institutions/imperfect information about other actors' state and attitude; error in predictions serving as a basis for actor's plan;
2. Fluctuation of the actor's intention, in the case of repeated decisions;
3. Rigidity and delay in the actor's adjustment to changed conditions.

Because in reality no system can exist in which adjustment takes place without any friction at all, the normal state of the market cannot coincide with the Walrasian equilibrium. For characterizing the normal state of the market new concepts and categories have to be introduced. The four most important – according to Kornai – are, on the one side, shortage and slack, and on the other, suction and pressure. But what does shortage mean? Kornai distinguishes four major forms of shortage:

1. A resource, good, or service is allocated by administrative rationing. The sum of claims exceeds the quantity available to the allocator. This is a 'vertical shortage' appearing in the vertical relationship between the allocator and the claimant.
2. A resource, good or service is sold by the supplier to the customer for money. The seller's supply does not cover the initial demand of his customers. This is a 'horizontal shortage' appearing in the horizontal relationship between seller and buyer – the 'sellers' market'.
3. A producer firm or a non-profit institution supplying a service free of charge does not have the inputs necessary to fulfil its plan. This is a shortage within a micro-organization: resource constraints are met.
4. Social capacity is utilized highly in production, or more generally by social activity. A shortage of capacity emerges. Continuing and expanding the activity involves sharply rising marginal social costs.

These four phenomena are *direct* manifestations of shortage, and are accompanied by many kinds of indirect effects. They frequently overlap and intertwine. All phenomena listed are included in the *collective concept* of 'shortage'.

But let us start with the investigation of consequences of friction. There is pressure in the market of a given product when the sellers queue for the buyers, when a positive aspiration tension appears for the sellers whose aspirations are not completely fulfilled. There is suction in the market of a given product when the buyers queue for the sellers, when a positive aspiration tension appears for the buyers whose aspirations are not completely fulfilled. There is Walrasian equilibrium in the market when the aspiration levels of the seller and the buyer are equal. Using these categories the following statements can be made:

1. In most of the actual economic systems there usually prevails either general pressure or general suction. Should the relations of market forces be different in the markets of the various products, with neither general pressure nor general suction prevailing, the markets of the individual products will still be characterized either by pressure or by suction.
2. In the case of pressure it is the seller and in that of suction, the buyer, who endeavours to reduce the tension, wishing his aspiration to be fulfilled. These forces acting towards equilibrium will assert themselves. However, the tension is continually reproduced.

According to Kornai, in the state of Walrasian equilibrium there is not and cannot be any competition. When the buyer's intention and actual purchase, and also the seller's intention and actual sale, are exactly identical there is nothing to compete for. In such circumstances, sellers can peacefully divide among themselves the purchasing power of the buyers, and the latter equally peacefully can divide among themselves the products of the seller. The concept of 'competitive equilibrium' – although a stock phrase with economist – is actually, according to Kornai, a complete paradox. Two types of *genuine* competition are possible. In the one the sellers court the buyers, in the other the buyers court the sellers. Both are genuine forms of competition because there are some who reach the goal and others who do not.

The various forms of monopoly, oligopoly, imperfect and 'perfect' competition are extensively treated in the literature. According to Kornai, it is of secondary importance. The primary question is whether there is pressure or suction in the market. The distinguishing characteristic of *competition* is that the aspiration of the organization can be fulfilled only at the expense of the competitors. In the case of pressure, competition exists only among sellers, and in that of suction only among buyers; in the case of equilibrium there is no competition.

The criterion of competition is that the aspiration of the organization can be fulfilled only to the detriment of its competitors. According to this definition, in the case of pressure the actual sales of one seller can approach his own aspiration only if one or several other sellers fall short of their own aspirations to an even greater degree. This is the essence of competition. In the case of suction, on the other hand, where the expansion of sales depends only on production the seller is able to find a buyer for all his products. He does not need to compete. Similarly, in the case of suction the buyer is able to fulfil his buying aspiration to a higher degree only if this is offset by other buyers' aspirations remaining unfulfilled to an even greater extent; he is competing with the other buyers. In the case of pressure, on the other hand, how much the buyer buys depends exclusively on his own resources and requirements, and he does not drive out the other buyers with his own purchases; he does not compete with them. This can be summed up in the following statement: *The character of competition is determined by the relative strength of market forces; the degree of monopoly or atomization in the branch concerned has only a secondary effect on the behaviour of buyers and sellers.* The positive and negative effects also depend on the *strength* of the pressure or suction in the market. Pressure on the market will be the greater, the greater the seller's aspiration tension.

Suction, too, can be treated in a manner analogous to the above description of pressure. The intensity of suction depends on the extent of the tension, that is, the dissatisfaction of the buyer. The higher it is, the more impatient is the buyer. Of course, impatience also depends on the harm caused to the buyer by the shortage; how intensively does he strive to fulfil his aspiration? Here we come to one of the most essential criticisms of the general equilibrium school – probably the most absolutely essential one. As a matter of fact, in this view – and Kornai has endeavoured to clarify this – what is desirable is not that demand and supply should be in equilibrium but that the aspirations of both sellers and buyers should be intensive and that one type of disequilibrium, namely pressure, should assert itself at this high degree of intensity. In connection with this he summarizes the main hypotheses as follows:

1. *The main shortage and slack indicators of the system show a certain degree of stability.* While the institutions and external conditions of the system are more or less stable, the intertemporal average of these indicators will also be quite firm. In what follows these intertemporal averages will be called the *normal values* of the indicators in question. He talks in this sense about the *normal shortage* and *normal slack* of the system. The question is not simply about the trivial point that these indicators – just as any other random variable – also have a mean value. His hypothesis is that in the system feedbacks and control mechanisms are functioning which drive shortage or slack deviating from the norm – either above or below it – back to their normal levels.

2. While it is a common property of all systems that these indicators are definitely positive, it is already *deeply characteristic of individual concrete systems what values the normal shortage and normal slack vectors take.*
3. Hypothesis 1 does not mean that a concrete system is once and for all tied to its own normal shortage and normal slack from which it cannot depart. The normal values of shortage and of slack *themselves are social formations which come about as a result of historical development and are made firm by social conventions.* Considerable changes in institutions, control mechanisms and, with these, also in social expectations and conventions may also entail modifications in norms.

It is appropriate here to make a few remarks on terminology. He does not endeavour to define abstractly and in general terms the expression 'normal state'. There is a system whose external conditions as well as internal behaviour exhibits regularities which are more or less stable. The 'regular' values of the main state variables of this system can be called the 'normal state'. Small external or internal disturbances in the system make the values of state variables depart from their normal levels, yet even with the fluctuations it is this 'normal state' that expresses the prevalent tendency.

We must avoid, he says, associating any value judgement – expressed or implied – with the term 'normal state'. A precapitalist society may have been stagnating for centuries. Obviously, that is its normal state. Nobody would think of calling this state 'good'. To assert that a system is in its normal state is neither praise nor rebuke; it is not condemnation, but not an excuse either. By this we say no more and no less than that a system functions in accordance with its own inner nature. It is an extremely important part of the scientific analysis of a system to understand what the normal values of the main state variable (or their normal path in time) are. The comparison of systems seeks to answer the question: How does the normal state of one system differ from that of another system?

RESOURCE-CONSTRAINED VERSUS DEMAND-CONSTRAINED SYSTEMS

The normal state of the market can be characterized in a different way in capitalism compared to socialism. Describing a system Kornai considers decisive the types of constraints which limit production. He distinguishes three types of constraints:

1. *Resource constraints.* These are *physical* constraints. Such are the material, semi-finished product and parts stocks instantaneously available to the firm, as well as workers with certain qualifications and other particular abilities who are present instantaneously, the functioning machines and equipment suitable for carrying out certain operations, and so on. These – and only these – are physical resources that can be used for production. At this point his approach is to include resource constraints on production, not just on the micro-level but on the *submicro*-level. He penetrates down to the *elementary* production events taking place in workshops at each moment. It is quite possible that, considering the whole of a big enterprise, tens or hundreds of thousands of submicro-level resource constraints do exist. And when he thinks of the whole of the national economy, their number is in the millions.

2. *Demand constraints.* Since he is examining instantaneous adjustment, prices (if they affect the buyer at all) can be considered as given. Given that, demands are also considered as given. The demand constraint exerts its effect on the producing workshop only in an indirect way. It is usually the firm's sales department that is in contact with the buyers. Employees of the firm in charge of sales forward the buyers' demand to the directors of the firm, or perhaps directly to the production managers. In any case, the producing workshops will perceive, relying upon instructions received from the directors of the firm or upon information transmitted by the sales department, whether they should increase manufacture of the product or reduce it or perhaps stop it entirely. In this way, under definite conditions, demand may restrict fulfilment of intentions to increase production.

3. *Budget constraints.* Under certain institutional conditions (for example, in a socialist economy) not just one but several budget constraints exist. Separately 'labelled' limits may be put on outgoings to be spent on wages or on investments or on imports. He includes under the heading 'budget constraint' the *total* expenditures and the *total* money available. The budget constraint, if it affects production, does so in an indirect way. It can prevent the firm buying physical resources: purchasing material and machines, employing workers.

Kornai's aim is to describe by the model *ex post* the actual functioning of the firm.

The following terms from the terminology of mathematical programming will be borrowed. For some constraints, given in the form of inequalities, equality holds in the solution. Production fully utilizes one or the other resource; sales may reach the limit of demand; expenses may exhaust the available financial resources. The constraint is *effective* because in fact it restricts the selected activities. Production would have been larger if it had not hit effective constraints. It can also be said that the effective constraint is in fact *binding*. For other constraints, however, inequality holds (they are 'not exhausted') in the solution of the programming problem. They are *non-effective* from the point of view of the instantaneous solution. It is as if they were not there at all, they do not influence the choice, they are 'redundant', that is they *do not bind* activities.

It is always the comparatively narrow constraints that are effective; it is they that restrict efforts at increasing production. Comparatively broad constraints are not effective.

For understanding the system other distinctions are needed, too. Resource constraints are of a *physical* nature. They express the trivial truth that it is impossible to make something out of nothing. It is possible to apply, instead of the first input–output combination, the second or third one; but some kind of combination of inputs will usually be needed, and this is constrained by the available quantities of resources. Therefore the resource constraints cannot be exceeded; they are hard as rock.

The situation is different with the demand and the budget constraints; these express not a physical necessity but a *behavioural* regularity. These are laid down by people, and people can transgress them. A programme within the constraints is satisfactory for the decision-maker, while he considers any overstepping unacceptable. He calls this type of constraint an *acceptance constraint*. The output stock, waiting for sale, has in normal circumstances a tolerance limit. Yet if it is exceeded, then it is exceeded. Transgression of the budget constraint means insolvency; this can also happen. *It depends on concrete circumstances, that is, on social relations enforcing observation of the behavioural rule, how hard or soft the constraint is.* The hardness of the behavioural constraint has a graded *scale*; it can be almost as hard as the physical constraint, or be of a medium hardness, or it can be expressly soft, that is, it can be violated without trouble or consequence. A hard behavioural constraint may be effective, but it is not necessarily so – it depends on whether other constraints are relatively narrow or broad. On the other hand, a soft behavioural constraint (disregarding certain exceptional cases) can never be effective. These are tools which should aid in describing the situation and behaviour of the firm. Kornai is dealing separately with the instantaneous and short-term adjustment of the producer, that is, with the long-term adjustment of the investor. But for clarifying the basic differences of different systems it seems to be enough to concentrate us on the characteristics of instantaneous adjustment of the producer.

After a survey of the constraints Kornai contrasted first two 'pure' types of system. One is the 'classical' capitalist firm. He takes into account the era before regular state intervention, that is, before Keynesian economic policy.

He disregards the peak of the upswing and centre the attention rather on the other phases of the cycle. The other 'pure' type is *the firm functioning in the traditional socialist economic management system*. Its activities are controlled by detailed central instructions; it lives in an atmosphere of growth at a forced rate. The most important comparisons between these two pure types are summarized in the Table 6.1.

Table 6.1

Type of constraint	Classical capitalist firm	Traditional socialist firm
Resource constraint	Rarely effective	Nearly always effective, more restrictive than demand constraints
Demand constraint	Nearly always effective, more restrictive than resource constraint	Rarely effective
Budget constraints	Hard	Soft
Production plan	Autonomous: the firm lays it down at the level of demand constraints; within resource constraints	Directive: prescribed by superior authority at the level of resource constraints; within demand constraints

The classical capitalist firm has a hard budget constraint. If it is insolvent, it will sooner or later become bankrupt. It can be granted a credit at best in advance of its future proceeds, which it has to pay back later with interest. It can buy only as much input as it can pay for from selling its products. Therefore it cannot produce more than it can expect to sell. It decides its production plans voluntarily at the level of demand constraints. As opposed to this, the budget constraint of the traditional socialist firm is soft. If it works at a loss that does not yet lead to real bankruptcy, that is, ceasing operation. The firm is helped out somehow: it receives additional credit, or its tax is reduced, or it is granted a subsidy, or the selling price is raised – and, finally, it survives financial difficulties. Accordingly, its demand is hardly constrained by solvency considerations. The firm, as *buyer*, tries to acquire as much input as possible in order that shortage should not hinder production. The other side of the same phenomenon is that the firm, as *seller*, faces an almost insatiable demand. At least that is the situation with firms whose buyers are themselves firms: demand from such buyers is almost impossible to satiate. This insatiable demand 'pumps out' the product from the firm. What is more, the superior authority determining the plan would also like to encourage the firm towards the largest possible production. The final result is that the production plan of the traditional socialist firm is set at the level of resource constraints. This proposition plays a central role in the whole train of Kornai's thought. He emphasizes three qualifications:

1. He does not claim that with the classical capitalist firm some of the resource constraints can never be effective – sometimes they can, but not often. And he does not claim either that with the traditional socialist firm some of the demand constraints can never be effective – the same can be said here: they can be effective sometimes, but not often. The statements are of a *stochastic character*: the probability of either one or the other type of event is prevalent with one or the other type of firm.
2. If a constraint is not effective, it is redundant and can well be omitted from the simultaneous equations. This holds here too for instantaneous adjustment, that is, for daily or hourly production decisions. Yet we must be aware that, indirectly and maybe with lags, non-effective demand constraints also affect the course of production. That is to say, one cannot say, for example, that production of the traditional socialist firm is perfectly independent of demand. It means only that at the next moment of production, when the production plan is already given, actions are not constrained by the buying disposition of the customer, nor by the size of output stock accumulation that the firm management and the superior direction are prepared to tolerate with a given knowledge of demand, but primarily and above all by the inputs available.
3. All that is said here is valid for the classical, traditional cases. The position of today's capitalist firm differs greatly from its classical predecessor. And the life of socialist firms in the course of economic reforms is not exactly the same.

PRICE IN SOCIALISM

Now it is worthwhile to recall some points of Kornai's criticisms concerning the general equilibrium theory. Kornai points out with great emphasis the important role of the so-called 'quantity' adjustment process in every economic system. This takes place without prices or at fixed prices – either way, without equilibrating and incentive effects or permanently changing and adjusting prices. The first part of *Economics of Shortage* (1980) while generalizing the experiences gained in socialist economies was intended to contribute to the better understanding of the nature of 'quantity' adjustment. The second part deals with adjustment in the presence of prices.

Although Kornai wants to give in his *Economics of Shortage* an all-embracing survey about the functions of price, he actually concentrates on experience gained in Eastern European countries during the prevailing socialist system. Vegetative control obviously prevails on a broader line in a socialist system that in a capitalist system. That is why *Economics of Shortage* gives very useful knowledge about how far the government can go with vegetative control. Those deliberations deserve greater interest, as they deal, first, with the responsiveness in firm decisions to price; secondly, with the price formation in the inter-firm sphere; and thirdly, with consumer behaviour in connection with price.

The majority of Kornai's propositions concerning the responsiveness to price is given as a function of the degree of hardness of the budget constraint. From this as a general rule, one can come to the conclusion that responsiveness to price is very weak because of the soft budget constraint. Since this set of problems is rather complex, Table 6.2 reproduces Kornai's table of issues to be discussed (1980, p. 324).

Rows 1 and 2 of Table 6.2 distinguish two classes of decision concerning *quantity* and *composition*. In terms of demand, this distinction is parallel with the well-known distinction in standard microeconomics between the

Table 6.2   A summary of types of a firm's responsiveness to price in different contexts

	1	2	3	4
	Instantaneous and short-term adjustment		Long-term adjustment	
	On the input side	On the output side	On the input side	On the output side
1. Decisions concerning total volume	Determination of the overall level of initial demand	Determination of the overall level of output		Determination of planned capacity
2. Decisions concerning product composition	Determination of composition of initial demand Revision of initial demand before forced substitutions Instantaneous and short-term determination of the composition of inputs	Instantaneous and short-term determination of the composition	Choice of technology	Determination of the composition of output

income effect and the *substitution effect* of a change in price. It is his aim to examine these effects, or the lack of them, under the conditions of a shortage economy.

Not all problems included in the table are treated in the same detail. The case defined by the entry in column 1, row 2 is treated at greatest length. This is the effect of relative prices on the firm's instantaneous and short-term demand and the actual input combination. It is not only the importance of the subject that justifies discussion in full detail, but also the fact that Kornai has developed for this purpose *analytical tools* which can also be used to examine other aspects. He generally disregards special issues related to the effects of export and import prices: they are treated only briefly with regard to investment.

He begins with the phenomenon that is called the *income effect* in standard consumption theory. How does the change in price affect the *quantity* demanded by the firm within the framework of instantaneous and short-term adjustment? What happens if it is not the price of a single input that changes but that of a whole group of inputs which are all substitutes? (For example, all kinds of raw material that can be used in the manufacture of a product.) Their prices increase simultaneously in the same proportion, while the prices of complementary inputs are unchanged. According to standard macroeconomics, demand for the group of inputs that has become more expensive ought to decrease, since the same budget can now purchase only a smaller quantity. This is true, however, only with a hard budget constraint. *In the case of a soft budget constraint the income effect does not materialize.* If the firm has a demand for any input which is on sale, it will buy that input in spite of the higher price. Where the increased costs cannot be covered within the limits of its budget constraint, it will sooner or later charge them to the buyer or the state.

The substitution effect is rather weak. It is absolutely not sure that the input demand 'A' will decrease if its relative price is increased compared to input 'B'. More generally: only if the budget constraint is hard will the firm respond to the changes of relative prices in respect of substitutable products. In that case the initial demand of all buyers is at the point most advantageous for the firm, the point of tangency between the isoquant and the budget line. For the sake of sharpening the contrast Kornai assumes – and gives several factors which may cause such a shift in initial demand – that when demand is not responsive to price it moves in the opposite direction to that in the price-responsive case.

The output level of the firm under perfect competition is controlled by price. The behaviour of the *traditional socialist firm* is radically different from the behaviour of firms in the models above. *Its output level is not controlled by price.* Powerful forces which are independent of prices drive the firm toward full capacity utilization. Full capacity is not the maximum production attainable by the firm in ideal conditions, but the maximum production attainable given the normal frictions of the system. Capacity is not a single, uniquely defined number, but rather a 'zone'. At every moment the firm hits certain bottlenecks on the input side; these resource constraints limit capacity. The traditional socialist firm is driven to taut capacity utilization by the output plan, by the quantity drive, and by the pressure of buyers queuing up for the product.

It may happen that price does not cover the marginal costs in the zone near full capacity utilization. This does not stop the firm increasing output. The budget constraint is soft. If the firm incurs losses through increasing its output, it can expect the state, or perhaps the credit system, to cover the loss in some way by giving price support, subsidies or special credits. Alternatively a price increase takes place sooner or later. *It is not volume that is adjusted to price, but much more frequently price is adjusted to the high costs caused by high output.* The standard microeconomic rules in practice never limit increases in total output. If it is restrained at all, it is by bottlenecks on the input side.

The responsiveness to output prices of a socialist firm operating in a resource-constrained system is very different from that of a capitalist firm operating in a demand-constrained situation. The firm bound by a demand constraint is forced to take the demand of its customers as determining the composition of output. It may be happy to manufacture a good which yields a relatively small profit as long as its inclusion in the production programme yields a positive marginal profit. That is because producing such goods allows the firm to enlarge its sales. On the other hand, in a suction economy, where chronic shortage prevails, the seller is not forced to do this, since he can sell his products anyway. Therefore, he can choose what to produce on the basis of profitability more than the demand-constrained capitalist firm can. If of two substitute products G and H the first is more profitable, the producer firm will give it preference, even if the customer would prefer H. The producer rightly expects that, since there is shortage, the buyer will finally accept G, if only as a forced substitute for H.

As a customer the firm gives in to the seller who decides what to produce according to relative prices. The customer does not even resist price increases because of its dependence. And the soft budget constraint enables the customer to charge the increase costs to its own customers or to the state.

There is a remarkable asymmetry between the input and the output side. While the firm as customer does not select inputs on the basis of their relative prices, on the output side its choice is strongly based on relative prices. This asymmetry follows logically from the nature of the resource-constrained shortage economy. In a seller's market the seller dictates and the buyer must conform. In fixing the composition of its output, a firm in the shortage economy can relatively easily be guided by the profit incentive, while it can hardly be so guided in fixing the composition of its inputs.

The investment input decision is not responsive to the relative price of inputs. The decision is not price-sensitive. In decisions between technological alternatives the cost-minimalization criterion plays a small roll. The budget constraint on investment expenditure is soft. The price of output made possible by the investment will sooner or later be adjusted to actual costs. It is not possible for an investment to be completed and then fail subsequently, in the sense that the firm goes bankrupt. The investment input decision – the input combination or technology chosen for the production activities specified by the output decision – is not responsive to the relative price of inputs. In the decision between technological alternatives the cost-minimization criterion plays a small role.

After examining the price-responsiveness of the firm on both the input and output side Kornai challenges a widely held opinion. According to this view the main cause of shortage phenomena (or at least one of their most important causes) is to be looked for in wrong relative prices. The refutation of this opinion follows from his analysis: *No change in relative prices is able to eliminate shortage in the firm sector.* Changes in the relative prices of products traded among firms may influence the intensity of shortage in the case of any single product. Since in terms of instantaneous and short-term adjustment the firm is responsive on the output side to relative prices to some extent, unfavourable prices may keep the firm from manufacturing certain kinds of products the shortage of which then increases. *Yet in the re-source-constrained system shortage depends not on the supply side but on the demand side.* Supply can be of any size if demand always tends towards infinity. And this is exactly the situation if the budget constraint of the firm is not hard enough and if no economic force operates to constrain demand. Under such circumstances the firm's demand for both current and capital inputs is almost insatiable. Whatever the relative prices of inputs, there are and always will be numerous inputs for which demand is unsatisfied.

His proposition has important theoretical and policy implications. Normative disputes about the relative prices of inputs are carried on in a vacuum if prices do not control the demand of the firm effectively. The explanations deserve greater attention with reference to how the firm affects prices. Most of the literature deals exclusively with price policy. Kornai's intention, however, is to demonstrate that price formation is the common result of central price policy and the efforts of firms: prices change or remain unchanged as a result of conflicts and compromises between these forces.

With some products price setting is quite an easy task. He calls this category *standard mass-produced goods*. Most raw materials, some semi-finished products and mass-produced traditional foodstuffs with a low degree of processing come into this category. Yet with other products price control is quite difficult. He calls this the category of *differentiated products of goods*. The number of standard mass-produced goods has not increased much even over a long historical period. On the other hand, the number of differentiated products increases continuously and rapidly. With a differentiated product the producer can impose a *hidden price increase* without much difficulty.

Kornai's standpoint concerning the correction of price statistics is closely connected with this point. Owing to cost–push or demand–pull, prices in the latter category may be rising, while with administrative prices the state can successfully counteract the tendency for price-drift. If price statistics are centred, understandably, on the observation of changes in prices of intertemporally comparable products, the price index will be biased downward.

COMMENTS

Up to this point Kornai's Theory has been faithfully reflected. I have quoted with almost no changes the pivotal concepts of his works *Anti-Equilibrium* and *Economics of Shortage* which, in my view, render substantive contributions to the body of economic thought. His ideas which were developed through a lifetime of elaborate research are, of course, not all incorporated in his two major works. Here, however, I decided to limit my focus on Kornai's major ideas, rather than furnishing a lengthy catalogue of all his contributions. I shall concentrate on emphasizing his contributions to economic thought, which I plan to make the centrepiece of my comments.

To begin with, I raise the question: How can Kornai's role be viewed within the mainstream of contemporary economics? Let him speak for himself (1971, p. 373):

> Macroeconomics and microeconomics have developed almost hermetically separated from each other. The same is true of formalized and literary economics, the economics of socialism and capitalism, the Walras-school and the behaviorists, econometrics and mathematical programming; these examples certainly do not exhaust the list of non-intersecting sets of sciences in the multidimensional space of economics. The time is ripe for a broader synthesis.

I start out from the same analytical base as the critics of the classical and neoclassical theory. Through the evaluation of the relations between individuals, the classical school made a distinction between *free goods* and *economic goods*. Within the framework of natural resources the distinction between free and non-free goods was the renewableness of resources. Since land was considered a non-renewable resource, economics had to extend its scope to its utilization. In contrast, water, air, sunshine and so on were considered free goods, as they used to be considered indestructible gifts of nature.

The classical theory started out by defining, first, that the objectives of economics were to carry out the activities of production, exchange, distribution, and consumption; and secondly, that economic goods are the fruits of labour. Then from the labour theory of value it followed that value is a product of labour, though despite that, the process of production requires the combination of land, labour and capital. This explains, according to the classicists, that on the one hand, economic laws derive from the labour theory of value and, on the other hand, that the use of 'free goods', which are available free of charge, is a basic principle of the economic act of production.

One of the basic frameworks of the classical theory is the theory of markets. In this theory the role of public goods has marginal significance, and they do not constrain the laws of free markets. But if we juxtapose the present state of knowledge with the teaching of the classical school, we can note without bias that socioeconomic development deviated in two significantly different areas from the classical school.

First, it has become clear that people do abuse, and even worse, destroy natural resources. The fallout on economics comes in the form of environmental damage, which is a by-product of mass production. Pollution occurs when the degree of productive and consumer waste exceeds the self-cleaning capacity of air and water. It has come to pass that natural resources which once were plentiful and available in unlimited quantities are only available today in limited supply. It was therefore necessary to extend the scope of economic goods to these new dimensions, in which the so-called environmental products made their entrance.

Secondly, with the extension of the dimensions of economics and goods the scope of the market has not increased but, rather, has been scaled down, not only because of the emergence of environmental goods, but also because the sphere of public good has gained ground successively compared to individual commodities. As is known, in the allocation of resources the market is workable only in the sphere of individual commodities.

Societies, whether organized under capitalism or under socialism, must take into consideration specific characteristics which derive from the three dimensional need of economic goods. They include: the theory of free markets; environmental economics; and the theory of public choice. These dimensions reveal certain inner consistencies. The equilibrium theory must emancipate the operation of these three dimensions, by integrating the markets with ecology and the theory of grant economics. The quality of life has to express the material and intellectual welfare of society, including environmental balance. If this is an acceptable proposition, then what Kornai refers to as 'integration' is nothing other than his effort to synthesize all available knowledge under an up-to-date market theory. This in itself poses a rather significant challenge. It seems then to be important to put his findings in the correct perspective.

But let me limit the scope of investigation to the prevailing contemporary market theory. Then one should raise the question whether it is necessary to eliminate the neoclassical theory, given that one accepts the theory of the 'normal state of the market'. I consider the clarification of this issue important, because what Kornai is offering us in this context is undeniably a significant contribution to economic theory, which opens up brand new vistas of comprehension of economic phenomena and the market theory. The main watershed in Kornai's views came when he moved away from his disequilibrium theory (*Anti-Equilibrium*, 1972) and concentrated the centre of his action on non-Walrasian equilibrium (*Economics of Shortage*, 1980). Thus the following question is of importance: Would it be possible to create an analytical base for economics with a twin-core equilibrium? I believe one should not exclude such possibilities. What then is the next step?

Economics as an autonomous discipline emerged through the back-up support of philosophy, which considers human freedom as an original and irrevocable part of the universal order. The classical school of economics presented a theory within whose framework economic phenomena were separated from social and economic policy. Through 'the momentum of the times' the terms 'free market', 'natural' and 'right' prices became synonymous. While the classical theory was initially drawn up by strong political undercurrents, it ultimately became a manifesto against any government interference into economic affairs. Its motto, coined by the physiocrat Vincent Gournay, '*laissez-faire*', became inscribed worldwide on the banner of free economies, which considered the best government to be the one which governed least.

In later stages of development the neoclassical economists were interested in developing the impact of rational human behaviour on economic phenomena. Rational human behaviour was always governed by the '*lex minimi*'. Then the General Equilibrium Theory simply packaged it into a uniform framework. Critics claim that neoclassical theory is marred by several flaws, such as approaching economic laws through generalizations which are subject to numerous exemptions. The latter is the basis for corrections summed up by Kornai under the heading of the 'reformist' approach. But none of these can alter the basic essentials: the economic motivation of the social process fundamentally derives from Hedonistic philosophy.[3] On this account, the validity of the Walrasian General Equilibrium Theory cannot be ignored by its continuous transmittals reflecting reality.

I further believe that the normal state of the market can be understood as a suboptimal state of the economy. In such a case, intensity of deviation from the Walrasian equilibrium could be interpreted as the degree of the deviation from the optimum. One can perceive the complementary and not exclusive character of the two kinds of equilibrium by the interpretation of an ecological equilibrium. Perfect ecological equilibrium prevails when the intensity of environmental pollution is equilibrated by the self-clearing capacity of natural resources (for example, free goods). In the world of mass production such an equilibrium is not attainable. But working towards a normal (tolerable) and controllable arrangement can rightly be expected. It would require the introduction of policies which would ban the production (or consumption) of technologies (products) particularly dangerous to the environment, and/or set tolerance limits on their application. Transgressors would have to be prosecuted under the legal codes governing the region that encompassed the violators' political boundaries. I don't believe I have deviated too far from Kornai's views, where with respect to the General Equilibrium Theory he states (1971, pp. 28–9):

> It would be entirely unwarranted ... to interpret the term 'general' ... as implying a 'real science' theory of general validity, a universal truth – valid, to a certain extent, for every age, country and system. In actuality, we are dealing with highly 'specialized' theory, valid only within, a highly restricted sphere, perhaps preferably expressed as a very 'special sphere'.

NOTES

1. V.V. Novozhilov, Nyedosztatok tovarov, *Scarcity of commodities*, Vesztnyik Finanszov, 1927, no. 5.
2. Edmond Malinvaud, *L'Expansion*, 8/21 March 1985.
3. From the '*homo economicus*' (Economic Man) principle.

APPENDIX I: CURRICULUM VITAE OF JANOS KORNAI

Born: 21 January 1928, Budapest, Hungary
Nationality: Hungarian
Married: Zsuzsa Dániel, economist

Current Posts

1967–	Head of Department, Institute of Economics, Hungarian Academy of Sciences, Budapest
1986–	Professor of Economics, Harvard University, Cambridge, Massachusetts

Past Posts

1947–55	Economics Editor, newspaper *Szabad Nep*, Budapest.
1955–8	Research Fellow, Institute of Economics, Hungarian Academy of Sciences, Budapest
1958–63	Head of Department, Institute of Textile Industry, Budapest
1963–7	Head of Department, Computing Centre, Hungarian Academy of Sciences, Budapest

Degrees

1956	Candidate of Sciences (CSc), Hungarian Academy of Sciences, Budapest
1961	Doctor of Economics (DrOec), Karl Marx University of Economics, Budapest
1965	Doctor of Sciences (DrSc), Hungarian Academy of Sciences, Budapest

Visiting Professorships

1964	London School of Economics
1966	University of Sussex
1968	Stanford University
1970	Yale University, Cowles Foundation
1972	Princeton University
1972–83	Institute for Advanced Study, Princeton
1973	Stanford University
1976–7	Stockholm University
1984–5	Harvard, F.W. Taussig Research Professor

Honours and Learned Societies

Econometric Society, *Fellow*, 1968; *President*, 1978
Karl Marx University of Economics, Budapest, *Honorary Professor*, 1968
American Academy of Arts and Sciences, *Honorary Member*, 1972
United Nations, Committee for Development Planning, *Vice-Chairman*, 1972–7
Hungarian Academy of Sciences, *Corresponding Member*, 1976; *Full Member*, 1982
American Economic Association, *Honorary Member*, 1976
University of Paris, *Honorary Doctor*, 1978
British Academy, *Corresponding Member*, 1978
University of Posnan, Poland, *Honorary Doctor*, 1978
Royal Swedish Academy, *Foreign Member*, 1980
F.E. Seidman Distinguished Award in Political Economy, USA, 1982
Hungarian State Prize, 1983
Alexander von Humboldt Prize, GFR, 1983
Finnish Academy of Sciences, *Foreign Member*, 1985
European Economic Association, *President*, 1987
J.S. McDonnel Foundation, *Distinguished Fellow*, 1988.

APPENDIX II: SELECTED LIST OF PUBLICATIONS IN ENGLISH

The ten most valuable works:

(1959), *Over-Centralization in Economic Administration*, Oxford: Oxford University Press. Also published in Hungarian.

(1965), 'Two-Level Planning', with Tamás Liptak, *Econometrica*, **33**, (1), 141–69.

(1971), *Anti-Equilibrium*, Amsterdam: North-Holland. Also published in Hungarian, Rumanian, German, Japanese, Polish and Serbian.

(1972), *Rush Versus Harmonic Growth*, Amsterdam: North Holland. Also published in Hungarian, Czech and Spanish.

(1980), *Economics of Shortage*, Amsterdam: North-Holland. Also published in Hungarian, Czech, French, Polish and Chinese.

(1981), *Non-Price Control*, Amsterdam: North Holland; Budapest: Akadémiai Kiadó. Editor of the volume with Béla Martos. Author or co-author of chapters 1,2,4, 10 and 12. Also published in Hungarian.

(1982), *Growth, Shortage and Efficiency*, Oxford: Basil Blackwell; Berkeley and Los Angeles: University of California Press. Also published in Hungarian, Chinese and Polish.

(1985), *Contradictions and Dilemmas*, Budapest: Corvina, 1985, Cambridge, Mass.: MIT Press. Also published in Hungarian, Japanese and Chinese.

(1986), 'The Hungarian Reform Process: Visions, Hopes and Reality', *Journal of Economic Literature*, **24**, (4), 1687–1737.

(1988), 'Individual Freedom and Reform of the Socialist Economy', *European Economic Review*, **32**, (2–3), 233–67.

7. Edward Leamer

Herman B. Leonard and Keith E. Maskus

The body of work produced by most highly productive and prolific scholars of economics can generally be characterized as having an integrating theme, an organizing principle. While most have worked in more than one area, it seems fair to say that the work they have done in different areas adds to our body of knowledge in similar ways. Scholars of public finance will concentrate for a period on taxation, studying the effects of different taxes, and will move to consider expenditure policies. A labour economist will study the impact of schooling on wages, extend the work to cover the impact of training, become interested in the impacts of unionization and investigate whether those impacts are felt through changes in training inputs. Many of the most highly regarded scholars have opened new areas of inquiry, by reframing old problems or inventing new ones, by bringing or developing a new tool that permits dramatic progress in our understanding of economic relationships.

The work of Edward E. Leamer, both in econometrics and international trade, could be characterized as fitting this general pattern. One could describe his work topically, pointing to the wide variety of different methodological problems he has identified and sought to resolve in econometrics and listing the variety of theoretical and empirical problems he has attacked in international trade. As with many other highly productive scholars, such a characterization would show a set of relationships among the topics that he has worked on, and would permit a description of a chronological or topical evolution with a substantial degree of thematic integration.

But such a description would also miss the essential story of the unfolding of Leamer's work. In most scholars we seek an explanation of how their interest was drawn from one topic to another, and we seek intellectual connections among the topics. The organizing principle for Leamer's work lies less in the topics he was studying and the things he was discovering about those *topics*, and more in the things he was learning about the *audience* he was trying to address. For Leamer's quest has not been motivated solely, or perhaps even principally, by a desire to add to what he knew or what, collectively, the profession knew in principle – rather, it has been directed at trying to get his audience to change how it behaved, how it learned from data. Where for others we might say, 'he *proved* ... ' or 'she *taught* us ... ' or 'he *showed* us ... ', with Leamer we must say 'he tried to *get us* to ...'. Thus, his inquiry has been directed at least as much by what he has learned about what would (and would not!) influence the behaviour of the profession as it has by his intrinsic interest in the individual topics he has examined, at least as much by what he discovered *about* us as by what he has discovered *for* us. His role has not only been that of discoverer of conditional truths (what we ordinarily refer to as theorems or conclusions or inferences), but also that of advocate for changing our approach to learning from examining data. He implicitly takes on, then, not only the task of discovering the methods, but also of trying to craft them in such a way that they become intuitive, powerful and attractive enough as tools to get us to pick them up and use them. As a consequence, his attention is drawn not only to the development of new ideas and the proof of new facts, but to the crafting of those facts and ideas in a form that penetrates the consciousness of the profession.

From the perspective of trying to review Leamer's work, this implies that the story of its evolution can be most effectively organized around his discoveries about what would influence the rest of us – we can identify the phases of his inquiry in terms of what he felt would most directly and successfully address *our* deficiencies, rather than the collective deficiency of knowledge in the profession. It also implies that from the perspective of trying to characterize the success of Leamer's work, it is not enough to ask how original and powerful the concepts developed have been; we must also ask how effectively they have penetrated the profession's consciousness and work habits.

In this context, we can identify four logically sequential assertions about why the economics profession is not using a more revealing approach to learning from data and Leamer's response to each. First, it is often difficult to translate theory into meaningful statistical hypotheses and this gap between theory and practice encourages the use of relatively empty empirical specifications. In such situations classical methods of statistical inference which, by virtue of training and availability, are easy to use, are inappropriate and provide inferences that may be seriously flawed. Leamer has consistently argued both for the rigorous use of economic theory in establishing a framework for empirical analysis and for the use of informed data analysis to develop more robust estimates. Thus, on both grounds the profession has lacked an adequate stock of methods in theory for conducting appropriate inference. Leamer's major contribution has been to develop a wide array of new inferential methods in econometrics to address this problem.

Secondly, the new methods may be too difficult to apply because they are not embodied in the standard statistical packages used by the profession for its inferential computations. In response, Leamer has developed a computer package that made it easier to carry out some of the techniques.

Thirdly, the profession may not yet have encountered sufficiently persuasive advocacy for the improved methods. Leamer has endeavoured to provide this persuasion, contributing a series of articles designed to convince and motivate economists who had yet to adopt his inferential approaches.

Fourthly, the profession may need more examples of how the better methods would work in order to see their value more clearly. Leamer tried to address this situation most prominently by applying his methods to an area of great practical interest – the explanation of international trade patterns. Other examples of how he thought inferential inquiries should be conducted have been advanced as well.

The phases appeared roughly chronologically in his work, and the main locus of his interests has moved through them more or less sequentially, though he has addressed himself to all four hypotheses in varying degrees throughout his work from the very start. The mix of his attention, however, has evolved over time more or less continuously.

BUILDING THE METHODS: FOUNDATIONS OF LEAMER'S ECONOMETRIC APPROACH

In the preface of his 1978 book *Specification Searches*, the capstone of his early work, Leamer describes his odyssey as having been prompted in part by the opportunity he was given as a graduate student at the University of Michigan in the late 1960s to observe the contrast between theory and practice in econometrics. He describes the 'schizophrenia' of those who 'wantonly sinned' in their practice of econometrics in the basement computer centre and who became 'highest of the high priests' as they ascended to the third floor to teach econometric theory.

Leamer found the classical theory of statistics and econometrics, as taught in the classroom, wholly inadequate to support the inferential conclusions on whose behalf it was invoked (given the way those conclusions had actually been reached in practice). Classical theory provided a nice, neat set of ways to characterize inferential ambiguity, but its conclusions were always conditional on the presence of information that the practitioners being observed by Leamer routinely behaved as if they knew they did not have. In particular, the classical theory lying behind parameter estimation for econometric models – the application he was daily witnessing in the basement – required that the model whose parameters were being estimated be known with certainty to be correct. But in carrying out the estimations to which they would attach classical statistical measures of inferential uncertainty, researchers routinely discarded dozens of model specifications in favour of those that seemed to be favoured by the data.

How, reasoned Leamer, could we apply a theory whose validity was conditional on our knowing with certainty in advance that the models we were estimating were correctly specified, when we regularly discarded one model after another if it didn't fit the data sufficiently well (or, more accurately, if we found another model that fit the data better)? It was possible, of course, that the *ad hoc* searches through alternative specifications always led to the discovery of exactly the correct, true model, in which case the invocation of the classical statistical model would be valid. But there was nothing that seemed to guarantee that the searches would terminate with the right model in hand; certainly, there was no theory of searching that could adequately describe or lead to confidence in the performance of these search methods that would give confidence that the t-statistics of the chosen model were in any way an adequate measure of the inferential ambiguity that should be attached to the parameters.

Indeed, there was a great deal of evidence to the contrary embodied in the behaviour of the profession. First, there was no sense or even argument that the models resulting from *ad hoc* specification searches were 'true' or 'right'; they were characterized as 'close', or it was said that they 'captured a lot of what was going on', but virtually no one would defend any particular specification as 'correct'. Secondly, the degree of confidence exhibited by researchers in their parameter estimates was often considerably less than that indicated by the classical statistical ambiguity measures. Finally, and perhaps most compellingly, there was very little faith exhibited by researchers about the parameter values estimated by others, at least as compared to the degree of faith that would seem to be required by the classically computed t-statistics. The profession was engaged in the widespread use of statistical methods for which it could give no sound theoretical explanation, and to the conclusions of which it accorded a healthy scepticism – beneath a veneer of polite interest in other researchers' empirical results and a tacit bargain to use uncritically the nominal mantle of classical statistical theory, even when essentially all researchers agreed that it did not apply to the circumstances in which it was being invoked. The implicit bargain not to criticize each others' research results, on the basis that they were not properly inferred from the perspective of the classical statistical model, amounted to a kind of Geneva Convention among the profession.

Unfortunately, Leamer also found the pure Bayesian theory taught in the mathematics department to be only imperfectly reconcilable with the practices he observed. Bayesians at least had a formal learning model – indeed, they claimed, somewhat evangelically, to have the *only* formal learning model. And adopting a Bayesian posture at least reduced the degree of conditioning on facts that were supposed to be known with certainty before inference began. But Leamer found that full-fledged Bayesian learning could only be conducted completely convincingly in relatively simple problems: inferential problems dramatically less complex than those Leamer saw his colleagues trying to draw inferences in.

Moreover, strong resistance by classical statisticians to the introduction by Bayesians of prior information into inferential problems had diverted a substantial component of the intellectual effort among Bayesians to the use of information-minimizing priors – that is, to the development of methods that were true to the Bayesian form of inference but that brought as little as possible in the way of prior information to the examination of data. Since what Leamer saw (in the basement!) amounted to a willingness to impose quite strong prior information – but an unwillingness to admit it – Bayesian theory, at least as it was then currently developing, did not seem likely to provide a fully satisfactory alternative. Leamer gradually became less hopeful about the prospects of a full reconciliation – or unification – and instead set out on a different track, one motivated by and sensitive to Bayesian approaches and concerns, but distinctively different, less rigidly wedded to a comprehensive formal learning model, more directly inspired by the need to provide a more robust framework for the practices he observed in the basement.

Leamer's approach has evolved over time, but the general shape of it was clear enough even early in his career. Concerned with the inadequacy of the widely invoked classical methods to characterize the degree of uncertainty that researchers should (and did) attach to the parameter estimates they derived, Leamer has recharacterized the problem as describing the 'ambiguity' that remains about an estimate after encountering a given body of data. Even an infinitely large amount of data might be insufficient to remove the ambiguity arising from a lack of definitive knowledge of what the correct model is, so the ambiguity measures should depend on the degree of certainty attached to the model and its specification as well as on how well the data 'fit' – that is, the size of residual errors or the percentage of variance explained by the model.

One way to recharacterize this problem, implicitly and explicitly adopted in much of Leamer's work, is to change the question the researcher is asking. Under the classical approach, the question is framed in terms of what 'the estimate' of a parameter is after encountering the data, and of how 'precise' that estimate is. By contrast, Leamer suggests framing the question in terms of the *range* of estimates that *could be* supported by the data, and of how that range depends upon (a) the size of the classical random error in the data, and (b) a variety of beliefs that the researcher has brought to the estimation process. When the range of estimates that can result from a given class of beliefs in a given dataset is 'small', the researcher should feel more confident about the estimate. (Here, 'small' must be defined in terms of the relevant decisions that would flow from the inference. If essentially the same decision would be made no matter which element of the range is selected as the basis for decision, then the range is small.) When the range is wide (whether because the classically indicated standard error of the estimate of the parameter is high, or because the estimate depends markedly on which among a plausible set of prior beliefs is imposed), then the researcher should reach only more tentative conclusions, and should either seek additional data (if the range of uncertainty is generated largely by classical statistical uncertainty), or seek alternative methods of narrowing the range of prior beliefs that should be regarded as plausible.

Another way of characterizing the problem faced by the researchers Leamer was observing in the basement is that they have too many possible explanatory variables and too little data. Indeed, they may (and generally will) be able to imagine a wide range of possible explanatory variables that might belong in any given relationship they are trying to estimate. They face data limitations in two dimensions. First, they typically will have data for only a small subset of the explanatory variables that plausibly might be included. Secondly, even if they could find data for all of the plausible explanatory variables, they have far too few observations to allow them to estimate all the parameters if they were to include all the plausible explanatory variables in the relationship. To put it succinctly, 'any researcher who has a positive number of degrees of freedom has had a terrible failure of imagination about what the explanatory variables might be'.[1]

If we view the typical econometrics estimation in this way, then the problem is that, given the scope of the available data, (a) there are many unobservable variables (some of them probably highly correlated with each other, and certainly highly correlated with the error term in any relationship that excludes them); and (b) the parameters in the equation are unidentified (given the number of available observations). In this situation, the range of estimates potentially supportable by the data is infinite. To narrow the range, the researcher must either apply more data or apply some form of prior restrictions. The activities of the researchers witnessed by Leamer in the basement amounted to the (rather casual and surreptitious) imposition of quite strong prior beliefs.[2] Thus, as Leamer framed the problem, the question was not whether to include prior beliefs – prior beliefs had to be applied to produce an identified model and to make the range of supported estimates finite. The question, instead, was how to apply prior beliefs, and how to characterize the dependence of the range of supported estimates on the beliefs imposed.

It was to these questions that Leamer turned his prodigious mathematical talents. In an extended series of papers stretching from his early work to the present, he has worked out the mathematics of the bounds on the posterior estimates implied by various forms of prior information in an array of common inference problems. He turned his attention first to the standard linear regression model, of which practising econometricians were so fond. The linear model with normally distributed errors is both particularly commonly used and relatively tractable under a variety of approaches to specifying prior information. Leamer painstakingly worked out the algebra and geometry of the bounds implied for the parameters of interest of a series of increasingly narrow specifications of information about the parameters of the model.

In an early paper in this series (Leamer, 1972), he presented the algebra of the mixture of normal prior and posterior information with various ways to parameterize the prior information, and applied the apparatus to the problem of estimating US import demand using a distributed lag equation. He also presented an argument for the use of sensitivity analysis – the examination of the extent to which conclusions depend importantly upon underlying assumptions – as a way to develop priors as well as a way to characterize results. Thus, he departed materially both from the classical tradition (by introducing prior restrictions explicitly) *and* from the pure Bayesian tradition (by treating the prior as imperfectly known, and examining how inferential conclusions depend upon which prior is chosen).

In an array of papers that followed, Leamer worked out similar results in the context of specific troublesome econometrics problems and extended the work to other classes of prior information. For example, he provided (Leamer, 1973) what he characterized as a Bayesian interpretation of multicollinearity. While this paper is Bayesian in spirit, it explicitly considers the impact of alternative priors, an approach that most pure Bayesians would regard as wholly unorthodox. In two papers with Gary Chamberlain (Chamberlain and Leamer, 1976; Leamer and Chamberlain 1976), Leamer extended the algebra and geometry of matrix-weighted averages and the implied bounds for posterior estimates and provided a Bayesian-spirited interpretation of pre-testing.

In the early work, the central focus of inquiry is the relationship between prior information imposed in the form of beliefs about model parameters, or, more generally, linear combinations of model parameters. In some cases, the focus of inquiry by the researcher is presumed to be specific, chosen linear combinations of the parameters (for example, individual parameters themselves, or sums or differences of two coefficients). In many models, linear combinations of coefficients have an economic interpretation, and therefore the researcher might be presumed to have prior information about them. For example, in estimating a log-linear production function, the researcher may wish to indicate prior information that the process exhibits constant returns to scale. This restriction can be imposed with certainty by estimating the regression with the coefficients constrained to add to 1.

The approach proposed by Leamer is to examine the implications of introducing this prior information by specifying a prior that a linear combination of the coefficients (in particular, their sum) is 1. The researcher can then explore the implications (in terms of the posterior location of the individual parameter estimates, or combinations of them) of imposing this prior with varying degrees of certainty.

In order to use prior information of this (rather classical Bayesian) form, the researcher must have a concrete idea of which linear combinations of the coefficients are relevant and of what the likely values of those combinations might be. Some researchers have proved reluctant to specify which combinations of parameters they have information about, or what that information is. To explore the implications of less-restrictive information, Leamer (1978a) developed the algebra of the 'extreme' bounds implied by all possible linear restrictions of the variables (holding fixed the location, generally chosen to be the origin). These bounds compute the extreme limits of the value that can be taken by a given linear combination of the model's parameters as estimated in a constrained regression imposing an arbitrary set of linear constraints.[3]

The capstone of this early work is the *tour de force* presented in Leamer's 1978 book, *Specification Searches*. The book pulls together the results of the explorations and findings of the early investigations of bounds, and provides many new results, details and illustrations. It also both presents an integrated critique of (the misapplication of) classical estimation approaches *and* recommends specific, usable alternative methods. Leamer describes the process of constructing models and inferences from data as the process of searching, more or less effectively, through alternative specifications. The classical approach to data analysis is unable to provide a theory for what such a process is doing or what its results will be, and hence is unable to provide any guidance for how it should be undertaken, because the classical approach conditions on prior certainty about the form that the model takes. Leamer confronts this rather odd classical conception of the researcher's information as he or she approaches the data: complete certainty about the form of the model, and no knowledge whatever about the coefficients of the model. To put it another way, the classical approach combines an absolutely rigid prior specifying that all variables that might have been included in the model, but that have not been, have coefficients of zero with absolute certainty, with an absolutely uninformative prior about the values of the included coefficients.

Leamer observes that the conduct of data analysis as it is carried out in practice is a clear and present refutation of what he refers to as the classical 'axiom of specification'. People are behaving as if they had nothing like the information the classical theory assumes they have. With what he would later characterize as a considerable 'theological fanfare', Leamer set out in *Specification Searches* to pull together, elaborate, develop, illustrate and provide rhetorical support for a coherent, consistent and accessible alternative approach to estimation applicable to a wide variety of problems. The central focus of the book is the linear regression model so commonly used in econometrics. Leamer presents the accumulated results of his development of bounds methods, together with new results. He considers special problems that develop in some applications (for example, the problem of 'multicollinearity'), and examines and reinterprets some impurely classical methods then in fairly wide use (for example, 'Ridge Regression'). He also considers a variety of other common estimation settings (for example, point hypothesis testing), and examines more general problems of learning from data simultaneously about the formulation of the model and the evidence supporting the model.

In Leamer's early explorations, capped by *Specification Searches*, the focus of both the inferential attention *and* the prior information imposed is the coefficients of the model themselves. In later research, Leamer extends his work seeking bounds as a function of prior information to other classes of prior restrictions and to other problems. Some of his papers develop ideas closely related to the earlier work on the linear regression model. For example, he worked out (Leamer, 1982) how the possible locations of posterior means depend on assumptions about bounds for the variance matrix of the prior distribution.

However, other work considers quite different types of models and classes of restrictions. Leamer (1978a) considered the standard simple errors-in-variables model, and showed that the maximum likelihood estimate of the relevant parameter is the median of the least squares estimate, the reverse regression estimate and the instrumental variables estimate (so long as all have the same sign). Though this paper is not couched in the language of discussing the dependence of the bounds of an estimate on prior assumptions, it is none the less a determination of how an estimate is bounded as a result of prior assumptions (in this case, the assumption that the instrument is uncorrelated with the measurement error). In a later paper (Leamer, 1987a) he extended this work to the more general errors-in variables setting of a linear system of equations, generalizing the computation of bounds under varying assumptions about the form and intercorrelations of the errors in measurement. Again, this paper is not couched explicitly in terms of bounds implied by the imposition of prior information, but it is an exploration of what the bounds are for the relevant parameters under varying assumptions about the measurement-error distributions, which amount to the imposition of prior information. In another exploration of the errors-in-variables model (Klepper and Leamer, 1984), he and Stephen Klepper showed how prior information on the size and form of the measurement errors can impose bounds on the permissible inferences.

Other work departs even further from the early research on bounds implied by restrictions on the parameter values. In a paper drawing together a long stream of work by early econometricians in the first half of the twentieth century, Leamer (1981b) showed how inequality constraints can partially identify the equations in the standard supply-and-demand curve simultaneous equations problem. With C. Zachary Gilstein (Gilstein and Leamer, 1983), he showed how to establish the robustness of estimates with regard to the assumption of normality in the error distribution. In an exploration of the dependence of results on yet a different form of restriction, Leamer (1981a) showed how to compute the possible estimates of the location of a distribution where the estimates are to be based on information contained in a sample drawn under various different assumptions about the independence or the interdependence of sample observations. Here, the 'prior' restrictions imposed are on the degree and form of interdependence of different elements in the sample, rather than, for example, restrictions on linear combinations of the parameter values. The spirit of the inquiry is, however, much the same: how does imposing prior information of a given form restrict the range of estimates that can result?

CONFRONTING INTRANSIGENCE: WORKING TOWARD GETTING THE METHODS USED

As Leamer developed the individual methods and the generic approach to estimation that he proposed, his interest was in more than mere codification of a critique and the presentation of an alternative. He wanted to change the way people in the profession interacted with data. Thus, almost from the beginning of his work he was concerned with understanding the sources of reluctance to adopt the new methods and with developing ways to overcome the apparent obstacles.

An immediate obstacle was that the early developments were of methods in principle, and using them often required taking on a substantial computational burden. The same might have been said of the use of multiple regression analysis before the advent of computer packages that reduced the algebra to the process of invoking a short series of commands. That problem had eventually been solved by people taking it upon themselves to write and disseminate the required computer code. By the time Leamer was observing the behaviour of his graduate-student colleagues and professors in the basement, complex regression models were easy to estimate. By contrast, adopting Leamer's early suggestions for how to make the interaction with data a more sensible process imposed a large computational burden in the form of having to write a computer code that carried out the non-traditional computations. Much later, the development of personal-computer-based matrix operations programs would make implementing some of Leamer's approaches much easier in practice, but in the 1970s there was no way for researchers to conduct the kind of analysis Leamer was suggesting with anything like the computational ease that new computer packages were providing for more standard estimations.

Accordingly, Leamer set out to develop a computer package that would make his approach to estimation in the context of the linear regression model simple and straightforward. Called SEARCH (*Seeking Extreme and Average Regression Coefficient Hypotheses*), the package accepted as inputs raw data and various alternative specifications of prior information, and produced as outputs a collection of implied bounds and posterior estimates. Some of the software was developed in the early 1970s, and early versions of the program were available by the mid-1970s. By the late 1970s Leamer was urging use of the approach embodied in SEARCH as a standard practice for the reporting of regression estimates. While some researchers sought copies of the package and presented reports based upon its output (see, for example, Cooley and Leroy, 1981), use of the package has still not widely penetrated the standard empirical practice of econometrics.

An additional obstacle to wider adoption of the kinds of practices Leamer was suggesting was, as he saw it, a simple lack of sufficient exhortation and persuasion. *Specification Searches* is a testimony to this view; it is replete with both exhortation and what Leamer would subsequently refer to as 'theology'. In 1983 Leamer published two papers (Leamer, 1983; Leamer and Leonard, 1983) that attempted simultaneously (a) to explain the methods concisely and in a widely accessible form (devoid of explicit Bayesian doctrine and theocratic discourse); (b) to interpret them as suggestions about how to report about and characterize the degree of belief that should attach to empirical estimates; and (c) to present reasonably well-developed, interesting examples where the methodology and approach to description of results appeared insightful.

In his provocatively entitled 'Let's Take the Con out of Econometrics', Leamer (1983) presented a convincing case that some of the standard panaceas (for example, randomization) are insufficient to avoid the kinds of post-data model construction problems he had so extensively explored. The article is deliberately rhetorical in character and presents no new methodology. It contains an interesting example focusing on the problem of assessing the deterrent effect of capital punishment. This is a problem to which different observers quite clearly bring very different prior beliefs, and Leamer used it to demonstrate the value of reporting the interaction of the data with various different priors. The results are illuminating. First, in the context of the data he was examining, Leamer found that the bounds of the estimate of the deterrent effect of capital punishment for any given prior ('right winger', 'bleeding heart', 'rational maximizer' and so on) were relatively wide. Thus, the data failed to provide strong confirmation (in the sense of yielding a narrow range of estimates) for most of the prior beliefs he examined. Secondly, the range of estimates across different prior beliefs was fairly wide. Thus, people who confront these data with different priors will reach different conclusions, but none of them should be very certain even after they have encountered the data. Leamer interpreted these results as suggesting that, in the context of the data he had at hand, the estimates of the deterrent effect were too 'fragile' – that is, too susceptible to alteration by different prior beliefs – to withstand the pressure of credulity. He argued that this is a dramatically more thorough and helpful way to characterize what we should think we have learned through an association with this dataset than would be given by the standard small table of regression coefficients and associated t-statistics typically published in economics journals.

In an article that appeared about the same time, Leamer and Leonard (1983)[4] took up the theme of fragility in the context of two additional examples, with less emphasis on rhetorical persuasion and a greater emphasis on characterizing the proposed methods succinctly. The explicit purpose of the article, reflected in its title, was to propose a standard approach to reporting how fragile a given estimate should be regarded. In a later reply to a comment by McAleer, Pagan and Volker (1985) about an article by Cooley and Leroy (1981), Leamer (1985) even more strongly takes up the challenge of defending the usefulness of his form of broad sensitivity analysis to establish the robustness of estimates. In a paper delivered to a European conference, Leamer (1991) summarizes both the methods and the arguments for them, propounding them to a new audience in the context of macroeconomic analyses.

Leamer's work in econometric theory has typically involved the use of illustrative examples. Yet even though his later work has been more overtly designed to persuade others in the profession to change their standard data analysis practices, the small number of 'serious' examples of interest to econometricians that have been developed may be insufficiently persuasive to effect major change. However, a significant body of applied work based on Leamer's fundamental approach is, in fact, available for inspection. This work constitutes Leamer's effort to use serious estimation techniques to examine certain basic questions in international trade, his area of greatest applied interest. To understand the role of his econometric development in the context of his work in international trade, it is necessary to examine the whole of his work in that area more fully.

LEAMER AS A PRACTISING APPLIED ECONOMETRICIAN: WORK ON INTERNATIONAL TRADE

It would be misleading to suggest that Leamer's research in international trade has been motivated solely by a desire to showcase his econometric methods for persuasive purposes. Rather, his interests in trade are sufficiently broad and his contributions to the literature sufficiently deep as to constitute a notable career in that field alone. Indeed, Leamer is an accomplished trade theorist in his own right. For example, in a series of papers best represented by a piece in the *Journal of Political Economy* (Leamer, 1987b), he has explored the process of growth in three-factor production and trade models under certain restrictive assumptions. One concept from this work, the 'Leamer Triangle', is emerging as a basic tool in trade theory.

Moreover, much of Leamer's research has reflected his impatience with the imprecise modelling characteristic of much of the existing empirical trade literature. Developing rigorous yet estimatable models of international trade in the context of realistic data analysis is a highly complex task. However, it is incumbent on researchers to push their models as far as possible in order to allow theory sensibly to guide estimation, rather than to adopt *ad hoc* intuitive specifications. A primary message of Leamer's criticism has been that intuition has often proved badly flawed when set against proper theoretical specification. This message has come through independently of his own empirical work.

Inevitably, however, Leamer's interests in applied trade analysis have come to be married to his econometric techniques for learning from data. There are many influential questions in trade toward which empirical work could be addressed with the expectation of more fruitful results than previous research accomplished, if it were carried out within a suitable theoretical framework. The most prominent example in Leamer's work is the specification of conditions under which international trade in goods is a linear function of excess resource endowments across countries, as discussed below. With theory as a roadmap, data may be analysed to provide inferences about sensible (that is, not obviously false) hypotheses about trade and endowments and to measure the effects of different variables on trade. Further, such inferences need to survive sensitivity analysis in various forms in order to be held confidently.

The development of Leamer's approach to empirical trade analysis has largely paralleled his work in econometric theory. For example, we noted earlier his disappointment as a graduate student at the gaps between theory and practice in econometrics. This disappointment carried over to his reading of much empirical research in international economics, which was often poorly motivated by theory and therefore vague in its inferential findings. That state of affairs motivated Leamer, while still a student and in conjunction with Robert Stern (Leamer and Stern, 1970), to write *Quantitative International Economics*, a short and incisive volume on problems with prevailing theoretical specifications for then-important problems in international finance and trade.

As one example, in the late 1960s regression models attempting to explain the cross-country or cross-commodity pattern of trade were in their infancy. A strand of literature had developed in Europe in which so-called 'gravity models' were used to estimate bilateral trade flows among developed countries. In these models, trade is expressed as a function of the sizes of trading partners in formulas suggested by gravitational attraction, with these formulas at times being augmented by the inclusion of other presumed trade determinants. While intriguing in some dimensions, such specifications were without firm foundation in trade theory. This situation induced Leamer and Stern (p. 3) to write, 'The lack of an explicit theoretical framework has been the greatest failure of these studies. Without such a theory the analysis tends to degenerate into a search for meaningless empirical regularities.' This statement presaged the thrust of much of the criticism Leamer has levelled at empirical work in trade throughout his career.

In their book Leamer and Stern attempted to specify empirical approaches suggested by economic theory for the problems they considered. Indeed, their reconsideration of the gravity models partially underlay recent attempts to 'rehabilitate' the approach (cf. Bergstrand, 1985). The volume was influential for at least a decade as practitioners in some research areas attempted to run their specifications through its critical filters and also to improve on its simple modelling approaches. We sense, however, that at least in Leamer's view it quickly became obsolete because its empirical recommendations were too wedded to conventional econometric practice. His interests rapidly were moving into exploring models interactively with thorough data analysis along the lines discussed earlier. The book had made its critical points; it was time to move on to specific analysis.

Throughout his career the primary focus of Leamer's empirical work in international trade has been the explanation of trade patterns, or the discovery of the sources of comparative advantage. In the early 1970s this literature was in great flux. The standard theoretical model of trade continued to be the Heckscher–Ohlin, or factor-proportions, model in which, under certain highly restrictive assumptions, countries would tend to export those goods that intensively used their relatively abundant factors. More correctly, countries would tend to export on net the services of their relatively abundant factors and import the services of their relatively scarce factors. However, alternative theories of the determinants of trade had been advanced based on patterns of demand, technological differences and barriers to international commerce. Empirical analysis to that point had achieved no consensus about the relative contributions of these influences to actual trade patterns.[5]

In an early (and often overlooked) paper, Leamer (1974) focused directly on the empirical issue of comparing these proposed trade determinants. The paper was noteworthy in two respects. First, as discussed below, the emerging practice in the literature (cf. Baldwin, 1971) of examining the factor-proportions model by regressing commodity trade on factor intensities in production across industries had a highly questionable basis in theory. Leamer revealed his preference for relating trade patterns to endowments across countries, rather than intensities across industries, because the former method is much closer to the actual relationships embedded in the factor-proportions theory. In retrospect, the profession should have paid more attention to this simple fact. Secondly, because the purpose of the study was to assess crudely the relative contributions of competing trade determinants to the pattern of international trade, it provided a vehicle for the simple use of Leamer's emerging data-analytic techniques. He was largely unsuccessful in discriminating among the likelihood of competing trade theories, due in part to the inability of his methods to separate the effects of various trade determinants under specified alternative scenarios. In our view, the inconsistent results were unfortunate in that they denied the paper its due in influencing later empirical work.

The bulk of Leamer's trade work came in the 1980s. His writings progressed from criticism of prevailing techniques in the literature to the specification of an empirically relevant theoretical framework for the factor-proportions model and the use of that framework to assess the apparent influence of endowments on trade. Prominent in the empirical research was the use of many of the econometric techniques Leamer has explicated.

To appreciate the impact this body of research has had on the empirical trade literature, it is necessary first to understand the methodological state of affairs to which they have been addressed. Because prevailing approaches to estimating or testing the factor-proportions model had been only loosely related to the underlying theory, it was difficult to know whether the model had any real empirical content. Indeed, 'tests' of the Heckscher–Ohlin trade model had been based on intuitively plausible yet theoretically false predictions. Further, a bewildering array of empirical specifications, all of which seemed acceptable due to the fuzzy link between theory and practical estimation, had yielded rather different inferences in similar datasets. In Leamer's terminology, these inferences were exceedingly fragile.

The former situation was most evident in the celebrated finding by Leontief (1953) that in 1947 the US production of a basket of import-competing goods was more capital-intensive than the production of a basket of exports, despite the obvious relative abundance of physical capital in the United States. The Leontief paradox, as this result quickly became known, seemed at odds with the predictions of the factor-proportions theory. Interestingly, this conclusion (and similar findings by later researchers) was not generally taken as empirical refutation of the theory but rather served to spur broader developments of the model that seemed more consistent with data. In this regard, Leontief's result was highly influential because it helped effect a substantive improvement in the sophistication of our explanations of the determinants of trade.

Ironically, however, the paradox was simply the result of inadequately specified theory, as Leamer (1980) pointed out. Leontief's two-factor approach does not pay sufficient attention to the implications of either the existence of multiple factors or imbalanced trade.[6] In such circumstances it is possible for a country to export or import on net both labour and capital. Relying on a set of equations developed initially by Vanek (1968), Leamer demonstrated that under the most appropriate definition of factor abundance, the factor-proportions theory predicts nothing in general about the comparison of capital–labour ratios in exports versus imports. Rather, the theoretically valid comparison is between the capital embodied in net exports relative to aggregate consumption and the corresponding labour-embodiment ratio. Under this criterion, Leontief's data themselves revealed the United States to have been capital-abundant and labour-scarce, overturning the paradox.

The latter problem of haphazard model specification was apparent in the variety of regression models that purported also to test the factor-proportions model. Much of the literature in this area had relied on the intuitively plausible yet (again) false notion that a regression of net commodity trade on factor intensities across manufacturing industries for a particular country would reveal that country's factor-abundance structure (cf. Baldwin, 1971; Harkness, 1978). The idea is simply that, other things being equal, a rise in capital intensity for an industry in a capital-abundant nation should result in greater net exports under the logic of the factor-proportions model. Thus, if the coefficient on, say, human capital intensity (typically, the ratio of capitalized wage differentials to employment or some measure of relative educational attainment by sector) in a cross-industry linear regression were positive, the researcher would infer the country to be abundant in human capital.

The results of such exercises were usually plausible, made all the more so by the disturbing presence of a negative coefficient on the physical capital-intensity variable for US trade, which was taken as another version of the Leontief paradox. This finding stimulated the two most prominent permutations to the regression approach. First, under the presumption that imported primary commodities might be highly capital intensive, numerous researchers have arbitrarily removed these industries from their calculations, a procedure that typically eliminated the paradox (cf. Stern and Maskus, 1981). Secondly, arguing that the Heckscher–Ohlin theory provides guidance only about the sign, rather than the volume, of an industry's net exports, Harkness and Kyle (1975) substituted a binary dependent variable into their regressions. For reasons that remain empirically unclear, this procedure also tended to remove the scarce-capital paradox.

As rough descriptive devices, such regressions may make some sense, though it is difficult to know what to make of the partial correlations that result. However, the practice in the profession was to treat the results as either implicit tests of the theory or, less strongly, as valid predictive devices for policy. For example, it was sometimes argued that, for a country with a positive coefficient on physical capital intensity, it would be possible to expand net exports through a programme of capital subsidies. Alternatively, if a negative coefficient on unskilled-labour intensity were taken to indicate labour scarcity, one might argue for tariffs to protect labour incomes.

The profession should have known better. It has been common doctrine in trade theory since Melvin (1968) to note that the factor-proportions model makes no predictions about the relative factor intensities of trade in particular commodities when there are more than two goods, implying that this regression approach was questionable from the outset. Further, for a large economy, such as the United States, factor intensities must be considered jointly endogenous with trade, a fact for which the simple regression procedures made no provision.

The most fundamental difficulty, however, was simply that the cross-commodity equations could not be derived from a theoretical specification of the Heckscher–Ohlin model. Again, it was Leamer, this time in conjunction with Chip Bowen (Leamer and Bowen, 1981) who pointed out the methodological shortcomings. In brief, such regressions reveal relative factor abundance only if the inverse regression matrix formed from factor intensities preserves the signs of a country's excess factor endowments, a condition that is extremely unlikely to hold. Moreover, the cross-industry regression approach was incapable of rigorously supporting policy conclusions of any kind. Conditions under which a change in endowments might be expected to expand net exports or a rise in tariffs might be expected to influence factor incomes in a particular way are considerably more complex in general equilibrium than simple regressions could reveal. Finally, Leamer and Bowen pointed out that, these substantial difficulties aside, no full 'test' of the theory could simply relate trade to factor intensities and infer factor abundance from the results. To do so is to accept the theory *ex ante*; instead, what must occur is a comparison of independent measures of trade, factor intensities and factor endowments.

Leamer's criticisms of both the Leontief paradox and the regression studies were based on his development (Leamer, 1980, 1984) of a simple general-equilibrium version of the factor-proportions model. The equations in this version rely on cost minimization by competitive firms, full employment of all resources, identical and homothetic preferences across countries, and identities relating production to resource supplies and trade to production and consumption. Further, countries are assumed to be in the same 'cone of diversification' in the sense that they produce enough goods in common to have identical factor prices and technology matrices. Under these assumptions, which are consistent with the basic Heckscher–Ohlin model, trade in factor services equals the difference between a country's factor endowments and its consumption of the world's endowments. By extension, if the number of goods and factors is the same so that the inverse technology matrix exists, trade in goods is a linear function of these excess or deficient factor supplies.

Each of these statements has provided a basis for more satisfying study of the relationships between resource endowments and trade. That an economy's net factor trade could be computed and then compared meaningfully to measures of excess endowments stimulated attempts to test the model rigorously both within the United States (Maskus, 1985) and across countries (Bowen, Leamer and Sveikauskas, 1987). These papers demonstrate clearly that actual data do not conform well to the model's strict predictions about the relationships among international trade, factor intensities and factor endowments. Predicted endowment ratios typically diverge from measured endowment ratios by margins that are too large to be reasonably ascribed simply to sampling and measurement error, though the econometric basis for this inference is murky. However, this conclusion is, in terms Leamer might prefer, methodologically unsurprising. The factor-proportions model rests on a series of incredible assumptions that cannot be expected to hold in any practical setting. These properly specified tests have succeeded essentially in demonstrating what was surely already known: the Heckscher–Ohlin theory cannot be taken as literally true, nor can differences in factor endowments be considered the only source of comparative advantage.

The more interesting question concerns the extent to which the international distribution of resource supplies seems capable of explaining the structure of foreign trade. This was the task Leamer set himself in his seminal empirical study of trade and factor endowments, *Sources of International Comparative Advantage* (Leamer, 1984). As noted above, the so-called 'even model', in which the number of factors and goods is assumed the same,[7] provided a theoretical justification for regressing net trade by commodity against excess resource endowments across countries. Various measures of 'goodness of fit' could be established to assess the contribution of factor supplies to trade in each good. Thus, the attempt was neither to test the literal factor-proportions theory nor seriously to establish a classical hypothesis-testing framework with firmly specified alternatives, but rather to see if the data could convincingly support the basic linear model. Clearly, Leamer's econometric methods, well-developed by that time, would play a large role in an inferential setup of this nature.

The book is a substantive contribution to both theoretical and empirical trade analysis. The initial chapter presents the fullest explication yet available of the linear relations among net trade flows and deficient or excess factor supplies (deviations of national endowments from levels needed for domestic production) that emerge from the multifactor trade model. Even more interestingly, Leamer explores within the framework of his basic model the implications of relaxing some of the incredible assumptions of the theory, demonstrating its fragility to different specifications. In truth, much of this analysis simply restates the results of previous authors. However, their appearance in a coherent framework makes the results more accessible. The chapter itself has become a common pedagogical device for teaching advanced trade theory.

Of greater interest is the empirical work. It is noteworthy in two respects. First, the book presents voluminous and carefully documented data compiled on 1958 and 1975 trade patterns, outputs and resource endowments for a cross-section of 58 of the most important countries in world trade. Endowments included physical capital (proxied by depreciated cumulative sums of past real investment flows), three labour types based on crudely defined skill differentials, four land categories, and three natural resources (proxied by current production values). Detailed trade categories were aggregated into ten commodity groups for the econometric analysis, where the aggregation was based on cross-country correlations of net exports. Inevitably such an exercise is plagued by the unavailability of some data and the inaccuracy (even in theory) with which data are measured. Leamer was unusually candid about the shortcomings of his dataset, perhaps because he used these problems to illustrate his preferred methods for estimation of the trade model.

This estimation is the second noteworthy feature of the empirical work. As noted, the data were questionable. Further, though the theoretical framework suggested a set of linear equations to serve as the basis for study, it could not be manipulated to yield a clearly defined and tractable theoretical alternative against which to test the model in the classical statistical sense. Thus, the empirical situation required, by the standards of Leamer's own econometric theory, the application of techniques that could extract convincing inferences from the data about the accuracy of the model.

To get an idea of the complexity of this task, consider a broad outline of the steps involved. First, because each excess factor endowment depends on all other factor supplies, including those that of necessity were excluded from the analysis, a regression on the original system would yield biased and consistent estimates. Leamer opted to estimate reduced-form equations with actual endowments on the right side, a compromise of some discomfort. Indeed, the first serious reservation could be expressed at this point. Leamer simply assumes that the included endowments are exogenous – an assumption subject to some debate in the trade literature – and uncorrelated with excluded factor supplies. Secondly, the reduced-form equations were estimated by ordinary least squares and then adjusted for unequal error variances as related to country size. Heteroschedasticity adjustments are important in any analysis of the factor-proportions model, which by its nature is scale-free. Empirical inferences that were dominated by the influence of large countries would be suspect. Similarly, the resulting weighted least-squares estimates were then subjected to a relatively simple sensitivity analysis for the influence of remaining outliers. This was performed by omitting from each equation each observation singly and checking for sign changes in the coefficients. Sign changes were sufficiently common and the influence of extreme observations was sufficiently strong in many cases to render the adjusted estimates 'suspicious'.

The third step was to check for the sensitivity of the estimates to measurement errors by running a series of reverse regressions as suggested by Klepper and Leamer (1984). In these, if the signs of the coefficients vary across the regressions there is evidence that collinearity in the measured variables may be so high that the true variables may be perfectly collinear. This situation appeared common in the data, implying that both the basic and adjusted regression estimates could not be regarded as believable with any confidence because they were inherently inestimatable.

In turn, this problem pointed to the need for imposing prior expectations on the regression coefficients as a way of expanding the information set and identifying the final estimates. Thus, true to form, Leamer's final task was to specify prior means and standard deviations for all 242 coefficients to be estimated, that is, to guess about the true influence of different endowments on various trade flows. This information was incorporated with the data to form Bayesian coefficient estimates, which Leamer seemed confident were reasonably robust. However, this conclusion was highly debatable since the coefficient signs often did not survive changes in the prior variance. Further, the factor-proportions model seemed, in this analysis, to perform rather well in explaining variations in international trade patterns. The author comments frequently that the results are 'surprisingly' favourable to the underlying theory.

In fact, Leamer's enthusiasm on this point was probably excessive. As others have noted (Anderson, 1987), the finding of a strong linear relation between excess factor supplies and trade does not demonstrate the truth of the particular relation predicted by the theorem. Put more starkly, Leamer's inability to relate independent measures of trade, endowments and factor intensities (the last variable being excluded from his analysis) implied that his approach was no more a 'test' of the theory than were previous efforts. In turn, it remains difficult to know what confidence to assign to the results, because no serious alternative hypotheses were considered in a consistent manner.[8] Leamer entertained the possibility of nonlinear relations between trade and endowments as competing models but that effort was relatively unconvincing in content. In this sense, his work also falls prey to many of the methodological criticisms Leamer himself has lodged against other practitioners.

In truth, this state of affairs is more a testament to the inherent problems in articulating sensible and refutable statistical hypotheses derived rigorously from underlying trade theory than a penetrating criticism of Leamer's study. Empirical trade is a difficult laboratory in which to work. Leamer's analysis of the factor-endowment basis of trade is a watershed because its insistence on serious data analysis bears some promise to effect important changes in the profession. *Sources of International Comparative Advantage* presents the most thorough and accessible example of learning from data in ways that help inform our understanding of the empirical content of an important trade question.[9] We should expect it to serve as a guide for others who wish to discover what data can reveal about trade matters. Indeed, a nascent literature based on its techniques is emerging.[10]

It must be admitted, however, that empirical trade analysts have been slow to adopt these methods and there is some doubt that they will ever come into standard use. It is of interest to ask why this is so, a question that receives a general treatment in the next section. The answer in trade cannot rely solely on the difficulty or unfamiliarity of Leamer's approach, since any talented and ambitious graduate student could implement them readily. Rather, there has emerged among international-trade scholars a systematic preference for work in abstract theory over empirical research. This is not wholly a question of methodological bias; there are good reasons to distrust the vast bulk of empirical work in international economics. The reasons are precisely those raised by Leamer in more general settings. Data are poorly measured, theory is inadequately transformed into estimation frameworks, and empirical work is too often aimed at refuting incredible hypotheses that we know to be untrue, such as the literal Heckscher–Ohlin model. Inevitably, the statistical inferences that result are doubtful and should, therefore, play little role in shaping the opinions of international economists.

Indeed, Leamer (1990) has argued that there have been only two influential empirical findings in international trade, the Leontief paradox (Leontief, 1953) and the fact that there is much two-way foreign trade within industries (Grubel and Lloyd, 1975) which is not easily explained in traditional trade models. They were influential not because the theory and techniques employed were esoteric (or, in retrospect, even correct) but because they discovered from data certain surprising empirical regularities that motivated economists to revise their modes of thinking. A trade economist's initial reaction might be to dispute these statements, but upon reflection it becomes difficult to disagree with them.

Seen in this light, Leamer's challenge to the trade profession becomes clearer. There are many important theoretical propositions in trade that remain without confidently held empirical content because the evidence brought to bear on them so far has been exceedingly fragile. The burden lies with empirical trade economists who must seek to remove that fragility. It may not be necessary to adopt Leamer's methods wholesale, but continued reliance on methods of inference that do not push the data to reveal insensitive information is likely to result in more frustration.

THE IMPACT ON PRACTICE

In international trade, Leamer's formulations of and approaches to problems of interest have generated a growing awareness of the value of his methods, but progress in using them has come slowly. In econometrics, Leamer has taught us a great deal more than we regularly use. His generic criticism of classical practice is widely accepted *in principle*. Few have tried to argue that what he tells us about the lack of theory behind classical estimation as actually practised is incorrect. Indeed, his critique is widely referenced and taught in graduate econometrics courses. But we have arrived at a rather odd equilibrium in our assimilation of his teaching. His name is regularly invoked in discussions of econometric results, and there is a general recognition that his proposed methods and reporting formats would aid discussion and learning, but the methods he proposes we use for developing and reporting estimates are not widely applied. Scholars have not adopted the techniques of exploring or reporting the degree of fragility of estimates, the width of the bounds for estimates implied by various alternative sets of prior beliefs. What should we make of this equilibrium?

First, we could conclude that Leamer simply hasn't done enough to develop, make accessible and publicize the methods, nor enough to convince us that we should take the trouble to use them. But reviewing the enormous body of theory, example and rhetorical support he has set before us makes this a thoroughly unconvincing explanation. The techniques are there. They can be (and even sometimes are) used. When they are, there are significant economies of argument about the empirical results – we don't have to have seven (or seventeen) different researchers conducting different analyses of the same data to find out how different the results can be under different approaches. To say, when we broadly accept the argument he has presented on behalf of the methods, that it remains his responsibility that we do not often apply them seems clearly a bankrupt explanation.

A second explanation is that the methods simply remain too difficult to use – that while using them might be widely regarded as a good idea in principle, in practice the cost is too high in terms of estimation effort and reporting space. Given the existence of a reasonably accessible computer package for carrying out at least the main suggestions for the most commonly used linear estimation model, this explanation must be interpreted as meaning that the intellectual task of forming, characterizing and revealing prior information is simply too demanding. While there is surely a good deal of truth in this, it clearly suffers from the economist's standard 'compared to what?'. Compared to the standard methods of abusing classical statistical theory, it is surely true that the approaches recommended by Leamer are intellectually arduous. But compared to other ways of trying to assess the robustness of estimates – for example, developing, searching over and reporting the results of *ad hoc* collections of alternative specifications of regression models – Leamer's techniques are at once more comprehensive and less difficult to apply.

A third possible explanation is that in practice the methods produce bounds that are distressingly wide, and therefore tend to undermine the apparent usefulness of the estimation process and the conclusions of proposed analyses. Many have raised this objection, for example, to the 'extreme bounds' methods, noting that the prior restrictions that give rise to the extreme estimates are difficult to interpret and (since they are constructed over the entire range of possible combinations of beliefs) are likely generally to embody rather strange information. Thus, knowing that the most extreme possible estimates that could arise from a given dataset are wide, but that those extreme estimates are associated with rather outlandish beliefs imposed with certainty may make the extreme bounds seem relatively uninteresting. This reaction, of course, has things almost exactly backwards. When the bounds are wide, Leamer agrees that one must seek a more limited and sensible class of priors, interior to those giving rise to the extreme bounds, within which to develop a narrower set of bounds. If no smaller class of priors that observers can agree are sensible can be found, then the results should be interpreted as too fragile to support conclusions. It is when the bounds are *narrow* that Leamer argues that the extreme bounds are most useful. When we can say that no matter what combinations of prior beliefs are imposed, the range of the implied conclusions is small, then we can conclude that the results are truly powerful; the fact that the range of beliefs over which we checked the implications includes outlandish combinations makes the conclusion more powerful.

None the less, there is again an important core of truth in this explanation – often the computed bounds are quite wide, and it is difficult to get interested observers to agree on a narrower set of prior beliefs that give rise to a narrower range of conclusions. When that is the case, how should we respond? A natural reaction might be to prefer a method that gives a narrower range – for example, the classical model and its point estimate, together with a classically computed standard error of estimate. But the time we discover that the irreducible area of agreement about priors, conjoined with a given dataset, leaves substantial ambiguity about the conclusions – that is, when the bounds are wide after we have tried to agree on a limited set of priors – is *precisely* when we should *not* substitute a method that provides a (false) sense that the range of possible outcomes is small (which is precisely what taking refuge in the classical approach would do). Thus, our approach to finding substantial fragility or ambiguity should be to redouble our efforts to narrow the range of possible prior beliefs, not to impose willy-nilly an *ad hoc* collection of much narrower and much less fully revealed prior restrictions in the form of throwing out variables and presenting classical estimates of the kinds of stripped-down models that result from an *ad hoc* classical specification search. This explanation, then, amounts to the statement that we simply prefer to delude ourselves about the degree of certainty that should attach to our estimates – a statement few would endorse, but many seem to affirm through their practices.

This brings us to the final explanation for why we might, as a profession, not be adopting more widely the practices Leamer has presented to us: we may not care enough about, or believe enough in, the empirical magnitudes we supposedly expend such large amounts of energy developing and purveying to one another. Our practices belie our (espoused) belief in our results. We report estimates based on small *ad hoc* searches over different models, aware – even expecting – that if we are lucky and our work attracts attention, other researchers may conduct different model searches and report quite different results. What meaning is there to reporting a small standard error of estimate for a result that we can expect to be confronted by a quite different alternative estimate?

One supposes that if we thought that important issues hung in the balance to be determined by the estimates we constructed, we might be much more careful to understand and characterize all the sources of uncertainty about the conclusions – the uncertainties due to our lack of prior knowledge of the relationships, as much as (or perhaps even more than) the uncertainties stemming from classical statistical errors of estimation. But the sociology of the profession – the value structure, the rules of academic discourse, the evaluation procedures for selecting articles for publication and for giving promotions in academic institutions – militates against such a stance by individual researchers. We are caught in a low-level equilibrium trap: poor practices based on a false application of classical statistical theory resulting in relatively fragile results. Wide appreciation of the fact that estimates are fragile leads to low credence being attached to estimates, which in turn provides little incentive for researchers to try to provide better estimates because few take them seriously anyway. Empirical estimation becomes merely a vehicle, an excuse for trotting out the work we really use to impress each other – new theory and methodology.

Leamer calls us on our act – and thus becomes something of an unwelcome guest at a masquerade party. He urges us to put aside the masks and to be candid with ourselves, each other and other interested parties. He urges us to pay more than lip service to the value of empirical results. To do that, we shall have to apply better methods for producing and reporting the degree of certainty that we and others should attach to our estimates. Leamer has first pointed out the direction, then paved the path to make it smoother, then exhorted us to try walking along it, and then walked down it himself to show us that it can be done. We should be embarassed to ask for more from him – though he should not (and undoubtedly will not!) hesitate to ask more from us.

CONCLUSION

Ed Leamer has had a substantial impact on what we know about econometrics and international trade. In the trade area, he has penetrated not only what we know in principle, but which problems we attack and how we go about subduing them. In econometrics, his impact on what we know has been enormous. He has constructed a wide and deep and coherent body of theory and suggestions about how we might more effectively learn from data. It is widely accepted as powerful in principle. It has not penetrated actual practice nearly as much as it has entered the consciousness of the field. His impact has been in the interstices – in how we describe specification searches; in how we characterize various specific problems (like multicollinearity); in how we comment on each other's work. The current equilibrium teaches us more about ourselves and our profession than it does about him or his suggestions.

NOTES

1. Leamer says that he never said this, though he wishes that he had. One author of the current paper (Leonard) thought he had heard it from Leamer, and doesn't think he coined it himself. Its source awaits identification.
2. We can think of the omission of a plausible explanatory variable (whether because we don't have the data or for any other reason) as the imposition of a prior restriction that its coefficient is zero with absolute certainty. This is very strong information to be applied with the casualness often demonstrated by practising econometricians.
3. Such a limit could be computed as follows. First, choose the linear combination, q', of the parameters, b, that is to be maximized or minimized. Now consider all possible linear restrictions of the model parameters (weighted linear combinations, r', of the coefficients adding to a prespecified value, typically chosen to be zero). Each such linear restriction, imposed with certainty, implies a constrained least squares estimate of the model (embodying that restriction with certainty), and thus implies a value for the constrained estimate of the linear combination of interest, q'. This creates a function mapping from the linear restriction r' to the value of the linear combination of interest, q'. Now maximize the value of $q'b$ with respect to the coefficients of the imposed linear restriction, $r'b = 0$. What Leamer worked out is the algebra that allows straightforward computation of such general bounds.
4. Leonard is a co-author of the present paper.
5. In fact, there is still no consensus today, although much progress has been made in understanding the empirical constraints that must be addressed in pursuing the question.
6. To be fair, Leontief's computation of the factor contents of $1 million each of exports and import-competing products was an attempt at forcing balanced trade on the computations. This procedure was inappropriate, however.
7. This assumption would be considered by most economists as patently false, even when liberal allowance is made for aggregation problems in defining goods and factors. Curiously, Leamer is little bothered by making it, believing that it can be made tolerable by supposing the existence of infinitesimal transport costs in goods to remove any theoretical indeterminacy in factor prices. This is a rather unappealing device, however, as noted by Anderson (1987).
8. But see Bowen, Leamer and Sveikauskas (1987) for an effort to improve on this situation.
9. However, two later efforts by Leamer (1988a,b) to use the basic model to investigate the effects of unobservable trade barriers were both less successful and less accessible.
10. For example, Maskus (1991) investigated the endowment basis for international trade in an independent data set covering 38 countries in 1984, replicating Leamer's finding of uncertainty as to the signs of most coefficients due to collinearity.

REFERENCES

Anderson, James E. (1987), 'Review of Edward E. Leamer, *Sources of International Comparative Advantage: Theory and Evidence*', *Journal of Economic Literature*, **25**, 146–7.

Baldwin, Robert E. (1971), 'Determinants of the Commodity Structure of U.S. Trade', *American Economic Review*, **61**, 126–46.

Bergstrand, Jeffrey H. (1985), 'The Gravity Equation in International Trade: Some Microeconomic Foundations and Empirical Evidence', *Review of Economics and Statistics*, **67**, 474–81.

Bowen, Harry P., Edward E. Leamer and Leo Sveikauskas (1987), 'Multicountry, Multifactor Tests of the Factor Abundance Theory', *American Economic Review*, **77**, 791–809.

Chamberlain, Gary and Edward E. Leamer (1976), 'Matrix Weighted Averages and Posterior Bounds', *Journal of the Royal Statistical Society*, **38**, 73–84.

Cooley, Thomas F. and Stephen F. Leroy (1981), 'Identification and Estimation of Money Demand', *American Economic Review*, **71**, 825–44.

Gilstein, C. Zachary and Edward E. Leamer (1983), 'Robust Sets of Regression Estimates', *Econometrica*, **51**, 321–33.

Grubel, Herbert G. and Peter J. Lloyd (1975), *Intra-Industry Trade: The Theory and Measurement of International Trade in Differentiated Products*, London: MacMillan.

Harkness, Jon (1978), 'Factor Abundance and Comparative Advantage', *American Economic Review*, **68**, 784–800.

Harkness, Jon and John F. Kyle (1975), 'Factors Influencing United States Comparative Advantage', *Journal of International Economics*, **5**, 153–165.

Klepper, Steven and Edward E. Leamer (1984), 'Consistent Sets of Estimates for Regressions with Errors in All Variables', *Econometrica*, **52**, 163–83.

Leamer, Edward E. (1972), 'A Class of Informative Priors and Distributed Lag Analysis', *Econometrica*, **40**, 1059–81.

—— (1973), 'Multicollinearity: a Bayesian Interpretation', *Review of Economics and Statistics*, **55**, 371–80.

—— (1974), 'The Commodity Composition of International Trade in Manufactures: an Empirical Analysis', *Oxford Economic Papers*, **26**, 350–74.

—— (1978a), 'Least-Squares Versus Instrumental Variables Estimation in a Simple Errors in Variables Model', *Econometrica*, **46**, 961–8.

—— (1978b), *Specification Searches: Ad Hoc Inference with Non-Experimental Data*, New York: John Wiley.

—— (1980), 'The Leontief Paradox: Reconsidered', *Journal of Political Economy*, **88**, 495–503.

—— (1981a), 'Sets of Estimates of Location', *Econometrica*, **49**, 193–204.

—— (1981b), 'Is it a Demand Curve, or is it a Supply Curve? Partial Identification Through Inequality Constraints', *Review of Economics and Statistics*, **63**, 319–27.

—— (1982), 'Sets of Posterior Means with Bounded Variance Priors', *Econometrica*, **50**, 725–37.

—— (1983), 'Let's Take the Con out of Econometrics', *American Economic Review*, **73**, 31–43.

—— (1984), *Sources of International Comparative Advantage: Theory and Evidence*, Cambridge, Mass.: MIT Press.

—— (1985), 'Sensitivity Analyses Would Help', *American Economic Review*, **75**, 308–13.

—— (1987a), 'Errors in Variables in Linear Systems', *Econometrica*, **55**, 893–909.

—— (1987b), 'Paths of Development in the Three-Factor, n-Good General Equilibrium Model', *Journal of Political Economy*, **95**, 961–99.

—— (1988a), 'Cross-Section Estimation of the Effects of Trade Barriers', in Robert C. Feenstra (ed.), *Empirical Methods for International Trade*, Cambridge, Mass.: MIT Press, pp. 51–82.

—— (1988b), 'Measures of Openness', in Robert E. Baldwin (ed.), *Trade Policy Issues and Empirical Analysis*, Chicago: University of Chicago Press, pp. 147–200.

—— (1990), 'The Interplay of Theory and Data in the Study of International Trade', paper presented at the 9th World Congress of the International Economic Association.

—— (1991), 'A Bayesian Perspective on Inference From Macro-Economic Data', in Marc Nerlove (ed.), *Issues in Contemporary Economics,* vol. 2: *Macroeconomics and Econometrics,* London: MacMillan.

—— and Harry P. Bowen (1981), 'Cross-Section Tests of the Heckscher–Ohlin Theorem: Comment', *American Economic Review,* **71**, 1040–3.

—— and Gary Chamberlain (1976), 'A Bayesian Interpretation of Pretesting', *Journal of the Royal Statistical Society* B, **38**, 85–94.

—— and Herman B. Leonard (1983), 'Reporting the Fragility of Regression Estimates', *Review of Economics and Statistics,* **65**, 306–17.

—— and Robert M. Stern (1970), *Quantitative International Economics,* Chicago: Alding.

Leontief, Wasily W. (1953), 'Domestic Production and Foreign Trade: the American Capital Position Re-examined', *Proceedings of the American Philosophical Society,* 332–49.

Maskus, Keith E. (1985), 'A Test of the Heckscher–Ohlin–Vanek Theorem: the Leontief Commonplace', *Journal of International Economics,* **9**, 201–12.

Maskus, Keith E. (1991), 'Comparing International Trade Data and Product and National Characteristics Data for the Analysis of Trade Models', in J.D. Richardson and P. Hooper (eds), *International Economic Transactions: Issues in Measurement and Empirical Research,* Chicago: University of Chicago Press.

McAleer, Michael, Adrian R. Pagan and Paul A. Volker (1985), 'What Will Take the Con Out of Econometrics?' *American Economic Review,* **75**, 293–307.

Melvin, James R. (1968), 'Production and Trade with Two Factors and Three Goods', *American Economic Review,* **58**, 1249–68.

Stern, Robert M. and Keith E. Maskus (1981), 'Determinants of the Structure of U.S. Foreign Trade', *Journal of International Economics,* **11**, 207–24.

Vanek, Jaroslav (1968), 'The Factor Proportions Theory: the N-Factor Case', *Kyklos,* **21**, 749–56.

8. Harvey Leibenstein

Mark Perlman*

INTRODUCTION

Harvey Leibenstein was born in Russia in 1922. Brought as a small child to Montreal, he received his initial education there. After a brief period at Sir George Williams University, he transferred to Northwestern University where he was awarded a BS in 1945 and an MS in 1946. He was at Princeton University from the autumn of 1947 until 1951, when he finished his doctoral studies. After ascending through the various professorial ranks at the University of California, Berkeley, from 1951 until 1967, he accepted an appointment at Harvard as the Andelot Professor of Economics and Population. He retired from Harvard some time after 1987 when it became apparent that the serious injuries he had received in an automobile accident precluded any early return to his normal teaching and research activities.

Recognized from an early stage as possessing both an original mind and considerable technical qualifications, Leibenstein was awarded numerous fellowships throughout his professional career.

THE EVOLUTION OF LEIBENSTEIN'S THINKING

In *Who's Who in Economics* Leibenstein described his contribution as:

> The microeconomics of human fertility, and X-efficiency theory (the non-allocative aspects of inefficiency). The latter attempts to develop a mode of analysis which relaxes the maximization assumption of conventional micro-theory, and substitutes postulates under which individuals are non-maximizers when there is little pressure on them, approaching maximizing behavior as external pressure increases. Behavior according to convention is an important aspect of this approach. Also, current research involves the application of the prisoner's dilemma paradigm to normal economic behavior.   (Blaug, 1986, p. 508).

The Legacy of his Training

One can easily see in Leibenstein's work evidence of the influence of certain teachers. The impact of two of his Princeton professors, Oskar Morgenstern and Frank Notestein, was apparent, particularly in the 1950s. Perhaps Morgenstern's influence lasted even longer, shaping Leibenstein's perception of what theory was about ('providing a framework for understanding'), the role of subjectivity[1] in contrast to 'objective rationality', and a taste for the kinds of demonstrations now associated with game theory and/or with experimental economics.

His taste for economic theorizing

Morgenstern's scholarly impact was clear in Leibenstein's 1950 graduate-student essay, 'Bandwagon, Snob, and Veblen Effects in the Theory of Consumers' Demand', published in the *Quarterly Journal of Economics*, well before he had completed his doctoral degree. This article, establishing Leibenstein's professional reputation for facile analysis, revealed the complex intertwining of ideas and exposition which has marked his contributions as having both a strong and an original strand. Although Leibenstein started that article with an incorrect Morgenstern assertion, that the market demand curve cannot be a summation of individual curves, the point of his effort was to show how one could construct a market demand curve illustrating *inter-dependent* as well as independent consumer preferences. In the process, Leibenstein differentiated goods wanted for the direct utility services they provide from goods wanted for ancillary (self-identification) reasons.

This differentiation was achieved by suggesting (but not performing) an experiment; different consumers were initially to be asked how much of a particular good or service each wanted at a variety of prices. Each consumer was then asked how much he/she would take if others' preference schedules were made known. Leibenstein conjectured that if an individual augmented his previously independently derived demand for any good, upon learning that others shared his preferences, that good had a 'bandwagon' quality. If that same bit of knowledge led to a reduced desire for the good, the result was a 'snob' effect. There was also the possibility of a *Veblen effect* which suggested that consumption *per se* of a good might carry some form of special prestige rather than utility; as such it was slightly different from the snob effect.

One important contribution was his proposed ingenious method of iterative questioning so that dependence or independence of response could be assured. It anticipated much of what is now occurring in the new-sub-field of experimental economics.

That article laid out the Leibenstein argument in two modes: one was literary, as in the Marshallian 'main text' form; the other was geometrical, as in the Marshallian footnote but also as in the Joan Robinson main text style.

His taste for observational generalizing close to the level of fact

His dissertational effort was in the Notestein tradition (Leibenstein, 1951). Notestein's interest was in problems, not in analytical or theoretical modes. Notestein, personally interested in the question of what he was convinced were too high birth rates in most parts of the world, depended not upon abstract analysis but on careful generalization as his research method. He is best known to a generation of American demographers for his attachment to the Demographic Transition hypothesis [in industrialized societies increases in life expectancy (lower death rates for every cohort group) precede lower fertility (and birth) rates by about a generation].

His Work on the Micro-economics of Human Fertility Decisions

Leibenstein's 1957 book *Economic Backwardness and Economic Growth* was an outgrowth of the published version of his earlier dissertation, *A Theory of Economic Demographic Development* (1954).[2] Here again, the Morgenstern–Leibenstein interest in the interdependency of individual preferences, manifested in a desire for personal (household) economic improvement, holds centre-stage. For reasons of brevity it suffices to note that understanding both the role of individual motivation and the fact that there are limits to human understanding about oneself (to say nothing about others) are clearly the points of entry into this work.

Leibenstein's approach involved studying in splendid detail the objective biological and economic factors which could shape fertility decisions. Yet he went beyond them to study the very nature of the reasoning behind the decision-making process. This work is well-recognized for his ideas about the institutional shifts from regarding more children as the pay-off for previous prosperity-inducing decisions to a more 'modern' situation where the responsibility of educating and otherwise preparing children for life in an industrialized society became costly, indeed overwhelmingly so. Later, in 1974, he was to attack the Chicago/Becker New School of Home Economics for its excessive reliance upon full specification and clear (read 'logical') reasoning in the case of fertility decisions. Leibenstein's position, as I interpret it, was not an attack on logic *per se* but on the belief that the logical method was mechanistic. In his view, reasoning itself was a process costly in many dimensions, and how rigorously or even extensively one used the process was itself a separate decision.

The book received full and even lengthy and favourable reviews in the *American Economic Review* (Hamberg, 1958), in the *American Journal of*

Sociology (Whitney, 1958) and in the *Annals of the American Academy* (Buck, 1958).

During this period he also worked with Walter Galenson on topics of national production functions[3] (a professional activity considered fashionable during the 1950s). Conventional wisdom, challenged by them, was that backward countries (a term then used without embarrassment) with high levels of disguised unemployment (that is, underutilized, particularly low-wage labour) were well-advised to introduce labour-intensive manufacturing methods (Galenson and Leibenstein, 1955). Rather, it was suggested by the two of them that *if these LDCs wanted to enter international markets*, it would be wiser to look for state-of-the-art technology.[4] In retrospect, it is clear that this conclusion was consistent with the point that individual motivation was the key to competitive economic performance; if the absence of individual motivation was a general problem, then, of course, capital substitution for labour made greater programmatic sense. What showed up was a pattern of differential national productivity increases. That was *the* phenomenon of the time.[5] But underlying their whole analysis was the premise that empirical evaluations (by their nature *ex post*) provided a kind of knowledge that could not be expected to exist *ex ante*.

Leibenstein's 1960 book, *Economic Theory and Organizational Analysis* (1960a), reflects his mind in mid-passage as it moved from concern with the practical parameters of rational maximization in fertility decisions and decisions relating to the embracing of the fruits of industrialization as compared to the traditional fruits of pre-industrial social wealth, to questions of how firms producing goods and services in the industrialized market operated. He seems to have been organizing intellectually what others had written, and what he made of it.[6]

The Development of the X-Efficiency Theory

Leibenstein's later and best-known contribution was his work on X-efficiency, a concept he introduced to explain the internal operation of firms, particularly under some external stress, although effective internal leadership, perhaps motivated by the Veblenian instinct of workmanship, could result in the same outcome.

What is the X-efficiency theory?

Among the most recent efforts Professor Leibenstein made to expound his ideas about X-efficiency theory, was the description he wrote in *The New Palgrave* (Leibenstein, 1987b). The 'concept' of X-efficiency, he writes, is one thing; the 'theory' explaining it is another.

The concept refers to a regularly observable phenomenon. It is that firms not only perform their productive functions with considerable 'preventable' waste, but that if one looks only at the 'molecular' unit (that is, the firm) one misses an important area of preventable waste. It is the interactive, but somewhat constrained, economically bargained decision-making among 'atomistic' individuals within the firm.

X-efficiency theory is an effort to explain this phenomenon at all levels. This loss to the firm (deviation from the 'optimal') is not only a result of technical (that is, technological) incompetence (refusal to abandon outmoded equipment and systems as well as other manifestations of psychological inertia or cultural or individual sloth); it also is a result of an inability and/or an unwillingness to achieve (or is perhaps a breakdown of) organizational fully specified (contractual) relationships and obligations, rights and responsibilities, co-ordination and focus.

In Leibenstein's words (1987, pp. 934–5):

> X-efficiency theory represents a line of reasoning based on postulates that differ from standard micro theory. ... The postulates of the theory ... [are:]
>
> [First:] *Relaxing Maximizing Behavior* such that it is assumed that some forms of decision making, such as ... habits, conventions, moral imperatives, standard procedures, or emulation, ... can be and frequently are of a non-maximizing nature. ... not depend[ing] on careful calculation ... Other decisions attempt at maximizing utility. In order to deal with the max/non-max mixture we use ... [the] psychological ... Yerkes-Dodson Law, ... at low pressure levels individuals will not put much effort into carefully calculating their decisions, but as pressure builds they move towards more maximizing behavior. At some point too much pressure can result in disorientation and a lower level of decision performance.
>
> [Second:] *Inertia*: ... functional relations are surrounded by inert areas, within which changes in certain values of the independent variables do not result in changes of the dependent variable.
>
> [Third:] *Incomplete Contracts*: ... the employment contract is incomplete in that the payment side is fairly well specified but the effort side remains mostly unspecified.
>
> [Fourth:] *Discretion*: ... [the] employees have effort discretion within certain boundaries, and ... top management has discretion with respect to working conditions and some aspects of wages. [The relationship between] the employees on the one side and management on the other ... jointly determine[s] the outcome. Thus, ... [there is] a latent Prisoner's Dilemma problem ... In general the Prisoner's Dilemma problem solution will be avoided ... [because] a system of conventions which depends on the history of human relations within the firm is likely to lead to an outcome that is usually intermediate between the Prisoner's Dilemma outcome and the optimal solution. ... for every effort option that employees choose the firm will want to choose the minimum wages and working conditions ... Similarly, for every [working condition level] the firm chooses, the employees will want [their minimum tolerated working-condition-level]. This ... [would be] the Prisoner's Dilemma outcome, which ... is not likely ... However, this adversarial-relations problem between employees and managers is com-

pounded by another free-rider problem. Every employee has a free-rider incentive to move to the [his tolerated] minimum level ... even though he or she might want others to work effectively. ... overall effort would be reduced to the minimum if they all followed their individual self-interest. Clearly, ... individual rationality cannot solve the Prisoner's Dilemma problem. Something akin to 'group rationality' ... is required to achieve an improved solution.

... conventions should be viewed as solutions to multi-equilibrium, coordination problems, and ... can provide superior solutions to the Prisoner's Dilemma outcome. ... A coordinated solution is superior to an uncoordinated outcome. However, the various [possible] coordinated solutions ... need not be equally good. ... [E]ffort ... and working-conditions conventions can bring about a non-Prisoner's Dilemma solution. ... Thus, the effort convention is a coordinated solution ... superior to uncoordinated individual behavior. Similar remarks hold for managerial decisions. Of course, the ... [minimum-working condition level] has to be viable in the sense that it must represent a long-run profitable outcome, although not necessarily the maximum profit level.

There is a difference between the creation of a convention and adherence to it. ... [C]reation may come [from] ... leadership of some managers, ... some employees, or ... some initial effort levels being chosen arbitrarily. Once established, a convention reduces the flexibility of employees' behavior. Thus, new employees will adhere to the convention, and possibly support it through sanctions on others.

Although stable to small changes of its independent variables, an effort convention need not stay at its initial level indefinitely. The concept of inert areas suggests that a large enough shock can destabilize a convention. Once destabilized it is no longer clear whether the dynamics of ready adjustment will lead to a superior or inferior situation for both sides, or a situation under which one side gains at the expense of the other. Such considerations (and fears) help to stabilize the convention.

... [U]nder low-pressure conditions the postulate of non-maximizing behavior ... explains why firm members may stick with their conventions and impose supporting sanctions even in situations where they would be better off not doing so. Non-calculating, situation-response behavior helps to shore up the convention-solution to the Prisoner's Dilemma problem, and to shore up the persistence of nonoptimal conventions ... [and] helps to explain the existence and persistence of X-inefficient behavior.

I draw on some of his other writings to expand the foregoing material. His emphasis on micro-micro analysis put the spotlight on the reaction of 'atomistic' individual motivation to various kinds of constraints. As noted, within every economic unit there are numerous individuals, each of whom prefers 'to do his/her own thing'. But what can be said about that 'thing'? It is a compromise between what the individual accepts as something with which he/she is culturally comfortable, which he/she personally prefers, and whatever must be done if the job is to be retained and/or the firm is to survive. What is true of workers as individuals is comparably true of management as individuals and even owners as individuals. Thus, those employing the X-efficiency thesis (unlike most economists) recognize the profession's basic unit, the firm, as a molecular *aggregate*, made up of individualistic atoms compressed under various kinds of pressure.

Under *usual* conditions these molecular aggregates operate at less than maximum efficiency because there are abounding disparate atomistic individual motivations (incomplete contractual specification permitting greater choice by the worker; inertia leading to the ignoring of rule-breaking; and/or the nature of the job allowing more or less personal discretion which permits individuals to choose their levels of effort). Under certain *unusual* conditions, particularly those arising from changes in external pressures, such as price competition from other firms, the firm is forced to reduce costs. The freedom for these disparate motivations to interact is then reduced, and the pressure to develop a lower cost system is increased. The very economic survival of the firm may require that what individuals *like or ought* to offer in the way of output gives way to what they feel they *must* offer. This shift to *unusual* conditions, whatever may precipitate it, means that management decides that neither it nor the workers can be left to follow former procedures. It could also mean that the owners (shareholders) can come to the same conclusion about management.

All of this goes beyond a mere power struggle. X-efficiency theory also states that even under pressure there are inert areas surrounding the existent levels of effort. These inert areas reflect the disutility of effort; the benefit to be gained by the change must exceed the cost of changing, or else the effort level will remain the same. Leibenstein defines 'inert areas' as areas of choice which are left untouched for a variety of very different reasons ranging from a sheer inability to penetrate to the high costs of penetration. There are, however, problems of bargaining standoff. These come under the game theoretic Prisoner's Dilemma rubric.

Under *usual* conditions firms produce[7] and consume without much serious attention to leakages in the output stream. In so far as the *usual* output varies from the *unusual* or 'might-have-been', assuming identical cost inputs are the same for the two contrasting sets of conditions, we can estimate quantitatively X-inefficiency, or the amount lost by the firm because of the impact of this aspect of worker and management individualism. That loss is X-inefficiency; or to put the matter the other way around, we can identify and estimate this 'X-efficiency gain' as the product of stringent pressure.

One point of X-efficiency theory is that firms do not maximize mechanically because each firm's managers are not completely in command of the full spectrum of the decision-making process. Management must cope with each worker's motivation preferences, and in some instances the latter are so complex, even at points contradictory, that a 'best' outcome is no more than management's collective (but no less subjective) conclusion that it has done as much as it can (and whatever that was) it was good enough to keep the firm economically afloat. '*Firms do not maximize because true maximization requires a level of control not consistent with "Free Will"*.' Leibenstein's work on X-efficiency surfaced in the *American Economic Review* in 1966 under what *ex post* was a transitional title, 'Allocative Efficiency vs. "X"-Efficiency'. It drew heavily on the work of many scholars trying to identify the losses in potential growth due to various kinds of traditional misallocations by management. These, Leibenstein concluded, were quantitatively trivial, 'frequently no more than $^1/_{10}$ of 1 per cent' (Leibenstein, 1966a, p. 397). But growth fluctuated much more than that small amount. What caused it? The answers, X-inefficiency as well as X-efficiency, are mentioned in passing, without any effort at definition except the implication that they are due to 'managements [not] bestirring themselves sufficiently, [unless] the environment forces them to do so'.[8] His data were drawn largely from LDCs, with considerable emphasis put on episodic reports. His conclusion reflects an early formative state of the theory (Leibenstein, 1966a, pp. 412–13):

[There are] three reasons for X-inefficiency ... These are (a) contracts for labor are incomplete, (b) the production function is not completely specified or known, and (c) not all inputs are marketed or, if marketed, are not available on equal terms to all buyers.

... [F]or a variety of reasons people and organizations normally work neither as hard nor as effectively as they could. In situations where competitive pressure is light, many people will trade the disutility of greater effort, of search, and the control of other peoples' activities for the utility of feeling less pressure and of better interpersonal relations. But in situations where competitive pressures are high, and hence the costs of such trades are also high ... [t]wo general types of movements are possible. One is ... towards greater allocative efficiency and the other ... involves greater degrees of X-efficiency. The data suggest that [often] the amount to be gained by increasing allocative efficiency is trivial while the amount to be gained by increasing X-efficiency is frequently significant.

In the years that followed Leibenstein expanded his X-efficiency theory, partly in response to comments on it and partly due to his desire to differentiate it from the work of others.[9] In 1975 the *Bell Journal* published a more polished rendition of the theory (Leibenstein, 1975a). *Inter alia*, it also distinguished Leibenstein's theme from Herbert Simon's idea of firms maximizing within areas of bounded rationality and the Cyert–March thesis that firms found it irrational (uneconomic/?) to fight currently dominant institutions (City Hall/? and certainly unions).

Two of Leibenstein's books (1976a and 1978a) came out in the late 1970s with the apparent intention of trying to lay out his whole thinking in detail. As I read them, the first was a major effort at locating his ideas within the profession's general perception of economic theorizing. The second book was an application of X-efficiency theory within the stream of development economics. *De gustibus non disputandem est*, but the tightness of the applied argument found in the latter has, for me at least, a special appeal.

In 1978 he published two particularly sharply focused articles on his theory. One, a reply to the voice of price-theory orthodoxy, Professor George Stigler, lays out in good natured (if biting) prose – almost matching Stigler's own style (Stigler, 1976) – Leibenstein's abhorrence of attempts to fit his theory into the Procrustean bed of the *original* Marshallian price system legacy (Leibenstein, 1978c), something Stigler had thought desirable to do, citing the high cost of individuals' foregoing their preference for leisure as they were driven to excise X-inefficiency.

The other is Leibenstein's assertion of the X-efficiency theory 'while standing on one foot' (1978b): 'In a budgetary permissive environment the looser the [*effort responsibility consequence* for any firm member i], for all i on the average, the greater the degree of X-inefficiency (i.e., the excess of actual over minimum cost).'

His general efforts, in my opinion, reached a more condensed, if not a new or higher, plane in his 1979 article, 'A Branch of Economics is Missing: Micro-Micro Theory' (Leibenstein, 1979a). There he discusses five important elements in his theory:

- *Selective rationality (degree of maximization deviation)*. This relates to individual decisions regarding the degree to which deviations, reflecting a variety of inner and external pressures, from the firm's goals occur. These are spelled out and then diagrammed.
- *Individuals are basic decision-making units*. Each individual joining the firm gets all sorts of signals from his peer group, from the hierarchy, and from historical influences.
- *Effort discretion*. Of course in addition to all of these signals (or, perhaps underlying them), are a set of economic pressures on the firm.
- *Inert areas*. Here habit takes over. Unless the firm's goals are dominant to the point of pure dictatorship nothing changes.
- *Organizational entropy*. The management must struggle using centripetal integrative energy against the centrifugal individualistic forces. Failure can occur.

In a second article published in 1979, he used tabular presentation, employed elsewhere, to contrast his theory (1979b). This is worth reproduction (see Table 8.1).

After 1979 Leibenstein wrote several other books and essays. Some were additions, emandations often prepared as response to comments in journals (1980a, 1980b, 1981b, 1981c, 1982a, 1982c, 1983a, 1985a, 1985b). And some tied X-efficiency to other theoretical *Gestalt* such as the economic theory of contracts (1982c), game theory (1981d, 1982c), and the general theory of organizations and management (1987a). The degree of refinement

Table 8.1   X-efficiency theory and neoclassical theory

Components	X-efficiency theory	Neoclassical theory[10]
Psychology	Selective rationality	Maximization or minimization
Contracts[11]	Incomplete	Complete
Effort[12]	Discretionary variable	Assumed given
Units	Individuals	Households and firms
Inert areas[13]	Important variable	None
Agent–principal	Differential interests	Identity of interests

increased, but the general outlines had been laid out earlier. Much of this work was in response to criticisms levied by both 'orthodox' neoclassical economists and some fellow heterodox types. Roger Frantz (1990), writing in the posture of assessing these criticisms, categorizes them under four headings: (a) assertions that X-efficiency theory can be subsumed under rent-seeking behaviour; (b) that the employees' leisure is one of the output products of the firm; (c) that in practice management is the residual claimant for undistributed profits; and (d) that X-efficiency theory can be subsumed under a theory of property rights. His last book *Inside the Firm: The Inefficiency of Hierarchy* (1987a) received mixed reviews: James D. Hess (1989) wrote that he shared Leibenstein's dissatisfaction with neoclassical orthodoxy, but he could not accept Leibenstein's formulation of an alternative; yet John Kenneth Galbraith (1988) shared the dissatisfaction common to Hess and Leibenstein and appeared to accept much of the latter's answer.

LEIBENSTEIN'S 'PIGEON-HOLE' IN THE HISTORY OF ECONOMIC THOUGHT

Reflecting the Marshallian Influence

Although neoclassical economics is associated these days with Hicks–Samuelson–Solow, Leibenstein basically draws on the original Marshallian approach, albeit with some of his criticisms. The Marshallian and Pigovian level of abstraction was intentionally lower than that employed by Hicks, and for the most part by Samuelson and Solow.

What Marshall thought economics was all about was how men in their ordinary pursuits of livelihood made decisions; he deliberately eschewed formal exposition, noting that intangibles were critically apparent in that decision-making process. Formal exposition, as seen by Marshall, was relegated to footnotes, where it did not interfere with the flow of his thinking but could be used as an explanatory device.

Leibenstein's thinking as well as his pedagogical preferences seem to parallel Marshall's. Moreover his method (choice of rhetoric) has that same quality of episodic empiricism (with a historical dimension). He shies away from the formalism of simple (purely rational) maximization, as found in mathematics, not only because it requires specification where specification (of intangibles) is impossible, but also because it employs a level of abstraction which negates the purpose of the analysis. Neither for Marshall nor for Leibenstein is a reasonable man necessarily logical; their man, having a mind influenced by cognition as well as imagination, lives in a dynamic and disequilibrating world, and does his 'level best' (which is a good measure short of perfect). Their reasonable man bases his decisions on habit, on his incomplete and otherwise imperfect subjective perceptions of his internal (cf. super-ego) pressures, and on what he must bend to because of the superiority of forces he cannot easily manage (or manage at all).

In the development of the history of economic thought Marshall's preferred example of the firm in competition was supplanted by firms in some other relation to the market. It is often forgotten that his *Principles of Economics* was essentially an unfinished product, and that Marshall clearly noted in its 'Mathematical Appendix' that conditions of increasing returns not only vitiated his simple competitive model theoretically, but also *in actual fact*. This point is commonly credited to Piero Sraffa and was popularized by Joan Robinson. But her method was far more abstract than Marshall's generally was. In terms of preferred rhetoric Edward H. Chamberlin's was closer to the level of observed fact; Leibenstein's rhetoric (where he has the space) is also close to the level of observed fact. However, in deference to the *mores* of our profession at the time of his own graduate training, Leibenstein usually lays out his argument *in the text* in geometric (formal) terms – Mrs Robinson's impact.

In his *Beyond Economic Man* (1976a), Peter J. Kalman co-authored with him a formal statement of the theory, employing much of the rhetoric of symbolic logic: 'Toward a Mathematical Formalization of X-Efficiency' (pp. 273–282, 291).[14]

What makes Leibenstein's work on population and on X-efficiency theory so 'Marshallian neoclassical' is something else as well. It is the role of attitude and how it is generated (created, manipulated and handled by incentive systems). Leibenstein's interest in individuals' motivations is central to his perception of the whole economic process – not only of production but also of distribution. Men, Leibenstein concludes, do not and often cannot maximize; Marshall put the point in another way when he remarked that economics was the study of man in the ordinary business of making a living.

Other economists have offered somewhat separate reasons for man's failure to maximize: (a) 'maximizing is perceived as economically too expensive (cf. Herbert Simon's costs of information and 'satisficing'); (b) maximization is theoretically impossible – absent *ex ante* perfect knowledge, there is no path to *ex post* optimization (cf. G.L.S. Shackle's 'uncertainty'); (c) the capacity to maximize is a limited resource – differential personal endowments or capacities create entrepreneurs and innovators (cf. Cantillon's and J.B. Say's 'entrepreneur' and Schumpeter's 'innovator'); (d) many have no taste, much less a penchant, for efficiency (cf. J.M. Clarke's 'an irrational passion for rationality'); and (e) the underlying contradictions within the specifications of the social contract and the government contract (cf. Thomas Hobbes, 1651; and Cyert and March, 1963).

However, Leibenstein suggests that, given sufficient market pressure, the individuals in the firm suppress some of their contrary or inconsistent motivations and are likely to get closer to the maximization process. This switch is one which seems to require the assertion of one set of priorities over all others – that is, the assertion of one set of individual preferences, cleaned up of its internal contradictions, over all the others. Survival pressures, to paraphrase Dr Johnson, 'powerfully clarify the mind'. *A measure of the presence of X-efficiency may be an inverse measure of personal liberty.*

As Part of the Morgenstern–Austrian Tradition Influence

There is also a neo-Austrian underpinning to Leibenstein's perception of theory. One key Austrian element is the role of subjectivity in the decision-making process. This element was perceived in the role of the consumer, whose tastes for consumer goods, according to Menger and his two 'students', von Wieser and Böhm-Bawerk, provided the 'first cause' for all economic activity.

Professor Wesley Clair Mitchell, in his Foreword to the English edition of von Wieser's *Social Economics* (1927, pp. ix–xii), puts his finger on the exact point. If things occur in the mind, how then does the mind operate? – a problem which von Wieser (and his group) eschewed, but which von Neumann and Morgenstern tried to handle as the mini/max. Leibenstein's X-efficiency theory leads us back to the wilfulness (that is, subjectiveness) of each of the parties in any economic activities. Leibenstein adds that given *sufficient* pressure, one man's decisions (the imposition of his ordered and consistent preferences) can and often will replace the others' subjectiveness with that decision, which in operation thus becomes interpersonally 'objective'. That management's decision can be said to be the 'entrepreneur-in-action'. Otherwise the entrepreneur, like everyone else, is quiescent, and production proceeds without much reference to the elimination of efficiency – the state of Leibenstein X-inefficiency.

It has recently been fashionable to categorize most modern economic theorists in sequential sets of pigeon-holes. One early division is between those studying tendencies towards equilibrium and those focusing on disequilibrium. Clearly Leibenstein's work fits better into the latter category.

So much of the former category draws upon the equilibration mechanism of Walrasian *tâtonnement* that it is pertinent to mention that X-efficiency theory not only eschews *tâtonnement* as meaningful in the interactions between the various individuals making up the firm, but seems to deny the simple rationality that Walras's and Pareto's general models required. Given outside pressures, individuals are driven to communicate according to comparative status, not according to negotiated interactions. The metaphor is not Walras's *tâtonnement*; it is Pirandello's *Six Characters in Search of an Author* (for author, read some compelling force like Hobbes's *Leviathan*).

But I think one can say more. The leading 'neo-Austrian' of our time, Professor Hayek, has of recent years come to see the importance of economic conventions as signalling systems or communications devices. Communications devices are precisely what Hobbes identifies as language itself. Language is partly what Hayek calls 'institutions', borrowing (knowingly or otherwise) the precise phrase John R. Commons used almost a century ago (cf. Perlman, 1986). The impact of these conventions/institutions is one of the external pressures which can force firms to diminish their levels of X-inefficiency. X-efficiency theory requires communications or signalling within the firm. That is what the theory is largely about.

Morgenstern and Hayek came from the same mould. That they were different in the end merely indicates that the mould is at the starting point. But were they so different? Morgenstern was, it may be unnecessary to recall, Hayek's successor at the Vienna Research Institute which they both left in the 1930s – the one to go to the London School of Economics, the other to Princeton. The linkage of Leibenstein to Morgenstern is clear; the linkage of Morgenstern and Hayek to the Austrian-subjectivist tradition is also obvious. The linkage of Leibenstein to the original Menger formulation is not clear; but there is a link to the Austrian post-Menger tradition. And that is where I would fit in Leibenstein.

Reflecting the 'Adam Smith Problem'

During the latter part of the nineteenth century there developed, particularly in Germany, great interest in purported contradictions between Smith's view of man as seen in his *Theory of Moral Sentiments* and in his *Wealth of Nations* (cf. Viner, 1926). In the former, man was perceived as usually having a gregarious nature (a 'herding' kind of 'animal'), and capable of continuous detached self-judgement of his actions, as planned and also with regard to likely consequence. In the *Wealth of Nations*, single-minded, efficiency-conscious 'economic man' emerged totally supreme.

X-efficiency theory can be presented as an effort to identify the active relationship between these two aspects of man. Why? Because Leibenstein's work on economic development as well as on X-efficiency theory explains the internal and the external pressures which cause man-in-the-production process to choose between what he would like to do (the Austrian subjective factor), what he thinks he ought to do (Smith's detached observer), and what efficiency considerations, under certain conditions, force him to do (the compromises he must make with true maximizations, in so far as he can grasp the latter).

I believe that his X-efficiency theory goes beyond this important point. It also explains what efficiency considerations cannot force him to do, and why. That is the rubric of inert areas. In this sense Leibenstein goes beyond Smith and *das Adam Smith Problem*.

In sum, perhaps one of the more useful ways to classify Leibenstein's contribution to economic theory is to note that in its initial grasp it was Marshallian neoclassical, but almost immediately he came to challenge the assumptions of simple rational maximization. He is not part of the Walrasian mathematical, purely logical neoclassicism. And in so far as this last is the mainstream of our time, his work has to be seen as part of contemporary heterodoxy.

NOTES

*Parts of this essay have been adapted from Perlman (1990).

1. Part of Leibenstein's dissociation from both Marshallian and Hicks–Samuelson neoclassical economics reflects the impact of Morgenstern's own brand of Austrian economics. In the flow of ideas early Austrian economics came to stand for many things: The role of the subjective, the importance of demand from which was derived supplies of consumer goods and supplies of higher order goods, resistance to mathematical formulations, a strong preference for 'free markets' and an opposition to socialism, etc. Morgenstern was intellectually very independent and differed greatly from many of his contemporary 'Austrians'. For one thing, he was from early on interested in quantification and headed a private research organization studying business cycles, albeit he was there as Hayek's successor. For another, he came to represent one type of formalism – the mathematics involved in the point theorem and game theory. What stands out about Morgenstern's brand of Austrian economics was its concern with how choices were made, particularly on the demand side. While not all the questions on which Leibenstein has written have that as the dominant theme, his work on interdependence of consumer choice, human fertility and, derivatively, X-efficiency theory do.

2. Interest in the determinants of fertility choices persisted. Whether it was the source of his interest in X-efficiency theory or has merely paralleled it is unimportant. But much of Leibenstein's bibliography comes under the heading of demographic economics, as such (cf. Leibenstein 1962, 1964, 1974b, 1974c, 1975b, 1975c, 1976a, 1976b, 1977a, 1977b, 1978a, 1979c, 1980b, 1981a).

3. Macroeconomics was emerging during the post-Second World War period. It turned attention to the work done on aggregate national constant-returns-to-scale production functions by Paul Douglas and Charles Cobb.

4. Part of the professional reaction they encountered was that this approach was exactly the hard-line 'little-or-nothing-for-consumers' policy which Stalin had pursued. Both men had always been anti-Stalinist. Their conclusions, implying that there was a hard logic to Stalin's cruel investment policy, came as something of a surprise. Many first reactions found expression in strong (if irrelevantly derived) criticism of them. Leibenstein spent a great deal of time refuting critics (cf. Leibenstein 1958, 1960b, 1962, 1963, 1966b).

5. Note the date; it was the era of fine-tuning. In that period the concept of an American annual productivity increase of about 4 per cent was accepted almost as a given. Fabricant and others spoke of growth cycles having replaced business cycles.

6. A 1962 article, 'Notes on Welfare Economics and the Theory of Democracy', seems to me to have reflected a more original and formative type of thinking. In it he introduces the concept of 'consent areas', a forerunner (?), albeit negatively phrased, of what later he was to term 'inert areas'.

7. I see no reason why X-efficiency theory should not be adapted to the purchasing and consuming activities of the household. Indeed, what is amazing to me is the number of times Mitchell's 'backward art' has been republished and cited, without anyone mentioning the underlying rationality conditions (cf. Mitchell, 1912).

8. The X-factor might well have referred to the unknown or residual factor in trying to explain the 'high' American annual productivity growth rate. In the course of my work I have found many claims to being the first to note that 'unexplained residual'. I am inclined to credit Professor Abramovitz with having been 'the last' to have discovered the unexplained phenomenon; thereafter it 'stayed discovered'.

9. Cf. Leibenstein 1969, 1972, 1973, 1974a, 1977c, 1980a, 1980b, 1981b, 1981c, 1981d, 1982a, 1982b, 1982c, 1983a, 1983b, 1985a, 1985b.

10. '[W]e [have] ended up with the unalloyed jewel known as the market in general equilibrium. In such a market the firm becomes a trivial and indeterminate entity. If price of inputs and outputs are known, and if the menu of techniques that translates inputs into outputs is known, then the firm can be presumed to behave quite mechanically' (Leibenstein, 1979b, p. 128).

11. Contracts are incomplete and can be asymmetrical – payment is specified, but work effort is not (ibid., p. 130).

12. The effort variable is 'made up of ... (A) activities chosen, (P) the pace of carrying out the activities; (Q) the quality of activities; and (T) the time sequence aspect. Assuming that A, P, Q, and T can be assigned values, we can then visualize the vector $APQT$ as an effort point' (ibid., p. 130).

13. 'We posit the existence of a psychological *inertial* cost of moving from one [effort] position to another. Thus an individual who finds himself in one effort position may not move to a superior effort position because the inertial cost is greater than the utility gain. Inertial cost should be viewed as a personality characteristic. An individual who is a maximizer would have zero inertial costs' (ibid., p. 130).

14. A much earlier effort at formal exposition was made by William S. Comanor and Leibenstein (Comanor and Leibenstein, 1969).

REFERENCES

Abramovitz, Moses (1956), 'Resource and Output Trends in the United States Since 1870', Occasional Paper 52, New York: NBER.

Blaug, Mark (1986), *Who's Who in Economics: A Biographical Dictionary of Major Economists, 1700–1760*, Cambridge, MA (2nd edn).

Buck, Philip W. (1958), Review of Leibenstein's *Economic Backwardness and Economic Growth: Studies in the Theory of Economic Development*, in *Annals of the American Academy of Political and Social Science*, **318**, 185.

Comanor, William and Harvey Leibenstein (1969), 'Allocative Efficiency, X-Efficiency, and the Measurement of Welfare Losses' *Economica*, N.S. **36**, (143), 304–9.

Cyert, Richard M. and J.G. March (1963), *A Behavioral Theory of the Firm*, Englewood Cliffs, N.J.: Prentice-Hall.

Fabricant, Solomon (1959), 'Basic Facts on Productivity Change', Occasional Paper 63, New York: NBER.

Frantz, Roger S. (1990), 'Ex-Ante and Ex-Post Criticisms of X-Efficiency Theory and Literature', in Klaus Weiermaier and Mark Perlman (eds), *Studies in Economic Rationality: X-Efficiency Examined and Extolled*, Ann Arbor, Mich.: Michigan University Press, 43–62.

Galbraith, John Kenneth (1988), Review of Leibenstein's *Inside the Firm: The Inefficiency of Hierarchy*, *New Republic*, **198**, 42.

Galenson, Walter and Harvey Leibenstein (1955), 'Investment Criteria, Productivity, and Economic Development', *Quarterly Journal of Economics*, **69**, 343–70.

Hamberg, D. (1958), Review of Leibenstein's *Economic Backwardness and Economic Growth: Studies in the Theory of Economic Development*, in *American Economic Review*, **48**, 1020–3.

Hess, James D. (1989), Review of Leibenstein's *Inside the Firm: The Inefficiency of Hierarchy*, in *Journal of Economic Literature*, **27**, 641–3.

Hobbes, Thomas (1651), *The Leviathan*.

Leibenstein, Harvey (1950), 'Bandwagon, Snob, and Veblen Effects in the Theory of Consumers' Demand', *Quarterly Journal of Economics*, **54**, 183–207.

—— (1951), 'Toward a Theory of Demographic Transition', a doctoral dissertation submitted to the Department of Economics, Princeton University.

—— (1954), *A Theory of Economic Demographic Development*, Princeton, N.J.: Princeton University Press.

—— (1957), *Economic Backwardness and Economic Growth: Studies in the Theory of Economic Development*, New York: John Wiley.

—— (1958), 'Underemployment in Backward Economies: Some Additional Notes', *Journal of Political Economy*, **66**, 256–8.

—— (1960a), *Economic Theory and Organizational Analysis*, New York: Harper.

—— (1960b), 'Technical Progress, the Production Function and Dualism', *Banco Nazionale Lavoro*, **13**, 345–60.

—— (1962), 'Notes on Welfare Economics and the Theory of Democracy', *Economic Journal*, **72**, 299–317.

—— (1963), 'Investment Criteria and Empirical Evidence – a Reply to Mr Ranis', *Quarterly Journal of Economics*, **77**, 175–9.

—— (1964), 'An Econometric Analysis of Population Growth: Comment', *American Economic Review*, **54**, 134–5.

—— (1966a), 'Allocative Efficiency vs. "X-Efficiency" ', *American Economic Review*, **56**, 392–415.

—— (1966b), 'Incremental Capital–Output Ratios and Growth Rates in the Short Run', *Review of Economics and Statistics*, **48**, 20–7.

—— (1969), 'Organizational or Frictional Equilibrium, X-Efficiency, and the Rate of Innovation', *Quarterly Journal of Economics*, **83**, 599–623.

—— (1972), 'Comment on the Nature of X-Efficiency', *Quarterly Journal of Economics*, **86**, 327–31.

—— (1973), 'Competition and X-Efficiency: Reply', *Journal of Political Economy*, **81**, 765–77.

—— (1974a), 'Comment on Inert Areas and the Definition of X-Efficiency', *Quarterly Journal of Economics*, **88**, 689–91.

—— (1974b), 'An Interpretation of the Economics Theory of Fertility: Promising Path or Blind Alley?', *Journal of Economic Literature*, **12**, 457–79.

—— (1974c), 'Socio-economic Fertility Theories and Their Relevance to Population Policy', *International Labour Review*, **109**, 443–57.

—— (1975a), 'Aspects of the X-Efficiency Theory of the Firm', *Bell Journal*, (Autumn), 580–606.

—— (1975b), 'The Economic Theory of Fertility Decline', *Quarterly Journal of Economics*, **89**, 1–31.

—— (1975c), 'On the Economic Theory of Utility: a reply to Keeley', *Journal of Economic Literature*, **13**, 469–72.

—— (1976a), *Beyond Economic Man*, Cambridge, Mass.: Harvard University Press.

—— (1976b), 'The Problem of Characterizing Aspirations', *Population and Development Review*, **2**, 427–31.

—— (1977a), 'Beyond Economic Man: Economics, Politics, and the Population Problem', *Population and Development Review*, **3**, 183–99.

—— (1977b), 'Economic Theory of Fertility: Reply to Cullison', *Quarterly Journal of Economics*, **91**, 349–50.

—— (1977c), 'X-Efficiency, Technical Efficiency, and Incomplete Information Use: a Comment', *Economic Development and Cultural Change*, **25**, 311–16.

—— (1978a), *General X-Efficiency Theory and Economic Development*, New York: Oxford University Press.

—— (1978b), 'On the Basic Proposition of X-Efficiency Theory', *American Economic Review Papers and Proceedings*, **68**, 328–32.

—— (1978c), 'X-Inefficiency Xists – Reply to an Xorcist', *American Economic Review*, **68**, 203–11.

—— (1979a), 'A Branch of Economics is Missing: Micro-Micro Theory', *Journal of Economic Literature*, 477–502.

—— (1979b), 'The General X-Efficiency Paradigm and the Role of the Entrepreneur', in Mario J. Rizzo, *Time, Uncertainty, and Disequilibrium: Exploration of Austrian Themes*, Lexington, Mass.: Lexington Books, 127–39; Israel M. Kirzner's 'Comment', 140–51.

—— (1979c), 'Comments on "Fertility as Consumption: Theory from the Behavioral Sciences" ', *Journal of Consumer Research*, **5**, 287–90.

—— (1980a), *Inflation, Income Distribution and X-Efficiency Theory*, London: Croom Helm.

—— (1980b), 'Notes on the X-Efficiency Approach to Inflation, Productivity and Unemployment', in Burton Weisbrod and Helen Hughes (eds), *Human Resources, Employment and Development*, vol. 3: *The Problems of Developed Countries and the International Economy*, Proceedings of the Sixth World Congress of the International Economic Association held in Mexico City, 1980, 84–96.

—— (1981a), 'Economic Decision Theory and Human Fertility Behavior: a Speculative Essay', *Population and Development Review*, **9**, 381–400.

—— (1981b), 'The Inflation Process: a Micro-Behavioral Analysis', *American Economic Review*, **71**, 368–73.

—— (1981c), 'Microeconomics and X-Efficiency Theory', in Daniel Bell and Irving Kristol (eds), *The Crisis in Economic Theory*, New York: Basic Books, 97–110.

—— (1981d), 'X-Efficiency Theory, Productivity and Growth', in Herbert Giersch (ed.), *Towards an Explanation of Economic Growth*, Symposium 1980, Kiel: Institut für Weltwirtschaft, 187–212.

—— (1982a), 'On Bull's-Eye-Painting Economics', *Journal of Post Keynesian Economics*, **4**, 460–5.

—— (1982b), 'The Prisoners' Dilemma in the Invisible Hand: an Analysis of Intrafirm Productivity', *American Economic Review Supplement*, **72**, 92–7.

—— (1982c), 'Worker Motivation and X-Efficiency Theory: a Comment', *Journal of Economic Issues*, **16**, 872–3.

—— (1983a), 'Intrafirm Productivity: Reply [to M. Shamid Alam in ibid.]', *American Economic Review*, **73**, 822–3.

—— (1983b), 'Property Rights and X-Efficiency: Comment', *American Economic Review*, **73**, 831–42.

—— (1985a), 'Comment [on the *World Development Report, 1984*]', *Population and Development Review*, **11**, 135–7.

—— (1985b), 'On Relaxing the Maximization Postulate', *Journal of Behavioural Economics*, **14**, 5–20.

—— (1987a), *Inside the Firm: The Inefficiency of Hierarchy*, Cambridge, Mass.: Harvard University Press.

—— (1987b), 'X-Efficiency theory', in John Eatwell, Murray Milgate and Peter Newman (eds), *The New Palgrave*, vol. 4, pp. 934–5.

Mitchell, Wesley Clair (1912), 'The Backward Art of Spending Money', *American Economic Review*, **2**, 269–81.

—— (1927), 'Foreword' in Friedrich von Wieser, *Social Economics*, trans. A. Ford Hinrichs with a Preface [*sic*] by Wesley Clair Mitchell, New York: Augustus M. Kelley, reprinted 1967.

Perlman, Mark (1986), 'Subjectivism and American Institutionalism', in [Lachmann, Ludwig M.], *Subjectivism, Intelligibility, and Economic Understanding: Essays in Honor of Ludwig M. Lachmann on his Eightieth Birthday*, ed. Israel M. Kirzner, New York: New York University Press.

Perlman, Mark (1990), 'The Evolution of Leibenstein's X-Efficiency Theory', in Klaus Weiermair and Mark Perlman (eds), *Studies in Economic Rationality: X-Efficiency, Examined and Extolled; Essays Written in the Tradition of and to Honor Harvey Leibenstein*, Ann Arbor, Mich.: Michigan University Press, pp. 7–25.

Stigler, George (1976), 'The Xistence of X-Efficiency', *American Economic Review*, **66**, 213–16.

Viner, Jacob (1926), 'Adam Smith and Laissez Faire', in John Maurice Clark *et al.*, *Adam Smith, 1776–1926*, lectures to commemorate the sesquicentennial of the publication of *The Wealth of Nations*, Chicago: University of Chicago Press.

Whitney, Vincent Heath (1958), Review of Leibenstein's *Economic Backwardness and Economic Growth: Studies in the Theory of Economic Development*, in *American Journal of Sociology*, **64**, 105–6.

9.   Charles E. Lindblom

Richard P. Adelstein

THE INTERDISCIPLINARIAN AS ECONOMIST

Is it strange to contend, as I shall here, that the scholarly contributions of a man who has served as president of the American Political Science Association and whose life's work has been respectfully given its due in the history of that discipline[1] should be recognized as an important part of the history of modern economic thought? If so, this is but a reflection of Charles E. Lindblom's uneasy relationship with economics, the field in which he took his PhD at the University of Chicago in 1945 and against whose institutional biases and professional tunnel vision he has struggled for some 50 years.[2] For amongst the economists, as Lindblom wrote (1957, pp. 252–3) from bitter experience in 1956:

> a tradition in recruitment has grown up through which those who will be happy within the limitations of economics are admitted to the brotherhood and others are commonly turned away. In the best training centers, with few exceptions no one can become an economist who does not come to value formal economic theory. Moreover, the boundaries of economics have been marked out with careful attention to those tasks to which theory can be applied [so that] economics has come close to defining an economist as one whose professional ambitions are limited to those for which formal economic theory is not seriously frustrating.

But from the beginning, Lindblom's own ambitions have pushed him well past the limits of this increasingly confining definition. Free of the sterile abstraction and fascination with optimization and equilibrium that dominate modern economics, his work has always had a strong interdisciplinary flavour, probing the artificial boundaries separating economics from political science and exploring the relationship between human knowledge and values and the central problems of social organization. Over the years it has taken him ever further from the optimistic, laboratory environment of neoclassical theory, a world of mathematical certainty and free, perfectly informed beings in full command of their own desires, toward the imperfect, imprecise world of exchange and power where real people live, a more

threatening realm of radical ignorance and uncertain interests, hostile manipulation and bureaucratic authority.

Still, for most of his career Lindblom has seen himself explicitly and, I
think, correctly as an economist, extending his discipline to address problems and phenomena not a part of its modern research agenda. If, as Woodrow
Wilson (1887) believed, politics is the search for the common good in
human affairs and political theory the reflection of this search in the domain
of analysis, then Lindblom reveals himself to be an economist in his consistent denial of a meaningful or intelligible collective interest and his corresponding commitments to political and methodological individualism. He is,
moreover, an economist in Friedrich Hayek's (1967) sense as well, focusing
inquiry on the patterns created by harmonizing processes of spontaneous
order rather than the particular outcomes they produce. Like Hayek and his
own teacher Frank Knight, Lindblom is deeply impressed with the prodigious
feats of organization achieved in the face of imperfect, widely dispersed
knowledge by 'mutual adjustment', the spontaneous reconciliation of conflicting values through self-interested behaviour. But he significantly deepens
their analyses of economic catallaxy (Hayek, 1976, pp. 107–32) by illuminating the co-ordinating power of mutual adjustment not just in a variety of
political contexts across the ideological spectrum, but in the social creation
of values and beliefs themselves.

In this, as in his lifelong focus on the actual institutions that direct and
constrain social life, the historical significance of Lindblom's economics is
best seen in the context of the great 'calculation debate', the passionate
conversation on the feasibility of large-scale economic planning initiated by
Mises (1920), carried on by Hayek (1935, 1948), Lange (1938) and Bergson
(1948), and resolved, if at all, only by the collapse of Marxist socialism in
Eastern Europe.[3] A persistent theme in Lindblom's work has been the contrast between the invisible hand of spontaneous mutual adjustment and the
conscious grasp of central planning and control, between 'epiphenomenal'
problem-solving through the decentralized play of interests and the rational-
ist ideal of 'synopsis', the faith that 'there are men in the society wise and
informed enough to ameliorate its problems and guide social change with a
high degree of success' (Lindblom, 1975, p. 26). In a life's work that can
usefully be divided into two distinct but interrelated areas of substantive
concern, Lindblom has developed the implications of this crucial dichotomy
in directions uncharted by others, and in the two parts to follow, I consider
the variations he has played on the theme of order and planning in both of
these areas.

The first encompasses Lindblom's early discussions of incremental decision making and mutual adjustment and their application to political problem
solving, and in Part II, I argue that this work fruitfully extends and synthe-

sises the complementary ideas of Hayek and Herbert Simon, economists similarly disrespectful of traditional disciplinary boundaries. All three share the conviction that economic theory is of little scientific value unless it accounts for the nature and limitations of real human beings as decision-makers, and each dismisses optimization on epistemological grounds, for Hayek in a denial of the possibility of rational central planning by the state, for Simon in a critique of the neoclassical theories of the consumer and the firm, and for Lindblom in a rejection of the synoptic method of public policymaking. But Lindblom's interlocking analyses of incremental, sequential decision-making by interdependent political actors and the adjustments they undertake over time to harmonize their decisions go much further, seeing in mutual adjustment not just a co-ordinating device but a spontaneous process of goal formation and global decision-making of immense practical value in a democracy. Values, interests and outcomes become the simultaneous, unplanned results of a complex interplay of partisan opportunism, accommodation and consent despite the cognitive limitations of its participants, and mutual adjustment an invisible maker of hard choices made tolerable by the absence of credit or blame.

Hayek's critique of planning assumes that individuals are not motivated to co-operate with the planners, a lack of alignment between rulers and ruled that denies the planning agency the information it needs to determine what the desired allocation of resources is and the steps needed to achieve it. But as Lindblom has always understood, planning can succeed even in a free society in the event of war or similar emergency where the necessary alignment of goals exists, and effective planning even without war is possible given citizens who, like Mao's 'new man', identify so completely with the objectives of the planners that they act as required without being told to do so. From the outset Lindblom has emphasized the ubiquity in industrial society of centralized economic and political hierarchy, public and private, and the distortions introduced into various processes of mutual adjustment by the inequalities of power and wealth these islands of planning create. He has thus been able to expand the critique of planning beyond that done by the state itself and to address not just the economics of large, bureaucratic systems of authority but the political attitudes and values that must be inculcated in the citizenry in order to ensure their success as well.

The principal result of this second line of substantive inquiry has been the highly controversial *Politics and Markets* (1977), a pessimistic, angry portrait of the American political economy in which the managers of large corporations enjoy a privileged position of authority and influence in all areas of public life and the people have been so deeply indoctrinated with the values of the ruling élite that they have largely surrendered to it whatever control they might once have had over their own destiny, unaware that they have even done so. Like the distinguished jurist Louis Brandeis half a century before him, Lindblom is understandably repelled by these shallow, materialistic values. But unlike Brandeis, Lindblom sees the gradual subordination of ordinary Americans to industrial hierarchy in the economic sphere and to the leadership of an élite dominated by business in the political as evidence of a kind of trick, a corrupt, shrouded effort on the part of that élite to make the people believe and desire things they wouldn't otherwise. In Part III I consider this claim alongside the contrasting view of Lindblom's distinguished predecessor, and argue, with Brandeis, that the nation's economic history since 1870 makes clear that Americans have been neither tricked nor manipulated into choosing these values, but have done so on their own, with open eyes.

But in recent years Lindblom too has explored the implications of his unsettling hypothesis and offered a different perspective, drawing heavily on his earlier work and lending his intellectual career a satisfying unity and (perhaps premature!) sense of closure. Venturing still further from the traditional territory of economics, he has turned his attention explicitly to the complex of social processes that govern the production of knowledge and culture, and in *Inquiry and Change* (1990) has come to see this indoctrination as part of a larger phenomenon he calls 'impairment' of individual inquiry. If it is clear that all social life demands some degree of consensus on fundamental values, Lindblom makes equally plain that the socialization that produces this consensus also imprisons our perceptions and blinds us to the liberating potential of values different from our own. Seeking to free our minds from impairment and our social life from debilitating pathologies we can neither diagnose nor address, Lindblom is drawn back to the contrasting ideals of centralism and pluralism. In a competition of ideas possible only in the latter, he finds the one, faint hope of intellectual and political liberation.

ECONOMIC POLITICS

Consider the neoclassical firm, an abstraction with a problem. More precisely, two problems: first, how to transform the inputs it buys into the output it sells, and then to determine how many units of each kind of input to buy and thus how many units of output to produce. What makes these questions 'problems' is that the firm has a specific objective it wants to achieve in answering them, so that the degree to which this goal is met determines which of the many possible answers to the questions is the 'best' solution to the problem posed by the governing objective. The range of possible objectives is wide; the firm might, for example, try to maximize sales or market share, or maximize the wages paid to its workers, or earn a reputation for producing only the highest quality goods. But the objective ascribed to the neoclassical firm is maximizing profit, selecting both the technology of production and the level of output that make the difference between the cost it pays for its inputs and the revenue it receives for its output as great as it can possibly be.

In making these decisions, the firm commands a great deal of relevant knowledge. It knows the state of the technological art and the price of each input, so it can choose from among all the available technologies the one that minimizes the cost of producing output and thus calculate the most favourable array of marginal costs, and it knows the price at which it can sell every unit of output it makes, so it can superimpose a marginal revenue function on the schedule of marginal costs. In the powerful light shed by this 'clarity of objective, explicitness of evaluation ... high degree of comprehensiveness of overview, and ... quantification of values for mathematical analysis' (Lindblom, 1959b, p. 173),[4] the firm can see just how much profit it will earn at every possible level of production, so that achieving its objective becomes a simple matter of mathematics, finding the output at which marginal revenue and marginal cost are the same.

In a series of related works published up to 1965, Lindblom has come to call this ideal of rational problem-solving 'synopsis' (1962a, p. 198; 1963, pp. 37–57; 1965, pp. 137–43).

> To adopt the term is to assume that a problem is solved by understanding it. Understanding requires a comprehensiveness of information and analysis. It is also to assume that one cannot be rational without first knowing what one wants and proceeding only thereafter to a comprehensive examination of alternative means to the attainment of what one wants.   (1965, p. 138)

But as both Ronald Coase (1937) and Chester Barnard (1938) had recognized in rather different ways before 1940, the difficulty with the synoptic method is that the real business firm is not an 'it' but a 'who', subject to all the many imperfections of the human condition as it goes about trying to formulate and achieve its objectives. By 1947 Herbert Simon had identified the cognitive obstacles to synopsis he would later call 'bounded rationality' (Simon, 1947, pp. 68–70, 80–84), limitations Lindblom also saw as rooted in

> the plain fact that, like Winnie-the-Pooh, [man] is an animal of very little brain. The number of alternatives man would need to consider in order to act rationally is very often far beyond his limited mental capacity [and] it is difficult to use such foresight as feeble brain and personality might otherwise permit because often one cannot judge between present goal achievement and future – partly because one cannot always know what he wants until he has tested the goal; concrete experience often is the only adequate test.   (Lindblom, 1953, pp. 60–61)

The interrelated inabilities of real men and women to specify in advance of the moment of decision the values and objectives that are to guide their choices and then to gather and assess the information needed to 'optimize' have thus been a major theme in the work of both Simon and Lindblom. But where Simon's interest in administration as such drew him toward a theory of 'satisficing', in which the question of value selection is resolved by assuming that the decision-maker is able to identify outcomes that will be 'good enough' and attention focused instead on the difficulties of securing the requisite information (Simon, 1957, pp. 204–5), Lindblom's lifelong interest in the intricacies of political organization and behaviour, and more specifically in the day-to-day operation of the decentralized, interlocking public and private institutions that govern the creation of public policy in a democracy, has led him in a different direction.

Policymaking, Lindblom argues, ordinarily contemplates only a range of alternatives that differ slightly from one another and the status quo (1958a, p. 300). It proceeds both incrementally, taking 'existing reality as one alternative and compar[ing] the probable gains and losses of closely related alternatives by making relatively small adjustments in existing reality' (1953, p. 82), and sequentially, so that each policy increment 'is tried, altered, tried in its altered form, altered again and so on' (1958a, p. 301). This is so because the preconditions of democracy itself, 'widespread consensus on fundamental values [and on] the general direction and character of desired social change', demand it.

> When an individual lives in a society marked by the kinds of consensus referred to and when he is dubious about the predictability of large-scale change, his demands upon political leadership and his response to their appeals to him will have the effect of buttressing incremental policies. (Lindblom, 1958a, p. 301)

The consensus to which Lindblom refers relates not to the short-term objectives of particular policies but rather to such fundamentals of democracy as a recognition that only those who have fairly prevailed in free elections can legitimately claim to rule, a broad tolerance of conflicting opinion, and a preference for persuasion and agreement as against violence or revolution (Lindblom, 1953, pp. 294–302). But experience makes clear that even within such a consensus, pluralism and vigorous partisanship usually flourish. People differ greatly in their preferences with respect to the specifics of policy despite their agreement on the fundamentals. How to allocate the budget? Where to put the new airport? Lower the gasoline tax? Raise the minimum wage? Questions like these, it might be said, could be resolved simply by reference to 'the public interest'. But 'there is no one public interest, as we all know. ... No social goal can be anything more than a compromise of conflicting individual goals' (Lindblom, 1955, p. 157).

> Politics is not an art or science pursued by philosopher-kings who find the public interest in the sky, but is a craft practiced by negotiators who know that the public interest can never be anything else but the common goals of different people. ... Hence, within a certain range the public interest is represented by an agreement among partisan interests, which is the way bargainers see it, not a goal or state of affairs having some validity other than as a practical bargained compromise.   (Lindblom, 1955, pp. 155–6, 158)

As in the firm, then, problem-solving in the realm of everyday public policy must always contend with the cognitive limits imposed by human frailty. But Lindblom distinguishes the firm from the policy-making agency in three crucial particulars. First, where the firm is free to make the radical changes in scale and organization that separate the short run from the long, the democratic consensus demands that public policy be made at the margin, in successive small steps. Secondly, where the pursuit of at least some positive profit confronts decision-makers in the firm with an easily appreciated, quantifiable organizational objective sufficiently compelling to motivate Simon's arguments for satisficing behaviour, the absence of an analogous, clearly defined public interest in the case of policy-making makes resolution of the question of which particular values are to be served by policy a critical element of the problem itself. And finally, if hierarchy and managerial technique make centralized decision-making at least a plausible aspiration for the firm,

> we can describe American national policy-making as fragmented rather than unified. It is a process much like the market process in important respects. Various groups, each viewing policy from a limited point of view, make decisions that reinforce or counter one another's. ... A series of mutually countering and reinforcing moves between ... groups can stimulate each to find that position in which a relatively high degree of goal attainment is possible without stimulating the other group to further countermoves. Because in a series of such moves each group often explores its own values at the margin, the moves themselves are necessary to the achievement of a mutually acceptable solution, and a centrally contemplated policy could not always find so satisfactory a solution. ... Fragmentation would seem to substitute politics for brains in problems of co-ordination that run beyond human intellectual capacity.   (Lindblom, 1958b, pp. 536–7)

Thus, the broad dispersal in all democratic systems of the effective power to influence, block or react to decisions made elsewhere among a host of public agencies and private organizations requires that all policy be to some extent the undesigned result of explicit accommodation and compromise of diverse partisan interests rather than the product of synoptic attempts at global problem-solving in the service of a single, collectively defined objective.

Policies are set as a resultant of ... conflict, not because some one policy-making individual or group achieves an integration but because the pulling and hauling of various views accomplishes finally some kind of decision, probably different from what any one advocate of the final solution intended and probably different from what any one advocate could comfortably defend by reference to his own limited values. (Lindblom, 1959a, p. 174)

Given consensus on the basic rules of the game, fragmentation in the political arena operates to produce policy in the face of conflicting interests precisely as the analogous decentralization operates in the market to allocate resources to competing ends given consensus on the fundamental principles of private property and free exchange. Both adapt to bounded rationality by allowing consensual solutions to large, complex problems to emerge epiphenomenally from the efforts of each decision-making centre to solve its own smaller, simpler ones. No one need solve, or even see, the big problem, with its enormous number of variables and its myriad of conflicting values; each centre confronts only the far smaller set of variables that touch its own narrow interests and seeks to promote them through a series of incremental adjustments conditioned by the similar actions of the others.

The sequentiality of adjustments, moreover, the play of move and countermove, allows the inevitable omissions and errors made by individual centres in calculating their interests and predicting the consequences of their decisions to be revealed and, in Lindblom's phrase, 'mopped up' (1965, p. 151) over time: 'Values neglected in one group's limited view of its problems often become central to the interests of other groups; and around important values felt to be neglected by all existing groups new groups form' (Lindblom, 1958b, p. 536). Like the market process, mutual adjustment becomes a 'discovery procedure' (Hayek, 1979a), a source of

powerful motives to mobilize information and analysis on the relations among possible decisions. To be sure, no one decision maker is motivated to undertake the comprehensive investigations envisaged by the advocates of an overview, but, taken together, a group of partisan adjusters may generate a great deal more information and analysis than will a central coordinator. (Lindblom, 1965, p. 174)

As in the market, then, initiative and self-reliance thus become important determinants of success for the individual; if there are interests touched by the problem at hand but overlooked or ignored by those currently engaged with it, new problems are created for those who hold them, and like competitors in a market where new technology has created new costs and new opportunities, they hold back from the fray only at their peril (Lindblom, 1959b, pp. 183–5).

In much the same way that Adam Smith had illuminated the co-ordinating powers of the invisible hand a full century before the marginalist revolution was able to offer a theory of individual behaviour consistent with his larger insight, Lindblom had himself identified mutual adjustment as the 'hidden hand in government' (1955) some years before he was able to formulate the theory of 'disjointed incrementalism' that lay beneath it. But by 1959 he had, in perhaps his best-known essay, systematized the pragmatic technique of problem-solving characteristically employed by real public administrators as 'the science of muddling through' and defended it as a *system*, 'not a failure of method for which administrators ought to apologize' (1959b, p. 188). Twenty years later he offered this summary of its most salient features:

> (a) limitation of analysis to a few somewhat familiar policy alternatives; (b) an intertwining of analysis of policy goals and other values with the empirical aspects of the problem; (c) a greater analytical preoccupation with ills to be remedied than positive goals to be sought; (d) a sequence of trials, errors, and revised trials; (e) analysis that explores only some, not all, of the important possible consequences of a considered alternative; (f) fragmentation of analytical work to many (partisan) participants in policy making. (Lindblom, 1979a, p. 239)[5]

Time and again Lindblom denies the synoptic postulate that values must be known before rational choices can be made, and stresses the 'intertwining' of the two, not just in policy-making but, more strikingly, in his interpretation of the paradigm of synopsis itself, the neoclassical theory of the consumer. 'The value problem is ... always a problem of adjustments at the margin. But there is no practicable way to state marginal objectives or values except in terms of particular policies' (Lindblom, 1959b, p. 177).

> The way in which we economists can, for our own professional purposes, conceptualize consumer choice obscures the great difference between what the consumer can be conceived of as having done but does not actually do – ascertain a function, then choose so as to maximize it – and what he actually does – simply compare policies at the margin and choose directly the preferred policy. Like the consumer, the incremental decision-maker in governmental affairs does not make use of a utility function [or] a social welfare function. ... He can hardly be said to know even a point or two on such a function because he does not think in terms of alternative social states; and, if he can be said to value one social state higher than another, this fact is more to be inferred from his choices than said to control them. He makes specific choices, as does the consumer, at the margin. (Lindblom, 1961, p. 307)

Thus, neither the consumer nor the administrator need 'try to analyze any values except the values by which alternative policies differ and need not be concerned with them except as they differ marginally. His need for information on values or objectives is drastically reduced as compared with [synopsis]; and his capacity for grasping, comprehending, and relating values to one another is not strained beyond the breaking point' (Lindblom, 1959b, pp. 178–9).

With the task of articulating the substance of disjointed incrementalism and developing its philosophical implications completed (with the help of David Braybrooke) in *A Strategy of Decision* (1963), Lindblom sought to close the circle of this 'large-scale model of democracy' (1962b, p. 59) with an exhaustive analysis of mutual adjustment in politics in *The Intelligence of Democracy* (1965). From the outset, he had shown his solicitousness for the spontaneous order of the market (1949, pp. 15–21, 215–27) and made clear his conviction that in politics too, 'though we perceive it only obscurely, private vice may be public virtue' (1955, p. 140). Now, unsatisfied with the relatively vague notion of co-ordination set forth in his earlier discussions of fragmentation, he would substantially deepen this inquiry by undertaking 'a systematic comparative analysis of centrality and partisan mutual adjustment among various kinds of political officials and leaders as competing methods for rational co-ordination of governmental decisions' (1965, p. 9). In so doing he would again replay the history of his discipline in the microcosm of his own career. The elaboration of the behavioural insights of marginalism into the modern notion of general equilibrium after 1871 had encouraged the welfare economists of the 1930s to replace Smith's qualitative description of the organizational wonders worked over time by an invisible hand that never stopped with a mathematically precise analysis of allocative efficiency in the stasis of general equilibrium. Similarly, with the behavioural theory of disjointed incrementalism in hand, Lindblom would lend greater rigour to his claim that decentralized mutual adjustment could co-ordinate the decisions of a multitude of political actors, but unlike the welfare economists, he would reject the seductive but artificial mathematics of equilibrium to focus, like Smith and his modern successors, on the process of mutual adjustment rather than its outcomes.

Lindblom's earliest attempts to evaluate the results of mutual adjustment focused on the fact of agreement itself in an environment of conflicting but unchanging interests and objectives. Under synopsis, he wrote in 1959,

> a decision is 'correct', 'good', or 'rational' if it can be shown to attain some specified objective, where the objective can be specified without simply describing the decision itself. ... But what of the situation in which administrators cannot agree on values or objectives ...? What then is the test of 'good' policy? For [synopsis], there is no test. Agreement on objectives failing, there is no standard of 'correctness'. For [incrementalism], the test is agreement on policy itself, which remains possible even when agreement on values is not ... In an important sense, therefore, it is not irrational ... to defend a policy as good without being able to specify what it is good for. (1959b, pp. 179–81)

The virtues of such a test, he went on, are not to be slighted. Stable democracy requires a continuing consent to its procedures that can often be won only by conceding to every interest whatever price it demands for its agreement to the policy at issue. In this sense, mutual adjustment can be seen as

> a process in which, when the intensity of frustration of group interests threatens democratic consent, the fact is plain; and the option is open to other groups to pay the necessary price. This is an aspect of mutual adjustment much to be prized. ... [even though] inconsistency in government programs is thus inevitable and part of the mechanism of partisan mutual adjustment.   (1961, pp. 317, 324)

But by 1965 Lindblom's normative claims for mutual adjustment had become considerably stronger, particularly when the alternative was the imposition, in the name of rationality, of a single organizing objective on a large number of independently motivated political actors.[6] In *The Intelligence of Democracy* the relatively simple notion of co-ordination implied by the fact of agreement on specific policies at specific times was expanded to encompass the entire chain of actions and adaptive reactions required to formulate policy in a world in which objectives and the means to achieve them are constantly changing. 'In incremental analysis', Lindblom had written in 1959, 'values are not simply formulae for the guidance of policy choices but interact with policy choices in such a way that each unendingly alters the other as more is learned about both values and appropriate policies from the results of each incremental alteration in policy' (1959b, p. 309). But this, as he now realized, calls the fundamental idea of policy-making as problem-solving itself into question, for it makes little sense to see the outcomes of mutual adjustment as 'solutions' if fluid values and shifting opportunities continuously redefine the 'problems' they are meant to address (1965, pp. 148–9). Individual agreements on specific policies, small islands of consensus between temporary coalitions that solve the problems of the moment, thus take on a very different significance than they had when values and objectives were assumed to be stable. No longer ends in themselves, they become, like the countless individual transactions in the market whose particular terms are conditioned by the transient circumstances of time and place under which they are made, simply way-stations in a larger process that continually creates new interests and new possibilities for exchange with no apparent purpose or destination in sight.

> In partisan mutual adjustment some strong tendencies toward Pareto optima are present in pairs of decisions or other sets of decisions. In his relations with some Ys every X is motivated by his own interests to ask whether there is a possibility of mutual gain, or at least gain to X without loss to Y. ... The freedom of participants in partisan mutual adjustment to undertake partisan discussion, compensation, and negotiation sets in motion a never-ending and detailed, even

if highly fragmented, search for possibilities of benefitting a multiplicity of Xs without disadvantage to a multiplicity of Ys. For what is negligible detail to a central co-ordinator is motivating self-interest to X.   (Lindblom, 1965, p. 195)

But the very fluidity that makes this process of mutual adjustment 'never-ending precludes the achievement of equilibrium. Like the market order, in which individual contracts are constantly formed, dissolved and formed again in a kaleidoscopic environment that continuously shows participants new opportunities and constraints but reveals no purpose or direction of its own, the process of spontaneous mutual adjustment continuously produces new values, new problems and new agreements that propel it toward an open-ended succession of outcomes no one could possibly have predicted or characterized before the operation of the process itself. This suggests not only the futility of synoptic planning but also that, in the absence of static equilibrium, normative claims for the superiority of such equilibria, analogous to the welfare economists' timeless mathematical analysis of Pareto-efficient allocation, cannot be sustained. Instead, the critical roles of sequential decision-making and reactive 'mopping up' emphasize the centrality of time in the analysis of spontaneous order and turn attention away from the properties of transient, unstable outcomes and toward the dynamic processes that first produce them and then render them obsolete.

Just as Hayek (1945) had argued with respect to the market, then, in mutual adjustment one 'cannot show directly that its outcomes are superior to other outcomes. As with most social processes, we argue the superiority of the outcome from the process, not the process from the outcome' (Lindblom, 1961, p. 323). And so, when he came at last to evaluate mutual adjustment as a means of rational decision-making in politics, the points he chose to emphasize were procedural rather than substantive. First, mutual adjustment achieves co-ordination in the sense that 'the adverse consequences of any one decision for other decisions ... are to a degree and in some frequency avoided, reduced, counterbalanced, or outweighed', even though we cannot say 'just when, where, which, and whose adverse consequences ought to be taken care of as a condition of calling a set of decisions co-ordinated' (1965, p. 154). Secondly, it is self-regulating in the sense that the most acceptable rules for repairing or restructuring the process in the light of perceived defects are most likely to be those produced by mutual adjustment itself (1965, pp. 300–2). And finally, to those who would damn mutual adjustment for its 'conservatism', Lindblom, again echoing Hayek (1979b, pp. 18–22), replies, 'Is [it] not prepared for a world of unremitting change ...? Once launched ... on a course of changing policy, where is the stopping-place? Is there any limit to the changes to which it might lend itself?' (1963, p. 108).

In 1975 Lindblom brilliantly summarized the arguments I have sketched in this part as he posed the dichotomy between the 'intellectually guided' society, with its commitment to reason and planning, and the 'preference guided' society, with its commitment to decentralization and mutual adjustment. The real issue between them, he said, was 'an opposing set of views on the maximum role of reason ... in social organization and social change' (1975, p. 24). But if his task there was 'not to debate the merits of alternative views but to clarify' them (1975, p. 25), his arguments none the less underscored a truth he, like Hayek and others, had made explicit many years before:

> Reason runs out, cannot bear the burdens imposed on it, therefore has to be employed in light of its limitations. A general prescription to employ reason in decision-making, however persuasive, is less wise than a prescription to use reason in establishing such decision-making machinery as reduces the demands made on reason and achieves a co-ordination of only partly reasoned decisions through processes of adjustment other than those that go on in the human mind. (Lindblom, 1961, p. 320)

PLANNING AND THE POLITICS OF VALUES

Consider the neoclassical firm once again. This time, assume that the problems of Part II have been solved, that the firm's unitary 'brain' has successfully determined the best production technology and calculated its profit maximizing output. Now, however, a new problem arises. How can the 'brain' be certain that the 'fingers' will do its bidding? How, that is, can the firm achieve the internal co-ordination and control over its various human constituents necessary to ensure that the production plan will be faithfully carried out? For production organized in the market, of course, there is no plan; order is created by the spontaneous mutual adjustment, mediated by flexible prices, of men and women with no common goal, and the absence of a single, guiding objective obviates the need for conscious control over production altogether. But in the firm, order means planning, the subordination of diverse individual interests to the specific objectives of the firm and the harnessing of effort in the service of those ends, and must therefore be achieved in some other way. How this is to be done might be called the 'planner's problem', and for some 40 years Lindblom has recognized its ubiquity and importance for capitalism and socialism alike.

Long ago, Lenin (1943, p. 84) dreamed of a time when 'the whole of society will have become one office and one factory', with the requisite tools of control 'within the reach of anybody who can read and write and knows the first four rules of arithmetic', because a new consciousness had brought the objectives of the planners and the self-perceived interests of every citizen into perfect alignment. But, as Lindblom suggested in *Politics, Economics, and Welfare* (1953) and the rapid industrialization of the Soviet Union after Lenin's death confirms, successful large-scale planning needn't await the higher phase of communism or the creation of Soviet Man. All that is necessary is the power and the will to enforce the effective suppression of individual interests in favour of such relatively simple organizing objectives as 'the development of productive capacity' (Lindblom, 1953, pp. 394–402), 'the crude growth of physical output' or a rough 'balance' between the principal sectors of the economy (Lindblom, 1966, pp. 69–71). Where allocative efficiency expressed in terms of consumer preferences is not an issue, the demands of production can determine the particulars of consumption and the price mechanism be largely dispensed with. Not even the concessions to individual interest implicit in Lange's (1938) socialism are required, for just as 'in a capitalist economy, in this kind of market socialism the consumer remained sovereign – at a time when most socialists, planners, and Communists were looking for ways to effect collective purposes and national goals, rather than individual preferences' (Lindblom, 1966, p. 70).

Nor must a free society rely on markets in every circumstance, for in time of war a people may well agree to substitute commands for prices so that the common objective of victory can be achieved without the delays and the unacceptably divisive distribution of burdens and profits the market would produce even in so rare an atmosphere of sacrifice and shared purpose as this (Lindblom, 1953, pp. 402–12). Still, all of these arguments, like those of Mises and Hayek in the calculation debate, contemplate an unrealistically simple world of just two alternative modes of economic organization, the polar cases of atomistic markets on the one hand and comprehensive state planning on the other. But modern capitalism is far more complex than this and, as the success of the huge private firms that dominate it makes clear, it is a mistake to associate central economic planning exclusively with the state. Islands of purposeful planning in a sea of imperfect competition, within their boundaries these firms too must somehow solve the planner's problem, but they, unlike the crumbling economies of state socialism in recent years, seem to have found a way to do so. But if concentrating solely on the economics of state planning has blinded Hayek to the relevance of his otherwise telling and prescient critique to large-scale planning in the private sector, the question of how the modern capitalist firm has achieved the degree of internal co-ordination and control it has without compulsion or war has been a major focus of inquiry for Lindblom. In extending the critique of centralism to address the realities of corporate planning, moreover, he has from the outset been drawn from the economics of prices and information to the politics of bureaucracy and authority and, more recently, to the political psychology of indoctrination and impairment.

One possible answer to Lindblom's question lies in the idea of profit maximization itself. The more profits there are, the more that can be distributed to owners, managers and workers alike, so it might plausibly be said that larger profits serve the independent interests of all the firm's many constituents. If so, this in itself would create a general alignment of purpose from top to bottom that is likely to induce general consent to the control exercised by the firm's planners, each individual seeing in the policy of profit maximization a means to his or her own unique ends. As Lindblom has stressed in the context of policy-making, if individuals with otherwise conflicting values each see their interests served in different ways by the same policy, agreement on that policy is likely despite the divergence of ultimate ends (1959b, p. 180). But though its underlying logic bears strong resemblance to that of this simple response, Lindblom's own explanation of how the modern corporation has solved the planner's problem, proposed first in *Politics and Markets* (1977) and elaborated in a series of pessimistic essays published in the early 1980s, has been a more complex, profoundly more disturbing one.

Lindblom's rich and far-reaching critique of American corporate capitalism defies brief summary. But the aspects of it that bear most directly on the planner's problem are encapsulated in the related notions of a 'privileged position of business' in the political economy of democratic capitalism and a 'circularity' in the operation of its institutions. A largely unappreciated consequence of the system of private ownership, Lindblom argues, is its extensive delegation to unelected managers of corporate enterprises of the power to decide matters of crucial importance to the great mass of citizens. Every society must somehow determine whether new investment is to be undertaken and how to finance it, how new technology is to be developed and deployed, how the work force is to be organized, how big plants will be and where they'll be located, and how executives are to be compensated; indeed, it is decisions like this that ultimately determine the entire structure of an industrial economy, from the configuration of its cities to the bureaucratization of its workplaces, and so they are 'public' questions, whoever is given the authority to answer them. But the prerogatives of private ownership mean that it is neither the people directly nor the government they elect who decides, but 'business'.

> Because public functions in the market system rest in the hands of businessmen, it follows that jobs, prices, production, growth, the standard of living, and the economic security of everyone rest in their hands. Consequently, government officials cannot be indifferent to how well business performs its functions. Depression, inflation, or other economic distress can bring down a government. A major function of government, therefore, is to see to it that businessmen perform their tasks. ... [But] although governments can forbid certain kinds of activity,

they cannot command business to perform. They must induce rather than command. They must therefore offer benefits to businessmen in order to stimulate the required performance. ... Every government in these systems accepts a responsibility to do what is necessary to assure profits high enough to maintain as a minimum employment and growth. ... Any government official who understands the requirements of his position and the responsibilities that market-oriented systems throw on businessmen will therefore grant them a privileged position. ... He simply understands, as is plain to see, that public affairs ... are in the hands of two groups of leaders, government and business, who must collaborate and that to make the system work government leadership must often defer to business leadership. (Lindblom, 1977, pp. 172–5)

All of this is premissed on a broad public consensus in favour of the material wealth and growth that lie largely within the discretion of business leaders to create. Without it, elected officials have nothing to fear from a failure to meet the incessant demands of business for inducements to produce and invest; with it, sluggish investment or rising unemployment put every official at risk. But as every successful American politician has understood for decades, precisely this consensus is the single most important feature of the political landscape; the electorate does not hesitate to hold government at all levels responsible for the performance of the economy. In Lindblom's view, the pattern of individual desires that produce this consensus are in every case a personal combination of principle, appraisal, judgement and opinion far too complex to be captured in the neoclassical economist's notion of 'preference'. Preferences are simply tastes, automatic responses at moments of choice for which no active thought is required and no reasons need be offered. For every individual, they are just 'there', waiting to be revealed and not to be criticized: *De gustibus non est disputandum.* But to understand the dispositions behind the consensus for growth in this way is to impoverish our thinking 'by imprisoning it in an unsatisfactory model of preferences taken as given' (Lindblom, 1982, p. 335). More than mere preferences, they are *created*, not discovered. They are the products of active intellect, 'complex choices on which deliberation is both possible and practiced', not objective facts to be found but 'emergent acts of will' that express not an uncritical self-interest but a sense of how things ought to be (Lindblom, 1977, p. 135).

Lindblom calls them 'volitions', though it is clear that they are very much like the 'values' that played so important a role in his earlier work, and has made them and their origins a major focus of inquiry. But, as Adam Ferguson might say, to call them the results of human action is not to call them products of human design. Are they 'grown', unintended outcomes of spontaneous processes, or 'made', creatures of purposeful design? And if they're made, who makes them? Is each person the sovereign creator of his or her own volitions, or are they created for us, and we manipulated into holding them so that interests of which we may not even be aware can be served? In the case of the volitions that support the consensus for growth, *Politics and Markets* offers a clear and deeply unsettling set of answers. They are made, Lindblom argues, but not by a free and informed citizenry. They are instead the handiwork of 'business', and we hold them not in our own interests, but in those of a ruling corporate élite.

'A key element of much democratic theory is the informed, active, rational participant, a point on which democratic theory can be suspected of being a form of wishful thinking' (Lindblom, 1977, p. 132). Those who would see clearly must therefore consider

> the ominous specific possibility that popular control in both market and government is in any case circular. It may be that people are indoctrinated to demand – to buy and to vote for – nothing other than what a decisionmaking élite is already disposed to grant them. The volitions that are supposed to guide leaders are formed by the same leaders. (Lindblom, 1977, p. 202)

These leaders 'undertake a steady propaganda designed to reduce any fundamental popular hostility to business needs ... both by teaching popular attitudes favorable to business and, more commonly perhaps, by teaching and in other ways inducing political acquiescence or docility' (Lindblom, 1983, p. 128; 1977, pp. 203–6). And it has worked:

> If the business message is getting through ... we should expect a somewhat narrowly constrained set of volitions that does not much question business enterprise, the corporation, private property, and other fundamentals. Just so. (1977, p. 208)
>
> Most thoughtful men now give some significant credence to Marx's argument that life in market societies powerfully affects the kind of personalities formed. Hence, if a man feels free, it is often because he has been shaped into just such a personality as he wishes to have and do what the market system permits him to have and do. (1980, p. 97)
>
> Take care to understand my argument. I do not point to measurable flows of indoctrinating communications, messages, indoctrinations, and then claim to judge their effect from the observed magnitudes. Instead I infer from the existence of a pattern – a pattern of agreement – that a pattern of indoctrination must have established the agreement. How else could it have come about? I can find no other explanation. (1983, p. 134)

In corporate capitalism, then, the planner's problem is solved not at the level of the individual firm, but in the political economy as a whole. Submission to the managerial control that must be exercised within the firm is won not by coercion but by inculcating in every ordinary man and woman a personal identification with the corporate planners' pursuit of profit. And this identification is achieved not by a common desire to prevail in war or by the invocation of some great collective purpose but by the purposeful creation of a citizenry so committed to the shallow ideal of ever-increasing material wealth that they willingly surrender their moral, economic and political autonomy to an élite and a system that promises to give it to them. Lindblom sees in all of this much cause for contempt, and understandably so. But in his anger at what he sees as the manipulation of the masses by the captains of industry and their allies in government, he seems to imply that had the people been truly free to form their own volitions, they would surely have chosen other, nobler values. Better, perhaps, to believe this than the alternative, that not liberty but wealth is what the people really want.

Louis Brandeis took a different view.[7] First as 'the people's attorney' in a variety of causes and then, for 23 years after his appointment by Woodrow Wilson in 1916, from his seat on the Supreme Court, Brandeis put his considerable powers of analysis and advocacy in the service of Jefferson's vision of free, self-reliant citizens joined in small institutions that placed a measure of responsibility in each of them, nurturing their talents and developing their capacities. 'Remember', he wrote in 1922, '... that always and everywhere the intellectual, moral and spiritual development of those concerned will remain an essential – and the main factor – in real betterment.'

> This development of the individual is, thus, both a necessary means and the end sought. For our objective is the making of men and women who shall be free – self-respecting members of a democracy – and who shall be worthy of respect. Improvement in material conditions of the worker and ease are the incidents of better conditions – valuable mainly as they may ever increase opportunities for development. (Brandeis, 1978, pp. 45–6)

But the rapid growth of huge, hierarchically organized industrial firms after 1870 posed a grave danger to this development, threatening to create what Brandeis called 'a nation of slaves', men and women who were little more than cogs in a mass-production machine driven by corporate bureaucrats. 'The proposition that mere bigness can not be an offense against society is false, because ... our society, which rests upon democracy, can not endure under such conditions' (McCraw, 1984, p. 109). Rather, Brandeis believed,

> by the control which the few have exerted through giant corporations individual initiative and effort are being paralyzed, creative power impaired and human happiness lessened; that the true prosperity of our past came not from big business, but through the courage, the energy, and the resourcefulness of small men; that only by releasing from corporate control the faculties of the unknown many, only by reopening to them the opportunities for leadership, can confidence in our future be restored and the existing misery be overcome; and that only through participation by the many in the responsibilities and determinations of business can Americans secure the moral and intellectual development which is essential to the maintenance of liberty. (*Liggett* v *Lee*, 1933, p. 580)

For Brandeis, then, the 'curse of bigness' was the threat it posed to the values that he, like Lindblom, held most dear, the moral development of the individual and the ideal of participatory democracy. He would not hesitate to use the full powers of government to reverse the trend toward bigness, shunning its material rewards for the developmental advantages of individual empowerment and small scale. Still, Brandeis understood that free men and women are never mere spectators of an autonomous drama that forces bigness upon them against their will. It is always within their power, as workers and consumers on the one hand and citizens on the other, to decide otherwise and manifest a volition for smallness either in the market or in popular legislation. But although the long, bitter struggle over the Sherman Act betrayed a widespread uneasiness with the advance of large-scale organization and the desire for material comfort that drove it (Letwin, 1965), by 1920 it was apparent to Brandeis that Americans had made their peace with them. Reflecting on his differences with Wilson, he said, 'In my opinion the real curse was bigness rather than monopoly. Mr Wilson (and others wise politically) made the attack on lines of monopoly – because Americans hated monopoly and loved bigness' (Brandeis, 1978, p. 482). Their unthinkable swap of personal autonomy for mass production had turned responsible, self-reliant Americans into 'consumers', whom he contemptuously described to George Soule as 'servile, self-indulgent, indolent, ignorant' (Brandeis, 1978, p. 92). 'It's clear, I think', he told Felix Frankfurter in 1925, 'that the gentle enslavement of our people is proceeding apace ... & that the only remedy is via the individual. To make him care to be a free man & willing to pay the price' (Brandeis, 1978, p. 193). But the people seemed to want the material bounty of corporate bigness more than the elevating rigours of liberty, and a short time later he angrily captured the essence of the matter:

> Isn't there among your economists some one who could make clear to the country that the greatest social-economic troubles arise from the fact [that] the consumer has failed absolutely to perform his function? He lies not only supine, but paralyzed & deserves to suffer like others who take their lickings 'lying down'. He gets no worse than his just deserts.   (Brandeis, 1978, p. 207)

Lindblom has described the displacement of the small firms of the nineteenth century by the corporate giants of our own in words he might just as easily have used to describe the covert triumph of the materialist values that have made it possible:

> Never much agitated, never even much resisted, a revolution for which no flags were raised, it transformed our lives during those very decades in which, unmindful of what was happening, Americans and Europeans debated instead such issues as

socialism, populism, free silver, clericalism, chartism, and colonialism. It now stands as a monument to the discrepancy between what men think they are designing and the world they are in fact building. (1977, p. 95)

But if this were ever true of Europe, the tortuous history of the anti-trust movement in the United States and the fruitless, frustrated struggles of those, like Louis Brandeis, for whom opportunity and self-reliance were still the animating ideals of the American experiment make clear that the decision for bigness in this country was made by a people fully aware of the choices before them. That Americans do believe the things the mass production of consumable wealth requires them to believe, that they have largely traded the independence and acceptance of personal responsibility Tocqueville admired for the narrow political vision and readiness to do as they're told that both Lindblom and Brandeis properly despise is not a sign that their democracy has denied them what they want. It is rather a sign that their economy has given it to them. As Brandeis knew, the world we live in has not been forced on us, nor have we been manipulated into wanting it. For good or ill, unwilling to sacrifice our material interests in consumption and employment for the older virtues of autonomy and responsibility, we and our predecessors in this century have chosen to create it.

But whatever one might believe about how the volitions we hold have come to be what they are, the relevant question now is how they can be changed, how we can come to realize the extent to which our perceptions about social life and our inquiries into its possibilities have been impaired and, in so doing, to bring about the general intellectual liberation needed to make meaningful social change possible. In *Politics and Markets* itself, still wed to the idea that volitions are 'made', Lindblom flirted briefly with the possibility that they might be *remade* by a charismatic, ideologically driven leadership and the energies thus released put to work at the task of achieving truly revolutionary social change. Just such an attempt, he said, had been a hallmark of Mao's China and, to a lesser extent, of Castro's Cuba. Lindblom called this the 'preceptoral' ideal:

a system of social control through highly unilateral governmental persuasion addressed not to an élite or to a bureaucracy alone but to an entire population. It is also a system for moving towards centrally desired aspirations, not a system for widespread participation in the establishment of social goals. ... Persuasion, information, indoctrination, instruction, propaganda, counseling, advice, exhortation, education and thought control constitute the range of methods used to induce the desired responses. ... [The system] is aimed first ... at the creation of the 'new man', [one] 'with no selfish interests, heart and soul for the people', ... who will 'autonomously' serve collective interests, that is, who will do on [his] own initiative what in other societies [he] must be commanded or induced to do. (1977, pp. 55–6, 277)[8]

Fully aware of both its practical difficulties and its potential for 'ferocious oppression', Lindblom argued none the less that

> some credence has to be granted to some conspicuously humane elements of the preceptoral vision of social organization. ... Maoist thought puts its emphasis on human spontaneity and consciousness rather than on technology. It is difficult to dismiss Mao's 'Of all things in the world, people are the most precious' as mere rhetoric. On some counts as humane as any other great vision of man in the history of human aspiration, the vision of an 'educated' citizenry is appealing on many counts [and] on some points more so than the vision of market man. (1977, pp. 61–2)

But in the end Lindblom could scarcely square this vision with either his head or his heart. As his own frank evaluation of the Chinese and Cuban experiments (1977, pp. 56–9, 276–90) made clear, the 'centrally desired aspirations' at its core and the radical concentration of power over men's minds it entailed both implied claims for the potential of synopsis that cannot be sustained in practice, and Lindblom is in any case far too critical and independent an intellect to be deceived about the kind of life the 'new man' would (and did) actually live under such a regime. And so he began to explore an alternative conception of volitions, one in which they are 'grown', not 'made'.

As early as 1958 Lindblom had distinguished the creation of knowledge about the social world from the active solution of problems, but saw both as governed by closely analogous processes of disjointed incrementalism and mutual adjustment (1958b). Now, building on ideas about the powers and limits of social science first expressed in *Usable Knowledge* (1979b), he began to ask: 'Who Needs What Social Research for Policy Making?' (1984). His response reflected his lifelong denial of the possibility of analysis and policy-making in the public interest, the erroneous assumptions that correct policy can be known and that, once known, it can be put in place by a unitary decision-maker. It was that everyone, and most especially dissidents ordinarily denied access to serious analysis, needs thoughtful, explicitly partisan analysis of social issues, and that once we have it, the search for truth itself can be committed to mutual adjustment, to the spontaneous, unpredictable give and take of the competition of ideas. 'All major social reforms, all great improvements in the welfare of humankind come from dissidents', and to do their work they need the services of professional researchers who will 'acknowledge and display their selection of values and interests – in short, their partisanship – and give up any pretense or appearance of speaking from Olympus, or as neutrals, or as representing a nonpartisan integration of interests that is for the good of all and injurious to none' (Lindblom, 1984, pp. 313, 316). Only partisan analysis can foster the vigorous competition of ideas essential to pluralism and, as in a court of law, only in the intellectual thrust and parry of partisans can 'usable truth' emerge. 'Imperfect as the process is, indeed there is no feasible better alternative way of reaching an approximation to truth for social problem solving' (Lindblom, 1984, p. 321).

But partisanship presupposes interests, and interests presuppose volitions. If the competition of ideas is to flourish, there must first be competing volitions, a state of affairs Lindblom had come by 1987 to see as precluded by 'a historical and continuing process of impairment of thought and discussion by indoctrination, as well as impositions that range from gentle intimidation to coercion, through which advantaged segments of society have sought, though usually not conspiratorially, to protect their advantages against slow erosion' (1987, pp. 12–13). Probing the 'pattern of agreement' that so disturbed him in *Politics and Markets*, he broadened and softened his analysis of indoctrination in *Inquiry and Change* (1990), incorporating it within a larger, normatively more ambiguous phenomenon, 'impaired' thought and inquiry that affected everyone, everywhere and at every moment in history. To be sure, conscious manipulation and indoctrination *are* important causes of our inability to recognize and solve social problems, but a deeper, more pervasive influence is 'socialization', the mental glue that holds society together. The concepts, rules and interpretative perspectives that comprise culture itself are communicated and enforced by a range of institutions, including family, school and church, and socialization succeeds precisely *because* it impairs critical inquiry and the creation of new volitions. The result is a 'convergence' of attitudes, values and beliefs that need not amount to consensus but that must to some extent limit the competition of ideas (Lindblom, 1990, pp. 59–77).

To what degree this convergence must be preserved and, conversely, to what degree it must be disturbed in order to promote the creation of new volitions and the competition of ideas, are questions that no single intellect can answer. And so they too must be committed to mutual adjustment, to a process of stimulation and probing of diverse alternatives that 'requires the participation of vast numbers of people [and] pervasive sustained inquiry at many levels of competence broadly distributed in the society' (Lindblom, 1990, p. 233). In the end, it is mutual adjustment, the decentralized, unpredictable competition of ideas itself that not only determines how far it will be permitted to extend and thus how much freedom people will be given to create their own volitions, but that also generates the very multiplicity of volitions that sustains the competition.

If all social theorists and practical men in public life acknowledge at some level the indispensability of both central and mutually adjustive transformation of diverse volitions, a great cleavage separates those who rely largely on centrality from those who rely largely on mutual adjustment. The conflict between the two positions poses a fundamental issue about social organization, and thus for the future of humankind. (Lindblom, 1990, p. 249)

Casting his lot here, just as he did in addressing the problems of policy, with those who would use reason only to create 'such decision-making machinery as reduces the demands made on reason and achieves a coordination of only partly reasoned decisions through processes of adjustment other than those that go on in the human mind' (1961, p. 320), Lindblom brings his intellectual journey full circle. His work, not unflawed, is a gift of real and lasting value to the new world struggling to be born as these words are written, a coherent vision of the good society in the great tradition of political economy.

NOTES

1. See, for example, Anderson (1978); Premfors (1981); and Gregory (1989).
2. In an introduction to a collection of his essays, Lindblom briefly recounts some of the professional difficulties he encountered at Minnesota and Yale early in his career as a result of his scholarly interests, and reflects, with no little regret, upon the distortions he sees them as having introduced into his work (Lindblom, 1987, pp. 15–19).
3. On the debate, see also Murrell (1983); Lavoie (1985); and Heilbroner (1990).
4. Cf. Lindblom (1965, pp. 137–8) and a very similar formulation in the context of individual utility maximization by James March and Herbert Simon (1958, p. 137).
5. A much fuller exposition of these points is Lindblom (1963, pp. 81–143); at p. 82, Lindblom explicitly likens disjointed incrementalism to Karl Popper's earlier notion of 'piecemeal social engineering'.
6. Cf. Hayek (1944, pp. 56–71).
7. On Brandeis' life and thought, see Strum (1984) and Adelstein (1989).
8. Cf. Brandeis's enthusiasm for a strikingly similar 'new man' (Adelstein, 1989, pp. 646–55).

REFERENCES

Works by Charles E. Lindblom

(1949), *Unions and Capitalism*, New Haven, Conn.: Yale University Press.
(1953), *Politics, Economics, and Welfare*, New York: Harper; (with Robert A. Dahl).
(1955), 'Bargaining: the Hidden Hand in Government', in Charles E. Lindblom, *Democracy and Market System*, Oslo: Norwegian University Press, 1988 (hereafter *DMS*), 139–70.
(1957), 'In Praise of Political Science', *World Politics*, **9**, 240–53.
(1958a), 'Policy Analysis', *American Economic Review*, **48**, 298–312.
(1958b), Tinbergen on Policy-Making', *Journal of Political Economy*, **66**, 531–8.
(1959a), 'The Handling of Norms in Policy Analysis', in Moses Abramovitz (ed.), *The Allocation of Economic Resources*, Stanford, Calif.: Stanford University Press, 160–79.

(1959b), 'The Science of "Muddling Through" ', *Public Administration Review*, **19**, 78–88; reprinted in *DMS*, 171–90.

(1961), 'Decision-Making in Taxation and Expenditures', in National Bureau of Economic Research, *Public Finances: Needs, Sources, and Utilization*, Princeton, N.J.: Princeton University Press, 295–329.

(1962a), 'Economic Development, Research and Development Policy Making: Some Converging Views', *Behavioral Science*, **7**, 211–22, (with Albert O. Hirschman), reprinted in *DMS*, 191–211.

(1962b), 'Democracy and Economic Structure', in William N. Chambers and Robert H. Salisbury (eds), *Democracy Today: Problems and Prospects*, New York: Collier Books, 80–121; reprinted in *DMS*, 25–66.

(1963), *A Strategy of Decision: Policy Evaluation as a Social Process*, New York: Free Press (with David Braybrooke).

(1965), *The Intelligence of Democracy: Decision Making Through Mutual Adjustment*, New York: Free Press.

(1966), 'The Rediscovery of the Market', *The Public Interest*, **4**, 89–101; reprinted in *DMS*, 67–82.

(1975), 'The Sociology of Planning: Thought and Social Interaction', in Morris Bornstein (ed.), *Economic Planning, East and West*, Cambridge, Mass.: Ballinger, 23–60.

(1977), *Politics and Markets: The World's Political-Economic Systems*, New York, Basic Books.

(1979a), 'Still Muddling, Not Yet Through', *Public Administration Review*, **39**, 517–26; reprinted in *DMS*, 237–59.

(1979b), *Usable Knowledge: Social Science and Social Problem Solving*, New Haven, Conn.: Yale University Press (with David K. Cohen).

(1980), 'Changing Views on Conflict Between Freedom and Equality', in *Freedom and Equality in Contemporary Society*, proceedings from an international conference, 'Japan and the World Tomorrow', Tokyo, 18–22; reprinted in *DMS*, 95–9.

(1982), 'The Market as Prison', *Journal of Politics*, **44**, 324–36.

(1983), 'Democracy and the Economy', in *DMS*, 115–35.

(1984), 'Who Needs What Social Research for Policy Making?', in *Rockefeller Institute Conference Proceedings*, vol. 1, 1–42; reprinted in *DMS*, 305–35.

(1987), 'Introduction', in *DMS*, 9–21.

(1990), *Inquiry and Change: The Troubled Attempt to Understand and Shape Society*, New Haven, Conn.: Yale University Press.

Other Works Cited

Adelstein, R. (1989), ' "Islands of Conscious Power": Louis D. Brandeis and the Modern Corporation', *Business History Review*, **63**, 614–56.

Anderson, C.W. (1978), 'The Political Economy of Charles E. Lindblom', *American Political Science Review*, **72**, 1012–16.

Barnard, C.I. (1938), *The Functions of the Executive*, Cambridge, Mass.: Harvard University Press.

Bergson, A. (1948), 'Socialist Economics', in H. Ellis (ed.), *A Survey of Contemporary Economics* 1952, Homewood, Ill.: Richard D. Irwin, Inc., 412–448.

Brandeis, L.D. (1978), *Letters of Louis D. Brandeis*, vol. 5, ed. M. Urofsky and D. Levy, Albany, N.Y.: State University of New York Press.

Coase, R.H. (1937), 'The Nature of the Firm', *Economica*, **4**, 386–405.

Gregory, R. (1989), 'Political Rationality or "Incrementalism"? Charles E. Lindblom's Enduring Contribution to Public Policy Making Theory', *Policy and Politics*, **17**, 139–53.

Hayek, F.A. (1944), *The Road to Serfdom*, Chicago: University of Chicago Press.

—— (1945), 'The Use of Knowledge in Society', *American Economic Review*, **35**, 519–31.

—— (1948), *Individualism and Economic Order*, Chicago: University of Chicago Press.

—— (1967), 'The Theory of Complex Phenomena', in *Studies in Philosophy, Politics and Economics*, New York: Simon & Schuster, 22–42.

—— (1976), *Law, Legislation and Liberty*, vol. 2: *The Mirage of Social Justice*, Chicago: University of Chicago Press.

—— (1979a), 'Competition as a Discovery Procedure', in *New Studies in Philosophy, Politics, Economics and the History of Ideas*, Chicago: University of Chicago Press, 179–90.

—— (1979b), 'The Errors of Constructivism', in *New Studies in Philosophy, Politics, Economics and the History of Ideas*, Chicago: University of Chicago Press, 3–22.

—— (ed.) (1935), *Collectivist Economic Planning*, London: George Routledge.

Heilbroner, R. (1990), 'After Communism', *New Yorker*, 10 September, 91–100.

Lange, O. (1938), 'On the Economic Theory of Socialism', in B. Lippincott (ed.), *On the Economic Theory of Socialism*, Minneapolis: University of Minnesota Press, 57–142.

Lavoie, D. (1985), *Rivalry and Central Planning: The Socialist Calculation Debate Reconsidered*, Cambridge: Cambridge University Press.

Lenin, V.I. (1943), *State and Revolution* (1917), New York: International Publishers.

Letwin, W. (1965), *Law and Economic Policy in America: The Evolution of the Sherman Antitrust Act*, Chicago: University of Chicago Press.

Liggett v *Lee* (1933), 288 U.S. 517 (1933) (Brandeis J. dissenting).

March, J. and H. Simon (1958), *Organizations*, New York: John Wiley.

McCraw, T. (1984), *Prophets of Regulation*, Cambridge, Mass.: Harvard University Press.

Mises, L. (1920), 'Economic Planning in the Socialist Commonwealth' (1920), in F. A. Hayek (ed.), *Collectivist Economic Planning*, London: George Routledge, 87–130.

Murrell, P. (1983), 'Did the Theory of Market Socialism Answer the Challenge of Ludwig von Mises?', *History of Political Economy*, **15**, 92–105.

Premfors, R. (1981), 'Review Article: Charles Lindblom and Aaron Wildavsky', *British Journal of Political Science*, **11**, 201–25.

Simon, H.A. (1947), *Administrative Behavior*, New York: Macmillan.

Simon, H.A. (1957), *Models of Man*, New York: John Wiley.

Strum, P. (1984), *Louis D. Brandeis: Justice for the People*, Cambridge, Mass.: Harvard University Press.

Wilson, W. (1887), 'The Study of Administration' (1887), in *The Papers of Woodrow Wilson*, vol. 5, ed. A. Link, Princeton, N.J.: Princeton University Press, 359–80.

10. Douglass C. North

Gary D. Libecap*

INSTITUTIONS AND ECONOMIC PERFORMANCE: AN INTRODUCTION

Perhaps no question facing economists or economic historians is more important than understanding the sources of persistent differences between rich and poor societies. There have been chronic differences in economic performance throughout history, and they exist across societies today. While these issues have provided puzzles for historians interested in explaining the past, contemporary economic development policies aimed at narrowing the gap between the rich and the poor have involved enormous transfers of capital and uncounted teams of consultants. Nevertheless, in large part these efforts to explain or promote economic growth have failed. In the search for reasons why, Douglass North has been one of the foremost economists in asserting that much more attention must be directed to the institutional structure of a society in general, and to its property rights arrangements in particular, for explaining variation in economic performance across societies and across time.

According to North, the sources of contrasting economic performance lie within the property rights and legal structures of the society that define the incentives for saving, investment, production and trade: 'Modern economic growth results from the development of institutions that permit an economy to realize the gains from specialization and division of labor associated with the sophisticated technology that has developed in the Western world in the last several centuries' (North, 1987, p. 422).

Douglass North defines institutions as humanly devised constraints on political, economic and social behaviour. Both informal arrangements, such as customs, norms of behaviour and traditions, and formal rules, such as constitutions, statutes and judicial rulings, make up the institutional structure of the society. They outline the array of benefits and costs, including both production and transactions costs, associated with the various alternatives available to individuals in economic decision-making. As such, they underlie all economic activities and shape the direction of economic change towards growth, stagnation or decline. Because of this critical role for institutions, North claims (1990, p. 2) that

> economic history is overwhelmingly a story of economies that failed to produce a set of economic rules of the game (with enforcement) that induce sustained economic growth. The central issue of economic history (and of economic development) is to account for the evolution of political and economic institutions that create an economic environment that induces increasing productivity.

Although Douglass North has been an important contributor to the intellectual momentum of the 'new institutional economics', he has remained a neoclassical economist, publishing his work in neoclassical journals. For the past 20 years, however, he has urged his colleagues in economics and economic history to relax their self-imposed devotion to the constraints of strict neoclassical theory and to broaden the scope of their investigations to include analyses both of the role institutions play in economic growth and of the process of institutional change. More recently he has called for consideration of the elusive concepts of ideology, fairness and path dependence in attempting to explain why some societies are successful in economic development, while for others sustained economic growth remains an elusive goal.

As an economic historian, North has been clearly aware of the limited ability of narrowly defined neoclassical economics to explain why some societies with favourable resource endowments fail to capture the gains from trade, while other less favourably-endowed economies appear to organize in ways that promote relatively efficient investment and production. The answer to the many puzzles of the selectiveness of economic growth in history and its limited and uneven progress in many societies today lies, according to North, in the institutional framework of the society. Neoclassical economics, however, by assuming zero transaction costs or static institutions has had little to say about their contribution in determining economic performance or about the process of institutional change.

Accordingly, although North has grounded his analysis of economic behaviour in the neoclassical paradigm and maintained individual maximization as a central postulate of his approach, he has relaxed the assumptions of zero transactions costs and of neutral institutions. In so doing he has integrated neoclassical theory into analyses of the way institutions modify choices regarding the use of resources. He has also sought to explain how these institutions are established and refined in response to new economic and political conditions.

By maintaining his links to neoclassical economics, North has enhanced his academic credibility and broadened the acceptance of his arguments.

Further, his students, particularly those from the University of Washington, and other scholars in economics, economic history and political science have joined him in extending the examination of institutions and their impact on economic performance across a variety of empirical settings. As this research record has accumulated, the influence of North's views has grown.

THE EVOLUTION OF NORTH'S RESEARCH ON INSTITUTIONAL CHANGE

Douglass North's stature within the economics profession has helped him direct the attention of economists and economic historians to transactions costs, institutions and institutional change in studying economic growth. He clearly has been one of the leading economic historians in the United States. He was involved in the monumental revision of *US Historical Statistics*; active in the National Bureau of Economic Research; co-editor of the *Journal of Economic History*, 1960–6; President of the Economic History Association, 1972–3; President of the Western Economics Association, 1975–6; and Fellow of the American Academy of Arts and Sciences, 1987. His graduate programme at the University of Washington was one of the largest and most successful in the country in the production of new PhDs in economic history. Indeed, a mark of someone of lasting influence on the profession is an ability to attract and inspire good students.

Along with William Parker, Richard Easterlin, Stanley Lebergott, Robert Gallman, Robert Fogel, Lance Davis and John Hughes, Douglass North was one of the founders of the new economic history in the late 1950s and early 1960s. The new economic history was an explicit attempt to use the techniques and insights of modern economic theory to frame the questions asked, to influence the hypotheses posed, and to suggest the nature and type of data to be collected. This was truly a revolution within the field of economic history. North and his colleagues were successful in redirecting the focus of research and the training of students towards more theoretically based analyses, using the tools of statistics and econometrics. With the advent of the new economic history the popularity of the field, especially among economists, boomed. Leading departments of economics around the US competed to hire new graduates in the discipline, and articles on economic history became much more common in major economics journals.

Perhaps more than any of the early leaders of the new economic history, North was the champion of the movement. He promoted it within the discipline while co-editor of the *Journal of Economic History* and took its messages to the broader economics profession. Two articles appearing in 1963 and 1965 in the *American Economic Review* outlined the philosophy of economic history, its contributions and, importantly, its potential to provide empirical tests for the grounding and revision of economic theory. North was particularly interested in developing a more adequate theory of economic growth to better explain the past, and it was here that he began to encounter the problems posed by the institutional structure of the society.

Douglass North's early interest in institutions was reflected in his University of California, Berkeley, dissertation on the development of the life insurance industry in the United States, which led to at least three papers appearing in *Men in Business*, edited by William Miller, *Explorations in Entrepreneurial History* and the *Journal of Economic History*, published between 1952 and 1954. The more explicit use of basic price theory in probing institutions and defining their impact on economic performance, however, came later with the publication of *The Economic Growth of the United States, 1790 to 1860* in 1961, which offered one of the first truly integrated discussions of the development of the American economy. *Growth and Welfare in American Past: A New Economic History*, published in 1966 with a second edition in 1973, demonstrated the power of the 'cliometric' techniques advanced by North and his colleagues in the new economic history.

Although the focus of *The Economic Growth of the United States* was on the roles of the staple thesis, comparative advantage and regional specialization in American economic growth, institutions were given an important though subtle role. For example, the staple thesis suggested that the structure of the economy was determined, in part, by the nature of the staple. Cotton production, for example, seemed to lead to the development of slave economies. Slave economies led to very different institutions in commerce, finance, education and politics than found in the northern US. These institutional factors, in turn, determined whether the economy would continue to rely on the staple or would diversify successfully to other products.

In *Growth and Welfare in American Past* North extended his discussion of critical issues in American economic development to include agrarian discontent, New Deal programmes and, significantly, the role of government in the economy. Reflecting his neoclassical views at the time, government was presented as basically a contract between citizens and politicians for the institutional arrangements needed to support economic growth. In this volume North was much more explicit in his presentation of property rights and their impact on economic efficiency and the conditions affecting their definition and enforcement. He defined the costs of maintaining and exchanging property rights as transactions costs and illustrated their impact on economic growth through their effects on technological change and investment in human capital.

In 1968, North's paper on productivity change in ocean shipping, published in one of the leading neoclassical journals, the *Journal of Political Economy*, reaffirmed his growing appreciation of institutional factors in explaining the pattern of economic progress. North found that productivity in ocean shipping improved dramatically in the eighteenth and early nineteenth centuries, but that new technology, the standard explanation, seemed to account for only a small portion of the improvement. The major advancements that he found were in reductions in turnaround time (reductions in transactions costs) and greater protection of property rights through the associated fall in piracy. As the British Navy, in particular, increased the security of shipping, insurance rates fell, and ships with greater hold and deck space could be developed to carry more cargo because cannon and other armaments were no longer needed. Additionally, with fewer sailors necessary to defend a ship, crew sizes fell to those required solely for sailing and handling cargo. Rather than the standard neoclassical prediction of markets translating technological change into economic growth, North's analysis of productivity change in ocean shipping suggested that the beneficial new technology came after necessary institutional changes. In 1968, however, North was not yet ready to develop fully this theme of a leading role for institutions in economic performance, and he turned to explore the neoclassical underpinnings of institutional change.

This direction of his research was signalled by two publications, 'Institutional Change and American Economic Growth: a First Step Towards a Theory of Institutional Innovation', appearing in the *Journal of Economic History* (Davis and North, 1970), and *Institutional Change and American Growth* (Davis and North, 1971). These publications were followed by a chapter, 'Government and the American Economy', in *American Economic Growth: An Economists' History of the United States* (Davis et al., 1972), where North began to outline his views about collective action, institutional innovation and their impact on the nature of government activity in the economy. He then used that framework to describe government policies in the United States from colonial times through the mid-twentieth century, addressing property rights assignment and enforcement, transportation improvement (reductions in transaction costs), education, commercial activities (adoption of incorporation laws and the like) and redistribution.

Other work on institutions followed shortly, including *The Rise of the Western World: A New Economic History* (North and Thomas, 1973), *Structure and Change in Economic History* (1981), and more than 30 journal articles or chapters on institutional change, transactions costs and economic growth between 1971 and 1989. During this same period, North was on the faculties of Cambridge University (as Pitt Professor), Rice University, the University of Washington, and Washington University where he became Luce Professor of Law and Liberty and Director of the Center in Political Economy in 1983. In 1985 he became co-editor of the Cambridge University Press series, *The Political Economy of Institutions and Decisions*.

Institutional Change and American Economic Growth clearly described the way in which North viewed institutions in the early 1970s. In the book North and Davis applied the principles of neoclassical price theory to the process of institutional change, in a way similar to that outlined by Demsetz (1967) for property rights. They argued that contracting and bargaining for property rights through voluntary or government organizations were natural responses to changes in relative prices, as individuals sought to respond to new economic opportunities to which the existing institutional structure was poorly suited. For them, the establishment or modification of property rights was the outcome of a rational decision-making or investment process, where rights were established in stages as individuals balanced their private marginal benefits and costs of contracting for institutional change: 'It is the possibility of profits that cannot be captured within the existing arrangemental structure that leads to the formation of new (or the mutation of old) institutional arrangements' (Davis and North, 1971, p. 59). In other words, property institutions evolved for efficiency reasons to economize on transactions costs. Davis and North illustrated the use of this framework with brief discussions of voluntary and government-organized institutional changes in American financial markets, in the distribution of federal land and the development of agricultural policies, and in the design of transportation subsidies for canals and railroads in the nineteenth-century United States.

The message in *The Rise of the Western World: A New Economic History*, however, was more complex, reflecting the problems of reconciling the simple neoclassical view of the origins of institutions with the historical record. In that book North and Thomas examined issues of institutions and economic growth in Europe within the same neoclassical framework outlined earlier by Davis and North. They presented the manorial system of the early Middle Ages as a valuable arrangement for defence and stability, given the sparse settlement of Europe at the time and the fear of attack from marauding Vikings, Magyars and Moslems. According to North and Thomas, the manor reflected an exchange relationship between the lord, who provided protective services and adjudicated disputes, and the peasant, who provided labour services. This view of the manor as an institutional arrangement with positive attributes for growth and welfare was modified somewhat by North later, but it nevertheless ran counter to the existing literature, which emphasized exploitation in the lord–serf relationship.

North and Thomas argued that, as time passed, new forces for institutional change emerged, leading to the demise of the manor. Exogenous factors, such as population growth and the rise of trading cities, led to the adoption of new institutions to facilitate exchange. The rise in the labour to land ratio by the mid-thirteenth century led to diminishing returns to labour, demands for monetary rather than labour payments to the lord, and efforts to obtain greater security of property rights to land. Finally, changes in military technology reduced the advantages of the manor and increased the optimal size of the state as mounted knights were replaced by archers and pikemen and, later, by soldiers using gunpowder. These factors contributed to the commercialization of exchange and the decline of the manor, and there could be no return to feudalism, at least in most of Western Europe. The fall in population in the fourteenth century due to famine and the plague served further to weaken the structure of feudal society and to encourage the expansion of markets and subsequent economic development in the fifteenth century.

The observed pattern of growth in the sixteenth and seventeenth centuries outlined by North and Thomas, however, was not uniform. Although they did not emphasize it at the time, this raised questions about the usefulness of the contractual model presented earlier in the book to explain the rise and decline of the manor. England and the Low Countries, less populous and less wealthy than their larger rivals France and Spain, were much more successful in economic growth. North and Thomas argued that these observed differences were due, at least in part, to differences in property rights arrangements and limitations on the arbitrary power of the state. In England the early appearance of effective political opposition to the monarchy was critical for developing an environment favourable to trade and mercantile activities. The success in England of restricting the coercive power of the state was so important and perhaps so unusual that North returned to examine the issue in more detail later in his career.

In contrast, in France and Spain absolutist monarchies faced few political restrictions, and they relied heavily on granting and taxing local monopoly privileges, such as the Mesta in Spain. These monopolies provided both revenue and political support for the state, but they limited the growth of trade and reduced the incentive for innovation. Despite these costs, which may or may not have been clearly evident at the time, the monarchies were fearful of adjustments to provide more open economies and to guarantee property rights for the encouragement of investment and trade. They did not want to undermine their political and economic base, even if such changes ultimately offered broad economic gains. In England and The Netherlands, where commercial interests were politically stronger, property rights institutions tended to be adopted that allowed for more fluid resource movement to promote and to respond to growing markets. Parliament placed constraints on the English monarchy, limiting its arbitrary power to redirect resources in inefficient ways. The growing security of property rights and the erosion of mercantilist restrictions combined to provide new opportunities for the organization of firms in domestic and international markets. The English government tended to be on a sounder financial basis than the government in Spain, where repeated bankruptcies between 1557 and 1746 brought desperate efforts to raise short-term revenue through taxing monopoly privileges and licensing and sale of occupations. The associated bureaucratic structure was hostile to entrepreneurship and the uncertainties it posed for the existing political arrangement.

The maintenance of ineffective institutions in France and Spain for distributional and political reasons at the expense of significantly greater economic growth seemed to be inconsistent with the predictions of the model used by North and Thomas to describe the life-cycle of the major. Under a strict neoclassical approach, institutions that were out of step with economic development would be eroded by market forces. With positive expected gains from change, a new contractual arrangement with the state would emerge. But that was not what North and Thomas observed, and accordingly North was forced to broaden his analysis of the determinants of the institutional framework in a society to better account for the persistence of seemingly perverse arrangements.

In seeking to understand these institutional issues, North's thinking on the matter evolved from the rational investment model of institutional change he and Davis outlined in 1971, which v. as at the same time too optimistic and too mechanistic. It accepted too much of the full-information, low-transactions-costs view of economic behaviour embedded in neoclassical theory. North began to turn his attention more explicitly to issues of transactions costs, the free rider, bounded rationality, interest-group formation and competition, control of government authority, and to the even more elusive concepts of ideology and path dependence.

North began with a more detailed consideration of transactions costs and their impact on production and exchange. His analysis of transactions costs was influenced notably by the work of Ronald Coase, whose papers 'The Theory of the Firm' (1937) and 'The Problems of Social Cost' (1960) not only defined many key institutional issues but made them legitimate objects of economic analysis. In particular, 'The Problem of Social Cost' made economists and economic historians more aware of the role of property rights and transactions costs in moulding economic outcomes.

According to Coase, transactions costs included the costs of bargaining, information, measurement, supervision, enforcement and political action, and they had a critical impact on how individuals responded to changing economic conditions. If transactions costs were low, the property rights assignment did not matter for efficiency, because rights could be voluntarily exchanged to promote increased production. The assignment of rights, however, did affect the wealth distribution. On the other hand, where transactions costs were high, the allocation of property rights became more crucial for economic performance, because transfers to higher-valued uses were more difficult. In these circumstances, which describe most cases of economic history and development, the assignment and enforcement of property rights would have profound and enduring effects on production and distribution.

In incorporating transactions costs in analysis of differential economic performance, North argued that transactions costs could rise with economic development. To facilitate additional growth, new institutions would be needed to lower transactions costs and promote production and trade. In subsistence, rural societies, where personal exchange among economic agents familiar with one another dominates and where production involves simple technologies, transactions costs will be small relative to the costs of production. On the other hand, in modern economies with the complex production and exchange associated with specialization, division of labour and impersonal trade, the costs of transacting will be relatively higher. Verification, measurement, monitoring and enforcement of production and trade agreements command significant resources through elaborate legal, political and commercial institutions. These institutions are needed to define property rights, direct economic exchanges and constrain individuals to adhere to contracts. North asserted (1987, p. 427) that 'the absence of such institutions when compared to their presence in successful developing countries provides essential clues for exploring production failures as a result of the high cost of transacting'.

For North, the structure of the state and transactions costs became intricately linked. He argued that to reduce transactions costs and to provide incentives for investment and production, property rights must be imbedded in a structure of law, both formal and informal, that is far removed from arbitrary confiscation or alteration. Enforcement officials must be impartial. With this security, economic agents are the residual claimants of their production and consumption decisions, and they have confidence in the durability of the contracts and production relationships needed for investment. Modern Western societies have assembled these institutional arrangements successfully, allowing for long-term contracts and well-specified property rights to provide motivation for productive behaviour and to allow for valuable complex economic relationships.

Another important influence on North's thinking about property rights was H. Scott Gordon, whose paper 'The Economic Theory of a Common Property Resource: the Fishery' (1954) outlined the basic problem of rent dissipation when valuable resources were exploited in the absence of well-defined and enforced property rights. Although Gordon's arguments and their refinements by Cheung (1970) were in terms of open-access fisheries, the implications generalized to other resources and economic settings. Gordon's paper described the essential problems of insecure property rights, and showed that societies plagued by them are unsuccessful in achieving economic growth.

Despite the critical role of property rights, effective arrangements have been exceedingly difficult to create and maintain. Property rights typically are the outcome of the political process, and since they necessarily involve a distribution of wealth and political power, they are controversial in their assignment and enforcement. Politicians forge links with influential interest groups to maintain their positions, but the basis of the wealth and political power of those groups may lie in arrangements that bring inefficiencies, such as those resulting from state-protected local monopolies. Hence, a reallocation and redefinition of property rights to achieve a more effective arrangement is likely to create winners and losers, bringing considerable uncertainty and risk for politicians. Moreover, the side payments devised in political markets to compensate those who expect to be harmed by the new arrangement are unlikely to be complete. The result is that major changes in property rights will bring a redistribution of wealth and political power. Under these circumstances, it may not be in the interest of most politicians to support institutional changes, even though there may be important aggregate benefits through greater production and wealth.

The coercive power of the state and the political influence of various interest groups allow for opportunism in statutes, court opinions and administrative rulings in redistributing wealth and property rights to those who are politically advantaged. There is no reason for this process to lead to a distribution of property rights that is consistent with social wealth maximization. Further, if the distribution of political power is unstable, property rights will not be secure and uncertainty will dampen incentives for productive behaviour. Those who make the decisions regarding resource use cannot be sure that they will capture the profits resulting from their decisions, so that social and private returns diverge. There is, then, an important paradox: while the state is essential for the establishment and enforcement of economic institutions, it also is the principal source for blocking the emergence of the very institutions necessary for economic growth. These problems led North to conclude (1987, p. 422) that: 'In fact, one of the most evident lessons from history is that political systems have an inherent tendency to produce inefficient property rights which result in stagnation or decline.'

Property rights definition and political bargaining have been studied by a number of scholars both within the strict neoclassical framework and under modifications similar to those adopted by Douglass North. Among them are Armen Alchian, Terry Anderson, Yoram Barzel, James Buchanan, Stephen Cheung, Louis De Alessi, Harold Demsetz, Eirik Furubotn, John Umbeck, Ronald Johnson, P. J. Hill, Gary Libecap, Mancur Olson and Gordon Tullock. The topics covered by this group are broad. The organization of interest groups for private collective action and for lobbying politicians for government actions in their behalf was analysed by Olson (1965) and Buchanan and Tullock (1962). Demsetz (1967) and Alchian and Demsetz (1973) outlined some of the theoretical and empirical issues involved in the establishment of property rights. Libecap (1978), Johnson and Libecap (1980, 1982) and Libecap and Wiggins (1984, 1985) examined empirical details of the success or failure of property rights to develop across a variety of settings, including mineral deposits, range land on Indian reservations in the American south-west, fisheries and oil reservoirs. These analyses helped to draw attention to the intricacies of institutional change, the complexities of interest-group negotiations in both private and governmental settings, and the impacts of different property rights arrangements on economic behaviour.

The evolution of Douglass North's views of transactions costs, property rights and political institutions is reflected in one of his most important books, *Structure and Change in Economic History* (1981). Here North attempted to develop a general framework for analysing economic history, beginning with a neoclassical model of growth and then incorporating transactions costs, a theory of the state, and the roles of politics, preferences and ideology in determining institutional forms. In his theory of the state North outlined a continuum ranging from the contractual state he had defined earlier with its positive welfare effects, to an exploitive or predatory state where resources were redirected by politicians for their own means or on the behalf of influential constituents. Unfortunately, North noted that there was nothing in the logic of the neoclassical theory of the state that would support a prediction about the kind of state that might emerge or its likelihood of providing institutions that supported economic growth. He speculated that the distribution among constituents and politicians of the potential to use violence was a determining factor of the type of state in existence at any place or time. Where the distribution of force was relatively uniform, a contractual arrangement was a likely outcome, but if the ability to use force was concentrated in a few, a predatory state would emerge. The details of the evolution of political institutions awaited later attention by North, but the problems of the state and the unclear process by which effective institutions might be adopted were issues that could not be ignored.

It was becoming clear in North's writing that there was no basis for the optimism inherent in the more standard neoclassical view he and others had previously held that institutions were subject to the same kind of competitive pressures found in goods and factors markets. With zero or low transactions costs, side payments would be made to buy support in the political market for institutions, and since the most efficient institutions provided the greatest potential to make such payments, they would tend to out-compete alternatives. History, though, was not providing support for this view. It was a measure of North's understanding of history and of his intellectual flexibility that he was able to move from this framework to a more useful view of institutions.

Although his thinking about the issue continued to develop and be refined throughout the 1980s, for North institutions were no longer portrayed as responding principally to the new opportunities made possible by technological change and movements in relative prices. Institutions that fostered economic growth were not inevitable. With his stature in the profession, North could take this message to his colleagues in economics and force them at least to consider the implications for analyses of economic behaviour and performance.

In North's message to his colleagues, the state was critical because of its coercive power to define and enforce property rights and to reduce transactions costs. North noted the paradox (1981, p. 20): 'The existence of a state is essential for economic growth; the state, however, is the source of man-made economic decline.' Political conflicts over the distribution of wealth and political power, the incentives of politicians to respond to the demands of constituents, and ideology had to be incorporated in a broader version of the neoclassical model to explain why governments typically failed to adopt property rights arrangements that encouraged productive behaviour.

Ideology was and remains a concept viewed with suspicion by most mainstream economists because it is so difficult to model satisfactorily, measure and test in an empirically refutable way. North argued that it could not be ignored because it has had an important impact on institutional development, enforcement and economic performance. He defined ideology as the set of individual beliefs and values that modified individual behaviour and, in particular, reduced the free-rider problem in collective action. Moreover, tastes or ideological beliefs regarding equity or fairness affected the stands taken by individuals in bargaining over the voluntary or government allocation and enforcement of property rights. For an ideology to be successful, it had to provide a comprehensive view of the world and be flexible enough to account for observed changes in external conditions.

Within this framework, pressures for state actions regarding property rights could come about because of both changes in relative prices and new perceptions regarding the fairness of property allocation. In these ways, North argued (1981), p. 57) that ideology served as a powerful force in the role of the state and the development of institutions for economic stagnation or growth: 'The major source of changes in an economy over time is structural change in the parameters held constant by the economist – technology, population, property rights, and government control over resources.'

The importance of limiting the power of the state to do mischief emerged as a central issue in North's study of economic development, and in this area he again turned his attention to the success of England. In North and Weingast (1989) he examined the evolution of constitutional arrangements in the seventeenth and eighteenth centuries following the Glorious Revolution of

1688 in England. North and Weingast argued that the institutional changes initiated at that time provided more security for property rights by reducing the ability of both the Monarch and Parliament to arbitrarily confiscate property. Royal prerogatives in the English economy were reduced and the basis for subsequent economic growth was established. New legal constraints on the state provided for more credible commitments by Parliament to live up to its legal and financial obligations.

The institutional constraints included the development of an independent judiciary to arbitrate disputes in the society in a more-or-less neutral manner, hence supporting the sanctity of property rights and contracts. Additionally, a central and equal role for Parliament and the Crown in the development of laws was inaugurated. Not only could Parliament act as a balance to the authority of the Crown, but it represented wealth holders, who had much to gain from the security of property rights and economic growth. These wealth-holding groups were sufficiently heterogeneous, including land-owners and new merchant interests, so that coalitions could not form over long periods to direct the power of the state to establish local monopolies and other restrictions on competition on their behalf.

An outcome of this process to define more secure property rights was the development of capital markets and the establishment of the Bank of England. With its arbitrary powers constrained, the government was forced to honour commitments in order to secure funds from lenders. The new environment encouraged experimentation with new financial institutions and instruments to marshall and channel funds for private and government activities at lower interest rates. North and Weingast point to the development of the English stock market to illustrate how the expansion of private capital markets occurred along with the development of institutions for raising government funds. While these changes helped to lead England to the Industrial Revolution, Spain during the same period had no similar institutional constraints on the power of the government, thus making arbitrary seizure and redistribution more likely. With a climate of uncertainty there was less opportunity for propertied and commercial interests to develop, and Spain began a long-term process of absolute and relative decline.

Besides analyses of the constraints on the coercive power of the state, North also turned his attention to those cases when institutions emerged successfully to reduce the transactions costs of exchange and production. In Milgrom, North and Weingast (1990) North examined the adoption of institutions to support the revival of trade in the early Middle Ages in Europe. With the gradual rise in exchange across regions, traders could no longer rely on a good reputation, personal knowledge or repeat dealings as guarantees for honest compliance with contracts. Additional institutional protections were required. To promote greater trade and the wealth it brought, a system of judges was established to enforce commercial law with limited information on individual traders. These judges and the private code of laws, the *Law Merchant*, adjudicated conflicts and encouraged traders to behave honestly by imposing sanctions on violators which included denial of access to critical trade fairs where most exchanges took place.

In two papers with John Wallis (Wallis and North, 1986, 1988) North examined transactions costs and their links to technological and institutional change in another setting. They argued that the application of science and technology in specialized production and trade in the late nineteenth-century United States required an enormous increase in the investment of resources to facilitate transactions in the society. By their calculations, the costs of transactions, which had been 25 per cent of national income in 1870, had risen to 45 per cent by 1970. Since much of the expanding transactions sector of the economy involved creating new government regulations and agencies, it contributed to the observed growth of government. Moreover, North and Wallis asserted that the expansion of transactions costs made existing measures of output and productivity growth in the US problematic. Much of the recorded expansion in per capita GNP was probably in the transactions sector and not in the production of new goods and services for consumption.

North's interaction with his colleagues and students at the University of Washington and, later, Washington University has been very important in the development of his ideas regarding the questions to be asked and the research agenda to be defined regarding institutions. He has been characterized as one who listens to his critics and learns from his mistakes. Discussions with University of Washington colleagues, such as Don Gordon, Yoram Barzel, John Floyd, Robert Thomas, Steven N.S. Cheung and Robert Higgs, helped North refine applied microeconomic concepts for use in research in economic history in ways that had not been done previously by economic historians. In the case of Robert Thomas, a close working relationship developed that spanned approximately ten years. Through these interactions North's views of the roles of property rights and other rules of the game in moulding behaviour crystallized. Further, these discussions helped North discover ways for modifying the neoclassical framework with consideration of transactions costs and ideology so that institutional change and economic growth might be analysed in a more satisfying way. At Washington University association with Barry Weingast and Kenneth Shepsle among others resulted in a more game-theoretic approach for analysing institutions as repeated games and more attention to path dependence and the rules through which politicians and bureaucrats responded to demands for institutional change.

While North was a fellow at the Center for Advanced Study in the Behavioral Sciences, he more explicitly incorporated the work of Brian

Arthur and Paul David on path dependence into the analysis of institutional development and economic performance. David's article (1985) attempted to explain the persistence of technological anomalies, such as the peculiar organization of letters on the typewriter keyboard, the use of narrow-gauge rails, and the success of AC over DC electrical current. Incremental technological changes, according to David, tended to be self-reinforcing, leading society to 'lock in' to a particular technological path, even though it might be less effective than the abandoned alternatives. Arthur (1989) extended these arguments to show the nature of the self-reinforcing mechanisms that contributed to path dependence in technological change. These included high fixed costs and associated increasing returns from expanded use of a technology, learning and co-ordination advantages and adaptive expectations. North saw these underlying contributors to path dependence in technological change also as factors in the process of incremental institutional change, and they became a basis for the continued refinement of his views on the interaction between institutions and economic performance.

North's stay at the Center for Advanced Study provided a transition for his move from the University of Washington to Washington University in St Louis. University of Washington students who received their PhDs from the mid-1960s to the early 1980s were also influential in the development of Douglass North's views of institutions. Not all worked in economic history, but these students had two common identifying characteristics: an understanding of the importance of basic price theory for framing questions for empirical analysis and an appreciation of the role of institutions in moulding economic behaviour. Although much of their research was not directed explicitly to institutional issues, it was firmly based on a price-theoretic framework and as such was critical in publicizing the usefulness of North's approach to economic history and development. A very abbreviated list of those who completed Washington PhDs in economic history or related fields and who followed North's approach includes Gary Walton, James Shepherd, Gerald Gunderson, Terry Anderson, Clyde Reed, Trevor Dick, Ben Baack, Taylor Dennen, Phil Coehlo, John Umbeck, Ronald Johnson, Sumner LaCroix, Lee Alston, Price Fishback, John Wallis and Barbara Sands. In one way or another, these students were influenced by Douglass North in the questions they asked of economics and in the development of their research agendas.

THE PROCESS OF INSTITUTIONAL CHANGE

According to North, the gains from reduced transactions costs and lower uncertainty and the resulting increased production and trade provide important incentives for the establishment and subsequent refinement of economic institutions such as property rights. The bargaining parties, which include private claimants, politicians and bureaucrats, are motivated by self-interest to capture a share of the gains from institutional change. The assumption of individual utility maximization as a guide for predictions regarding economic and political behaviour is drawn from neoclassical theory.

The contracting process by which institutions are created or changed is initiated by shifts in relative prices, changes in production and enforcement technology, and (with the modifications added by North) changes in preferences, ideology or other political parameters. Any of these factors can upset the prevailing institutional framework and raise the returns from contracting to change property rights. An increase in an asset's relative price, for example, will raise the stream of rents attainable from ownership and encourage new competition for control. Old property rights enforcement mechanisms will no longer be adequate and rent dissipation will result. The corresponding rise in ownership uncertainty and transactions costs lowers incentives for long-term investment, production and exchange. Hence capturing a portion of any rents that can be obtained through collective action can motivate individuals to organize in private and political groups to adjust property rights to respond to new conditions.

Whether determined within informal, private groups or through more formal legal structures, property rights changes involve a wealth assignment typically requiring some redistribution. When many competing interests are involved, each attempting to maximize their share of aggregate wealth, the process of change can be very controversial. There will be both winners and losers and, in developing a position regarding any proposed change, each party compares its position under the status quo with its expected position under the new arrangement. Competing parties, politicians and bureaucrats have a stake in the outcome, and the political process often involves searching for agreements that will compensate influential parties. Political influence depends on the wealth, size and homogeneity of the groups. Current asset owners as vested interests probably have important advantages in contracting because of established ties to politicians, sunk organizational costs and an understanding of the political process. Their influence gives politicians incentives to maintain the status quo or to modify it only incrementally.

Crafting agreements on institutional change involves devising side payments to mollify opposing parties, but political side payments are difficult to construct. There are questions of who should pay, who should receive, how much should be transferred, and the form payment should take. As North and others have shown, these are formidable issues, and the complete side payments necessary to facilitate major institutional changes are unlikely to be the outcome of political bargaining. Accordingly, agreements are most apt to result in relatively minor institutional changes. This, of course, will not be the case if there is a major shock to the status quo through the introduction of dramatic new technology or if pent-up demands for change due to past failures to adjust institutions bring revolutionary pressures that swamp existing arrangements. These dramatic changes, however, are not characteristic of the general process of incremental institutional change.

In determining their expected gains from institutional change, the various interests who have a stake in the old and new arrangements attempt to gain information on the aggregate benefits and their expected share in them. With this information they attempt to maximize their share of those benefits through bargaining in the political arena. This manoeuvring, however, affects the nature of the property rights that ultimately are adopted and the aggregate benefits that can be obtained. Calculating and comparing their positions under the status quo and the proposed change is complicated by information problems and the uncertainty associated with forecasting future benefits. The process of net gain calculation is affected by the anticipated size of the aggregate gains, the number and heterogeneity of the bargaining parties, the length of time involved in implementing the new institutional arrangement, and the likely allocation under the proposed institutions. Limited adjustments are easier to agree to because expected shares can be determined more clearly when the impacts on any party are relatively small. This reinforces the conservative, incremental nature of most institutional change.

North has correctly emphasized the path dependence of institutional change, which he argues is 'more than the incremental process of institutional evolution in which yesterday's institutional framework provides the opportunity set for today's organizations and individual entrepreneurs (political or economic)' (1990, p. 16). Existing institutions determine the prevailing allocation of wealth and political power and in turn define who the economic and political actors are, their stakes in the system, and the costs and benefits from organizing to lobby for institutional change. Past distributions of property and the ease of entry into the economic and political systems establish precedents for the process and expectations for the success of collective action for institutional change. The reinforcing mechanisms of path dependence in institutional change also include the large initial set-up costs of legal and political institutions, which offer subsequent increasing returns; learning and organizational gains as individuals and organizations adjust to and mould the opportunities provided by the prevailing institutional framework; informal constraints that blend with and modify formal rules; and the adaptive expectations formed by economic agents within the current institutional structure. North argues that with increasing returns, institutions matter and shape an economy's long-run path. Since the markets in which political trades are made to adjust institutions are likely to be very incomplete with high transactions costs, ideologically based bargaining stands and incomplete information, this long run-path can persist, even if it is seriously inefficient. In these ways, the process of institutional change and hence the performance of the economy are inexorably tied to the economic and political institutions that previously were put into place.

In the last ten years Douglass North has repeatedly argued that the historical record of uneven and limited economic growth indicates that the process of institutional change is so complex that the emergence of institutions which support economic growth cannot be taken for granted. Distributional conflicts, which must be resolved in the political arena, mould the process of institutional change and help to account for the wide diversity in arrangements and economic performance observed across societies and time.

This is a much less optimistic view of political contracting and institutional change than that outlined by Becker (1983) who argued, for example, that among the possible regulatory arrangements those that offer the lowest deadweight losses will be adopted. Libecap's (1989b) study of crude oil regulation in the United States provides a counter example of policies that explicitly raised production costs in responding to influential constituents.

In a wealthy society, such as the United States, the incremental costs imposed by regulation can be absorbed within the broader economy, which is characterized by relatively high productivity. According to North, however, where inefficient institutions are the common social condition, the aggregate wealth effects will have a compounding impact on the performance of the economy and the well-being of the population.

CONCLUDING REMARKS

Douglass North has successfully drawn the attention of his colleagues in economics and economic history to the role of institutions in determining economic performance. The most promising area for new research appears to be in examining the details of the political framework in which negotiations for institutional change occur. This involves identifying interest groups, their links to politicians and bureaucrats, and how the manoeuvring of all parties, including politicians and bureaucrats, affects the institutions that result. Only through micro analyses can we see exactly how institutional arrangements are promoted or blocked.

This has been the thrust of recent research by Alston and Ferrie (1989), for example, who examine the institution of paternalism in the American South and how political support for it in Congress helped to block the adoption of welfare legislation until the 1960s. Welfare programmes threatened southern paternalism and the labour relations it fostered. By the early

1960s, according to Alston and Ferrie, the mechanization of southern agriculture meant that paternalism was no longer needed, and opposition by southern members of Congress to welfare legislation subsided.

Douglass North has demonstrated that economic history provides an ideal laboratory for such studies. Important historical questions remain to be addressed, and data sources are available for detailed examinations. Attention must be directed to the opponents, proponents and the underlying determinants of their positions for understanding political contracting and why particular historical institutions resulted. He has challenged the economics profession to adopt more elaborate and complex views of economic and political behaviour and to recognize their interdependencies if the puzzles of economic growth are to be understood and useful policy options devised. History and contemporary experience have shown that there is nothing automatic about economic growth. There appears to be no process by which efficient institutions eventually crowd out inefficient ones. The costs of contracting and reaching agreement on compensation to those who might be harmed by institutional change in order to build a political consensus for socially beneficial change are high. Political side payments seem only rarely to be solutions to the distributional conflicts inherent in any important adjustment in economic institutions. Although this may be a pessimistic conclusion, it is nevertheless a necessary realization if progress is to be made in the study of the relationship between economic growth and institutions. More than any other economist or economic historian, Douglass North is responsible for educating and directing his colleagues to the study of the new institutional economics.

NOTE

*This essay was prepared with the help of students and colleagues of Douglass North, including Lee Alston, Price Fishback, Robert Higgs, Shawn Kantor, Barbara Sands and John Wallis.

REFERENCES

Alchian, Armen and Harold Demsetz (1972), 'Production, Information Costs, and the Theory of the Firm', *American Economic Review*, **62**, 777–95.
Alchian, Armen and Harold Demsetz (1973), 'Property Rights Paradigm', *Journal of Economic History*, **33**, 16–27.
Alston, Lee J. (1984), 'Farm Foreclosure Moratoria: a Lesson from the Past', *American Economic Review*, **74**, 445–57.
Alston, Lee J. and Joseph P. Ferrie (1989), 'Social Control and Labor Relations in the American South before the Mechanization of the Cotton Harvest in the 1950s', *Journal of Institutional and Theoretical Economics*, **145**, 133–57.

Anderson, Terry and P.J. Hill (1975), 'The Evolution of Property Rights: a Study of the American West', *Journal of Law and Economics*, **18**, 163–79.

Anderson, Terry and P J. Hill (1990), 'The Race for Property Rights', *Journal of Law and Economics*, **33**, 177–98.

Arthur, Brian W. (1989), 'Competing Technologies, Increasing Returns, and Lock-in by Historical Events', *Economic Journal*, **99**, 116–31.

Barzel, Yoram (1989), *Economic Analysis of Property Rights*, Cambridge: Cambridge University Press.

Becker, Gary (1983), 'A Theory of Competition among Pressure Groups for Political Influence', *Quarterly Journal of Economics*, **98**, 371–400.

Buchanan, James M. and Gordon Tullock (1962), *The Calculus of Consent*, Ann Arbor, Mich.: University of Michigan Press.

Cheung, Steven N.S. (1970), 'The Structure of a Contract and the Theory of a Non-Exclusive Resource', *Journal of Law and Economics*, **26**, 1–22.

Coase, Ronald H. (1937), 'The Nature of the Firm', *Economica N.S.*, **4**, 386–405.

Coase, Ronald H. (1960), 'The Problem of Social Cost', *Journal of Law and Economics*, **3**, 1–44.

David, Paul (1985), 'Clio and the Economics of QWERTY', *American Economic Review*, **75**, 332–7.

Davis, Lance E. and Douglass C. North (1970), 'Institutional Change and American Economic Growth: a First Step towards a Theory of Institutional Innovation', *Journal of Economic History*, **30**, 133–49.

Davis, Lance E. and Douglass C. North (1971), *Institutional Change and American Economic Growth*, Cambridge: Cambridge University Press.

Davis, Lance E. *et al.* (1972), *American Economic Growth: An Economist's History of the United States*, New York: Harper & Row.

De Alessi, Louis (1980), 'The Economics of Property Rights: a Review of the Evidence', *Research in Law and Economics*, **2**, 1–47.

Demsetz, Harold (1967), 'Towards a Theory of Property Rights', *American Economic Review*, **57**, 347–59.

Furubotn, Eirik and Svetozar Pejovich (1972), 'Property Rights and Economic Theory: a Survey of Recent Literature', *Journal of Economic Literature*, **10**, 1137–62.

Gordon. H. Scott (1954), 'The Economic Theory of a Common Property Resource: the Fishery', *Journal of Political Economy*, **62**, 124–42.

Higgs, Robert (1971), *The Transformation of the American Economy, 1865–1914: An Essay in Interpretation*, New York: John Wiley.

Johnson, Ronald N. and Gary D. Libecap (1980), 'Agency Costs and the Assignment of Property Rights: the Case of Southwestern Indian Reservations', *Southern Economic Journal*, **47**, 332–47.

Johnson, Ronald N. and Gary D. Libecap (1982), 'Contracting Problems and Regulation: the Case of the Fishery', *American Economic Review*, **72**, 1005–22.

Libecap, Gary D. (1978), 'Economic Variables and the Development of the Law: the Case of Western Mineral Rights', *Journal of Economic History*, **38**, 338–62.

—— (1986), 'Property Rights in Economic History: Implications for Research', *Explorations in Economic History*, **23**, 227–52.

—— (1989a), *Contracting for Property Rights*, Cambridge: Cambridge University Press.

—— (1989b), 'The Political Economy of Crude Oil Cartelization in the United States, 1933–1972', *Journal of Economic History*, **49**, 833–55.

—— and Steven N. Wiggins (1984), 'Contractual Responses to the Common Pool: Prorationing of Crude Oil Production', *American Economic Review*, **74**, 87–98.

—— and —— (1985), 'The Influence of Private Contractual Failure on Regulation: the Case of Oil Field Unitization', *Journal of Political Economy*, **93**, 690–714.

Milgrom, Paul R., Douglass C. North and Barry R. Weingast (1990), 'The Role of Institutions in the Revival of Trade: the Law Merchant, Private Judges, and the Champagne Fairs', *Economics and Politics*, **2**, 1–24.

North, Douglass C. (1952), 'Capital Accumulation in Life Insurance between the Civil War and the Investigation of 1905', in William Miller (ed.), *Men in Business*, Cambridge, Mass.: Harvard University Press, 238–53.

—— (1953), 'Entrepreneurial Policy and the Internal Organization in Large Life Insurance Companies at the Time of the Armstrong Investigation', *Explorations in Entrepreneurial History*, **5**, 139–61.

—— (1954), 'Life Insurance and Investment Banking at the Time of the Armstrong Investigation', *Journal of Economic History*, **14**, 209–28.

—— (1961), *The Economic Development of the United States, 1790 to 1860*, Englewood Cliffs, N.J.: Prentice-Hall.

—— (1963), 'Quantitative Research in American Economic History', *American Economic Review*, **53**, 128–9.

—— (1965), 'The State of Economic History', *American Economic Review*, **55**, 86–91.

—— (1966), *Growth and Welfare in the American Past: A New Economic History*, Englewood Cliffs, N.J.: Prentice Hall.

—— (1968), 'Sources of Productivity Change in Ocean Shipping, 1600–1850', *Journal of Political Economy*, **76**, 953–70.

—— (1978), 'Structure and Performance: the Task of Economic History', *Journal of Economic Literature*, **16**, 963–78.

—— (1981), *Structure and Change in Economic History*, New York: W.W. Norton.

—— (1986), 'The New Institutional Economics', *Journal of Institutional and Theoretical Economics*, **142**, 230–7.

—— (1987), 'Institutions, Transactions Costs and Economic Growth', *Economic Inquiry*, **25**, 419–28.

—— (1990), 'Institutions', working paper, Department of Economics, Washington University, St Louis, Missouri.

—— and Robert P. Thomas (1973), *The Rise of the Western World: A New Economic History*, Cambridge: Cambridge University Press.

—— and Barry R. Weingast (1989), 'Constitutions and Commitment: the Evolution of Institutions Governing Public Choice in 17th Century England', *Journal of Economic History*, **49**, 803–32.

Olson, Mancur (1965), *The Logic of Collective Action*, Cambridge, Mass.: Harvard University Press.

Olson, Mancur (1982), *The Rise and Decline of Nations*, New Haven, Conn.: Yale University Press.

Sutch, Richard (1982), 'Douglass North and the New Economic History', in Roger L. Ransom, Richard Sutch and Gary M. Walton (eds), *Explorations in the New Economic History*, New York: Academic Press.

Umbeck, John (1977), 'The California Gold Rush: a Study of Emerging Property Rights', *Explorations in Economic History*, **14**, 197–226.

Williamson, Oliver (1975), *Markets and Hierarchies: Analysis and Antitrust Implications*, New York: Free Press.

Wallis, John J. and Douglass C. North (1986), 'Measuring the Transaction Sector in the American Economy, 1870–1970', in Stanley L. Engerman and Robert E. Gallman (eds), *Long-Term Factors in American Economic Growth*, Chicago: University of Chicago Press, 95–148.
Wallis, John J. and Douglass C. North (1988), 'Should Transactions Costs be Subtracted from Gross National Product?', *Journal of Economic History*, **48**, 651–4.

11. John Roemer

Jon Elster*

John Roemer's intellectual profile is unusual. He is without doubt the outstanding Marxist economist of the post-war period, if we limit ourselves to economists who are Marxist in their scholarship and not just in their politics. However, while staunchly Marxist in his value orientations and basic assumptions about society, Roemer is equally unflinching in his espousal of neoclassical economics and, especially, General Equilibrium Theory. Indeed, the school of thought to which he has made crucial contributions has, among other names, been referred to as 'neoclassical Marxism'. His work shows that this phrase is no oxymoron and that, on the contrary, the analytical tools of neoclassical economics are not only appropriate but indispensable for tackling a number of classical Marxist problems.

Yet this characterization leaves much out. A simplified periodization of his career might go as follows: before 1980 Roemer was Marxist but not fully neoclassical; between 1980 and 1985 neoclassical Marxism came into full bloom; and after 1985 the neoclassical elements have come to the forefront while the Marxist ones have receded. As the discussion below will show, things are more complicated, but there is an important core of truth in the simplified story. Roemer's relentless commitment to truth and rigour has, over time, proved fatal for a number of his politically inspired convictions. In this respect he differs importantly from other economists who explore Marxist ideas with a mathematical or even a neoclassical tool-box, and whose work proves that skill and technique do not immunize against obscurantism.[1] Rather, what is needed is the ability and willingness to play the devil's advocate; to lean over backwards in exposing one's most cherished ideas to critical scrutiny. Reading Roemer, I have always been equally impressed by his penetrating and original intellect and by his willingness to acknowledge – indeed, to point out before anyone else – flaws or ambiguities in his own reasoning. These are never technical flaws; as far as I can judge (and relying on others whose judgement is better than mine) he is a superbly skilled mathematical economist. However, as we shall see below, problems sometimes arise in interpreting the results.

In trying to retrace Roemer's intellectual Odyssey over the last decade, a convenient starting point may be the state of academic Marxism *c*.1978 in the United States and other Western countries. As a rough generalization – a more adequate description would have to include several exceptions and qualifications – it seems fair to say that Marxist scholarship at the time was in a pretty dismal state. The dominant explanatory modes were functionalism and structuralism, the former arguing that social institutions and behaviour patterns can be explained in terms of their benefits for capitalist class domination; the latter, that structural constraints leave no room for individual choice behaviour. Methodological individualism and rational choice theory belonged to the 'bourgeois' conceptual universe and were incompatible with Marxism, as also were analytical philosophy, statistical data analysis and mathematical economics. Causal analysis was 'mechanical', and inherently inferior to the 'dialectical' study of social change.

G.A. Cohen's *Karl Marx's Theory of History* (1978) and John Roemer's *Analytical Foundations of Marxian Economic Theory* (1981) were the two main publication events that shattered this sectarian universe.[2] Before proceeding to discussion, let me note that Roemer himself had to no small extent been guilty of the fallacies that, later on, he was to denounce. In one early article he violated methodological individualism, by arguing that 'What typifies working class collective action is the adoption of a new paradigm – collective rationality replaces individual rationality' (Roemer, 1978, p. 158). In another, he appealed to naive, unsupported functionalism when he argued that wage discrimination exists because it is in the interest of capitalism. Although the article purports to provide 'microfoundations of a Marxian theory of wage discrimination', its basic premiss is that 'psychologies are endogenous, and in fact are manipulated in such a way as to produce an equilibrium outcome beneficial to capitalists' (Roemer, 1979, p. 704).

Roemer (1981) takes an extremely clear and explicit stance on these issues.[3] In the introductory chapter he insists that Marxian economics needs *microfoundations*, defined as 'deriving the aggregate behavior of an economy as a consequence of the actions of individuals, who are postulated to behave in some specific way' (p. 7). Furthermore, he argues against the two main varieties of functionalist explanation prevalent in Marxism: the idea that 'if the occurrence of X will further the reproduction of capitalist relations, then X occurs' and the idea that 'if the occurrence of X is necessary for the *demise* of capitalism, then X will come to pass' (pp. 8–9). Although Marxist scholars had been deploying such 'heads I win, tails you lose' arguments for a long time, Roemer was, I believe, the first to draw attention to this two-handed practice.

As a substantive piece of writing, the book has the curious status of being an outstanding contribution to a decaying research programme. (In my view the same is true of Cohen's book.) The labour theory of value and the theory of the falling rate of profit are dissected and dismissed with exemplary lucidity and generality – a useful accomplishment, but not one that will inspire much further research. To my mind, the most valuable discussions concern the relationship between class and technology. In Section 2.7, on 'The interaction of class consciousness and the choice of technique' Roemer argues that exploitation of workers may require the use of suboptimal techniques, namely, if the most efficient technique has the side-effect of enhancing the ability of workers to organize themselves. In Section 6.4, on 'Technical change and class struggle' a similar argument is made within a somewhat different framework.[4] Both discussions, however, are highly abstract, without much attention to details, mechanisms and real-life examples. Recent work in bargaining theory shows how Roemer's intuitions could be spelled out, for example, by appealing to the idea that heavy investments in fixed capital makes the firm more vulnerable to strikes (van der Ploeg, 1987). Roemer's habit of viewing all economic phenomena through the lens of General Equilibrium Theory (see Roemer, 1981, pp. 9–10) probably deflected him from exploring models of this kind. Although Roemer (1988a, 1990) eventually did turn to bargaining theory, he did so mainly for methodological purposes, not for the sake of positive analysis.

Roemer's first book was largely a scholastic exercise, brilliantly if somewhat pointlessly performed. His next book, *A General Theory of Exploitation and Class* (1982), was a masterpiece. Before offering a summary and a discussion, I want to observe that the title is severely misleading, since the book offers *two* distinct, largely unrelated accounts of exploitation. I have argued elsewhere (Elster, 1982) that the 'unequal exchange theory' offered in Parts I and II of the book is much more interesting and powerful than the 'withdrawal theory' of Part III. I shall therefore limit myself to the former.

For Roemer (in the unequal-exchange version), exploitation is a predicate, not a relationship. Using general-equilibrium techniques, and assuming that all labour is homogeneous, we first calculate the labour content of all goods. For any given individual, we can then ask two questions. How many hours does he work? How many hours of labour are embodied in his consumption bundle?[5] We then compare the answers to the two questions. If a person works more hours than are embodied in his consumption bundle, he is exploited. If he works fewer, he is an exploiter. This induces a partition of society into an exploited class and an exploiting class, with a tiny band in the middle consisting of individuals who expend exactly as many hours of work as they get back in the form of consumption goods.

The definition is entirely classical, yet Roemer shows that it has surprising (that is, non-classical) consequences. Most strikingly, there can be exploitation without class formation or a labour market. One can easily imagine an economy in which independent producers with different initial endowments engage in trade that results in some of them being exploited and others emerging as exploiters. (Indeed, as argued in Roemer (1983b), unequal exchange between countries can be understood on this model.) The capital-rich producers can specialize in capital-intensive lines of production, whereas those who are poorly endowed with capital must specialize in labour-intensive activities. As a consequence, the former work fewer hours than the latter in order to obtain the same consumption bundle. Conceptually, the result is important because it drives a wedge between exploitation on the one hand and class struggle and dependent labour on the other. It is not invariably the case that exploitation is made possible by extraction of surplus value in the process of production. The phenomenon is more general.

In most of the book, however, Roemer's concern is with exploitation that does arise through the labour market.[6] In these chapters, Roemer introduces a stunning conceptual innovation that, for me at least, had the effect of completely changing my perspective on classes and class formation.[7] Class membership, in his models, is determined endogenously as a result of optimizing labour market behaviour, not given exogenously through birth or fate. The agents, in his model, have the options of selling their labour, hiring labour and working for themselves. These options yield five different classes,[8] distinguished by their optimizing behaviour.[9] Depending on their endowments, some individuals (the landlords) will optimize by hiring others to work their capital; others (rich peasants) will both hire others and work themselves; still others (middle peasants) will only work for themselves; a fourth class of individuals (poor peasants) will work some of the time for themselves and some of the time for others; while those in the final category (agricultural labourers) work all the time for others. In what is perhaps the climactic passage of the work Roemer (1982, p. 73) adds:

> The names in parentheses are added as a historical curiosus: they are the names Lenin and Mao Zedong gave to the five classes of peasantry. The identifications are not specious, as these writers defined the five classes the way they are defined here – for instance, a poor peasant was someone who worked his own land, but also hired himself out; a rich peasant worked his own land, but also hired others; a landlord only hired others; and so forth. For Lenin and Mao, the ordering of the five classes as listed here also was the ordering according to the degree of wealth, and therefore the degree of exploitation of the various classes of peasantry. That result is a theorem in this model.

Before I discuss that theorem, let me point out that Roemer's imputation of his ideas to Lenin and Mao is slightly inaccurate. In their view, a poor peasant (say) is someone who *actually* works his own land and also hires himself out. In Roemer's model, the poor peasant is someone who *has to* choose these options to optimize. Class-membership, in other words, is a matter of *endowment-necessitated behaviour* rather than simply of observed behaviour or – as in much of the earlier Marxist literature – of endowments.[10] The self-proletarianized student, for instance, is not a member of the working class, because he is not forced to sell his labour.[11] This implication of Roemer's definition is not a trivial one. Any definition of class has to be assessed in terms of its usefulness, that is, whether class membership is correlated with other things we want to explain, such as participation in collective action. Roemer's definition is useful if bonds of solidarity are strongest among those who *have to* sell their labour; it less useful it if turns out that actual labour-market behaviour is more highly correlated with collective action. Or we might look to the ideological views of people who sell their labour-power, to see whether there is a stronger affinity between the views of those who do so because they have to than within the group as a whole.

The analytical core of Roemer's book is the *class-exploitation correspondence theorem*, which spells out the link between the partition of society in terms of exploitation status and the partition in terms of optimal labour-market behaviour. In itself, the theorem is unsurprising. It asserts, roughly speaking, that the exploiters are members of the class who optimize by hiring labour-power, whereas the exploited optimize by selling their labour-power.[12] It is nevertheless a beautiful result, because it lays bare the mechanism – the competitive market with optimizing agents sorting themselves out into different categories – that reveals why things have to be the way intuition tells us they are. When I was asked to write an opinion for the blurb of the book, I said that it had the 'ex post obviousness characteristic of all good science'. Ten years later, my opinion remains the same.

The concept of exploitation is, first and foremost, normative.[13] But what, exactly, is wrong with exploitation? In *A General Theory* Roemer never confronts this issue. He does not, for instance, consider whether exploitation is wrong in circumstances in which the surplus extracted from workers is used for reinvestment in new production which ultimately benefits the workers. Nor does he consider issues of desert, that is, whether it is wrong to exploit others on the basis of superior material endowments when those endowments have been earned through hard work and saving. In later articles these issues are met head-on. The upshot is the conclusion that exploitation is not a fundamental moral concept. When exploitation is morally wrong, as it often is, it is not *qua* exploitation, but *qua* exploitation conjoined with some other factor or factors. In the absence of these other factors, there may be morally unobjectionable exploitation.

To illustrate this proposition, and to convey a flavour of Roemer's method of reasoning by simple numerical examples, I reproduce a vignette from Roemer (1985a). Suppose that there are two ways of producing corn, the Farm technology and the Factory technology. At the Farm, 3 days of labour and no capital produces 1 bushel of corn. At the Factory, 1 day of labour plus 1 bushel of seed corn produces 2 bushels of corn. There are two producers, Karl and Adam, with preferences over bundles (C,L) of corn and labour. Karl has an initial endowment of 1 corn and Adam of 3 corn. Their preferences imply, among other things, that Karl would rather have $^2/_3$ bushels of corn and not work at all than to work 1 day and consume 1 bushel, and that Adam would rather work 4 days and consume $3^1/_3$ bushels of corn than work 3 days and consume 3 bushels.[14] Let me now quote from Roemer (1985a, pp. 58–9):

> Now note that Karl can achieve (1,1) by working up his 1 corn in the Factory in 1 day; he consumes 1 of the bushels produced and starts week 2 with his initial 1 bushel. Likewise, Adam can achieve (3,3) by working up his 3 bushels in the Factory with 3 days' labor; he consumes 3 of the 6 produced, and replaces his initial stock for week 2. But this solution is not Pareto optimal. For now suppose Karl lends his 1 bushel to Adam. Adam works up the total of 4 bushels in 4 days in the Factory, produces 8 bushels, and pays back Karl his original bushel plus $^2/_3$ bushel as interest for the loan. This leaves Adam with $3^1/_3$ bushels, after replacing his 3 bushels of initial stock. Thus Karl can consume $^2/_3$ bushel and work not at all, which he prefers to (1,1), and Adam consumes the bundle ($3^1/_3$, 4) which he prefers to (3,3). We have a strict Pareto improvement. (The interest rate charged is the competitive one; for if Adam, instead of borrowing from Karl, worked on the farm for an extra day he would make precisely $^1/_3$ bushel of corn.) This arrangement may continue forever: Karl never works and lives off the interest from Adam's labor. According to the unequal exchange definition of exploitation, there is no shadow of doubt that Karl exploits Adam. However, Adam is richer than Karl. On what basis can we condemn this exploitation?

The answer is that in this case there is nothing wrong with exploitation. As the exploitation can be traced to the fact that the agents have different preferences, it is unobjectionable. In the standard case, with the labour transfers going from the poor to the rich, exploitation can be traced back to the fact that the agents have unequal endowments. To the extent that the latter inequality can itself be traced back to different preferences, the exploitation remains unobjectionable. As pointed out by Roemer (1985a, pp. 48–9), even if X and Y start out with equal endowments, X's high aversion to work might induce him to eat up his seed corn and thus make it optimal for him to sell his labour to Y rather than go working on the Farm. He can't complain, because he could have acted differently and, in fact, could reverse the situation at any time by working on the Farm and accumulate more seed corn. The only morally objectionable form of exploitation is that which originates in endowment differences that are not themselves the outcome of free, voluntary transactions among initially equal agents.

In presenting these examples I have gone beyond Roemer's own statements. In Roemer (1985a), the claim that Karl's exploitation of Adam and Y's exploitation of X are unobjectionable is merely backed by intuition. The more general argument that exploitation is objectionable if and only if it rests on different initial endowments is not explicitly made. An argument of that kind is made in Dworkin (1981), however, although not with explicit reference to exploitation. Part I and Part II of Dworkin (1981) are concerned, respectively, with equality of welfare and equality of resources as varieties of egalitarianism. Dworkin rejects equality of welfare as an ideal for distributive justice, on the grounds that the relevant interpersonal comparisons of welfare cannot be carried out, and argues instead for the idea of equality of resources. The argument has two parts. With respect to external, alienable resources, Dworkin argues that all agents should receive the same bundle of goods and then trade to equilibrium. With respect to internal features of the agents, he makes a sharp distinction between inborn endowments (skills and talents) on the one hand and preferences, ambitions and tastes on the other. Distribution ought, he claims, to be 'endowment-sensitive' but not 'ambition-sensitive' (Dworkin, 1981, Part II, p. 311). To ensure that the final distribution is endowment-blind, we can implement the outcome of an insurance scheme behind the veil of ignorance, and award the handicapped or less-talented the amount they would have taken out in insurance, given their preferences (including their risk aversion) and the costs of insurance.

Although only mentioned in passing in Roemer (1985a), Dworkin's article was to lead him down the path to a wholly different research programme. In the very same year he published an article (Roemer, 1985b) devoted to refuting the part of Dworkin's theory that concerns the rectification of unequal natural endowments. Dworkin considered two schemes for neutralizing the effects of unequal talents. The first – giving each person equal property rights in everybody else's labour – is rejected because it amounts to 'the slavery of the talented' (Dworkin, 1981, Part II, pp. 311–12). In fact, it would make the talented worse off than others, since their time would be so valuable that they would have to work very long hours to earn enough to buy it back and get some leisure. The second is the insurance scheme referred to above. Roemer (1985b, pp. 170ff.) showed that this mechanism, too, leads to the slavery of the talented: with optimal insurance for talent the talented end up working more and being worse off than others. In fact, he produces a numerical example showing that the talented could be even worse off under the insurance scheme than under the equal-property scheme. (I shall return to the fact that Roemer here assumes what Dworkin denies, namely, the possibility of interpersonal comparisons of welfare.)

Roemer's analysis of Dworkin, although important as a critique, was mainly a stepping stone towards the more ambitious and constructive result offered in Roemer (1986a), 'Equality of Resources Implies Equality of Welfare'. This article is the centrepiece in Roemer's third and, to simplify again, post-Marxist stage. In addition to the substantive result announced in the title, it introduces a novel methodology for the axiomatic treatment of welfare economics. I begin with the latter.

Roemer's treatment is reminiscent of axiomatic bargaining theory and social choice theory, with the difference that in his system the axioms are defined on much more complex objects.[15] In bargaining theory, a state of the world is represented by an n-tuple of utility numbers. Certain states are available as feasible agreement points, and in addition one state is singled out as the disagreement point. The axioms impose (roughly speaking) optimality and consistency conditions on potential solutions to the bargaining game. In social choice theory a state of the world is an n-tuple of individual preference rankings over the feasible alternatives, which are assumed to be atoms without any internal structure. The axioms are (even more roughly speaking) conditions that constrain the relation between these rankings and the social ranking of the same alternatives.

The central concept in Roemer (1986a) is that of an *economic environment*, defined as an n-tuple of available resources (specific amounts of n different resources) and two utility functions defined over these resources. (I follow Roemer in limiting myself to the two-person case, since all theorems are true for any finite number of agents, with the same proofs.) Any given allocation of the resources among the agents will give rise to a utility pair. The article examines the mechanisms which map economic environments into feasible allocations of those environments. Given an economic environment, an allocation correspondence will select a set of feasible allocations. However, Roemer restricts himself to correspondences that select all and only the allocations associated with a single point in utility space; to those correspondences, in other words, that induce a function from the economic environment into utility space. The substance of the article is an investigation of various constraints that, in the perspective of resource egalitarianism, should be imposed on those correspondences. The conclusion, announced in the title, is that the only correspondences that satisfy all the constraints are those that select allocations each of which gives equal utility to both agents. Hence, Roemer concludes, Dworkin's equality of resources collapses into equality of welfare.

The theorem cannot be faulted, but perhaps its interpretation can. Roemer himself notes (1986a, p. 776) that if one denies the possibility of interpersonal comparisons of welfare, his theorem turns into an impossibility theorem: 'We have, then, two results: if welfare is interpersonally comparable, then the only coherent conception of resource equality requires equalizing welfare; if welfare is noncomparable, there is no coherent conception of resource

equality.' This is not the most serious qualification, however. A more fundamental objection is raised by Thomas Scanlon (1986), who charges that
Roemer (in his 1986b) inappropriately imposes a welfarist framework on
resource egalitarianism. The axiom of resource monotonicity, for instance,
'says that whatever equality-of-resources means, it must at least require that
no agent's welfare diminishes as total resource endowments increase'
(Roemer, 1986a, p. 761). Scanlon replies (1986, p. 112) that although 'any
principle of resource equality requires some means of comparing bundles of
resources as "larger", "smaller", or "equal" ... it would be question begging
to assume at the outset that this standard of comparison must be just the
amount of utility which a bundle produces'. And he concludes (ibid.) that
'The idea that "if the total bundle of resources increases, neither agent's
utility falls" ... might be thought to express an optimistic (welfarist) attitude
towards the consequences of economic development rather than a necessary
tenet of resource egalitarianism'.[16]

Scanlon also advances similar objections to the other axioms, but these
need not detain us here. The more fundamental question is whether the
axioms are reasonable constraints *on resource egalitarianism*, or simply
represent more general intuitions about fair distributions. If, as I believe, the
latter is the case, Roemer's results appear in a different light. One might
object that any general intuition about fairness ought also to constrain resource-egalitarian theories, but this would be to overlook the fact that our
full set of pre-analytical intuitions about fairness certainly are inconsistent.
(Nobody ought to suffer and everybody ought to get what they deserve.) A
resource-egalitarian theory is one that singles out certain intuitions as more
fundamental than others from its particular vantage point. If Roemer had
wanted to model that theory, he should have asked himself whether his
particular constraints are such that they would appeal specifically to the
resource-egalitarian. I believe Scanlon is right in arguing that they do not.

The argument in Moulin and Roemer (1989) can be used to reinforce this
point. Here the authors propose an axiomatic model of public ownership,[17]
based on 'public ownership of the external world and private ownership of
self'. Unlike the model in Roemer (1986a), this approach deals with production and allocation, not only with the latter. One axiom of this model is that in
a world of two agents, one skilled and the other unskilled, the unskilled should
be no worse off than he would be in a world in which the other agent were as
unskilled as he. Commenting on this axiom, the authors (ibid., p. 354) remark:
'We lack a clear motivation for this axiom from the property rights we wish to
model, but we think it is attractive nevertheless.' I agree with both points. The
axiom is prima facie attractive, but so are many others. And it is not connected
with public ownership of the external world or with private ownership of self.

Mutatis mutandis, the same point could be made with respect to several of the axioms used to model resource egalitarianism.[18]

The normative arguments discussed so far constitute, I believe, the main, continuous thread of Roemer's work. I now consider two of his more recent contributions to positive theory, both of them arising out of his concern with normative issues.

As mentioned earlier, Roemer's claim that equality of resources implies equality of welfare cannot even be stated if welfare or well-being cannot be compared across individuals. The possibility of such comparisons constitutes a long-standing and largely unresolved issue in economics and philosophy. The method of empathy seems methodologically unsound; some would argue that the whole idea of comparing the welfare of different individuals is meaningless. To look more closely into the question, Roemer and I recently organized two conferences on interpersonal comparisons on well-being, the proceedings from which are found in Elster and Roemer (1991). In his contribution to that volume (co-authored with Ignacio Ortuño-Ortin), Roemer constructs an ingenious mechanism that might, at least in theory, actually allow us to carry out such comparisons.

Earlier, Allan Gibbard had suggested an approach which relies on overlap between segments of lives rather than on empathy with whole lives. Each of us will, through our experiences, form 'hypotheses about how the intrinsic reward of a course of a life depends on a range of combination of features of the person and the life he leads. Call these *personal hypotheses*' (Gibbard, 1986, p. 185). If there are at least two points of overlap between the personal hypotheses of two individuals, they can be used to calibrate the degrees of intrinsic reward on a common scale. Now, for a randomly chosen pair of individuals such overlap seems implausible. Ortuño-Ortin and Roemer (1991) develop an approach designed to overcome this difficulty. They argue that each person, through empathy or experience, can compare his well-being with that of persons sufficiently similar to himself. From such local comparisons one can then under certain conditions piece together a comparison between two persons who differ from each other in so many respects that pairwise comparison or even pairwise overlap would be impossible. I believe this approach provides a valid, affirmative answer to the question whether interpersonal comparisons are at all meaningful. It does not, however, bring us any closer to practical measurement and comparison of utilities. And even if it did, it is not clear that it could serve for purposes of distributive justice (Elster and Roemer, 1991).

With the exception of the early work in Roemer (1978), his main concern over the years has been to show that (or to discuss whether) people *ought to* abolish capitalism and exploitation, not to discuss the conditions under which they *will* do so. In Roemer (1985c, 1988b), he describes a game between 'Lenin and the Tsar' that suggests some answers to the latter question. Whereas in Roemer (1978) he solved or evaded the free-rider problem for revolutionary behaviour by stipulating a mystical 'collective rationality', he now simply brackets the issue by acknowledging its existence and assuming that it has, somehow, been solved.[19] The assumption is heroic; excessively so, in my opinion, as it does away with most of the hard and interesting problems by fiat.[20] This being said, Roemer's treatment is, as always, superlatively clear and succeeds in illuminating important aspects of the problem.

The pre-revolutionary situation is modelled as a distribution of income. Lenin proposes a new distribution of income, whereas the Tsar proposes a set of penalties – fines, to be precise, with current income as the ceiling – for those who participate in a revolution that fails. Assuming that the Tsar moves first, the task is to characterize the equilibrium strategies of the two parties.

A coalition against the Tsar is said to be formable if the expected income of every member of the coalition exceeds his present income, taking into account the chances of success, the size of the gain in case of success and the size of the penalties in the case of failure. The chances of success, in turn, are a function of the size and membership of the coalition (assuming that it has formed) and of the penalties. This function is subject to three constraints:

- *Coalition monotonicity*: Chances of success never decrease as more people join a coalition;
- *Penalty monotonicity*: Chances of success never decrease as penalties become more severe;
- *Lean and hungry*: Adding a poor person to a coalition raises the chances of success at least as much as adding a richer person does.

The first condition, Roemer says, 'needs hardly to be motivated'. It is not impossible, however, to imagine situations in which it would not be satisfied (Elster, 1989, pp. 190–1). More importantly, the third condition could, as Roemer himself notes, easily fail to obtain. The efficacy of an individual in collective action depends both on motivation and on resources. As the former is a decreasing function of income and the latter an increasing function, the net effect of income on efficacy is in general indeterminate. The second condition might appear to be paradoxical, but this impression is dispelled as soon as we note that it holds only for coalitions that have succeeded in forming. High penalties will, other things being equal, make fewer coalitions formable, but increase the chances of success for those that have been formed. I believe this is a valid and important insight. With characteristic frankness Roemer asserts (1985c, p. 88) that it 'is assumed in order to make the Tsar into a nontrivial player', as if its only role in the argument were to allow Roemer to display his skills. I believe, however, that the East European events of 1989 underscore the substantive validity of the assumption. As Roemer remarks (ibid.), 'The more tyrannical the regime is, the more incensed people become and the more successful revolutionary attempts are likely to be.' In this sense the assumption of penalty monotonicity rests on 'the psychology of tyranny'. In addition, severity of penalties serves as a signal to each potential revolutionary that the regime believes itself to be in trouble, and hence that he is not as isolated as he might otherwise have believed himself to be. If (as argued in Roemer, 1985c, p. 90) the potential revolutionaries have assurance-game preferences, knowledge that one is not isolated is exactly what is needed to trigger revolutionary action.

Roemer shows, first, that if the penalty monotonicity condition is strengthened a little bit, so as to assert that every increase in penalties will actually increase the chances of success (as distinct from not decreasing them), it never pays for a rational Tsar to impose maximal penalties, since their deterrence effect is always smaller than the effect from the psychology of tyranny. (If *per impossibile* Ceausescu had read Roemer, he might still be around.) He next introduces the additional assumption of 'relative severity': if the Tsar raises by a little bit the penalty of someone who is already punished severely, the probability of success increases more than if the penalty of someone who is less severely threatened is raised by the same amount. Under this assumption, which is 'like a second-order condition on the psychology of Tyranny' (Roemer, 1988b, p. 237), Roemer shows that the Tsar's optimal strategy is to impose more severe penalties (relatively to their income) on the poor than on the rich. The main result proved about Lenin's optimal strategy concerns the conditions under which it is rational for Lenin to propose (quite independently of any ideological justification) a 'progressive' redistribution of income, that is, one that takes from the rich and gives to the poor. In this context the axiom of 'lean and hungry' is replaced by the stronger axiom of 'symmetry', according to which the probability of success is a function simply of a coalition's size, with the incomes of its members making no difference. Roemer then shows that under this assumption, something like (but weaker than) progressivity can be proved. There is no need to give details, as I find Roemer's findings about Lenin less interesting than his analysis of the Tsar.

If I were to summarize the intellectual qualities of Roemer's work in a single phrase, the one that comes to mind is *good taste*. He has consistently chosen to work on important problems and, more importantly perhaps, has consistently approached them using models that are simple, natural, novel and profound. Physicists often talk about beauty, elegance and simplicity as important guides to truth. In the mathematical part of the social sciences, too, this concern is paramount. This is not a matter of technical skills, but of mathematical intuition. Among mathematicians, John von Neumann was second to none, I believe, as far as skills go, yet he is reported to have been deeply envious of the more intuitive André Weil. As far as can be judged by someone who is not himself a mathematician, Roemer possesses the deep delight in *going with the grain*, of finding the simple and *ex-post*-obvious approach that lays bare the nature of things in an unstrained and effortless manner. There may be an element of Hegelianism in this view of the world, 'the Rational is the Real'. I am probably too much of an empiricist to appreciate it fully. I have increasingly come to see the social sciences as closer to chemistry than to physics, more concerned with inductive generalizations that with logical deduction (Elster, 1989, p. 1). But I can understand the attraction and the beauty of the more austere approach, of which Roemer is an outstanding practitioner.

Roemer's political views are, in their way, no less uncompromising. I believe it is a roughly true generalization that mathematicians tend to be radical in their politics, and I conjecture that the reason has to do with the absolute freedom with which they move within their professional domain. The mathematician is less subject to friction and resistance than anyone else. He is constrained at most by the principle of contradiction, and even that he can finesse in various ways. Turning to politics, he may naturally approach it in the same spirit. (For some elaborations on this piece of amateur psychology, see Elster, 1990, ch. 4.) Roemer's political views are radical both in the sense of occupying a place at the very left end of the political spectrum, and in the sense of being concerned with first-best principles rather than with practical compromises. However, his radicalism never leads him seriously astray: his willingness to listen to argument and objections is too highly developed for any kind of dogmatism to take over.

Roemer's views are also radical in the further sense of being at the very *left*, rather than at the very right, end of the spectrum. This, however, is a matter of compassion with the disadvantaged and indignation with those who take unfair advantage of them, not of intellectual style. These attitudes pervade his work, yet are never allowed to dominate it. He is, in my view, a model of the *engaged scholar*.

262   *New Horizons in Economic Thought*

NOTES

* I am grateful to Karl O. Moene and John Roemer for their comments on an earlier draft of this article.

1. In reading mathematical Marxist economists, one often has the impressions of theorems in search of assumptions: the belief in the conclusions stems from political conviction and wishful thinking, not from belief in the premises on which they are based. (The innumerable attempts to make non-trivial sense of 'the transformation problem' can be cited as an example.) Now, in several places Roemer (1982, p. 153; 1988a, p. 233) defends an apparently similar practice, the use of 'proof-generated assumptions'. In his case, however, the idea is that pre-analytical intuitions about what is to be proved can guide us to assumptions that will then be come to be seen as independently plausible and hence justify their ancestors. Belief in assumptions need not be independently formed to be independently plausible.

2. Judging from the references in Roemer (1981), this work was written before he had read Cohen. Although not simultaneous, the two were independent of each other.

3. It should be noted, though, that he apparently believed (see Roemer, 1981, pp. 7–8) that his earlier efforts (in Roemer, 1978, 1979) were compatible with his new research programme.

4. Both arguments can be seen as ways of spelling out the Marxist idea that capitalism is a 'fetter' on technical change. In Section 4.3, on 'The effect of technical change on the rate of profit', Roemer argues that the capitalist goal of minimizing *paid* labour, rather than labour *tout court*, can also lead to the adoption of socially undesirable techniques. The argument is criticized in Samuelson (1982), with a rejoinder in Roemer (1983).

5. Or, more generally, how many hours of labour are embodied in the consumption bundles that his income will buy him? Because the prices of goods are not in general proportional to their labour content, the answer to that question provides a range of amounts of labour embodied rather than a unique amount. In the following I shall abstract from the various complications that follow from this fact.

6. He also devotes a chapter to exploitation arising in economies with a credit market but no labour market, showing that the partition of producers into exploiters and exploited is the same as in a pure labour market economy. I conjecture, however, that this isomorphism would disappear in more fine-grained models, because the principal–agent problem between managers and workers differs from that between banks and firms.

7. At least with respect to pure competitive economies. In ch. 6 of Elster (1985) I discuss whether Roemer's approach may be extended to pre-capitalist economies, to economies with state ownership, and to economies with large corporations. The results are ambiguous, and certainly do not approach the compelling transparency of Roemer's work.

8. Abstractly speaking, there are eight different cases. As an agent who neither works for himself nor hires himself out nor hires others would not survive, that case can be dismissed. Roemer shows that if an agent has an equilibrium solution in which he both sells his labour and hires labour, he also has a solution in one of the five classes mentioned in the text.

9. In the model under discussion here, agents minimize labour time subject to a consumption constraint; hence the option of not working at all can be optimal. In other models, where the goal of the agents is to accumulate as much as possible subject to a constraint on working hours, everybody will work in equilibrium and there are only four different classes.

10. Cohen (1978, pp. 70ff.) already observed that possession of some means of production is compatible with the owner being a member of the proletariat, if they are insufficient to enable him to gain his living without selling his labour.

11. I'm skipping a step here. To conclude that the worker is forced to sell his labour-power, it is not sufficient to show that this is his optimizing solution: one must also argue that he is forced to optimize.

12. In addition, Roemer shows that exploitation status and class status are correlated with wealth, in the natural way.
13. It is implausible to think that the idea of exploitation could be used for explanatory purposes, e.g., by entering into the motivation for collective action. Since the determination of whether one's exploitation status is positive or negative would require a horrendously complicated labour time accounting, this status is unlikely to matter for subjective motivations. Yet the class-exploitation correspondence theorem tells us that exploitation is correlated with the immediately observable and clearly motivating labour-market status.
14. Actually, as Roemer shows, these 'local preferences' might be part of the same overall preference schedule.
15. Later Roemer applied his apparatus to restate bargaining theory (Roemer, 1988b, 1990) and social choice theory (Donaldson and Roemer, 1987). Lack of competence prevents me from assessing these results.
16. Scanlon is guilty of some confusion here, since the idea that a bundle 'increases' must be seen as a statement about comparative statics, not as a statement about change. But I do not think this slip vitiates his criticism.
17. Their conclusion is that public ownership, as characterized by their axioms, must equalize welfare. In other work Roemer (1989) has explored different approaches to the concept of public ownership, with the emphasis on the design of efficient mechanisms rather than on the axiomatic treatment of outcomes. I shall not discuss this work here, since it falls outside the line of development I have been trying to trace.
18. In Donaldson and Roemer (1987, p. 268) a compelling counter-example is produced to show that even on welfarist terms the axiom of resource monotonicity is ethically dubious.
19. Roemer (1988b, p. 234). Roemer (1985c, p. 90) defends the assumption by stipulating 'a change in agents' preferences from those of the prisoner's dilemma to those of the assurance game', while acknowledging that 'we do not fully understand' how this transformation comes about. As observed below, however, assurance-game preferences by themselves will not bring about action unless they are known to be shared.
20. For a sketch of regime-opposition dynamics in a revolutionary situation, with major emphasis on the free-rider problem, see Elster (1990, pp. 20–8).

REFERENCES

Cohen, G.A. (1978), *Karl Marx's Theory of History*, Oxford: Oxford University Press.
Donaldson, D. and J. Roemer (1987), 'Social Choice on Economic Environments with Dimensional Variation', *Social Choice and Welfare*, **4**, 253–75.
Dworkin, R. (1981), 'What Is Equality?', *Philosophy and Public Affairs*, **10**, 185–246 (Part I) and 283–345 (Part II).
Elster, J. (1982), 'Roemer vs Roemer', *Politics and Society*, **11**, 363–74.
—— (1985), *Making Sense of Marx*, Cambridge: Cambridge University Press.
—— (1989), *The Cement of Society*, Cambridge: Cambridge University Press.
—— (1990), *Psychologie politique*, Paris: Éditions de Minuit.
—— and J. Roemer (eds) (1991), *Interpersonal Comparisons of Well-Being*, Cambridge: Cambridge University Press.
—— and —— (1991), 'Introduction', to Elster and Roemer (eds) (1991).
Gibbard, A. (1986), 'Interpersonal Comparisons: Preference, Good, and the Intrinsic Reward of a Life', in J. Elster and A. Hylland (eds), *Foundations of Social Choice Theory*, Cambridge: Cambridge University Press, 165–94.
Moulin, H. and J. Roemer (1989), 'Public Ownership of the External World and Private Ownership of Self', *Journal of Political Economy*, **97**, 347–67.

Ortuño-Ortin, I. and J. Roemer (1991), 'Deducing Interpersonal Comparisons from Local Expertise', in Elster and Roemer (eds) (1991).

Ploeg, F. van der (1987), 'Trade Unions, Investment and Employment', *European Economic Review*, **31**, 1465–92.

Roemer, J. (1978), 'Neoclassicism, Marxism, and Collective Action', *Journal of Economic Issues*, **12**, 147–62.

—— (1979), 'Divide and Conquer: Microfoundations of a Marxian Theory of Wage Discrimination', *Bell Journal of Economics*, **10**, 695–705.

—— (1981), *Analytical Foundations of Marxian Economic Theory*, Cambridge: Cambridge University Press.

—— (1982), *A General Theory of Exploitation and Class*, Cambridge, Mass.: Harvard University Press.

—— (1983a), 'Choice of Technique under Capitalism, Socialism and "Nirvana" ', Working Paper no. 213, Department of Economics, University of California at Davis.

—— (1983b), 'Unequal Exchange, Labor Migration and International Capital Flows: a Theoretical Synthesis', in P. Desai (ed.), *Marxism, Central Planning and the Soviet Economy: Economic Essays in Honor of Alexander Ehrlich*, Cambridge, Mass.: MIT Press, 34–60.

—— (1985a), 'Should Marxists be Interested in Exploitation?', *Philosophy and Public Affairs*, **14**, 30–65.

—— (1985b), 'Equality of Talent', *Economics and Philosophy*, **1**, 151–88.

—— (1985c), 'Rationalizing Revolutionary Ideology', *Econometrica*, **53**, 85–108.

—— (1986a), 'Equality of Resources Implies Equality of Welfare', *Quarterly Journal of Economics*, **101**, 751–86.

—— (1986b), 'The Mismarriage of Bargaining Theory and Distributive Justice', *Ethics*, **97**, 88–110.

—— (1988a), 'Axiomatic Bargaining Theory on Economic Environments', *Journal of Economic Theory*, **45**, 1–31.

—— (1988b), 'Rationalizing Revolutionary Ideology: a Tale of Lenin and the Tsar', in M. Taylor (ed.), *Rationality and Revolution*, Cambridge: Cambridge University Press, 229–44.

—— (1989), 'A Public Ownership Resolution of the Tragedy of the Commons', *Social Philosophy and Policy*, **6**, 74–92.

—— (1990), 'Welfarism and Axiomatic Bargaining Theory', *Recherches economiques de Louvain*.

Samuelson, P. (1982), 'The Normative and Positivistic Inferiority of Marx's *values* paradigm', *Southern Economic Journal*, **49**, 11–18.

Scanlon, T. (1986), 'Equality of Resources and Equality of Welfare: a Forced Marriage?', *Ethics*, **97**, 111–18.

12. Tibor Scitovsky

Peter E. Earl

INTRODUCTION

Tibor Scitovsky was born in Budapest in 1910, the son of a senior civil servant. The kind of economist that he has become and, indeed, the fact that he became an economist at all both owe much to his lifestyle in childhood and adolescence. In his (forthcoming) paper on his life philosophy he explains how his parents used his father's high income to provide a private tutor for him in a house that was replete with antiques and often the location for great parties. They also took him on their travels to countless museums, exhibitions and artistic performances in many countries. But he also became aware of the plight of those who were less fortunate, for he often travelled through the slums of Budapest and had many occasions to see his mother serve as a fairy godmother to anyone she knew who was in difficulties. This gulf between rich and poor, and his awareness of the ways in which career paths in Hungary were dominated by social connections, eventually led him to revolt against his mother's desire that he should become a banker. Wanting to stand on his own feet, and interested by the economic problems of the day, he left Hungary in 1935 to enrol at the London School of Economics. Thus began an academic career in which the sources of economic power and the nature of human satisfaction have often provided a focus for his attention.

It is no easy task to organize a chapter on this remarkable economist's work, for his half-century of books and articles contain many interlocking ideas and he kept coming back to some topics after long periods occupied in other areas. The structure that I have chosen involves some sudden changes of direction between sections but wherever possible tries to make the most of theoretical linkages between his contributions. We begin with his works on the welfare and the competitive process, which provide the microfoundations for many of his macroeconomics contributions. There is then something of a jump to his famous attempts to infuse psychology into economics and his controversial critique of the American way of life. These discussions lead us back, finally, to macroeconomic issues.

WEALTH AND WELFARE

The distributional implications of changes in policy for the underlying structure of the economic system have been one of the most frequent points of focus in Scitovsky's works. He caused controversy very early in his career by uncovering problems with Kaldor's (1939) confident claim that economists assessing the desirability of particular projects could avoid interpersonal welfare comparisons by seeing whether or not gainers could potentially compensate losers. Scitovsky (1941b/1964, pp. 136–7) took note of earlier debates in relation to the use of Paasche's and Laspeyres's rival formulae for estimating cost of living index numbers and pointed out that Kaldor's criterion for an increase in social income was merely one way of viewing things: an alternative test would be to see whether or not potential losers would be willing to offer potential gainers a bribe big enough to deter them from supporting the contemplated change. If they were not that willing to pay to preserve the status quo then it could be said that the change represented an increase in social income.

The 'losers bribing gainers' criterion that Scitovsky suggested is obviously open to the criticism that the willingness of losers to pay others not to disturb their positions is constrained by their wealth. As an extreme case, consider the position of primitive tribespeople in confrontation with logging companies who wish to cut down the rain forests in which they live. No matter how highly the tribespeople value their existing lifestyles they are unlikely to be in a position to compensate the latter for the profits that will fail to materialize if the rain forests are not logged. But the point of raising this criterion may really have been just to show that matters were not quite as straightforward as Kaldor had asserted, for Scitovsky had two further objections to Kaldor's criterion. First, it is unlikely that compensation will *actually* be paid in free enterprise economies to those who are prejudiced by change (1951a/1964, p. 182); hence recommendations made on the basis of potential Pareto improvements involve a value judgement in favour of those who stand to gain. Secondly, even if they can expect compensation to be paid, economists should recognize that their efficiency-orientated recommendations 'are not independent of value judgements between alternative income distributions either. For, going out of their way to preserve the existing distribution of income, they imply a preference for the *status quo*' (1941b/1964, p. 126).

Not surprisingly, Scitovsky's views provoked a heated debate, a detailed discussion of which is provided by Dobb (1969, chs 5 and 6). Attention should also have been given to some of his insights on how the competitive process might affect income distribution. For example, in another of his early papers (1945/1964, pp. 200–1) he pointed out that if firms practise price discrimination against the wealthy this will tend to reduce differences between rich and poor in terms of the physical consumption of commodities. But he also noted that this effect will be somewhat reduced in so far as the dividend incomes of the rich are inflated by higher profits resulting from price discrimination. Moreover, although the rich may end up paying at a higher rate for the characteristics they consume, any negative attitudes of the rest of society towards their conspicuous consumption are none the less likely to be a function of the nominal expenditure involved, for this serves as a proxy for the money incomes that the rest of society might have enjoyed. Preferences of better-off consumers for differentiated products can also be seen as a matter for concern if they result in goods being made to order rather than for stock, causing economies of large-scale production to be lost and prices to be higher (1958, pp. 28–30).

Doubts about the use of price as a rationing mechanism arise once we recognize that costs and benefits reflect the existing distribution of income. Suppose that it is thought necessary to limit entry to a national park in order to avoid undue strain on fauna and flora. The conventional policy is to set an entry fee at a level high enough to keep numbers down to the tolerable level. But this approach is a recipe for turning a visit to the park into what Hirsch (1976) labels as a 'positional' good. Scitovsky (1964, p. 261) therefore canvasses a policy of making access difficult by providing very poor-quality access roads. In this case, rich and poor alike will have to decide whether they value access to nature highly enough to tolerate a long, rough drive in order to get to the park. (It is probably no coincidence that this suggestion appears to anticipate Hirsch's thinking. The two economists were friends and it was Scitovsky who actually encouraged Hirsch to write about the social problems of economic growth: see Scitovsky, forthcoming.)

In trying to decide how economist might best make policy recommendations Scitovsky (1964, ch. 16) assigns a central role to the ways in which the public at large view the concept of equity. His interpretation of how people decide whether something is fair implies a lexicographic criterion in keeping with more recent discussions about 'basic needs' and the use that Lutz and Lux (1979) have made of the 'idea of a hierarchy of needs' proposed by the psychologist Maslow (1954). (Scitovsky himself makes no reference to Maslow's well-known contribution.) He suggests that 'the first dictate of people's consciences is that the prime necessities of life should be generally available and distributed in an egalitarian way. Even great inequalities of income and wealth will not be considered oppressive as long as necessities are cheap and plentiful enough to be generally available; whereas slight inequalities of income may be considered unjust if one or more necessities are short – that is, scarce and expensive enough to become the privilege of the well-to-do.' In other words, 'most people consider equitable an economic system or economic organization that leads to an egalitarian or near-egalitarian distribution of the necessities of life' (1964, p. 254). The use of local reference standards is also implied in his analysis of how people judge what is fair: he portrays people as judging their lists of necessities very much with a view to the state of development of the economy of which they are members (1976, pp. 115–20). In affluent societies the list of necessities includes the assurance that retirement will not see a plunge in a person's living standards (1964, p. 258) and that 'one will be able to continue to enjoy one's accustomed level of comfort in the future' (1978a, p. 229). These views of equity figure in his analysis of inflation. So, too, do his writings on market processes, to which I shall now turn.

INFORMATION AND ECONOMIC EFFICIENCY

One of the unusual things about Scitovsky's work on the efficiency of capitalist economies is his recognition of the role of expectations in determining whether or not an economic system will deliver the goods that consumers would most prefer and whether it will achieve equilibrium following a disturbance without undergoing major adjustment costs. This role is crucial, since the real world, unlike the world of much General Equilibrium theorizing, is a place that has neither complete futures markets nor consumers who are born with well-defined preferences.

If tastes are acquired rather than innate, preferences will depend upon experiences of consumption, either at first hand or via the observation of others. Mindful of this, and despite his concern with the effects of product differentiation on average costs and hence on income distribution, Scitovsky (1960/1964, p. 237; 1962/1964, p. 245) argues that the supply of a wide variety of products is essential for social well-being. He points out that if poorly informed consumers comprise the majority, they may fail to discover better ways of spending their money unless the minority of better-informed consumers with 'good tastes' can set an example. This requires that the minority have access to the sorts of products they wish to buy. However, problems of access are likely to arise if costs can be reduced by large-scale production and if domestic producers are sheltered from competition from overseas producers whose home markets have different tastes. If the biggest domestic producers do not face such competition and only supply products that are consistent with what their market research tells them about the existing tastes of the majority, there is no mechanism by which they can discover whether they could be meeting underlying needs better by being more imaginative with their offerings. They could end up pandering to a mythical majority – just as Hollywood and Detroit did before the importation of foreign films and cars showed them just how wrong were their interpretations of market preferences (Scitovsky, 1962/1964, p. 247). (With hindsight it appears Scitovsky was a bit premature in assuming that American car producers had actually learnt from the success of smaller, less-powerful imported cars: witness the recent ascendancy of Japanese products.)

Scitovsky's thinking on the issue of the attainment of equilibrium has much in common with Richardson (1960), who discussed this problem at greater length and whose contribution is only lately being given the attention it deserves. (Scitovsky (1990, p. 142) himself has recently noted Richardson's contribution without mentioning its similarities with some of his own work.) The essence of the problem is that payoffs to competitive and/or complementary investments depend on future market conditions but in the absence of futures markets the market only transmits information about the current state of affairs (Scitovsky, 1951b, p. 243; 1971, pp. 238, 284).

Most introductory texts use the 'cobweb diagram' to illustrate what may happen if a state of excess demand arises in a market: widespread optimism can result in excessive capacity creation and losses for all concerned, whereas payoffs to competitive investments can be handsome if caution leads to relatively small expansions in capacity. However, such texts rarely seek to explain how or when chaos is likely to be avoided. In his discussion of the problem in the context of a wartime economy Scitovsky suggests that it is likely to be most acute following a sudden, major price change, and when the authorities encourage the prompt adjustment of production plans to the new conditions (Scitovsky, Shaw and Tashis, 1951, pp. 272–4). He also anticipates Richardson by noting the co-ordinating role of nonmarket sources of information about production plans, such as might exist in government publications and trade journals. Elsewhere, he raises the possibility that a history of past co-ordination disappointments might eventually produce sufficient hesitancy on the part of some producers as to facilitate an orderly, sequential expansion of capacity (1951b, p. 238; 1971, p. 234). Recently, however, (1990, p. 142) he has supported Richardson's view that barriers to entry associated with market power may serve a socially beneficial role by limiting the number of possible players in a market and allowing incumbent price-makers to respond to quantity signals such as their own waiting lists.

Complementary investments are discussed by Scitovsky in his work on balanced growth (1959/1964), European economic integration (1958, p. 19) and external economies (1954/1964, pp. 78–83). Here, one sees him rather moving away from the idea of a system tending toward equilibrium. Like Myrdal (1957), he recognizes that if one firm's investment expenditure improves the profitability of its customers' activities (for example, by reducing the cost of their inputs), then the latter may undertake investments which have beneficial repercussions for others, and so on, in a virtuous circle.

However, each firm will normally be thinking only of its own profits when it decides how much to invest. It is easy to see how inflationary bottlenecks could arise in multistage production and distribution processes if producers at one stage in the chain only make tentative, incremental expansions of their operations because they are not sure of the price elasticity of demand for their output or because they are afraid of excessive capacity creation. The only benefits likely to come of such bottlenecks are innovations designed to reduce the need for the inputs that are in short supply (1959/1964, p. 108). These considerations made Scitovsky pessimistic about the results of investment decision-making in systems involving large numbers of specialist producers, leading him to see potential benefits in moves towards indicative planning and the integration of decision-making units in order to 'internalize' external economies.

The notion of internalization is now commonplace in industrial economics, where mergers and moves toward vertical integration are seen as the responses to difficulties in using the market to handle externalities. But such perspectives owe little to Scitovsky: despite his pioneering use of the term, he did not attempt to follow the lead of Coase (1937) and portray the firm as an institution which uses an internal managerial command system for dealing with co-ordination problems. It is a pity that when he was preparing the revision of *Welfare and Competition* (1971) he did not take heed of Graaf's (1965) comments about the narrowness of his earlier work on externalities. Had he done so, something more akin to Williamson's (1975) analysis may have been the result.

Williamson's work is worth mentioning at this point for another reason: there are other aspects of Scitovsky's views about the nature of market processes which closely resemble key themes in Williamson's writings, but with no reference being made to Scitovsky, and vice versa. One obvious case is Scitovsky's (1950/1964) view that ignorance is a source of oligopoly power, to which he has returned in some of his latest work (1990). His early discussions focus on the relationship between firms and the buyers of their products, noting how incumbent producers often try to deter customers from switching to new, unknown suppliers by pursuing advertising policies which highlight the complexity of the product and its production process, along with the resources needed to design it and provide after-sales back-up. Potential competitors may thus be deterred by the marketing costs which they will need to incur if they are to build up customer goodwill (1950/1964, p. 207). Forty years later, we find him arguing that 'today, superior knowledge and earlier knowledge are the main sources of monopoly power' (1990, p. 138). However, we do not find him attacking monopoly power in general, even though, by extending his early observations about the growing importance of highly complex, differentiated goods (1941c, pp. 679–80) and the tendency of buyers to judge quality by price (1945), we might nowadays expect that it may take more than just a competitive price to enter someone else's market. Rather, he offers a more intricate, evolutionary view of the competitive processes.

Modern-day consumers may find it difficult to make choices between complex products but, as workers, they often enjoy information advantages that go with experience in a specialized job. They have countervailing power in so far as they know more about their jobs than do their employers or would-be occupants of their job-slots. Scitovsky does not note similarities between his views about the consequences of specialization and those of Williamson (1975). Nor does he recognize the possibility that workers may be able to enjoy total benefits in excess of their transfer fees if they can conceal the fact that they are working below their potential: it is indeed surprising to find no discussion of Leibenstein's famous (1966) work on 'X-inefficiency' in either the 1971 edition of *Welfare and Competition* or his more recent works on the performance of economic systems. (The closest he comes to an implicit discussion of X-inefficiency is a recognition (1971, pp. 463–4) that *managers* may need to be motivated by the pressure of competition if their firms are to achieve technological efficiency.) However, his later work does look more penetratingly at dynamic efficiency in a somewhat Schumpeterian way. He emphasizes that, although the complexity of modern products and production processes may give firms information advantages over their customers and potential competitors, these advantages are often the result of innovations which, in time, others may copy. In the absence of a prospect of temporary monopoly profits, firms might not develop the products for which customers may initially be asked to pay a premium price. But firms may also be unlikely to be very innovative if they can hold on to their information advantages indefinitely. From this standpoint it appears that patent rights are necessary (1985/1986, p. 98), along with anti-trust legislation to promote nonprice competition and regulations concerning truth in advertising (1990, p. 146).

PRICE-MAKERS AND PRICE-TAKERS

Scitovsky's first book *Welfare and Competition* (1951b; rev. ed, 1971) introduced the terms 'price-maker' and 'price-taker' in economics. The analysis of price determination in his book is an extension of his earlier articles (1945/1964, 1950/1964) on the effects of incomplete information on market processes, and this analysis has itself been extended in more recent articles (1978a, 1985/1986, 1990). But it is useful to begin a discussion of his views in this area much as he does in his book, by recognizing that since each buyer must trade with a seller, four types of trading relationships are possible.

One is the case assumed in theories of perfect competition, where both sides of the market treat the price as parametric; it leaves unanswered the question of who actually sets the price. Though he accepts the idea that perfectly competitive markets are valuable as a reference point for discussions of efficiency, Scitovsky emphasizes that there are few real-world examples of markets in which both buyers and sellers are price-takers; these are confined largely to commodity exchanges in which large numbers of expert buyers and sellers confront each other in a centralized trading area. A second case is that of bargaining, where both buyers and sellers try to act as price-makers, putting forward take-it-or-leave-it suggestions as to the terms on which trade should be conducted. The practical importance of bargaining is limited by the negotiation costs it involves – in terms of both time and investment in the skills required to know which concessions it would be wise to make. A third possibility, nowadays most familiar in the context of corporate takeovers, involves a buyer stating a price for a specified commodity and offering to buy as much or as little as sellers are prepared to make available. Finally, and most importantly for practical purposes, there are exchanges in which the seller makes a take-it-or-leave-it offer and the buyer decides how many, if any, units to purchase.

Scitovsky sees the question of who takes the initiative in setting the price as one to be answered with reference to information problems. In real-world instances of perfectly competitive markets both buyers and sellers are professionals and the commodities in terms of which they are dealing are standardized. There is thus no confusion as to whether or not changes in price reflect changes in quality rather than altered market conditions. The geographically centralized nature of trading means it is practically impossible for an individual seller to get away with an attempt to charge a market price higher than the going rate: it is easy for buyers to check price offers. Bargaining, likewise, will normally involve experts on both sides of the market: there is little point in trying to engage in bargaining if one has no basis for deciding whether to accept an offer as the best that one is likely to get, or to continue to try to beat one's opponent down. Costs of acquiring information will be relatively small where buyers and sellers operate in close proximity to each other and frequently have occasion to deal with each other. But they will tend to become prohibitive if (a) an individual only wishes infrequently to trade a particular commodity, especially if its quality is difficult to judge; and (b) there are many transactors with whom potential deals could be negotiated before it becomes clear where the best deal is to be obtained. Hence Scitovsky predicts one-sided price-making behaviour in markets for non-standardized commodities in which both the number of buyers and sellers and their expertise are not evenly matched. (If both sides of a market lack expertise, Scitovsky predicts the emergence of intermediaries.) The price-takers will be those whose numbers are largest, for the economies of gathering expertise are on the side with the smaller number of traders. The specialists forgo potential costs and benefits associated with striking individual bargains and instead use their expertise as a basis for selecting sufficiently profitable price/product packages to offer to the non-specialist market as a whole.

If non-specialists become passive quantity adjusters rather than incurring the costs of becoming expert traders and haggling over prices, they still need a basis for deciding to whom they should give their custom when they are unsure of the relative qualities of the goods that are on offer or the prices at which goods of a given quality normally change hands. Their relative ignorance and reluctance to risk disappointments limits the range of situations in which price-makers will opt to compete on the basis of price. Yet it also means that competition on the basis of product quality is by no means assured of success. For example, a reduction in price unambiguously signals a better deal only to buyers who are regularly incurring the costs of checking on conditions in the market and who therefore know what the previous price was; if infrequent buyers use current prices as indicators of quality, the price reduction can lead to reduced sales. Similarly, if 'the proof of the pudding is in the eating' it may be very difficult to signal in a credible manner that better value for money is being offered via a quality upgrade. The situation is very different if new models are introduced at the same price as those they supersede and can *easily* be seen to offer more – particularly if the old ones continue to be offered but at a lower price than before (1945/1964, pp. 195–7).

If we compare *Welfare and Competition* with Scitovsky's recent (1985/ 1986, 1990) work it is evident that he has only lately recognized a key element in the answer to this question of how price-makers might rationally compete if uncertainty makes value-for-money judgements difficult for consumers to make. He now highlights the relatively limited success of discount warehouses that offer little by way of customer services, and focuses on those aspects of non-price competition which involve the price-makers in *providing their customers with the information* they will need to make risk-free judgements and with services that it would be more expensive for the price-takers to procure for themselves. Relevant elements here are warranties and professional accreditations of suppliers; the variety of goods in stock and the displays, comfort and opening hours of the shopping environment; well-informed staff who readily make refunds and do not try to pressurize people into buying; and the availability of credit and insurance. This view of how frictions between buyers and sellers can be lessened is close to that found in the marketing literature. But Scitovsky (1985/1986, p. 104, my italics) surely goes too far when he asserts that these aspects of non-price competition make shopping a '*completely* frictionless and even enjoyable task'.

INFLATION: ITS CONSEQUENCES, CAUSES AND POSSIBLE CURES

A good deal of Scitovsky's more recent output applies his views about the competitive process to the economics of rising prices (1978a, 1978b, 1982, 1983). This research has been concerned primarily with the causes of inflation, rather than its effects which are considered in his earlier work (1941a/ 1964; Scitovsky and Scitovsky, 1964). One is left with a rather mixed picture of the effects of inflation, but this is to be preferred to the typical economist's stance of assuming it is a problem without bothering to stop to consider why. On the one hand, we are told that 'relative prices are a very poor index of the relative urgency of wants when the price-level as a whole is galloping up or down' (1941a/1964, p. 46), and that, since inflation is unlikely to involve simultaneous equiproportional movements in all prices, it is likely to lead to managers and consumers having to spend more time studying market conditions and to feel a greater need to use intermediaries (Scitovsky and Scitovsky, 1964, pp. 460–1). On the other hand, Scitovsky and Scitovsky, (1964, pp. 460, 463) note how wage lags in times of inflation may aid economic growth by increasing the profits share, with inflation facilitating relative price adjustments in a world in which wages are downwardly sticky. They also (p. 459) highlight the difficulties of finding instances in which moderate inflation has caused resource misallocation and suggest that such costs were not spectacular even during Germany's hyperinflation. Here, they may be paying insufficient attention to the possibility that difficulties involved in sizing up future relative prices in an environment of uneven inflation may lead entrepreneurs to avoid investing in the wrong line of activity by not investing at all, or to focus their attention on the gains to be had from financial speculation rather than from the creation of new physical capacity (cf. Leijonhufvud, 1977).

In analysing the causes of inflation, Scitovsky focuses on incompatibilities within the economic system. He sees excess demand inflation in a pretty conventional way, except that he does stress its tendency to arise due to disruptive events on the supply side (such the diversion of workers to fight in a war, or bottlenecks in the supply of capital goods) rather than an increase in monetary demand (1982, pp. 1–3). What most of us call 'cost–push inflation' Scitovsky thinks of as 'excess claims inflation' which is due to an incompatibility between prices of factors and products and which can occur regardless of the level of aggregate demand. His thinking about the latter appears originally to have been inspired by work of scholars such as Schultze (1959) and Eatwell *et al.* (1974) which centred on the role of differences in productivity or demand growth among sectors of an economy, and on the desire of workers to maintain their wage relativities.

Firms that are doing particularly well may be able to pay more to their workers without increasing their prices. However, other workers may then insist on similar increases to maintain parity even if their living standards have not been threatened. The latters' employers may only be able to maintain their real mark-ups if they can pass on their higher costs into higher prices. This in turn restores the abilities of the leaders to concede higher wages and so the process continues. As Scitovsky (1983, p. 224) points out, this hardly fits in with general equilibrium analysis. The general equilibrium framework would not lead one to expect chronic inflation, but instead the dissipation of any price-rising disturbance as lateral processes of substitution led it to affect more and more markets. Rather, 'Everything we know about inflation suggests that ... a multiplier-type vertical transmission process must be at work, which generalizes an isolated price increase into a general price increase and gathers enough momentum to keep the process going.' The key to explaining why a process of inflation keeps up its momentum lies in the presence of asymmetric market power between buyers and sellers and the fact that buyers in one market are often sellers in other markets (1982, p. 6; 1983, pp. 229–32).

Scitovsky's insight here involves an application of his price-maker/price-taker analysis. For example, suppose producers are price-makers in their product markets and opt to increase their prices. If they are also price-makers in their labour markets they can prevent workers from attempting obtain higher wages to restore their living standards. A change in income distribution is effected via a one-off hike in the price level, not ongoing inflation. Similarly, inflation would not be expected in an economy in which producers were price-takers in both their product and factor markets: faced with tougher terms on which labour or other inputs could be obtained, firms would simply have to suffer reduced profit margins and/or cut back their rates of output to viable levels. However, all too often producers are price-makers only in their product markets, and workers (or other factor suppliers) – the producers' victims in the product markets – can retaliate because they call the tune in factor markets.

A price-making producer that is presently setting its price by equating its marginal cost and marginal revenue will find it costly to concede workers' demands for higher pay: at the present price the price elasticity of demand must be greater than one, so a raising of that price in an attempt to recoup higher marginal costs will be only partially successful (1982, p. 5). Ideally, therefore, the producer should stand firm, but it is unlikely to be operating in a first-best environment in which it can coolly make a wage offer on a take-it-or-leave-it basis. Even if it judges that its workers would eventually give in and accept its original terms, it must take account of the costs of disruption that they could impose in the interim.

Rather than discussing the ways in which protagonists bargaining over factor prices can impose costs on each other (for such a discussion, see Tylecote, 1981), Scitovsky simply argues that if such a producer opts to concede demands for higher pay it may be indicative of a second-best solution which the firm has adopted because its market power is greater in its product market than in its factor market. He might also have been wise to add some discussion of the likelihood of the firm expecting its demand curve to shift to the right. This could happen due to (a) its rivals making similar concessions, and/or (b) the demand for its product being affected by increases in nominal purchasing power as a result of wage inflation in the economy as a whole. Both of these factors could reduce or altogether eliminate the loss of real profits resulting from payment of higher factor prices.

An implication of Scitovsky's analysis is that it may be fruitful to explore factors affecting countervailing power to understand why inflationary tendencies differ on a cross-sectional or time series basis (here, too, it may usefully be read in conjunction with the excellent book by Tylecote, 1981, which not only has many parallels in theoretical terms with Scitovsky's bargaining-oriented approach but also includes a wealth of comparative institutional case studies). For example, we may consider explaining the increasing pushfulness of workers in the late 1960s and 1970s in terms of 'increasing affluence and social security having led to conflicting power relations in different markets' (1978b, p. 228): compared with their forebears who were living financially on the margin, modern-day affluent workers will be more willing to embark on industrial action that may involve the risk of a lengthy strike. The willingness of an individual firm to give in to its workers' demands will change as its market situation changes: the more discretion it has over the prices that it charges, and the more market goodwill it stands to lose if it suffers supply disruptions, the more willingly it may be expected to give ground to its workers.

Changes in the technology of production may also affect the willingness of management to keep on the side of their workers by granting pay increases – even if they see themselves as wagemakers because their workers are not tending to engage in collective bargaining. Here, Scitovsky (1982, p. 6; 1983, pp. 236–7) contrasts old-style, repetition-based factory work and work in modern, mechanized environments where workers enjoy positions of responsibility and have to be attentive, always on the lookout for unexpected breakdowns or lapses of quality. The latter situation is one in which the worker's task cannot be fully prespecified in a hiring contract and where it may be rather difficult to find a replacement if the worker quits. It is thus particularly important that management maintain the morale of workers in such positions. Firms in leading sectors may be able to do so by offering better remuneration packages without reducing their profits to sub-normal levels; less prosperous firms will then find themselves having to follow if they are to maintain the morale of their workers and hence their productivity levels. All this may happen without such workers needing to belong to a trade union or threatening strike action.

To the extent that inflation arises from excess claims on an economy, measures aimed at reducing it will only succeed if they can, directly or indirectly, reduce the sum of claims to realizable levels. Scitovsky (1978b, p. 229; 1982, p. 8) argues that if restrictive monetary policies are not merely to lead to higher levels of unemployment their beneficial effects on inflation are likely to arise as a result of their making people more cautious and choosy – not merely because this will mean less-aggressive bargaining by workers but also because fussy buyers reduce oligopolistic restraint and encourage research, development and innovation. Though this might appear to suggest that, in the long run, monetarist policies may achieve their desired results by their effects on incentives, we do not find Scitovsky concluding that a Thatcher/Reagan-style of policy towards inflation is inherently the most desirable. He recognizes that an environment of tight money is likely to deter investments aimed at encroaching on the territory of other market participants and that there are other ways of stepping up competitive pressures in an economic system that may not involve the creation of 'short-run' unemployment – measures such as more aggressive anti-trust policies, and assistance to would-be market entrants who might otherwise find their access to know-how rather restricted. However, in the light of his (1990) work, we must note that policies aimed at reducing excess claims inflation by reducing price-makers' market power need to be used with caution: innovation may suffer if the ease of entry makes would-be innovators pessimistic about the chances of getting an adequate return on their investments.

INTERNATIONAL ECONOMICS

Scitovsky has made a wide variety of contributions in the general area of international economics: on the theory of tariffs (1942/1964, 1987b); on the effects of import substitution policies (Little, Scitovsky and Scott, 1970); on economic integration (1958, 1964, ch. 6); and on the more general operations of the international monetary system (1964, ch. 17, 1965, 1966, 1969).

The usefulness of this work to economists in the 1990s varies considerably. Those who might hope to find his 1950s thoughts on European economic integration to be of great assistance in analysing the possible effects of the creation of the unified market within the European Community in 1992 are likely to find his thinking rather dated: for example, a modern-day investigation would pay much more attention to the effects of multinational firms and to the ways in which licensing, subcontracting and joint venture arrangements may be used to achieve a reasonably even spread of growth around a set of small economies each of which is below the minimum efficient scale required for balanced growth. Given Scitovsky's great insights into the ways in which information problems affect competitive processes, I also find it rather surprising that his writings on trade are not themselves integrated with the dynamic, knowledge-based theories of trade produced by economists such as Posner (1961) and Vernon (1966). Where I find his writings on international economics at their most impressive is in the general area of the management of payments disequilibria. In particular, his delightfully titled satire 'International Payments in Laputia' (1964, ch. 17) is a remarkably clear analysis of the deflationary bias of the world economy, similar in vision to subsequent contributions by Robinson (1966) and Stewart (1983). It retains its freshness and relevance despite being written during the Bretton Woods era when exchange rates were difficult to revise.

The central problem with today's international economy, as with the Bretton Woods system, is that the financial community has been unwilling to recognize that it could be far more efficient to remove payments imbalances by forcing action on the part of nations with financial surpluses, rather than by those that suffer from deficits. The latter have typically lacked bargaining power in international negotiations, since bankers regard deficits as signs of faulty economic policies or economic weakness. Bankers fail to see that a payments surplus involves 'a squandering and improductive hoarding of national resources' (1964, p. 269). Moreover, in addition to attributing blame in a one-sided manner, money managers tend to be more concerned with price stability than with full employment; yet they fail to see the role of a balance of payments deficit as an anti-inflation device in a fully employed economy. Hence their inclination towards insisting that countries in deficit eliminate the imbalance by cutting domestic activity levels, rather than suggesting that countries in surplus should take steps to increase their activity levels and hence their imports. If countries with surpluses expanded their economies, the deficit nations would only need to reduce their domestic demand levels if they were already at full employment or if the additional export demand would make them hit the full employment output ceiling.

In addition to arguing that pressure should be placed on surplus countries to dispose of their surplus reserves, Scitovsky proposed an ingenious new role for the International Monetary Fund as a benevolent issuer of an international reserve currency. He saw a larger supply of international liquidity as necessary so that deficit countries can weather their difficulties until the surplus nations wake up to the consequences of their surpluses in terms of higher inflation or the under-employment of their resources. Some might argue that, since the time he was writing, the development of the eurocurrency market has removed the need for such a reserve currency, for it is now far easier for nations to continue to run deficits – too easy, in fact, given the international debt crisis that has emerged. However, an IMF reconstituted as Scitovsky proposed over a quarter of a century ago appears well placed for helping to sort out that mess that has emerged in the interim. His new version of the IMF would put its international reserve currency into circulation in ways which would benefit poor nations: some would enter in the form of aid to these nations, some would be used to buy on the open market securities representing debts of the poor countries. The IMF could put upward pressure on the currencies of surplus countries by choosing to do its open-market buying of bonds in their money markets.

Such measures for the correction of international payments disequilibria are based on the premise that the disequilibria are 'the joint responsibility of all countries affected' (Scitovsky, 1969, pp. 183–4). As such, they are open to abuse by countries that opportunistically choose to 'live beyond their means' in the expectation that their deficits will ultimately be absorbed by the IMF. However, flagrant behaviour of this sort could be responded to by the IMF in its choice of markets in which to inject the international reserve currency.

TOWARDS THE INTEGRATION OF PSYCHOLOGY AND ECONOMICS

At the age at which most academics are thinking of retiring, Scitovsky chose to challenge established economic doctrine by writing *The Joyless Economy* (1976), a book which calls for the integration of economics and psychology. Readers of the preface to that book could be forgiven for thinking his belief that economists would be unwise to continue to try to get along without psychology was something which had emerged only in the early 1970s. However, since he actually raised psychological issues on a number of occasions in his earlier work, we might be wiser to see his controversial book as representing the culmination of a process of mental adjustment that had been going on for many years. To judge from the preface to his (1986) collection of papers and from his (forthcoming) essay on his life philosophy, his fascination with the psychology of human satisfaction probably originated in his decidedly non-puritanical upbringing in Hungary, which contrasted strongly with the lifestyle he was later to observe in the United States. The idea that many Americans are best seen as puritan income maximizers, not utility maximizers, certainly crops up frequently in his writings on motivation and welfare. However, it was the issue of price expectations that provided the first sign of his recognition that economists may need to take account of psychology.

In one of his earliest papers, on unemployment and inflation, we find Scitovsky (1941a/1964) considering the possibility of what we would now call a 'real balance effect' or 'Pigou effect' (after Pigou's work, also of 1941) and stressing the role of the community's psychology in the determination of the general price level and orderly functioning of the economic system. Scitovsky pointed out that a changing price level would fail to exert a stabilizing effect on the level of real aggregate demand if its initial impact on the value of money balances led to expectations of a further change in the same direction. But this would not always occur, since the 'limit to the degree of price-flexibility, beyond which it would destroy the belief in a normal price-level seems to be analogous to the "threshold of consciousness" which must be surpassed by a sensation to become perceptible to our senses' (1941a/1964, p. 50). In other words, people would only become aware of the changing value of money if price movements become 'very general or very drastic' (p. 52); otherwise, price changes will be seen merely as temporary fluctuations. So long as the threshold is not crossed, a belief in normal prices would tend to be self-sustaining, the more so in the presence of technical and organizational factors that make prices difficult to change.

A couple of years later Scitovsky was questioning economists' assumptions about the motivation of entrepreneurs. The idea of a profit-maximizing entrepreneur involves a lexicographic kind of psychology: a single-minded concern with making money, with no willingness to hold back from the pursuit of profit in order to find time to consume the fruits of one's business success (1943/1964, pp. 170–2). It might be in order to assume such a way of thinking in cases where puritanical backgrounds led entrepreneurs to desire money as an index of their success in life rather than as something to be spent. But until empirical investigations were undertaken one would have to recognize that the population of entrepreneurs might include many, even a majority, who, with rising success, would tend to relax their efforts, either because their wants were satiable or because they wanted time for leisure.

That this critique of the notion of profit maximization needed further development was evidenced in his (1958, p. 23) work on European integration, which saw him pondering the effects of freeing trade between nations with very different work ethics: if other European Community members might *have* to adopt German work ethics, at the cost of lost leisure, in order

not to be swamped by German competition, then one might equally well argue that a puritanical entrepreneur within an individual economy would tend to force rivals to adopt a similar life philosophy or go out of business. In the European case, Scitovsky failed to note the slack permitted to leisure-orientated nations by exchange rate adjustments, but by the second edition of *Welfare and Competition* he was more careful to point out that entrepreneurs would need some protection of their market positions if they wished to take a more relaxed approach to business (1971, p. 153; contrast with 1951b, p. 147). Given his insights about the origins of market slack, it is strange that he did not make more use of behavioural or managerial theories of the firm (such as Cyert and March, 1963; Williamson, 1964) in his subsequent discussions of welfare: a less taut competitive environment may work wonders for entrepreneurial well-being at the expense of that of consumers and yet neither *Welfare and Competition* nor *The Joyless Economy* includes an index entry on stress, executive or otherwise.

Despite Scitovsky's willingness to embrace psychology, he has made little use of the literature associated with the work of Herbert Simon which abandons maximization altogether on the grounds of its logical impossibility and cognitive complexity. This is surprising, given his interest in the role of information in the competitive process. It is particularly puzzling since he came close to a satisficing perspective at a very early stage in his career (1945): in his analysis of how people decide what to purchase in economies whose growing complexity is making them increasingly bewildered, he suggested that buyers rely on reputation and assume that quality is a function of price or of the size, age or financial success of the manufacturer; and that the more affluent consumers are, the more casual they are likely to be in their shopping activities.

His neglect of the literature on bounded rationality should not be taken to imply that he was oblivious of links between psychology, complexity and human welfare. On the contrary: when he later returned to the question of the implications of the increasing complexity of modern economies, he actually (1964, pp. 227–9) drew on the work of Erich Fromm and other members of the American neo-Freudian school of psychologists to paint a picture of parents who are at a loss to answer their children's questions about the nature of every day objects, and who, as a result of increasing specialization in the workplace, feel dependent on distant officials and gigantic, mysterious organizations. But he did not address a question that mainstream economists might want to ask in order to avoid facing up to the need to include psychology in welfare analysis: if people do feel alienated by modern society and technology, should we not expect media entrepreneurs to come to their rescue by offering information-orientated television programmes rather than soap operas and gameshows?

The links between macroeconomics, psychology and welfare were high-lighted in his joint paper with his (then) wife Anne Scitovsky (1964) for the Commission on Money and Credit. They note the capacity of inflation to provoke anxiety, particularly for the middle classes who find their savings being eroded as speculators make quick bucks (p. 468). The importance of upbringing in shaping how well people cope with unemployment is canvassed via the suggestion that those with a puritan ethic will find unemployment a particularly distressing experience because they lack skills for coping with enforced idleness (pp. 433–5, 469). Even those who do not lose their jobs may suffer reduced welfare in times of unemployment in so far as they fear that they too could join the ranks of the unemployed and suffer social humiliation. Feelings that one is unwanted and of resentment towards the economy will be most acute if unemployment is concentrated on an ethnic basis. Worse still, if unemployment reduces feelings of independence, self-assurance and self-reliance, or if policymakers do not try to reduce the distress caused by unemployment associated with economic transitions, then rates of innovation and growth may suffer.

GROWTH AND WELFARE

It is the question of the *effects* of growth on welfare that provides the focus for Scitovsky's (1976, 1986) most extensive use of psychology. However, I must stress that by 'extensive' I mean the range over which he has sought to apply psychology, not the range of inputs from psychology that he uses. As in his early discussions of complexity and economic development, he makes no use of the extensive literature on decision heuristics and biases; and he is seemingly unaware of branches of cognitive and social psychology which complement his perspectives on how people go about their lives (cf. my review of the broader literature in Earl, 1990). This has made his contributions easier for orthodox economists to digest and less of a challenge to their work but, despite this, his ideas are yet to filter into the core of modern welfare economics.

Scitovsky's particular focus is on economic implications of Daniel Berlyne's (1960, 1971) optimal arousal model of behaviour, a stance which he seeks to justify with reference to the empirical work that has demonstrated the model's robustness in a variety of contexts. The essence of the model is neatly summarized by Middleton (1986, p. 397), in one of the few papers in an economics journal which attempts to follow Scitovsky's lead and even uses it as a basis for econometric work. Middleton notes that the optimal arousal model 'hypothesizes that a certain general type of utility is a function of the degree to which the distribution of events in an experiential

"frame" is "new" in the subject's experience. Utility increases with "subjective novelty" up to a point, then decreases, and then is replaced by disutility and anxiety. Subjects prefer intermediate degrees of novelty.'

Scitovsky illustrated this hypothesis with reference to a diverse range of examples such as tolerance of types of music and other art forms (originally discussed in his 1972/1986 paper), theme parks, gambling, fashionable clothing, and even economics texts such as his own which would be ignored if either saying nothing new or too different from the mainstream. Middleton (1986, p. 409) has gone further, suggesting that changes in the amount of new information flowing in financial markets may affect the mood of investors: 'It may be very pleasurable to trade in a market with a certain amount of dynamic surprise, while highly surprising markets are known to cause investors anxiety.'

Awareness of the extent of novelty in a situation that one is confronting affects one's level of physiological arousal and the sensation of excitement that one feels. In his (1981/1986) paper, Scitovsky portrays the effects of novelty on arousal as arising in so far as a stimulus is strong enough to threaten or challenge one's position and demand that one acts. He sees uncertainty about one's physical or intellectual capacity for dealing with the new situation as a major precondition for any situation to represent a challenge, whether to one's life, limb, health, economic well-being, prestige, status or self respect. All this fits in very well with the recent psychology literature on stress (such as Hanson, 1987; Hurrell *et al.* (eds), 1988). Our bodies have limited capacities for dealing with high levels of arousal. Sustained challenges over long periods lead to 'burnout'. On the other hand, people will 'rustout' if they do not choose to place themselves in a sufficiently challenging environment. For people to function most efficiently in physical and mental terms they need to position themselves somewhere between these two extremes. So long as they are not fully constrained by their environments, people can choose how much excitement/arousal/stress to confront.

Scitovsky argues that people in relatively primitive societies did not need to seek out excitement: it was often thrust upon them by difficulties in meeting their basic needs. However, the major uncertainties of life were made bearable by its normally sedate pace and the availability of time to spend engaging in folk art and cultural rituals. In advanced economies, by contrast, people may find it necessary to set out to find excitement in so far as their jobs become boringly repetitive whilst providing them with economic security. They can seek to meet this need for excitement by trying new forms of entertainment; in do-it-yourself or travel; by switching, as many are, from being mere spectators to become sports participants or political activists; or by indulging in gambling, violence (whether as participants or by watching it on screen) and drugs.

Many of these activities display similarities with work, in that they are both rewarding and onerous. But they vary considerably in their social implications, depending on the kinds of externalities they involve: the differences between participation in adult education classes and other cultural and sporting activities, as opposed to vandalism, violence and coping with addicitive forms of stimulation, are so obvious as not to need elaboration. These externalities point to a need for policies aimed at crowding out antisocial activities with substitutes that provide risk, danger and excitement and at the same time have positive spill-over effects on the rest of society. Scitovsky (1981/1986, p. 134) places a lot of faith in changes in relative prices as a means to produce such substitutions, claiming that 'There is no reason to believe that the poor practice violence rather than dangerous sports because they prefer it and not because it is cheaper.' I suspect that major propaganda expenditure is also necessary to realign attitudes and reduce the extent to which people conform to antisocial pressures from their peers.

In addition to varying between societies at different stages of development, preferences in respect of excitement may vary through time for an individual (even an elderly person who normally leads a sedate life may be attracted by a challenge involving a burst of great uncertainty so long as its duration is certain to be short) and between individuals at similar life-cycle stages. The latter possibility arises because the way people feel about a given situation will depend on whether they believe they possess the skills required to cope with it. For example, someone who has grown up in a Swiss mountain village might not be greatly aroused by the prospect of skiing, whereas to someone who has never tried to ski before the very idea of a skiing holiday could seem far from ideal as a way of winding down. Choice is thus path-dependent, affected both by past experiences resulting from choices based on the exercise of personal imagination and by the social and informational environment in which the individual comes under pressure to try particular activities and picks up ideas about what may be exciting.

The choice of how much arousal to aim for is, in Scitovsky's view, a choice about how *comfortable* one's life is to be. How *pleasurable* it will be is an altogether different matter, for experimental work by neurophysiologists suggests that feelings of pleasure arise as a result of *changes* in one's *level* of arousal, particularly changes which move the level of arousal towards its optimum. The distinction is a major one for normative purposes: to experience pleasure, one must first have sacrificed comfort (by choice or force of circumstances) and moved away from one's position of optimal arousal.

This conflict was already much on his mind during the preparation of the second edition of *Welfare and Competition*: there (1971, p. 244), he notes that 'Instinctive behaviour is not always the one that yields most pleasure; and when it is not, self discipline and the sophistication of going against one's instinct are required to obtain the best satisfaction.' Consumers may thus feel that despite their increasing affluence their lives are not particularly pleasureable – are joyless – without realizing that this is the result of their having chosen to spend their extra money and time in ways which only involve them in facing as much novelty as is necessary to keep themselves at an optimal level of arousal. The consumers who find that increasing affluence makes their lives more satisfying may be either the ones for whom it provides the means to increase the amount of novelty in their lives and bring them nearer to their optimal level, or those who use greater affluence as a means of obtaining periods of stimulation in which they depart temporarily from their positions of greatest comfort.

THE AMERICAN WAY OF LIFE

Had Scitovsky suggested that economists should merely try to use physiological psychology to make better sense of differences in the behaviour of individuals and as a basis for discussions concerning matters of public policy such as merit goods, *The Joyless Economy* would have raised controversy merely because of its challenge to mainstream methods of theorizing. However, he also raised the hackles of his peers by choosing to use the psychological material, along with a mass of comparative statistics and his long-held view of the United States as an overwhelmingly puritanical society, as a basis for contrasting the lifestyles and feelings of satisfaction of Americans and their more bohemian European counterparts. Criticisms of how he did this may have served a useful smokescreen role for those who were unsettled by his message that economics could do with an infusion of psychology.

Economists should have been well-prepared for his lengthy critique of American lifestyles since, a few years before, he had already set out his views in three articles (1972/1986, 1973a/1986, 1973b/1986) – albeit with the first two being based more on the implications of puritanism rather than on an extensive psychological discussion. His concern there was with the tendency for American consumers to hand over passively to producers or intermediaries the key decisions concerning the quality of goods and the basis for choosing them – the result being a diminution in the range of goods on offer as producers sought to mould tastes in favour of products that would enable them to obtain economies of scale. A lack of education in matters of taste in respect of leisure pursuits – the result of a puritan education focused on the development of workplace skills – resulted in consumption being a defensive activity, aimed at avoiding 'pain, effort, discomfort, boredom, the unknown and the uncertain' (1972/1986, p. 41) and in the stereotypical *nouveau-riche* style of life of affluent Americans.

The detailed portrayal of the American lifestyle offered in *The Joyless Economy* was brilliantly summed up by Peacock (1976, pp. 1278–9) in his review of the book:

> Look around you Yankees and see what a miserable lot you are, wholly inexpert in the art of living, laughing and loving. The normal ambiance for a meal resembles the atmosphere of a filling station – it frequently is a filling station – rather than a pleasant communication of connoisseurs. Speech is for rapidity of communication and not leisurely mind-stretching converse. You have no music in your soul. All that leisure time you have created by labor saving devices is used up in being glued to the TV, and when social pressures demand the allocation of some of it to the European Grand Tour, your cultural background is so exposed in its inadequacy that you seek protection in the encapsulated package deal, only too glad at the end to return to the homelier pleasures of coffee and apple pie. Travel broadens your feet but not your mind. Your lack of faith in the quality of your domestic decision-making drives you into the arms of an array of predators, such as home decorators and psychiatrists. In short, the Puritan Ethic haunts you ...

Non-Yankees may find it difficult not to have some sympathy with Scitovsky's imagery and yet agree with Peacock's criticism that it is misleading since it seems to treat the whole of the United States as a single unit. Mainstream economists would also be expected to find comfort in Peacock's observation that, contrary to the impression Scitovsky gives in his theoretical analysis, there do exist sophisticated neoclassical models which recognize sources of (dis)satisfaction derived from intangibles such as social interaction and the nature of work environments (p. 1279).

Aufhauser's (1976, p. 913) criticism that Scitovsky's analysis ignores alternative historical and institutional explanations is potentially more powerful in methodological terms. To make this point Aufhauser used the fact that Americans eat less fresh fruit and vegetables than the French:

> The book would have us think that this results from our Yankee avoidance of gustatory pleasures. But if the author had thought for a moment in historical or institutional terms, it would not have been difficult to find that Americans' consumption of fresh produce has been declining ever since the big agribusiness companies began taking over that sector of the economy (U.S. Department of Commerce, *Historical Statistics of the U.S.*, Washington, 1961, p. 186). According to Scitovsky's line of reasoning, however, the decline would have to be attributed, absurdly, to a revival of puritan anti-sensualism during the period.

Given that the author of *The Joyless Economy* had not long since revised *Welfare and Competition*, it is most surprising that, in looking at the state of consumer dissatisfaction, aspects of industrial organization were not raised in conjunction with the socio-psychological material. However, it may also be said that Aufhauser leaves open the question of why the agribusiness giants could get away with their policies. If the typical American consumer were less passive and more inclined to connoisseurship, food consumption patterns might well have been very different.

UNEMPLOYMENT IN AFFLUENT SOCIETIES

Since Scitovsky's formative years as an economist coincided with the unemployment of the Great Depression and the emergence of Keynes's theoretical analysis of its causes, it is not surprising that he has maintained a concern with the origins of unemployment and a broadly Keynesian perspective on what might be done about it. He has always been careful to point out that standard approaches to the notion of efficiency are essentially the 'The Economics of a Fully Employed Economy' (this was the subtitle to the first edition of *Welfare and Competition*, and its absence from the second edition is actually the result of a typesetting omission that he failed to spot at the proof stage; the message is still very clear from its opening chapter). Rather than seeing stagflation as implying the need for a return to the sort of equilibrium analysis advocated by many economists of the Right, he has looked for features of modern economies that cause aggregate demand and supply problems which Keynes did not anticipate. His distinctive perspective only appears to bolster mainstream views through its suggestion that status-conscious people are reluctant to accept jobs that they see as beneath their stations in life (1986, p. 121 and ch. 11). In conjunction with subsidies for high-level training and the availability of unemployment benefits, this 'excess demand for job importance' may help account for the co-existence of unemployment amongst professionals and unfilled vacancies for more lowly positions.

The issue of status was also on Scitovsky's mind when he chose the occasion of his Fred Hirsch Memorial Lecture to make one of his most thought-provoking contributions on unemployment, reframing some of Keynes's concerns in a modern context. He began by airing the possibility that the satiation of wants in affluent societies might pose a threat to the continuation of economic growth. Certainly, basic needs are already more than satisfied for many affluent consumers, who demonstrate this by dieting and jogging. But consumption demand might none the less remain buoyant due to spending on needs associated with the attainment of social standing and personal fulfilment. In his (1987a) Hirsch lecture, naturally enough, he concentrated only on the means by which people seek to meet their social needs but, as far as the latter is concerned, we should note his discussions elsewhere (1976, pp. 78–82; 1981/1986, pp. 130–1) of the increasing extent to which people are engaging in do-it-yourself activities – in other words, internalizing the production of goods and services they could have purchased in the market – in order to obtain excitement and stimulation. Do-it-yourself activities may contribute towards a stagnationist tendency in so far as people who undertake them save money and do not spend more elsewhere.

According to Scitovsky, macroeconomic problems arise from social needs because the modern consumer strives to attain status not by purchasing more goods of a particular kind – the typical person is, after all, disgusted by the Imelda Marcos's extravagence in owning 3000 pairs of shoes (1987a, p. 3) – but by seeking to increase his income regardless of whether he can get around to spending it all, and by concentrating his spending on exceptional items, goods that are prestigious because they are in short supply and thus command high prices. In the extreme case, as with homes in prime locations, antiques and old masters, the act of spending on such items involves no direct demand for new production save that for the services of auctioneers and other dealers in such commodities, and for maintenance and restoration services. It is a form of spending that is akin to hoarding one's flow of income as cash or leaving it as a bank deposit rather than placing it where it might increase the supply of funds that others would like to borrow. However, unlike an excessive preference for liquidity, the preference for hard-to-reproduce positional goods exerts an inflationary impact on the price level as well as a deflationary effect on the demand for labour (1987a, pp. 10–11), all the more so since the predictable rise in prices of such goods makes them attractive as hedges against inflation and diverts funds away from investment in new business activities.

This was a most timely analysis, coming as it did during the mid-1980s boom in conspicuous consumption and real estate prices; yet one can see it very much as an extension of ideas rehearsed in his (1940/1964) study of interest and capital. However, Scitovsky did not consider the underlying process as carefully as in the earlier paper. He neglected to note that for each buyer of a positional good there must be a seller. If a seller uses the proceeds towards buying an alternative higher-status good, he must find another seller. If funds are to move into supply-inelastic positional goods markets at the expense of sales in markets for reproducible commodities, we must have a situation in which sellers of the former are choosing to keep liquid rather than spending their capital gains on reproducible goods or on newly issued financial assets. (If someone sells a piece of prime real estate and uses the proceeds to purchase existing financial assets, the buck is merely passed to the seller of these securities.) So unless this argument is to hinge upon timelags in the buying and selling of assets causing a rise in the transactions demand for money, we need a more detailed flow of funds analysis to see whether the end result is as Scitovsky proposed. His story works fine, for example, if a yuppie withdraws a bank deposit that he otherwise would have used to purchase some current output and buys instead into the market for positional goods *and* if the seller in this market banks the proceeds as a means of financing a less-ostentatious lifestyle, such as early retirement (though here we also have a reduction in labour supplied!). The analysis would also hold if the rise in prices of non-reproducible assets led to a rise in the propensity to save of people who desired to accumulate enough – for example, a house deposit – to get on to the first rung of the positional ladder, or who, at the expense of would-be purchasers of reproducible goods, took out bigger loans to do so and then had less left over each month to spend on newly produced goods and services.

Scitovsky's view of the origins of at least part of observed unemployment makes the macroeconomic policies of both Reagan and Thatcher seem particularly unhelpful. Policies aimed at promoting greater equality would have been much better than tax cuts for the rich, for the demand for positional goods would thereby have been reduced and the structure of aggregate demand would have been shifted more in the direction of unsatiated needs for personal comfort. Furthermore, if the supply of positional goods is inherently difficult to expand, the Reagan/Thatcher 'justification' for cuts in marginal rates of income tax – that they would lead to an increase in the supply of labour and thus to the expansion of output and reduction of inflation – is wrong-headed: it would have been better to reduce the demand for employment and to spread employment around more equitably by encouraging part-time working and job-sharing. So long as policy-makers are dealing with fairly small changes in the average number of hours worked per week, Scitovsky does not feel they need to worry about causing the psychological problems that can arise when people are not skilled in filling their leisure time in an active manner.

Today, as environmental problems are beginning to be taken seriously, it is becoming more difficult to believe that environmentally responsible governments are going to be able to offer their entire able-bodied populations the prospect of full-time employment. So far, though, little attention has been given to the practical issue of how one ensures an equitable distribution of part-time/shared work and sets about ensuring that people receive education in making the most of their extra leisure. Most politicians are yet to abandon the goal of full-time full employment and set about trying to produce a similar paradigm shift in the minds of voters. It is here that Scitovsky's integration of psychology and economics is potentially most significant: his (1979/1986) message to the American public is that if they acquire skills for enjoying a non-puritan lifestyle they will be able to reduce their expenditure on consumption (and hence their need to work) and at the same time find greater fulfilment in their lives.

CONCLUSION

If we take a broad view of Scitovsky's contribution to economics it is difficult to avoid the conclusion that, despite a very extensive record of being cited, it has not had the kind of impact it deserves. His works are well-known and yet do not seem to have affected fundamentally the way in which the vast majority of economists nowadays teach or research the subject. Most modern-day economists probably now see *Welfare and Competition* as nothing more than an intermediate-level textbook on microeconomic theory and welfare economics, not as something presenting a much more complex view of the functioning of economic systems than is found in many more-recent and more technically demanding texts. To the extent that economists have started to recognize that market power has informational foundations they appear to have been reinventing Scitovsky's wheel rather than recognizing this persistent theme in his work. *The Joyless Economy* has been cited mainly by non-mainstream economists or by scholars in other fields; it has made little impact on welfare economics. As Scitovsky (1988, p. vii) himself points out, his work has tended to foster the creation of a distinct psychological branch of economics rather than 'infuse some psychology into the general framework of the discipline'.

Part of the answer to the question why his work has not had the impact it deserves is probably to be found in its very novelty, which presents too much of a challenge to established research practices. It is not just the unfamiliarity and diversity of the literature of psychology that he is asking economists to take on board which makes them uncomfortable but also the kinds of models towards which it points. Differences in knowledge are inherently difficult to capture in mathematical models, while deterministic conclusions about matters such as consumer sovereignty become difficult to achieve if tastes are seen not as genetically given but as affected by external factors including tradition and education as well as advertizing. Scitovsky (forthcoming) himself thinks that part of the explanation of resistance to his analysis of the deficiencies of modern economies lies in a mistaken view that he is an élitist: he stresses that one can achieve sensory stimulation outside the workplace by many means other than intellectual activity.

No less important as a factor hindering the impact of Scitovsky's work may be the way it has been packaged and served up to the economics profession. It needed to be better linked to other works that seek to challenge the mainstream, and its various components themselves needed to be more thoroughly integrated. In this chapter one of my aims has been to give pointers as to how these things might have been done. But what we really need is a third edition of *Welfare and Competition* which pays careful attention to recent contributions by others on the effects of information on the operation of economic systems (such as the transactions cost literature) and which explores the welfare implications of his socio-psychological view of consumer behaviour.

REFERENCES

NOTE: Entries marked * are reprinted in Scitovsky (1964), and those marked ** are reprinted in Scitovsky (1986). All page numbers of citations refer to the reprinted versions. I am grateful to Tibor Scitovsky for supplying me with a bibliography of his writings and copies of his latest works.

Aufhauser, K. (1976), 'Review of T. Scitovsky (1976) *The Joyless Economy*', *Economic Journal*, **86**, 911–13.
Berlyne, D. (1960), *Conflict, Arousal and Curiosity*, New York: McGraw-Hill.
Berlyne, D. (1971), *Aesthetics and Psychobiology*, New York: Appleton-Century-Crofts.
Coase, R.H. (1937), 'The Nature of the Firm', *Economica*, **4** (new series), 386–405.
Cyert, R.M. and J.G. March (1963), *A Behavioral Theory of the Firm*, Englewood Cliffs, N.J.: Prentice-Hall.
Dobb, M.H. (1969), *Welfare Economics and the Economics of Socialism*, Cambridge: Cambridge University Press.
Earl, P.E. (1990), 'Economics and Psychology: a Survey', *Economic Journal*, **100**, 318–55.
Eatwell, J., J. Llewellyn and R. Tarling (1974), 'Money Wage Inflation in Industrial Countries', *Review of Economic Studies*, **41**, 515–23.
Graaf, J. de V. (1965), 'Review of T. Scitovsky (1964) *Papers on Welfare and Growth*', *Economic Journal*, **75**, 803–4.
Hanson, P. (1987), *The Joy of Stress*, London: Pan Books.
Hirsch, F. (1976), *Social Limits to Growth*, Cambridge, Mass.: Harvard University Press; 1977, London: Routledge & Kegan Paul.
Hurrell, J.J., L.R. Murphy, S.L. Sauter and C.L. Cooper (eds) (1988), *Occupational Stress: Issues and Developments in Research*, New York: Taylor & Francis.
Kaldor, N. (1939), 'Welfare Propositions and Interpersonal Comparisons of Utility', *Economic Journal*, **49**, 549–52.
Leibenstein, H. (1966), 'Allocative Efficiency vs. X-Efficiency', *American Economic Review*, **56**, 392–415.
Leijonhufvud, A. (1977), 'Costs and Consequences of Inflation', in G.C. Harcourt (ed.) (1977), *The Microeconomic Foundations of Macroeconomics*, London: Macmillan, 265–312.
Little, I.M.D., T. Scitovsky and M.F.G. Scott (1970), *Industry and Trade in Some Developing Countries*, London and New York: Oxford University Press.
Lutz, M.A. and K. Lux (1979), *The Challenge of Humanistic Economics*, Menlo Park, Cal.: Benjamin/Cummings Publishing Company.
Maslow, A. (1954), *Motivation and Personality*, New York: Harper & Row.
Middleton, E. (1986), 'Some Testable Implications of a Preference for Subjective Novelty', *Kyklos*, **39**, 397–418.
Myrdal, G. (1957), *Economic Theory and Underdeveloped Regions*, London: Duckworth.

Peacock, A. (1976), 'Review of T. Scitovsky (1976) *The Joyless Economy*', *Journal of Economic Literature*, **14**, 1278–80.

Pigou, A.C. (1941), *Employment and Equilibrium*, London: Macmillan.

Posner, M.V. (1961), 'International Trade and Technical Change', *Oxford Economic Papers*, **13**, 323–41.

Richardson, G.B. (1960), *Information and Investment*, Oxford: Oxford University Press.

Robinson, J.V. (1966), *The New Mercantilism: An Inaugural Lecture*, Cambridge: Cambridge University Press; reprinted in J.V. Robinson (1973), *Collected Economic Papers*, vol. 4, Oxford: Basil Blackwell.

Schultze, C.L. (1959), *Recent Inflation in the United States*, Study Paper no. 1 prepared for the Joint Economic Committee, Washington, D.C.: Government Printing Office.

Scitovsky, T. (1940), ' A Study of Interest and Capital', *Economica*, **7**, 293–317*.

—— (1941a), 'Capital Accumulation, Employment and Price Rigidity', *Review of Economic Studies*, **8**, 69–88*.

—— (1941b), 'A Note on Welfare Propositions in Economics', *Review of Economic Studies*, **9**, 77–88*.

—— (1941c), 'Prices under Monopoly and Competition', *Journal of Political Economy*, **49**, 663–85.

—— (1942), 'A Reconsideration of the Theory of Tariffs', *Review of Economic Studies*, **9**, 89–110*.

—— (1943), 'A Note on Profit Maximization and its Implications', *Review of Economic Studies*, **11**, 57–60*.

—— (1945), 'Some Consequences of the Habit of Judging Quality by Price', *Review of Economic Studies*, **12**, 100–105*.

—— (1950), 'Ignorance as a Source of Oligopoly Power', *American Economic Review*, **40**, 48–53*.

—— (1951a), 'The State of Welfare Economics', *American Economic Review*, **41**, 303–15*.

—— (1951b), *Welfare and Competition: The Economics of a Fully Employed Economy*, Chicago, Ill.: Richard D. Irwin.

—— (1954), 'Two Concepts of External Economies', *Journal of Political Economy*, **62**, 143–51*.

—— (1958), *Economic Theory and Western European Integration*, London: George Allen & Unwin.

—— (1959), 'Growth: Balanced or Unbalanced?', in M. Abramovitz *et al.* (eds) (1959) *The Allocation of Economic Resources*, Stanford, Cal.: Stanford University Press*.

—— (1960), 'Standards for the Performance of our Economic System: A Critique of Present and Proposed Standards', *American Economic Review* (supplement), **50**, 13–20*.

—— (1962), 'On the Principle of Consumers' Sovereignty', *American Economic Review* (supplement), **52**, 262–8*.

—— (1964), *Papers on Welfare and Growth*, Stanford, Cal.: Stanford University Press.

—— (1965), 'Requirements of an International Monetary System', *Princeton Essays in International Finance*, no. 49, November.

—— (1966), 'A New Approach to International Liquidity', *American Economic Review*, **56**, 1212–20.

—— (1969), *Money and the Balance of Payments*, Chicago, Ill.: Rand-McNally.

—— (1971), *Welfare and Competition*, rev. edn, Chicago, Ill.: Richard D. Irwin.

—— (1972), 'What's Wrong with the Arts is What's Wrong with Society', *American Economic Review* (supplement), **62**, 1–19**.

—— (1973a), 'The Producer Society', *De Economist*, **71**, 225–50**.

—— (1973b), 'The Place of Economic Welfare in Human Welfare', *Quarterly Review of Economics and Business*, **13**, 7–19**.

—— (1976), *The Joyless Economy: An Inquiry into Human Satisfaction and Consumer Dissatisfaction*, London and New York: Oxford University Press.

—— (1978a), 'Asymmetries in Economics', *Scottish Journal of Political Economy*, **25**, 227–37.

—— (1978b), 'Market Power and Inflation', *Economica*, **45**, 221–33.

—— (1979), 'Can Changing Consumer Tastes Save Resources?', in I. Adelman (ed.), *Economic Growth and Resources*, London: Macmillan, 34–45**.

—— (1981), 'The Desire for Excitement in Modern Society', *Kyklos*, **34**, 3–13**.

—— (1982), 'The Real Side of Inflation', *Korea Development Institute Seminar Series*, no. 82–02.

—— (1983), 'The Demand-Side Economics of Inflation', in D. Worswick and J. Trevithick (eds), *Keynes and the Modern World*, Cambridge: Cambridge University Press, 223–38.

—— (1985), 'Pricetakers' Plenty: a Neglected Benefit of Capitalism', *Kyklos*, **38**, 517–36**.

—— (1986), *Human Desire and Economic Satisfaction*, Brighton, Sussex: Wheatsheaf.

—— (1987a), 'Growth in the Affluent Society', *Lloyds Bank* Review, no. 163, 1–14.

—— (1987b), Entries on 'Balanced Growth' and on 'Tariffs', in J. Eatwell, M. Milgate and P. Newman (eds), *The New Palgrave: A Dictionary of Economics*, London: Macmillan, 177–9, 586–8.

—— (1988), 'Foreword' to P. Albanese (ed.), *Psychological Foundations of Economic Behavior*, New York: Praeger.

—— (1990), 'The Benefits of Asymmetric Markets', *Journal of Economic Perspectives*, **4**, 135–48.

—— (forthcoming), 'My Life Philosophy', in M. Szenberg (ed.), *The Life Philosophy of Eminent American Economists*, Cambridge: Cambridge University Press.

—— and A. Scitovsky (1964), 'Inflation versus Unemployment: an Examination of their Effects', in Commission on Money and Credit, *Inflation, Growth and Employment*, Englewood Cliffs, N.J.: Prentice-Hall, 429–70.

—— , E. Shaw and L. Tarshis (1951), *Mobilizing Resources for War: The Economic Alternatives*, New York: McGraw-Hill.

Stewart, M. (1983), *Controlling the Economic Future*, Brighton, Sussex: Wheatsheaf.

Tylecote, A. (1981), *The Causes of the Present Inflation*, London: Macmillan.

Vernon, R. (1966), 'International Investment and International Trade in the Product Cycle', *Quarterly Journal of Economics*, **80**, 190–207.

Williamson, O.E. (1964), *The Economics of Discretionary Behavior*, Englewood Cliffs, N.J.: Prentice-Hall.

Williamson, O.E. (1975), *Markets and Hierarchies: Analysis and Antitrust Implications*, New York: Free Press.

13. Amartya Sen

Michael McPherson*

Amartya Sen combines two intellectual characteristics that too often are kept apart by economists. Sen possesses a remarkable technical virtuosity, a set of mathematical and analytical skills of a very high order, which have been used to good effect in the more technical of his writings on social choice theory and decision theory. At the same time, Sen possesses a lively awareness of the depth and complexity of the phenomena of human psychology and morality. In keeping both these orientations in play, one might say that Sen attempts to be rigorous without being *reductionist*. An enterprise of this sort is fraught with intellectual tension – tension which, in Sen's case, has proved a bountiful source of creativity.

That tension between rigour and non-reductionism relates closely to another, namely the divergent pulls of the need for simplification in theorizing and the demands of realism and relevance. Sen (1985a, p. 341) has characterized it as follows, in his typically understated fashion:

> The choice of behavioral assumptions in economics tends to pull us in two different – sometimes contrary – directions. The demands of tractability can conflict with those of veracity, and we can have a hard choice between simplicity and relevance. We want a canonical form that is uncomplicated enough to be easily usable in theoretical and empirical analysis. But we also want an assumption structure that is not fundamentally at odds with the real world, nor one that makes simplicity take the form of naivety. There is a genuine conflict here – a conflict that cannot be easily disposed of either by asserting the need for simplification in theorizing or by pointing to the need for realism. What we have to face is the need for discriminating judgment, separating out the complications that can be avoided without much loss and the complexities that must be taken on board for our analysis to be at all useful.

Most of our profession has opted whole-heartedly, and often naively, for simplification in the underlying behavioural and moral assumptions. One motive for this choice has been the (largely unexamined) belief that any attempt to move away from convenient simplifications in the interest of greater realism would quickly render the whole subject intractable. In an odd way it seems often to be true that the minority of the economics profession

who have insisted on greater realism and complexity have implicitly acqui-
esced in the judgement that the extreme simplifications of neoclassical economics are essential to its analytic tractability. The minority response – as
suggested in much of the work of the institutionalists – has been to abandon
formal analysis in favour of more discursive modes of inquiry. In this light,
Sen's sustained attempt to live with the tension is all the more interesting.

In this chapter, I shall explore this theme through examination of three
interrelated aspects of Sen's work. First is his development of a more complex analysis of individual motivation and behaviour than the standard self-
interested picture of 'economic man'. Second is Sen's development of a
novel view of the concept of 'personal well-being' as a set of 'achievements'
or 'functionings' of a person rather than a level of utility'. Finally, I shall
consider Sen's distinctive and important analysis of the role of 'rights' in the
moral evaluation of conduct and states of affairs.

In focusing on these areas, I leave aside several other major areas to
which Sen has made important contributions. These include the bulk of his
work in the theory of social choice, his research into the axiomatic measurement of poverty and real income, and his contributions to the field of economic development, including his highly influential work on poverty and
famines. I remark briefly on each of these areas of research in the concluding
section.

THREE CONTRIBUTIONS

Committed Behaviour

As Sen has noted in his widely reprinted and highly influential essay, 'Rational Fools' (1977a), the standard economic view of human beings as self-
interested utility-maximizers has been variously judged to be testable and
plainly true, testable and plainly false, and tautological.[1] For many purposes,
however, it is less interesting to try to decide the question of whether the
standard view is refuted, or indeed refutable, than it is to ask how useful,
illuminating or limiting it is. It is certainly possible for those who feel a
powerful commitment to seeing people as self-interested to stretch the notion
of self-interest to include, say, the pleasure of serving others, thus moving
the theory toward tautology. Or, instead, one can protect the standard view
by arguing that contradictory evidence is in fact evidence of irrationality,
while the theory is properly concerned only with rational behaviour.

But whether or not this theory can be saved, the question remains whether
we can, for some purposes, do better with a theory that allows for more
complexity of individual motivation.[2] The standard view has the effect of

collapsing some important dimensions of individual conduct which might usefully be distinguished. To see this, it may be helpful to characterize this 'standard view' a little more explicitly. According to the version of utility theory which prevails in economics, a person's preferences are said to be 'revealed' by his or her choices. That is, by definition, as between two alternatives, a person is said to prefer whatever he or she in fact tends to choose. If the set of preferences so defined is internally consistent, the person is then said to be rational. Moreover, it is standard to equate a person's welfare with the satisfaction of her preferences. In this way a very tight definitional link is made among four different notions: choice, preference, rationality and welfare. (It's not much of a further step to say that a person's self-interest is to maximize her welfare; taking this step brings the theory close to tautology – the only way to avoid being self-interested is through being internally inconsistent.)

These notions are not nearly so closely linked in everyday usage as they are in this scheme of definitions. It is surely not unusual for someone to say, 'I would have preferred to go to the movie, but I chose to stay home with the kids since somebody had to do it.' Or to say, 'She chose to help her friend rather than look out for her own welfare.' And so on.

Now, while the term preference in the standard theory of 'revealed preference' does not *by definition* relate to any psychological or perceptual or welfare features (only to the actual choices made: x is revealed preferred to y only if x is chosen and y is rejected in some choice), the significance and reach of the concept of revealed preference depends substantially on the plausibility of interpreting the choice-based revealed preference as being identical with – or closely related to – 'preference' in the more substantive sense. That is the way in which the revealed preference theory has in fact been used in the literature, and welfare conclusions have been drawn by interpreting 'revealed preference', given by actual choice, both as preference in the substantive sense and also as the indicator of individual welfare of the person herself. There are at least two important distinctions about individual motivations to be made here that are obliterated on a 'revealed preference' view of individual behaviour. The first is a distinction between one's *personal well-being* and one's concerns for other people's welfare. Clearly a person – a parent, say – may care about his children's well-being as much or more than his own. It's reasonable to say that the parent's welfare depends both on his personal well-being and on that of his children. We want to think of the parent's utility function as having these different components: utility derived from his own consumption, and utility derived from the well-being of his children. This notion, and its generalization to other forms of altruistic concern for others, is missing from standard accounts but is a fairly straightforward extension of them.[3]

The second distinction is more of a challenge to the standard view. People sometimes act out of a sense of 'duty' or, to use the less-high-minded and broader term suggested by Sen, a sense of 'commitment'. Sometimes people's actions seem most naturally or plausibly explained as acting on principle or acting out of loyalty to a group. Often motives are mixed. A guard may stay alert at her post partly from fear of punishment, and partly from a desire to protect the fellow soldiers she cares about – she may be advancing her welfare once we take account of this concern for others. But another element may enter: she may stay at her post because she considers it her duty, and she would do so even without the threat of punishment and even if the personal cost of doing so would outweigh the gain in personal welfare she would experience from protecting her colleagues. The motivational information contained in a story like this is simply steamrolled by revealed preference theory: we deny ourselves any access to these motivational complexities by adopting that theory to describe behaviour.

The conceptual poverty of the revealed-preference approach becomes clearest when preference and commitment conflict. Suppose it happens that on a cold rainy night when there is little risk of attack or of a surprise inspection the guard is staying on the post out of duty. The natural thing to say is that her *preference* would be to go inside and warm up, but her *choice* is to do her duty. She is not in fact trying to maximize her personal well-being, or even her welfare, taking into account her concern for the safety of her colleagues; she is doing her duty. 'Committed' behaviour provides important instances of 'counter-preferential choice' – a category that simply doesn't exist in neoclassical economics but which, as Sen has argued convincingly, is an important feature of our lives.

But many economists would object that this kind of formulation runs afoul of the requirement that theory be based on 'observable' behaviour. If our knowledge about what people want is grounded in observation of what they choose, how can we make any use – or any empirical sense – of the idea of 'counter-preferential choice', or more generally of claims about different motives that may underlie behaviour? Sen's reply is that there simply is no good reason for economists to limit their inquiry into people's motivations to observation of their non-verbal behaviour, and in particular their market choices. To do so is, after all, a rather extraordinary act of self-denial. Even behavioural psychologists regard people's speech – their 'verbal reports' – as observable behaviour.[4]

Part of the reason for economists' scepticism about people's accounts of their motives and concerns is a strong suspicion that people always maximize self-interest, so that in general they will give the utility-maximizing, rather than the truthful, answer to a question. Yet while it is certainly smart to be careful about incentives that may exist in particular situations for people to give misleading answers to questions, it is extravagant of economists to deny to themselves all the information about personal motivations and concerns that might be obtained by talking to people – or indeed by reflecting on the motives behind their own behaviour (Sen, 1973).

Does this category of committed behaviour matter economically? Very likely it does.[5] The problem of controlling externalities and supplying public goods continues to grow in importance as economies develop. Although individual incentives and government regulation have important roles to play, often enough getting people to do their duty rather than serve their preferences is indispensable in looking after the supply of public goods and the control of externalities. A commitment not to litter is an obvious example. Even more telling is the willingness to pay taxes without cheating. Clearly, few people pay their taxes because of their altruistic concern for others. (The federal government in fact invites taxpayers to add an extra contribution to help their fellows, and has few takers.) Some people pay out of a fear of prosecution, and pay only what they might get caught for not paying. But a successful tax system relies on most people paying their taxes simply because it is their duty to do so.

Sen has argued that committed behaviour is also important in explaining the performance of firms. Worker motivation is an enormously important variable in explaining the differential performance of firms both within and across countries. Again, as with taxpaying, it is obvious that incentives and monitoring matter. But it is equally obvious that the sociology of the workplace and the society matter as well. Workers may work out of loyalty to the firm or to their fellow workers; their willingness to 'do their duty' is likely to depend heavily on their perception of the fairness of productive and distributive arrangements. We have little understanding of how these forces work in practice, and certainly labelling them 'committed behaviour' is not a substitute for the hard work of learning what determines the strength and the character of commitments. It does, however, prevent us from making the phenomenon disappear from sight, as the neoclassical analysis of individual motivation tends to do.

Capabilities and Well-Being

Although most economists may think they have shaken off the utilitarian heritage of their discipline, that heritage in fact exerts a powerful influence on the way in which normative or moral judgements are conceived in economics. Even though the *content* of these judgements may differ somewhat from those of classical utilitarianism, the *structure* of the problem of moral evaluation is very much that of utilitarianism. It will be useful to describe

Sen's characterization of this structure before proceeding to discuss some important ways in which he has proposed to modify and enrich it.

Sen has noted that utilitarianism as a moral doctrine can be characterized by three successively more-restrictive commitments: those to consequentialism, welfarism and sum-ranking.[6] These say, respectively,

1. that the only thing that matters morally in judging an action, a policy, a personal disposition or whatever is the goodness of the *consequences* that flow from taking the action, adopting the policy, developing the disposition, and so on;
2. that the only feature of the consequences of actions, policies, etc. that is of ultimate moral importance is the *welfare* levels for individuals that result from them; and
3. that the way to aggregate these welfare consequences for moral judgements is simply to add together the welfare levels.[7]

Owing to misgivings about interpersonal utility comparisons, economists are reluctant to endorse the third feature of utilitarianism, but they are enthusiastic and often unreflective supporters of 1 and 2. In particular, Paretian welfare economics is a thoroughly 'welfarist' doctrine.

A commitment to welfarism implies that all features of the world other than personal welfare levels derive any moral value they have strictly from their tendency to promote welfare. Thus, for example, personal virtues like courage or integrity, public activities like the protection of rights, and social achievements like the reduction of illiteracy are all to be appraised strictly according to their welfare-promoting tendencies. They are of no intrinsic value.

Not surprisingly, this is a daring and controversial position in moral theory, one that has distinguished defenders but no-less-distinguished and effective critics. It is interesting that economists, who for the most part make few claims to expertise in matters of moral theory, have in effect taken a strong stand on this difficult issue.

In the following section, we shall see how Sen's treatment of rights and liberty challenges this 'welfarist' outlook. Here we focus on the important problem in normative evaluation of measuring and comparing levels of individual well-being. Sen's approach puts much emphasis on the varied *purposes* to which assessments of levels of (or changes in) well-being might be put. He has no argument with the claim that some of these purposes are well-served by utility measures, and indeed he has argued forcefully that economists are too sceptical about producing interpersonal comparisons of utility in contexts where those might be useful (Sen, 1970c).

However, Sen argues that for some of the central political and moral purposes of measuring well-being, utility notions are much too weak. How do conceptions of individual well-being figure in problems of moral and social evaluation? One critical use is that of assessing the strengths of persons' claims on social resources. If we wish to distribute food or basic education to those whose needs are greatest, we need some means of assessing who is needier (or worse off). Similarly, if we want to provide resources to those whose well-being will be most improved by that provision we need some agreement on how to measure well-being. A closely related purpose in measuring well-being is that of settling on a standard of equality. To whatever extent a political or moral theory aims to combat inequality, it needs to set out a standard of what is to be equalized.

Sen has identified two principal shortcomings of utility measures when used for these purposes.[8] First, measures of the amount of utility an individual receives may depend on features of the person and her situation that should be irrelevant from a moral or political point of view. Thus, some people may have developed preferences that are very costly to satisfy. A person who is miserable unless he sleeps on satin sheets might, from a view that equates well-being with utility, be judged 'needier' than a hardy soul who sleeps well out-of-doors. Even more discomforting is the thought that persons who are deprived of material prosperity may come to adapt their preferences to their meagre allotment – learning not to want what they cannot have (see Elster, 1983). If well-being is equated with preference satisfaction, these adaptive preferences may wind up helping to justify the deprivation.

Sen's second objection to the use of utility to measure well-being is tied up with an aspect of personhood whose value Sen emphasizes. This is the interest persons have in acting, in doing, in accomplishing things. Equating utility with well-being emphasizes the consumption-orientated aspect of human life. As Rawls once suggested, a utilitarian view suggests the image of persons as vessels into which satisfactions are poured. But a tradition at least as old as Aristotle emphasizes the importance for human flourishing of individual achievements. Persons have projects they wish to carry out, goals they wish to achieve.

Now plainly a utility-based view of well-being can permit these goals and achievements to be valued, but they can have value only to the extent that they contribute to the utility or preference satisfaction of the agent. They are not valued intrinsically, but only as means to the end of higher utility. Sen objects that there is no reason why, from a political or moral point of view, we have to accept that measure of the value of these achievements.

Sen proposes as an alternative to a utility-based view of well-being a *capabilities*-centred view. From this point of view, an agent's well-being is a function of all the various things that he is able to do: walk about, eat, read, engage in political activity and so on. Some capabilities may be central to the utility levels persons can attain, and this will be one source of their value. However, other capabilities, such as basic literacy or the opportunity to run for political office, may be judged morally or socially important independently of whether they are an important source of satisfaction to the individuals involved.

This conception of well-being responds to both of Sen's objections to a utility-based standard. First, it puts stress on the active, achieving aspect of personhood, as a utility-based standard does not. Secondly, it avoids the kind of 'subjectivism' that a utility-based standard is vulnerable to. Thus, adaptive preferences may lead people who have no access to schooling to disvalue the ability to read. But their lack of literacy is an objective fact which will figure in a capabilities-based assessment of their well-being.

Sen's approach builds on and generalizes (while it also modifies) other objective approaches to the measurement of well-being. John Rawls' highly influential volume *A Theory of Justice* (1971) suggests that, for the purpose of determining the justice of basic institutions, individual advantage should be measured by the amounts of primary social goods people have claims to. These goods are seen by Rawls as 'universal means' – items that are needed for an individual to advance any conception of his own good.[9] Also related is the 'basic needs' approach to well-being measurement that has been advocated in the development literature (Streeten *et al.*, 1981). This approach assesses countries' living standards and economic accomplishments by measuring how well certain basic needs are met for the society's most deprived citizens. Both Rawls's approach and the 'basic needs' approach are similar to Sen's in their detachment from preference satisfaction and in their striving for greater objectivity in making assessments and comparisons.

Sen's approach is both more inclusive and in a certain sense more abstract. In principle, the range of capabilities to be included in an index of well-being is extremely broad and the capabilities of relatively privileged people matter too. But not all capabilities are equally important, so a central issue in developing an index of well-being is to agree on weights to be attached to different capabilities. It is important to stress that agreeing on such weights is by no means a technician's 'index number' problem (nor, obviously, is it to be resolved by determining how much utility people derive from the various capabilities!). It is instead a process involving public argument and deliberation. The argument would, in fact, be about what capabilities are of greatest importance in achieving a good life within the society in question. It may be that Sen's greatest contribution in this area is to remind us that *this*, and not the issue of how much utility people get, is the fundamental subject matter of theories of human well-being.

Rights and Liberty

We consider finally some of the contributions Sen has made to introducing notions of rights and liberty to the moral discourse of economics. The 'welfarist' commitments of standard economics discussed above yield a particularly narrow conception of the role of rights and liberty in the evaluation of economic outcomes and arrangements. Rights, whether moral or legal, have strictly instrumental value on this conception: they amount to rules that should be followed only in so far as following them has the effect of promoting greater utility within society. Analogously, the value of protecting individual liberty is simply whatever instrumental value such protections have in promoting welfare (including whatever subjective satisfactions individuals may derive from enjoying liberty).

This conception of the role and value of liberty and rights is in considerable tension with important aspects of the liberal tradition with which neoclassical economics is associated. Moreover, our moral intuitions seem to acknowledge an intrinsic importance to liberty and an intrinsic badness to rights violations which are not captured in the welfarist framework. Preservation of liberty is a morally valuable thing in its own right, and not simply because it helps us achieve other ends.

Sen brought this tension to the fore some decades ago with his striking formulation of the 'paradox of the Paretian liberal' (Sen, 1970b). It is natural to think of the economist's endorsement of the Pareto principle – make all changes that benefit some without hurting anyone – as a way of acknowledging the importance of liberty. Indeed, the move from utilitarian to 'Paretian' welfare economics is often seen as making modern economics more 'libertarian' than its utilitarian ancestors. Yet Sen showed through simple examples how easy it is for the Pareto principle to come into conflict with respect for personal liberty, and he proved a theorem which showed that the conflict is inescapable on even a minimalist view of personal liberty.

The conflict arises when people have preferences concerning the 'private' activities of others – as, for example, if I prefer you not to read pornography (while perhaps you think it would do *me* some good to read a sexy novel). Any plausible conception of personal liberty would leave it up to each of us to choose our own reading, but given the interdependence in our preferences the resulting set of choices may easily fail to be Pareto optimal.

This simple insight has given rise to an enormous literature, mostly aimed at trying to solve, resolve or dissolve the paradox. A number of illuminating points have emerged from these efforts, which have been ably surveyed by, among others, Wriglesworth (1985), Suzumura (1983) and Seabright (1989).[10] Yet the aim of making the paradox disappear, which animates much of this writing, may be misplaced. What Sen's theorem and examples show is that the Pareto principle and the principle of respecting personal liberty appeal to different moral concerns. The first appeals to helping people to get what they want, whatever that may be, and the second to respecting individuals' rights to have their preferences govern within certain spheres. That these are different dimensions of concern is not easy to see from within the neoclassical view because of its tendency, discussed above, to equate preferences, choices, welfare, personal well-being and self-interest.

Sen has argued here, as in the treatment of 'committed' behaviour discussed earlier, that to begin sorting all this out requires distinguishing the motives that lie behind preferences. There is an important moral distinction between my wanting to decide what I read and my wanting to decide what you read. There is no reason to think that a theory which places those 'preferences' on a par will be able to respect any notion of personal liberty. Nor is there likely to be any straightforward mechanical or formal procedure for handling these conflicts: they will necessarily be the subject of moral deliberation.

If rights aren't simply instruments for promoting utility, how are they best captured in an overall scheme of moral evaluation? Here again Sen has made important contributions. To see what is at stake, it is useful to contrast the instrumental view of rights with Robert Nozick's (1974) view of rights as absolute side-constraints on action. Nozick's view is radically anti-consequentialist: rights 'come on the scene' *before* any evaluation of consequences; any action that would violate such a pre-existing right is simply ruled out. Further, the scope and content of these rights is not determined by any sort of consequential evaluation, but must instead be determined by some version of a 'natural rights' argument.

But this alternative seems unacceptably strong. While the instrumental view suffers from a failure to recognize the intrinsic importance of rights, Nozick's view suffers from a failure to recognize that assessment of the overall consequences of a system of rights figures in the determination of what rights there are and in judging the importance of particular rights.

In several important essays, Sen (1982b, 1983b, 1985c) has laid out the elements of a scheme for acknowledging the value of rights in a more adequate way than either of these alternatives. Here again, Sen's approach is to elaborate a formal scheme to allow for the complexities of the problem. One such complexity is an elaboration of the notion of consequences. On the standard economic view, the only consequences that count in evaluating a state of affairs are the resulting welfare levels of individuals. Any other features of the situation, such as the number and severity of rights violations, enter simply through their impact on welfare levels. But there is no reason, except the commitment to welfarism, to define states of affairs so narrowly. If respecting rights is intrinsically important, then rights violations will enter negatively into our evaluation of states of affairs, independently of whatever welfare consequences they may have. This kind of formulation allows us to recognize the 'disvalue' of rights violations, while still trading off protection of particular rights against other items we value, including welfare and protection of other rights.

Even this elaboration, however, misses one dimension of the 'logic' of rights. Suppose I am in a situation where I can prevent two rights violations by committing a rights violation myself. (Perhaps somehow by torturing a prisoner I can learn things which will let me rescue two prisoners who are going to be tortured.) From an impersonal standpoint, the state of affairs where I do the torturing is better – having one fewer rights violation – than the state of affairs where I refrain from torturing. But this does not capture the force of the notion that the prisoner under my command has a right not to be tortured and that I have an obligation not to torture. Even though it may on balance be right for me to go ahead with the act of torture (say I can save 10,000 people) there is still, for me, a special weight to the obligation on me not to torture which is not captured in the impersonal evaluation.

Sen has proposed that we allow for this dimension by recognizing the notion of *agent-relative* moral evaluation of states of affairs. In my evaluation of states of affairs, *my* acts of torturing do not (and should not) count equally with those of others. It may turn out, then, that the right thing for me to do is not the thing that would be best from an impersonal point of view. Yet, unlike Nozick's view, my rights violations will not have infinite negative weight in my evaluation. Enough good consequences (including prevention of other rights violations) may outweigh the prohibition against my torturing someone.

Some would see the difference between different agents' moral evaluations of states of affairs as an unacceptable feature of a moral view, or as a mark of irrationality. Sen's reply, however, is similar to his insistence on complexity in other aspects of analysis. This tension between the viewpoints of different agents, or between an agent-centred and an impersonal viewpoint, is real. Like the tension between personal liberty and the Pareto principle, or between maximizing personal well-being and doing one's duty, this is a feature of our real situation which theory should highlight and clarify rather than obliterate.

THE SIGNIFICANCE OF SEN'S CONTRIBUTIONS

Each of the pieces of analysis reviewed here, all too elliptically, has its own significance, as I have tried to make clear. Is there anything more general to be said about the nature of these contributions, and the value of Sen's general outlook toward work on the borders of ethics and economics? I would venture two broad points.

First, although the impulse to simplify is of clear intellectual importance both in science and everyday life, it may well be that the greatest need in moral thought today is for what might be called the perspicuous treatment of complexity. This continues an ancient debate in moral theory, with Plato on the side of searching for deep theoretical simplicity and Aristotle on that of recognizing the many-sidedness of moral concerns. Some of the most evocative writing in contemporary moral philosophy is devoted to attending to these moral complexities – combining precision in argument with a resistance to the reduction of moral judgement to a few dimensions (Williams, 1985; Nagel, 1986; Nussbaum, 1990; Anderson, 1990). Much of Sen's work shows the potential for the analytical tools of economic theory and social choice theory to be used in this way: to reveal and clarify complexity.

My second generalization concerns the role of formal technique in moral reasoning. It is perhaps natural to suppose that one might hope that formal analysis could be used to *solve* moral problems – in effect, to substitute some algorithmic procedure for the messy process of moral judgement. Certainly neoclassical welfare economics seems to have that structure – identifying precisely what one would need to measure in order to find the optimum. It is striking that many of Sen's contributions have a different structure. Often their tendency is to identify those points at which moral judgement is needed, and to state more clearly just what the moral judgements are about. Thus, Sen's proposal to measure personal well-being through an index of capabilities invites and requires social deliberation about the importance to good lives of different kinds of capabilities. His consequence-sensitive analysis of rights calls for moral weighing of the importance of different kinds of rights violations as against one another and as against other morally valued outcomes. Sen's treatment of commitment is a little different in this regard, since that analysis is concerned more with the description and explanation of behaviour than with its moral evaluation. However, the analysis of committed behaviour does show an important way that people's judgements on moral matters can enter into the determination of their conduct – something that is difficult to find room for on the neoclassical account of behaviour. In general, Sen uses formal analysis to enrich and inform, rather than supplant, moral reflection.

CONCLUSION

Although the range and originality of the material reviewed in this essay is exceptionally large, it covers only one aspect of Sen's work. Neglected here are, among other things, most of Sen's technical contributions to the theory of social choice, his important theoretical work in development economics, and his influential empirical and analytical studies of poverty and hunger. In all these areas Sen's studies have been marked by the same respect for rigour and the same concern for the moral dimensions of economic issues which mark the writings surveyed here.

Without trying to characterize the full range of Sen's writings on social choice, it is worthwhile here to identify two persistent themes. One of these is a continuing search for ways to make social choice theory more useful by limiting the generality of its claims. Sen has, for example, argued that various kinds of partial comparability of the utility levels of different individuals may be available, even if full cardinal comparability is not feasible (Sen, 1970c). A second theme has been the need to attend to the variety of purposes for which social choice theory can be employed. In particular, Sen has stressed the distinction between the use of social choice mechanisms to arrive at particular decisions (as, for example, in voting on referenda) and their use in constructing evaluative weightings (as in trying to arrive at some collective moral judgement). Clarity about such matters is very helpful in appreciating the genuine contributions as well as the limits of formal social choice analyses.[11]

Sen's work on development is also closely tied to his interests in moral problems.[12] Sen has brought his expositional and analytical skills to bear on the problem of measuring poverty and income inequality.[13] His arguments for a 'capabilities' conception of well-being, discussed above, find a natural application in assessing living conditions in developing countries. Sen has contributed importantly not only to the conceptual discussion about how to assess such conditions but also to actual efforts at measuring and comparing such conditions. He has put special stress on the important issue of attending to gender inequalities in the distribution of resources within families (Sen, 1985d, 1989 and 1990a).

Finally, Sen has made strikingly important contributions to the literature on hunger. His 1981 book *Poverty and Famines* argued that famines are often the result not of absolute shortages of food but of maldistribution of entitlements to food. In work since then, culminating in his joint 1989 work with Jean Drèze, *Hunger and Public Action*, Sen has accumulated considerable additional evidence about the incidence and sources of both famines and malnutrition, and has assessed the effectiveness of alternative public remedies for these maladies. There are few better examples of a morally informed analysis of a fundamental economic problem than Sen's sustained work on this subject.

Sen's work is a landmark attempt to recover the position of economics among the moral sciences without yielding its reputation for rigour in formulation and precision in argument. Sen's work has ranged widely across moral philosophy as well as (in the case of his work on gender inequality and on famines) sociology and demographics. It is striking that Sen confronts work in these related disciplines with real respect and understanding: there is nothing in his outlook that corresponds to the 'academic imperialism' that is all too common among economists who extend their reach to other disciplines. Equally to be admired is Sen's willingness and capacity to engage in problems that range from the most highly abstract and theoretical to the most practical and urgent. Although few among us could hope to match the range and depth of Sen's work, we may hope that more economists will attempt to emulate its constructive and morally engaged spirit.

NOTES

* My thanks to Henry Bruton, Dan Hausman, Warren Samuels, Morty Schapiro, Amartya Sen and Gordon Winston for helpful comments on an earlier draft.

1. The hold of what I call here the 'standard' view of preference and choice on the economics profession has weakened somewhat over the last two decades, partly as a result of Sen's work. To some extent, then, one can see the following pages as contrasting Sen's view with the standard economist's view as it would be had Sen never written.
2. I discuss Sen's view of the self along with the related views articulated by Albert Hirschman and Tom Schelling in McPherson (1984b).
3. See, for example, Collard (1978) and Sen (1966).
4. In addition to Sen (1977a), see Sen (1971) and (1973).
5. For further discussion of the economic significance of moral commitments, and references to the literature, see McPherson (1984a) and Hausman and McPherson (forthcoming).
6. For Sen's description and critique of welfarism, see his 1979b, 1979c, 1987a, as well as Sen and Williams (1982, Introduction).
7. When policies may affect the number of people, one can distinguish versions of utilitarianism that aim to maximize *average* or *total* utility.
8. For material in this and the following paragraphs, see Sen (1985b, 1987b and c) and 'Equality of What?' (1982a, pp. 353–369). See also the discussion in Sen *et al.* (1987).
9. Sen has explained his differences from Rawls' position in Sen (1990b).
10. See also Sen's discussions of these issues in Sen (1976c and 1983a).
11. For excellent overviews of social choice theory, see Sen (1977b and 1986b). See also Sen (1986a).
12. See the essays in Sen (1984).
13. Among his most prominent contributions to the literature on the axiomatic measurement of poverty and inequality are Sen (1976a, b and 1979a).

REFERENCES

Anderson, Elizabeth (1990), 'The Ethical Limitations of the Market', *Economics and Philosophy*, **6**, (2), 179–207.
Collard, David (1978), *Altruism and Economy: A Study in Non-Selfish Economics*, New York: Oxford University Press.

Drèze, Jean and Amartya K. Sen (1989), *Hunger and Public Action*, Oxford: Clarendon Press.

Elster, Jon (1983), *Sour Grapes: Studies in the Subversion of Rationality*, Cambridge: Cambridge University Press.

Hausman, Daniel and Michael S. McPherson (forthcoming), 'Taking Ethics Seriously: Economics and Contemporary Moral Philosophy', *Journal of Economic Literature*.

McPherson, Michael S. (1984a), 'Limits on Self-Seeking: the Role of Morality in Economic Life', in David Colander (ed.), *Neoclassical Political Economy: The Analysis of Rent-Seeking and DUP Activities*, Cambridge, Mass.: Ballinger.

McPherson, Michael S. (1984b), 'On Schelling, Hirschman, and Sen: Revising the Concept of the Self', *Partisan Review*, Spring, 236–47.

Nagel, Thomas (1986), *The View from Nowhere*, Oxford: Clarendon Press.

Nozick, Robert (1974), *Anarchy, State and Utopia*, New York: Basic Books.

Nussbaum, Martha (1990), *Love's Knowledge: Essays on Philosophy and Literature*, Cambridge, Mass.: Harvard University Press.

Rawls, John (1971), *A Theory of Justice*, Cambridge, Mass.: Harvard University Press.

Seabright, Paul (1989), 'Social Choice and Social Theories', *Philosophy and Public Affairs*, **18**, (4), 365–87.

Sen, Amartya (1966), 'Labour Allocation in a Cooperative Enterprise', *Review of Economic Studies*, **33**, 361–71.

—— (1970a), *Collective Welfare and Social Choice*, San Francisco, Cal.: Holden-Day.

—— (1970b), 'The Impossibility of a Paretian Liberal', *Journal of Political Economy*, **78**, (1), 152–7.

—— (1970c), 'Interpersonal Aggregation and Partial Comparability', *Econometrica*, **38**, 393–409.

—— (1971), 'Choice Functions and Revealed Preference', *Review of Economic Studies*, **38**, (3), 307–17.

—— (1973), 'Behaviour and the Concept of Preference', *Economica*, **40**, (158), 241–59.

—— (1976a), 'Real National Income', *Review of Economic Studies*, **43**, (1), 19–39.

—— (1976b), 'Poverty: an Ordinal Approach to Measurement', *Econometrica*, **44**, 219–31.

—— (1976c), 'Liberty, Unanimity and Rights', *Economica*, **43**, (171), 217–45.

—— (1977a), 'Rational Fools', *Philosophy and Public Affairs*, **6**, (4), 317–44.

—— (1977b), 'Social Choice Theory: a Re-examination', *Econometrica*, **45**, (1), 53–89; reprinted in A. Sen (1982a, 158–200).

—— (1979a), 'The Welfare Basis of Real Income Comparisons', *Journal of Economic Literature*, **17**, (1), 463–88.

—— (1979b), 'Personal Utilities and Public Judgments: or What's Wrong with Welfare Economics?', *Economic Journal*, **89**, (355), 537–58.

—— (1979c), 'Utilitarianism and Welfarism', *Journal of Philosophy*, **76**, (9), 463–88.

—— (1981), *Poverty and Famines: An Essay on Entitlement and Deprivation*, Oxford: Clarendon Press.

—— (1982a), *Choice, Welfare and Measurement*, Cambridge, Mass.: MIT Press.

—— (1982b), 'Rights and Agency', *Philosophy and Public Affairs*, **11**, (1), 3–39.

—— (1983a), 'Liberty and Social Choice', *Journal of Philosophy*, **80**, (1), 5–28.

—— (1983b), 'Evaluator Relativity and Consequential Evaluation', *Philosophy and Public Affairs*, **12**, (2), 113–32.

—— (1984), *Resources, Values and Development*, Cambridge, Mass.: Harvard University Press.

—— (1985a), 'Goals, Commitment, and Identity', *Journal of Law, Economics, and Organization*, **1**, (2), 341–55.

—— (1985b), *Commodities and Capabilities*, Amsterdam: North-Holland.

—— (1985c), 'Well-Being, Agency and Freedom: the Dewey Lectures 1984', *Journal of Philosophy*, **82**, 169–221.

—— (1985d), 'Women, Technology and Sexual Divisions', *Trade and Development* (UNCTAD), **6**.

—— (1986a), 'Foundations of Social Choice Theory: an Epilogue', in Jon Elster and Aanund Hylland (eds), *Foundations of Social Choice Theory*, New York: Cambridge University Press, 213–248.

—— (1986b), 'Social Choice Theory', in K.J. Arrow and M.D. Intrilagator (eds), *Handbook of Mathematical Economics*, vol. III, Amsterdam: Elsevier, 1073–181.

—— (1987a), *On Ethics and Economics*, Oxford: Basil Blackwell.

—— (1987b), 'The Standard of Living: Lecture I, Concepts and Critiques', in Sen *et al.* (1987, 1–19).

—— (1987c), 'The Standard of Living: Lecture II, Lives and Capabilities', in Sen *et al.* (1987, 20–38).

—— (1989), 'Women's Survival as a Development Problem', *Bulletin of the American Academy of Arts and Sciences*, **43**, (2).

—— (1990a), 'Gender and Cooperative Conflicts', in Irene Tinker (ed.), *Persistent Inequalities*, London: Oxford University Press, 123–49.

—— (1990b), 'Justice: Means versus Freedoms', *Philosophy and Public Affairs*, **19**, (2), 111–21.

—— John Muellbauer, Ravi Kanbur, Keith Hart and Bernard Williams (1987), *The Standard of Living*, ed. Geoffery Hawthorn, Cambridge: Cambridge University Press.

—— and Bernard Williams (eds), (1982), *Utilitarianism and Beyond*, Cambridge: Cambridge University Press.

Streeten, Paul *et al.* (1981), *First Things First: Meeting Basic Needs in Developing Countries*, New York: Oxford University Press.

Suzumura, Kotaro (1983), *Rational Choice, Collective Decision and Social Welfare*, New York: Cambridge University Press.

Williams, Bernard A.O. (1985), *Ethics and the Limits of Philosophy*, Cambridge, Mass.: Harvard University Press.

Wriglesworth, John (1985), *Libertarian Conflicts in Social Choice*, New York: Cambridge University Press.

Index

New Horizons in Economic Thought

Appraisals of Leading Economists

This landmark book appraises the contribution of important economists whose work represents the best, the most promising and the most innovative in contemporary economics. Together, they have generated vast new substantive and interpretive horizons in economics. Between them they have made seminal contributions at the frontiers of the subject including economic history, social choice, justice, economic development, history of economic thought, microeconomic and macroeconomic theory, organizational theory, political economy, economic psychology and econometrics.

New Horizons in Economic Thought will rapidly become established as an essential reference work on some of the leading economists of the 20th century.

Warren J. Samuels is Professor of Economics at Michigan State University, US.